Critical Thinking

An Introduction to Reasoning and Living Well

CHARLES V. BLATZ
University of Toledo

 KENDALL/HUNT PUBLISHING COMPANY
4050 Westmark Drive   Dubuque, Iowa 52002

p. 34
Excerpts by Federico García Lorca, translated by James Graham-Lujan and Richard L. O'Connell, from *Three Tragedies*,
copyright © 1947 by New Directions Publishing Corp. Reprinted by permission of New Directions Publishing Corp.

Cover images © 2005 by Photos.com

Copyright © 2005 by Charles V. Blatz

ISBN 0-7575-1596-7

Printed in the United States of America
10 9 8 7 6 5 4 3 2 1

Contents

Preface

There is no excess of critical thinking in the world today. There is more than there has ever been, no doubt. Still, there is considerable room for improvement. And because of that, people suffer. They miss out on much, and they are taken advantage of. They are maimed or killed by wars, and they fail to make the most of peace. This is not to condemn the human species. It is just to note what seems to be fact. But things need not be this way. They need not, in spite of how hard it is to bring critical thinking into practice in the world and even in one's own life, and in spite of how many there are who would prefer to resort to power or to control by manipulation. Still, the alternatives to critical thinking have such a poor track record that it seems worth the effort to strive toward being persons, communities and societies living critically. This book is written in response to these assessments.

The discussion to follow attempts to approach critical thinking as if it belongs in every minute of our life; as if it is important to living well and to reasoning well for everyone, everywhere. Critical thinking is not a sometime requirement—something for the used car lot but not for interacting with a loved one, something for the boardroom but not for seeking to assess whether you belong in the boardroom. This may not be obvious since many applaud critical thinking as a set of skills that will keep others from taking advantage of us. Also, it might seem that critical thinking is faddish, a late-comer on the scene in the universities and colleges and high schools of the United States. Neither of these things is really true.

Critical thinking has a long history and a complex culture. It provided what in ancient times might have been called wisdom. It made the industrial revolutions socially possible, as well as the social contract. It found a home and was raised to high art in the early universities. And it was one 19th century prescription for improving society. (The English philosopher John Stuart Mill made much of it in connection with proper education.)

Further, while critical thinking can be found in the use of a variety of skills of reasoning, it is not just a certain way of doing things. Nor is critical thinking just following a set of rules or recipes that apply to specific problems. It encompasses both more than and something different from what are merely set ways of doing things. It involves creativity, a certain outlook or a set of attitudes, a set of values, a set of objectives, courts of judgment and appeal and correction, as well as a number of approaches and concerns that are shared and a number of practices that are not shared across communities of inquirers. Furthermore, critical thinking is the province of no one in particular and yet of everyone. Critical thinking is more a way of living and reasoning, more a constant responsibility than a process or set of procedures. And in all of these aspects, *critical thinking is not just in the service of reasoning and living well; rather, in very important ways, it **is** reasoning and living well.*

Perhaps this seems to include in critical thinking much more than belongs there. Perhaps something seems to be left out in this quick inventory. Perhaps. But the work of the discussion to follow will have to determine that. The answer lies in the details. Still the message should be clear that what follows is not intended to be a quick summary of some skills that can be learned and applied mechanically to keep people out of thinking troubles or to protect people against con artists and bad politicians. Critical thinking is so much more than that, it is not that at all. But again that is a promise to be made good in what follows. You as a critical thinker will have to be the judge of whether the author succeeds.

Studying critical thinking just might prove to be unlike any other scholarship you have been involved in. There are facts to learn, but the important thing is to learn how to use them and to take them to heart, not just to remember what they are so as to be able to demonstrate your powers of memory. There are skills to acquire, but again the point is not to prepare to demonstrate these in so many performances. Rather the point is to learn how to analyze and to assess and generally to think about what comes your way, not just in this class but in other classes, on the job, in your personal life, and in your life as a member of our society. You will be challenged to think about thinking and in doing so to prepare yourself to think about other things. You will be invited to reflect on your own life, your own values, and your own approach to the world. You will be offered assistance and support in coming closer to reasoning and living well. And you will be expected to prepare to offer the same to others, whether your own children, your fellow workers, the next generation of voters, or whomever.

If this much sets the tone of the discussion, still, as always, there are debts to acknowledge and a bit of history to tell. I am indebted first to the many students and teachers I have worked with and from whom I have learned much about what critical thinking is, as well as about what place it has in our lives. Fellow teachers in this endeavor have included many teaching assistants, recently and notably, Charles Carlson, Jeanne Kusina, team leader, and Michael Larson, and in other classes, Christa Jiamachello. I am deeply indebted to many colleagues from whom I have learned about the nuances and the knots in the theory of reasoning that is the study of critical thinking, and about the teaching of critical thinking. Among these are persons whom I have heard and conversed with over the years, including Robert Ennis, Donald Hatcher, Ralph Johnson, Steve Norris, Perry Weddle, and Mark Weinstein. Some years ago, Robert Ennis had a special good influence on some of my views in his role as outside evaluator of a National Endowment for the Humanities (NEH) project called Wyoming's Critical Thinking Project, which I directed. I am grateful for the funding of that project which in fact supported some of the reflections leading to views expressed here, just as I am grateful for Ennis's influence. David Hoch and Randy Bohn, current University of Toledo colleagues, recently conducted a National Conferences on Undergraduate Research and Leslie E. Lancy Foundation student-research-focused project on inquiry in science and the humanities and saw fit to include me as a discussion leader. I am indebted to them for comments on my work for that project, some of which has evolved into more recent work to be published by the Midwest Philosophy of Education Society. Parts of that Lancy related writing, like parts of the NEH work, show up in what follows. Another Toledo colleague, Roger Ray, has been my partner in conducting a local secondary-level school reform project in the humanities that has served to bring critical thinking to the classroom in many guises. This project has enjoyed funding from numerous sources including the National Endowment for the Humanities and the Clement O. Miniger Memorial Foundation. Further, the present work is the expression of the influence of several others who helped form my views at an early stage, notably, George Miller, William Todd, and Irving Copi.

At many places in the discussion you will encounter reports and references to scholarly work or to other texts in the area of critical thinking. This might be something of a departure from standard fare for introductory textbooks. However, it is included for several reasons: some of this is work I draw on and so it is important to note that; also, it is important to relate the present work to some others in the field to indicate points of convergence; it is important to relate this discussion to current research in other fields like psychology and the study of consciousness to indicate some connections and to relate important insights that help the understanding of critical thinking; and it is important to convey, I believe, that the study of critical thinking is a live and creative undertaking into which all who have something to say are invited—yes, even you, the student. The passages you encounter from other work will have appropriate references for you to follow up on if you are interested. These are quoted with permission which is hereby gratefully acknowledged.

This project would not have been undertaken when and as it was, had it not been for the interest and support of Michelle Weaver, Acquisitions Editor for Kendall-Hunt. I appreciate her faith in the project and her guidance.

One of the dominant themes defended in what follows is that critical thinking is a social undertaking, engaged in within communities of inquiry. Such communities are both smaller and larger. My hope is that this book will be the vehicle for many, many critical thinking learning-communities over the years to come and that these have a lasting good effect on all their members. That is my wish for the public life of the work. But also these reflections have a place in my personal life. Perhaps the most intimate community I am a member of I sustain with my soul mate, life partner, and best critic Sally Caldwell Blatz. This book is recognition of that community, its vitality, and its measureless value.

CHAPTER I

What Is Critical Thinking, What Does It Take, What's the Pay Off?

SECTION 1

What Is Critical Thinking?

> **Critical thinking is the careful attempt to arrive at well-supported beliefs, decisions, and plans of action, and to take these to heart so that we live accordingly and well.**

There is a lot packed into this initial definition. And you will need to get clear about these details as you go along in the remainder of this book. But three **central themes** stand out:

- **Critical Thinking is *an undertaking* or a pursuit.** Critical thinking is a form of striving for a goal, a way of organizing our inquiry so as to effectively and efficiently achieve that goal, an undertaking, and so it is something we can attempt and get right or wrong. Critical thinking is not a fixed and mechanical or automatic reaction we undergo. It is not something that happens to us, it is something we seek to do.

- **Critical Thinking is *goal oriented* seeking to separate good from bad, true from false.** Critical thinking seeks to separate good from bad beliefs, decisions, and actions or ways of proceeding, and it does this in a way that is supported by evidence or reasons for the distinctions it leads us to.

- **Critical Thinking is *value driven* and so works in connection with or is coordinated with our desires and feelings.** Critical thinking is not separated from feelings and emotions—at least not if such reasoning matters to and makes a difference in one's life. No matter how "hard and cold" reasoning is, if this thinking is going to influence life, thinkers still need to take up the results of reasoning into their hearts, or to reflect these results in their desires and emotions. So for example: scientists, passionate about knowing how things work, or fascinated by some organism or process, seek the best supported explanations and understanding; consumers seek to figure out the best deals they can make given what they are interested in; students eager to pass a course or to derive the greatest benefit the course has to offer study the materials in a critical way to gain understanding of them.

These themes will show themselves as you go along throughout this book. And so these three points will be touchstones by which to check your thought. Stay on the lookout for these themes and they will help you think about critical thinking as more than just a set of definitions, or a set of dos and don'ts to learn. They will help you apply what you study to your own life.

SECTION 2

The Cultural Heritage of Thinking Critically— Why Bother with Critical Thinking?

Critical thinking is not a recent cultural development, even though some of its expressions, such as those found in new scientific fields, are recent. In fact the themes the above definition emphasizes show up prominently in ancient plays—the equivalent 2500 years ago of our current thrillers. Perhaps no story illustrates this point and shows the cultural heritage of critical thinking better than one told by Sophocles in his play *Antigone* (apparently first performed around 441 B.C.). The story makes clear this text's thematic concerns and it also helps one see how very important critical thinking is to personal and social life. The story presents us with a clash over deeply felt values, and raises two questions: can reason which is guided by feelings of what is right or what is needed to achieve some valued end, itself be used to resolve conflicts of values? And, can reason be relied upon to guide thinkers in conflict-ridden decisions, for example, in ruling a state and leading the citizens to a good and decent life?

The answer to the first question seems to be that the shared value of relying on reason—even when reason is put in the service of conflicting values—is the best humans have to drive and guide their actions and reflections.

It is their most productive way to organize their lives together, even if reason itself cannot always find common ground and resolve particular value disputes.

And so, in answer to the second question, one must learn to depend upon a shared faith in reason as the basis of the mutual respect and consideration needed to help keep humans living together, even in the face of their disagreements.

Why not take a quick look at the play to see how these answers about the importance of critical thinking bubble to the surface?

The story unfolds in ancient Thebes shortly after Oedipus has discovered that he killed his father and married his mother. This discovery led to madness and chaos as Oedipus's mother/wife (Jocasta) killed herself, Oedipus scratched out his eyes, and his brother Creon, who had been ruling with Oedipus and Jocasta, took over the rule of the country. Thebes was at war with Argos. Oedipus's two sons took up opposite sides and killed each other in battle. Etocles, who fought for Thebes, is brought in for proper honors and burial while Polynices was left for the wild dogs to eat. Creon has forbidden anyone to bury Polynices, yet Oedipus's daughter Antigone, against the advice of her sister Ismene, has done just that. When Antigone is caught in the act of reburying her brother, Creon condemns her to death by starvation, chained inside a cave. Haemon, Creon's son and Antigone's fiancé, seeks to intervene, but Creon rejects him, saying that as ruler he must be tough and follow reason, not what he calls feeling (sympathy for family members rather than concern for the state), in matters pertaining to state security. Thus the conflict is between public spiritedness and familial loyalty or sympathy. Both Creon and Antigone think they are following reason and that the other is driven by the wrong values. Later, Creon sees the results of his decision in favor of public spiritedness—Haemon's suicide and Antigone's death. Creon is devastated by this outcome. And the play's internal commentators (the chorus) sum it up by urging that humans learn too late to bring all of reason and feeling, both public spiritedness and personal familial concern, together into a life well led. What a mess! And how could one rely on critical thinking to get back on the right track?

Four crucial passages highlight what seem to be pivotal points in the thinking of Creon, Haemon, and Antigone[1]:

ANTIGONE'S JUSTIFICATION: ➡	CREON'S STAND:
Nowise from Zeus, methought, this edict came,	Never, my son, let for a woman's sake
Nor justice, that abides among the gods	[out of love for your betrothed]
In Hades, who ordained these laws for men,	Reason give way to sense, . . .
Nor did I deem *thine* edicts of such force	But she shall die. Let her appeal to Zeus,
That they, a mortal's bidding, should o'erride	And sing the sanctity of kindred blood—
Unwritten laws, eternal in the heavens.	What then? If in my own house I shall nurse
Not of to-day or yesterday are these,	Rebellion, how shall strangers not rebel?
But live from everlasting, and from whence	He who to his own kith and kin does right,
They sprang, none knoweth. I would not, for the breach	Will in the state deal righteously with all.
Of these, through fear of any human pride	(p. 121)
To Heaven atone. (p. 115)	

HAEMON'S REPLY:	➡	ANTIGONE'S PARTING WORDS:

Beside the torrent's course, of tree that bend
Each bough, thou seest, and every twig is safe;
Those that resist are by the roots up torn.
. . . Cease from thy wrath; be not inexorable:
For if despite my youth I too may think
My thought, I'll say that best it is by far
That men should be all-knowing if they may,
But if—as oft the scale inclines not so—
Why then, by good-advice 'tis good to learn.
(p. 123)

So by my friends forsaken I depart,
Living, unhappy, to dim vaults of death.
Yet I transgressed—what ordinance of heaven?
Why to the gods, ill-fated, any more
Should I look up—whom call to succour—since
Impiety my piety is named? (p. 128)

Antigone claims the backing of eternal ethical rules demanding that she, as the family's oldest functioning member, bury her family's dead. The duty is hers no matter what orders of state she is under. Creon, however, is leader of a state. Justice means aiding and celebrating our friends, and harming as well as reviling our enemies. Thus in war Creon is duty bound by his office to protect the state. And those who threaten the state by fighting against it, family or not, are traitors and not worthy of decent treatment. He needs an example of firmness to show others that if they test him they will meet with the harshest of treatments. Creon felt that humans must protect reason from personal oriented emotion that might weaken us to our enemies, even if this protection expresses cruelty and anger, emotions suited to closing themselves off against all who do not stand with them.

Creon's son seeks a more measured response, a consideration of the possibility of something lying between favoring us or favoring them. The thing about simple lines separating the good from the bad is that you must be very knowledgeable—perhaps even all knowing—to draw them. And does anyone, at least any human, qualify for this task? Reason is important, but one must be honest enough to admit that just where reason calls for her or him to draw that line is not always clear. In fact, if humans do not let their values and emotions into the mix, why will reason draw the line anywhere? If nothing matters, nothing is good. And if nothing is good, nothing is bad. So, one must not be carried away with those powers of reasoning he or she has, and be taken to the point of thinking that these are all powerful. Instead one must suit reason to serve values and to limit those values by wise judgments. Which values? The play seems to suggest that in this conflict facing Creon and Antigone, the conflict of the public/state values with the personal/familial values, one must seek a way that is guided by both of the conflicting value sides.

Nevertheless, all this is too late for Antigone. Condemned, she can find no approval in the words of the gods. But that is not surprising since she was out to follow eternal rules not coming from the gods. She is not buying into Creon's requirement to leave her brother to be mauled and eaten, and then rotted away in the open air. And she cannot find any friend or relative to call upon for comfort or support as she goes to meet her fate. Once reason is separated from family concerns and put entirely in the service of the state, as Creon did with his orders about Polynices's body, public opinion offers no friendship for the condemned Antigone. Antigone appealed to the justice given in eternal rules, not Creon's justice of looking out for friends and harming enemies. And Antigone was as unwilling to work with Creon to try to find a harmonious path both could travel as he was unwilling to work with her. By both, reason was treated as only a tool of her or his values, not as something important in itself and so able to possibly limit the claim of the competing values of state and family. And so Antigone made the authority of reason separate from some values (separate from her feeling for the state) just as Creon did (when he divorced reason from personal feeling amongst family members).

Haemon seems to have been the champion of critical thinking here—let the life of reason itself be valued and so let reason be favored wherever it works in the service of more particular values that can be supported themselves. Reason seems to work best when all concerned can respect each other, come together, and seek agreement, even if their individual feelings and (defensible) values threaten to drive a wedge between them.

So this is a story that carries many of the traditions or inherited views on critical thought.

§ **Critical thinking is vitally important in times of adversity or in the face of danger**—perhaps the only real defense humans have. (Creon and Antigone and Haemon agree here!)

§ **Critical thinking should not be put at the service of only selected conflicting and otherwise defensible values.** Critical thinking should take equally seriously both public or official issues of knowledge and policy and personal or intimate concerns like those within families. (Haemon)

§ **Critical thinking is a social enterprise of give and take that considers various possible beliefs and choices one might take up and the reasons for them.** So humans need a society where policy and interactions and relationships support critical thinking in the form of such a dialogue. (Haemon)

§ As critical thinkers humans must not only maintain and use their own views of things but must be ready to respect the views and values of others if there is reason to do so. **One must not only maintain integrity, but must also be respectful or charitable in the recognition of others who differ from them in defensible ways.**

§ **Critical thinking is an undertaking that might have no final and correct endpoint, but rather it might be tentative and alterable in its conclusions.** (Haemon)

§ At some important level, **critical thinking is always striving more toward wise judgment than discovery of a final truth.** (The play's Chorus)

§ So **critical thinking calls upon us to be open and honest in thought processes and in consideration of the information and attitudes that come along.** As critical thinkers humans should not just seek knowledge claims they feel comfortable with because they are dictated by the aims and assumptions of their roles and group memberships. **They must be ready to be skeptical about what is assumed or taken for granted and must be open to learning by challenging their own views, even if they do not change these views after they have checked them out.** (This Creon was unwilling to do.) And so, as critical thinkers, people must participate in creating a world of relationships wherein they think critically about their own concerns and those of others. (Haemon and the Chorus)

SECTION 3

Thus the Basic Idea Is . . .

§ **People are dependent upon reason, operating in close relation with values,** in a give and take inter-personal fashion, aimed at finding support for claims that offer the cautious (and possibly revisable) solutions of problems of what to believe, what to decide upon, and what to do.

§ Not all cases of critical thinking are about practical matters such as what to do in a case like that of Creon and Antigone's conflict. Often the question is one of a matter of fact, or a question that people have some more or less universally or widely agreed upon procedure to settle as true or false, correct or incorrect. Here the values are values of knowledge, not ones of politics or ethics. Still, the story coming out of the play *Antigone* presents a unitary heritage. There are close connections of detail as well as framework in what is said about addressing questions of what is so, and questions of what should be. Much of the remainder of the book deals with separating good from bad beliefs and decisions concerning what is true or correct as opposed to false or incorrect. But as things go on in the book it will become clear that **most of the lessons you learn about critical reasoning in connection with what is true or false, correct or incorrect (about what is the case, in fact), also hold up with little modification in applying reason to questions of ethics specifically (in asking about what is good and bad, what should be done or not, and so on).**

§ One last aspect of the basic idea is this: **not all operations of the human mind or consciousness are matters for attention in studying critical thinking.** Sometimes, feelings and beliefs are just concerned with matters of opinion like: what is the best flavor of ice cream, or the best looking automobile, or the best alternative-punk-rock band. This is not to say one might not try to give the support of reasons for views in these matters or even draw conclusions about them from our cherished assumptions. **Rather, the point is that views of what we believe or care about as a matter of mere preference or whim form no part of what we and**

others recognize as a set of beliefs or decisions or actions it is important to separate out as good or bad. At least part of the reason for this is there seems to be no source of evidence or reasons for these beliefs and choices that goes beyond individual preference. Your view of what is, overall, the best (or coolest) alternative-punk-rock band need rest on nothing more than your personal preference at the moment. When this is so, since there is no source of evidence for your view which is separate from your individual whim of approval, and since a mere personal preference is just that—the holding of an opinion in the absence of any way to check for good versus bad, correct versus incorrect beliefs, then reasoning does not come into play here (with or without feeling and emotion). Here, unlike factual disputes and real ethical or political disputes, there are no recognized ways of going wrong or getting it right. But **if critical thinking has a place, it is precisely where there are recognized ways of going right or wrong in the thinking that leads to belief, decision, and action.**

So this investigation of critical thinking will move ahead leaving aside cases of the exercise of mere personal preference.[2] Later the discussion will return to the distinction between reasoned choice and mere preference. For now the discussion is concerned more generally with critical thinking or critical reasoning.

As critical thinkers people are in the business of picking out the true claims from the false and from the ones they do not know how to categorize—true or false, correct or incorrect, or, who knows? So critical thinkers can accept a claim, reject it, or simply withhold judgment.

Thinking critically, people reach conclusions on the basis of evidence and they come to find their beliefs, decisions, or actions more or less acceptable depending upon the degree and quality of that evidence.[3] To understand critical thinking then, the discussion needs to look carefully at how people reach conclusions, or arrive at beliefs or decisions, on the basis of evidence and at what might be sources of such evidence. **The challenge is to think carefully about thinking itself, trying to understand when it is good as opposed to bad.** This focus of inquiry will carry through the rest of the book.

SECTION 4

Social and Personal Conditions for Critical Thinking

As you proceed to think about good versus bad thinking, you will put to use background information, procedures of reasoning, and rules of proof. This is clear in situations like those found in the courtroom where two attorneys struggle over what are the facts of some crime as they present evidence and reasoning according to strict rules of procedure. But it is also true of your doctor trying to figure out whether you have a bacterial or a viral infection. And it is true of you as you think about how to do a mathematics problem, or as you are designing a house, or trying to figure out what your boss meant by that remark the other day. Consider house building. People know a lot about what stresses and strains there are on building materials in different applications and about what materials arranged in what ways will bear what loads. People have a lot of background knowledge of the properties of building materials and of the techniques through which they might bring these materials together into structures. And so they can play with the way a house might look—within those limits of construction techniques and material strengths. Do not build a straw bale home without putting in some kind of foundation if you live in a wet area and without covering it with some form of plaster or stucco facade. Do not put twelve floors on a single thickness of thin boards in the basement. But, yes, you can put windows in the corners of the house, if they are properly framed and if the weight is supported at some point besides at that corner. And so on. Thinkers rely on background information, procedures, standards, and past examples of good reasoning about the issues of interest to them in order to arrive safely at claims they want to affirm. And, they even organize themselves into groups studying common problems from common viewpoints in order to most efficiently and reliably get at the best set of background assumptions, beliefs, and reasoning procedures to serve their shared purposes of critical thinking.

This should all be very familiar to us. It is reflected in the division of learning into subject matters, and university education into major areas of concentration. You declare a major in order to say what particular problems you want to learn how to think about—using the systematically developed procedures and assumptions of the field. That is no mystery! But what is often overlooked is that this whole endeavor would not work if thinkers did not live in a certain sort of social setting, and if they did not have certain personal traits. These social and personal conditions of critical thinking are what the discussion turns to now.

Recall that critical thinking is a social enterprise involving the giving and checking of evidence and reasoning. Now this social process can go wrong on a number of fronts and in a number of ways that limit or even shut down critical thinking. What are some of the ways in which the organization of society and aspects of the psychology of human interactions in society can limit or support critical thinking? What are some of the most important ways in which a society and a personal psychology might limit or empower critical thinking? First you will look at some of these and then you will try to apply them to your own life and society.

Social Conditions for Critical Thinking

Social Condition I

People have to be free to think. Now in terms of society this means that a lot of things have to be true. For example, if a child is underfed, or confused because of lack of sleep, or ill, that child will not be able to think, let alone think critically. And if this was so from birth, if, for example, there was protein deficiency, the child's brain might not have developed properly, limiting her or his critical capacities. So, people who would be critical thinkers must meet their own and their child's basic needs for food, housing, health, and rest. And, whether or not these are met depends in part upon how a society organizes itself. If wholesome food, decent housing, and effective education are available only at a premium, or opportunity is not open to all who have the qualities needed to take advantage of it, then we can be assured that basic needs will not be met uniformly, and that some, perhaps many, will be removed from the social conditions of freedom needed to be critical thinkers.

Also, if the child or adult is ignored or not given what is needed for her or his self-esteem as required to assert beliefs and to have confidence in reasoning abilities, she or he will not function as a critical thinker. So again, part of freedom in a society is making sure that persons have the self-esteem they need.

And again, if someone is fearful because of the violence around her or him, or is working so hard that he or she does not have a minute to reflect, to think seriously about things, he or she lacks the freedom necessary to think critically. So other important aspects of freedom for critical thought are the security and the leisure that are necessary to reflect constructively on what to believe and decide.

If people are interested in critical thinking in society, they must think about how to organize it so as to provide or assure all these things—basic needs, self-esteem, personal security, and the leisure needed to reflect on beliefs and decisions. Does your society do that today? Does any society across the globe? If not, how can people expect a nation or world of critical thinkers?

SOCIAL CONDITION II

People can learn all they need in order to think about the issue in question. Now some of the capacity to learn is up to individuals—up to their personal effort—and some is dependent upon how people organize society. For example, consider sources of information. There are libraries and newspapers and the Internet, and all sorts of sources of information. Some of these, like libraries and the Internet, are supported, in effect, by the public, by society. So society has a role in whether people are free to think critically here too. If there are not the sources of information people need, or if these are not available to them and they cannot access them, or schools or other sources of socialization, enculturation, and education do not equip people to use these sources, then society has let them down and they are less effective as critical thinkers than they would otherwise be.

Does society provide sources of information, methods of access, and support of people's abilities sufficient for them to collect and use what information is needed to think critically and constructively about issues? What do you think about this? Do all children have good schools and understanding of how to use computers so that they can research on the Internet? Does everyone know how to check out the reliability of a source on the Internet? A recent review reported on National Public Radio that the general reading level of most information on the Internet, around an eighth grade level, is **too high** for the general public! This suggests a failing of the schools perhaps. But is that the problem and how does a society fix that?

Reflection Question: Are people efficient and effective critical thinkers in terms of information gathering and processing? For example, should libraries stop buying entertainment videos to loan and spend the money on computer literacy and research lessons for people in their neighborhoods?

SOCIAL CONDITION III

The problems at issue are open to reasoning. Some issues or focal points of dispute and critical thinking seem to be impossible to understand and reason about in a productive way. Some of these are matters of pure personal preference. These one does not have to worry about after he or she has noted that they are matters of preference only. Others are so central to one of many conflicting viewpoints that they seem beyond the reach of critical thinking. For example, when does a human offspring become a human being with rights? When is a home situation so abusive that a child has to be removed from it? How far should a physician be allowed to go in trying to save a patient? When is careful observation in the field science? When is a hypothesis well-supported in a field of study like sociology or physics? When can someone trust the predictions of an economist or should they ever be taken as more than hints at possible trends? Different societies might have honest differences over such issues and sometimes their views have to change by continued conversation and evolution, not by critical thinking settling the matter right now. Look how views in industrial countries have changed on child labor—whether it is allowed and how much is acceptable. Look at how societies have changed their views about what are the facts of the nature of disease and the best practices for dealing with it.

Other issues call for answers that are impossible to implement. For example, how can people resolve conflicts like in the Middle East, without people being willing to compromise? And, whether they are willing to compromise is surely in part a social matter.

Still as a society people must organize issues or the focal points of inquiry and dispute into those questions that are open to reasoning and those that are not. And they must organize their fields of inquiry and study so that how they may reason about these matters is clear and functional. If they do not, then they will not be free to think critically about them. Different countries have different educational systems with different aims, different organizations for their scientific or other forms of inquiry, different funding schemes, and different places in important social functions served by these systems. Just how these organizations work has affected what it means for someone to be free to recognize that problems are or are not open to critical thinking and then to pursue that critical inquiry. Think about the so-called science carried on by Nazi scientists aimed explicitly at showing the inferiority of whole peoples or economic groups. And think about how funding is assigned in the United States only to projects or studies approved by establishment scientists in the various fields involved.

Reflection Question: How do humans assure that society is organized so that they are properly free to separate out those issues they can think critically about—free of bias due to politics, personal power struggles, and other interfering factors?

SOCIAL CONDITION IV **People must be able to communicate on the issues.** Part of this is a technical issue—how can thinkers arrange communication in a society such as the United States of America, so as to effectively and efficiently run their democracy as a free exchange of ideas open to critical thinking? That is a question about the social conditions of critical thinking. But also there is a more basic communication issue here. If individuals cannot be understood or understand others, then they will not be able to share ideas and to critically exchange reasons for believing or deciding an issue. And as they mix more and more cultures, more and different economic experiences, more and more knowledge bases, and professional concerns, it becomes less and less easy to really understand others and to be understood, in all ways important to critical thinking. Again this raises questions of information management and education. But it also takes the discussion into issues of how a society organizes itself in being open to strangers and how it makes possible their functional assimilation, even if divergent groups of people wish to remain culturally separate. MTV has done much to make global communication possible on issues of consumption. But has it really done much to help people understand where others are coming from culturally, religiously, politically, economically, in terms of diet, in terms of family and other social relations lived in the day to day? It may bring people together in the products they consume, but does it bring them closer in understanding what others care about and why and how that bears upon what each other thinks? I believe not. And if it has not, then MTV has not helped create a world in which people are better critical thinkers because they are better able to communicate with others over issues that they need to think about critically.

Reflection Question: What do you think? Has MTV helped people to really communicate and become closer? Is anything else doing this across the world?

Social Condition V

People need to be accountable to each other. People need to be accountable to each other if critical thinking is to work. People need to stand ready to answer to others and explain why they believe or decide what they do. They need to (critically or carefully) accept others as authorities in their lives with respect to what is good thinking for the purposes at hand. Simultaneously, they must stand ready to play the same questioning roles themselves with respect to the thought of others and they must be accepted in that role—empowered as authorities in the thinking of others. Not everyone will be an authority in everyone else's life on every matter. Networks of critical authority are complex and shifting. For example, one is accountable to her or his supervisor for the quality of work performance, but not to her or his grocer. Whereas the grocer is accountable to her or his supervisor and, within limits, to the customer. But where appropriate, thinkers must take part in the process of insisting on proper thinking and all that follows in belief or decision, or else the rules and processes of critical thinking will have no life, no reality; they will not be taken up personally by thinkers and thinkers will do no more than conform to them in some rote fashion.

Reflection Question: How many people are you accountable to, in your thinking—your significant other, your boss, some of your teachers, your friends, your religious leader(s), your parents? And on what matters are you accountable to these others?

More and more, society in the United States has drifted and lurched away from taking accountability relationships seriously. This has seriously undermined both responsibility and critical thinking. And thus an emerging social structure and function without accountability is arguably making people less able to think critically.

SOCIAL CONDITION VI

People must be ready and able to reach common decisions. People must be ready and able, that is, emotionally as well as politically and socially, to reach common decisions. This is hard. You do not believe it? Try to reach a consensus on a significant matter in your department, or home, or religious organization. From where to go to the movies, to whether to build a new religious structure, consensus or even compromise and agreement is hard to reach. It is hard to get clear together on what each person wants and hard to get clear with oneself on what is an acceptable point to settle on. And once people get clear on these things then they have to think about implications and go on to seek some form of agreement. This work next requires a readiness and a spirit consistent with making the accommodations, compromises, and limitations of executive power required by the process of coming together. All right, two people cannot both have it their way in every detail, then who is to decide and at what price? It is not enough that the issue is something they can reason about. The issue must also be such that they can come to some agreement and coordinate their actions by that agreement. So they must be able to rest their agreement on a common enough set of standards, background beliefs, and a common enough perspective so that they can reach together a decision or belief that is agreed to be reasonable, rational, and the best, and one they all buy into. And people must reach this end on the basis of a commonly accepted, if not single, set of reasons.

Reflection Question: How often do you reach such a special space of agreement with others you work with or live with, instead of just swallowing resentment and your beliefs that the other is a blockhead or evil, or . . . ? Can you name one issue and fellow critical thinker on that issue where you agreed in this good way? What would that be?

SOCIAL CONDITION VII

People need to be able to coordinate their actions, and to act in collaborative ways. People need to be able to get their acts together, not just as individuals but also as members of a group, to a degree that is sufficient for putting into action the results of their agreed-upon thinking. And they need to go on to act in a way that is effective and efficient for the task or issue at hand. Even if thinkers agree on a belief or decision, if they do so for their own reasons, they might not be able to carry it out and then critical thinking will have come to nothing in practice, and they will not be able to enforce it or to get people to take it seriously. It is one thing for members of an accountability network—whether that is a society or a part of a society—to talk and think productively about, for example school funding, and it is another for them to agree on a course of action. Yes, schools need more funding and more equal funding, but how are we to do this? In spite of a State Supreme Court decision several years ago, Ohio has been unable to agree on how to proceed to equalize school funding. And once they have agreed on what to do or believe, it is quite another thing for them to put that agreed-upon belief or decision into practice in a way that works, a way that is effective and efficient. If thinkers cannot do that, critical thinking will have no social reality and will fall into disrepute. But if they are able to put it into practice, it will be because in part, they believe and act on the same reasons for the same decisions and they are seeking to uphold the same beliefs and values. It will be because their thinking will be coordinated in the reasons and processes leading to it, as well as some of the emotions behind it. And it will be because it can be coordinated in this way and still leave room for people to act freely.

Reflection Question: When was the last time you were involved in a social or group project that required coordinated or collaborative thinking and planning and then follow through? Did it go smoothly and come to the end you thought you had agreed to? If not, why did it break down? If it did succeed, what were the thinking and agreements in thinking (what were the agreements in reasons and thought processes) that helped that happen? And what was the organization of the group that allowed for these thought processes and feelings to carry the day? Could this organization be carried over into society at large? If not, how far could it be generalized between diverse groups? If you can answer these questions you have an excellent handle on this social conditions of critical thinking.

Mastery Exercises I.1

Thinking in terms of the social conditions of critical thinking just reviewed, state what seems to have gone wrong in each of the following scenarios. List which condition has been broken and give an explanation of what needs to be done to get things back on track.

1. The planning commission took the position that the mayor had no right to block the funding for the sewers in the new subdivision they had approved. And they refused to discuss it with her. So the project was put in limbo.

2. "The teacher said that she would provide the paper guidelines one week after the paper assignment topics were given out. But that was three weeks ago and still no guidelines, and what's more it is due next week."

3. The teacher went on and on about how lazy the students were and told them they had to get it in gear or they were all going to flunk the course with no one to blame but themselves.

4. Communications broke down on 9/11/2001 and none of the agencies involved at ground zero was willing to relinquish their own command to any other agency. This cost lives.

5. "No, we couldn't agree. She wanted to have a big church wedding and I wanted to go to the Bahamas for a wedding ceremony and honeymoon. We just couldn't seem to get on the same page. She just meant by wedding something else than what I did. And she just wouldn't come around to thinking in my terms."

6. "Well, I have tried and tried and I still cannot get him to realize that red is the only color to have on a convertible. We can agree on the brand of the car, but he just won't see that red is the only color to have. I guess we won't get a new car this year. Nothing I said would convince him."

7. Because of their controversial content, we will not allow books endorsing the theory of evolution to be taken out at this library. They are reserved for the exclusive use of clergy.

8. "No, I don't think we should raise the minimum wage because that would result in people having to work fewer hours and then what would they do? They should not be allowed extra free time; that only leads to trouble in society."

9. "No, I don't think that people should be allowed to meet in coffee shops without police being present and taking pictures since that is the kind of thing that leads to crimes being planned or revolution being undertaken."

10. "Are you crazy? Why should I meet with those people? If I did then I would have to show why I didn't agree with them or reach some compromise and that is not what my financial supporters and Board of Directors are paying for!"

(Answers in Appendix II.)

Mastery Exercises I.2

ASSESSMENT
CHECKUP

> **OBJECTIVES:** The first purpose of this exercise is to provide practice at thinking about our thinking about further issues. The second aim is to provide practice at verbalizing your thinking about thinking.

INSTRUCTIONS: Look at the issues listed below. Pick *one,* and in no more than five paragraphs over no more than one and one-half standard, double-spaced typed pages, explain why we, in our society, have *not* been successful in thinking critically about that issue. Explain by reference to *all* the relevant Social Conditions of Critical Thinking reviewed above. Then hand in your response as directed, and at the appropriate time.

Remember: The assignment is not to solve the problem or say why we haven't been able to put yours or any other solution into practice. The problem is to think about why we, in our society, cannot seem to think about the issue using critical thinking—and to identify and explain why we can or cannot in terms of the social conditions of critical thinking sketched above. If you think we *can* think critically about the issue you have chosen as your focus, explain how that has been possible while taking into account all of the social conditions of critical thinking.

So for each and every condition explain why it is or is not met in our society and explain how that impacts upon the possibility of thinking critically about the issue you selected.

Issues:

1. Whether it is a fact that we evolved from some form of apes and they from lower forms of life?

2. Whether women do have the right to choose to have an abortion?

3. Whether it is a fact that public schools are funded unfairly and we need to change the funding basis, in your home state?

4. Whether it is a fact that people who are not law enforcement officials should be allowed to carry concealed weapons?

5. Whether it is a fact that the death penalty is ethically acceptable?

The criteria by which these papers will be graded are, in general, the following (obviously you might meet these criteria more or less completely and well):

1. Your paper should comment on whether or not each and every one of the social conditions is met for thinking critically about the issue you selected.

2. Your paper should not try to address the issue itself, saying what should be done about it, but rather your paper should address the question of whether or not the social conditions for thinking critically about the issue are met.

3. Your paper should focus on a single issue from the assignment.

4. Your paper should be well and clearly stated and well organized.

5. Your paper should effectively explain, or else give reasons for, why the social conditions for critical thinking are or are not met for the issue you choose to write about.

Personal Conditions for Critical Thinking

PERSONAL CONDITION 1

Critical thinkers must be honest. They must be honest about what they know and do not know, about what they think and about what evidence they do and do not have supporting a belief, decision, or the undertaking of an action. Unfortunately, it is often not to one's advantage to divulge what he or she knows the support for a belief or decision or action to be. In some contexts like the courtroom or the board room one would be considered foolish or engaging in bad practice to do so. Does this mean that in practicing law and in making business transactions people should not or cannot think critically? No, it means that the accountability group in such cases does not include all other parties to a person's practice, at least not fully. If you are selling your house and it has carpenter ants, and you know that, you have to tell potential buyers, in some areas of the country. But you do not have to tell them that the expensive windows throughout the house were ones you bought for a song at an estate auction and that your brother-in-law put them in for free! Thus critical thinkers still have to be honest with others and tell them what they know or what support they have for a belief or decision, but that is true only within the rules governing interactions with others and only within the accountability groups where these thinkers operate under those rules. If buyer and seller are under the same laws, then they must think together as necessary to abide by the letter if not the spirit of those laws. Beyond that they are accountable only to those who are stakeholders or otherwise are importantly related to what they are doing that requires critical thought.

Further, being honest in the required way calls for thinkers to be patient and perseverant enough to do what is called for by the tasks of critical thought at hand. Of course, like honesty in the sense of being straightforward as just spoken of, honesty in putting forward proper effort and care will vary depending upon the task at hand, the age and skill level of the thinker, the stakes, and the time available. The third grader preparing to take the science test faces a lesser expectation of patience, and so care, and a lower expectation of perseverance than the high school senior or the college student taking a test or the rocket scientist preparing to make a suggestion about how to land a satellite on an asteroid.

So thinkers face individual expectations of engaging fully in appropriate social interaction as they think and so in sharing their thoughts. And they face expectations of proceeding carefully and with the effort needed and available to make the best contribution possible to such interactions.

Reflection Question: Can you describe a situation in which you were not honest with yourself or others in these ways and critical thinking was hampered because of this? For example, have you ever been trying to decide what to do with someone and deliberately not told that person something important in order to make the decision go your way?

Perhaps you did not tell that person that the ballgame tickets you had were in the hot sun even though you knew that person sunburns very easily? Such cases of the absence of this personal condition of critical thinking can undermine critical thinking in the moment and beyond that when it ends a friendship!

PERSONAL CONDITION 2

Critical thinkers must seek appropriate clarity. If anyone is to effectively and efficiently separate the true from the false and the well-supported from the not well-supported, then he or she must be very clear about what is under consideration and what is at stake. This is not just a matter of understanding the language in which the issues and beliefs or options of decision or action are stated as one takes them up. To be sure, that understanding is important and will be discussed later on. But also clarity is a matter of understanding the implications of believing or deciding or acting in some way as opposed to another. That is, it is a matter of grasping what else will be true or well supported if one takes up one belief or decision or action. Beliefs do not come in isolated units. If someone believes that a storm is coming he or she can expect the ground to get wet and the seats of her or his automobile to get soaked if its windows are open. With these expectations one might want to cover the ground, for example, if he or she is the groundskeeper at a major league baseball park with a game scheduled shortly after the rain passes through. And, if one has a car, he or she might want to shelter it or close the windows. Thus there are causal and practical connections between beliefs or decisions thinkers might come to and others that they might not think through. Also there are logical consequences and what might be called "knowledge empowerments" that come with picking out beliefs or decisions as good ones. Thus the critical thinker will infer or draw conclusions from the truth of beliefs or from the acceptability of decisions or actions. For example, the truth that it is about to rain also means that one can expect a change in the barometric pressure, and this enables those who have sinus troubles to rationally expect a headache. Thus those with such troubles would know that they might want to take a tablet to avoid the discomfort of a headache.

If a thinker were not aware of any such causal, practical, or logical consequences, then this person could not be said to be clear, as a critical thinker, about the belief, decision, or action under consideration. And, within limits that vary with the issue and the context, the less the thinker is aware of such consequences, the more unclear this person could be said to be about the issue.

Absence of clarity of consequences is important to critical thinking because these consequences are things one might need to check out to provide further checks on the truth or degree of support for a belief or a decision or action. Consequences can be stated as what else is true or well-supported if some belief or decision is, and if these consequences are not true or acceptable, then this will cast doubt on what they are a consequence of. For example, suppose I believe that rain is good for my cactus plants and so lots of rain must be very good. I put them out in the heavy storm only to find that they do poorly with all the water they soak up. Then the truth of the belief that a large amount of rain hurts cactus plants casts doubt on my original belief that rain is good for cactus plants.

Clarity is something thinkers must strive for by trying to learn all they can about the consequences of what beliefs, decisions, and actions they are entertaining. Clarity of this sort is hard work, and getting clear in this way on many matters is something that could take much longer than people want to spend or might take them far beyond their abilities. Still, all in all, such consequential clarity is something thinkers must strive for. Without it thinkers will be reduced in their capacity to be reflective and critical in the sense that is so important to being a critical thinker.

Reflection Question: Have you ever done something without thinking it through clearly and found that the consequences were not at all what you thought or wanted? Have you ever formed a belief or made a decision and then later found that you were thereby committed to believing or deciding something else you had no idea of and no interest in? How many times have you said, "if I only knew then what I know now, I would not have gone ahead?" All of these questions indicate the same sort of demand for clarity on critical thinkers, as given in the old carpentry saying, or should I say the old carpentry saw, "measure twice, cut once."

Critical thinkers must ask, "why?" If thinkers are to get clear about what they are considering, then they must ask why things occur as they do and what this will lead to. Also they must ask why they should believe one way or another, or else why they should decide in one way as opposed to another. If they do not then thinkers will not learn the consequences of what they are thinking about. "Why questions" are key to asking for the sorts of considerations that might serve as evidence. Why would that lead to or be followed by this? Why is that true? Why do you think that is a sound decision? Why did you do that? All of these questions (under one reading) amount to asking what is your evidence for thinking that something is true, or a sound decision, or a permitted or obligatory action to perform? "Why" sometimes asks for an account of what brought something about. Thus seeking what causal consequences events might have is a part of the critical thinker's way to get clear. And a "why" that asks for support for believing or for acting or deciding is another part. Requests asking for support are requests for evidence or, in general, **reasons** to believe, decide, or do something in some way.

Reflection Question: Can you think of other things thinkers ask for besides causal consequences and evidence or reasons for a belief or a decision when they ask "why" about something? Might they be asking for something that would clue them into what is the importance of believing or deciding in one way or another in the case in question—what are the practical consequences here? And, is asking for an explanation of some occurrence the same as asking for evidence of that occurrence taking place? Compare: Why did the soufflé fall? Why do you or, what makes you, think the soufflé fell? Why did the government prosecute that protestor? Why do you think the government prosecuted that protestor—that is, what makes you so sure it did?

PERSONAL
CONDITION 4

Critical thinkers must think for themselves. This is not just to say that critical thinkers must investigate and come to their own conclusions about what to believe, decide and do—which they must to the extent they can. But it is also to say that critical thinkers must exercise a certain amount of good spirited skepticism toward the views and decisions of others, standing ready to challenge these in their own mind or else overtly and explicitly, whichever is appropriate and productive. It is clear that critical thinkers are not mere conformists and when unable to check out some matter open to critical reasoning, thinkers must accept beliefs or decisions only tentatively and subject to revision or rejection at a later time. But what seems less and less clear in everyday life today is that *it is not just perfectly appropriate but is in fact an obligation of critical thinkers both to expect others to arrive at their views and actions only after careful thought, and also to hold others accountable for doing that.* (And here, "others" includes the self in that odd way that "thinkers think to themselves" in reflecting upon a belief or decision.) A society of critical thinkers cannot exist unless this happens; and, as we saw, individual critical thinkers cannot exist without such a society.

Skepticism cannot be carried to the point that the accountability relationship breaks down, of course. For that would have the same negative result as no challenge to others. But within reasonable limits of sociability, of time constraints, and of the energy of all concerned, as well as within the limits of the familiarity and opportunity provided by the accountability relationship itself, critical thinkers will hold others to account for evidence for their beliefs and decisions and the defense of their actions.

For example, at a press conference reporters are expected, on behalf of their corporate sponsors and their readers or viewers to ask tough and revealing questions of the politician or others holding the press conference. But decorum, common decency, the rules of critical thinking, and the tone set by the openness, style and familiarity of the person asked the questions all limit and shape the nature and way of asking questions that critical thinkers may engage in.

Finally, everyone must depend on others for most of what he or she believes and for some of the major influences expressed in decisions and actions. Saying that critical thinkers must be independent is not to deny that. It is instead to say that to the extent feasible and reasonable in the circumstances, critical thinkers must check their evidence and engage in inquiry to check their sources and the consequences of what they consider.

Reflection Question: Is there an area of belief or action where you do not now "think for yourself"? What is that area? Why is there such an area? Is this a matter of necessity, or a matter of the way you were brought up, or a matter of the rules of the community in which you would have to raise the questions? In those areas where you do not think for yourself, do you rely on a recognized authority whose credentials you can be sure of?

PERSONAL CONDITION 5

Critical thinkers must be ready to recognize, and to challenge, authorities when appropriate. The mention of how important it is to be ready to challenge an authority's credentials must be balanced against the need to be ready to recognize a presumption of authority in oneself and others as thinkers worth taking seriously. This presumption is only that and needs to be checked up on when possible. But the idea is that, in general, thinkers cannot proceed expecting others to prove everything to them at every turn.

Thinkers share or, when it is of interest, they can obtain some idea of common knowledge in most everyday matters and even in some technical fields where they must intrude. With this in hand they can proceed, and very quickly get the idea of whether or not someone is or might be a reliable authority in the field. In fact there is common knowledge on how to recognize someone who is a phony, a liar or otherwise is not to be trusted as a guide to belief or decision. For example, thinkers can always ask the person in question to explain or they can ask others about that person and thereby get some idea of how responsive and knowledgeable that person really is. This is a procedure some students use in selecting instructors. They go into the professor's office to ask about the course and if the reply is unclear, unresponsive, or uninterested, then the student might think again about signing up. Or the student might ask someone else who has had the class and so tap into the grapevine concerning the class and professor. But when all is said and done, the student, like all people seeking expert knowledge on various matters, must form a judgment about whether the identified authority really is an expert.

The discussion will explore more of that later. In fact authority is just one source of the beliefs and decisions people have or make and it is just one source of evidence for these. As you go along, you will look at several sources of evidence—such as "the evidence of our senses" or common experience, to see some of the restrictions there are on accepting evidence from such a source. But what is important here is that if you have some good reason to accept someone as an authority and there is not a reason to question that person's authority, then you should leave well enough alone, accepting the good fortune of interaction with someone you have reason to take as an expert.

Reflection Question: Can you identify three people in your life that you take as authorities? How do you rely on them? Could you get along as well without them? What reason do you have for accepting them as authorities? How would you respond to challenges to their authority? Would you consult still other authorities or do independent research yourself? Can you ever take someone's word for being an authority?

The critical thinker must be ready to think creatively. Critical thinkers then are not ones to follow some rote or routine set of procedures to separate the truth from alternatives, the well-supported from the not. As discussed, critical thinkers are seeking to think on their own, and in the best way possible in a field of inquiry, or as the problem calls for. And critical thinkers seek to arrive at a grasp of defensible beliefs and decisions and to do so in a way that is sensitive to the consequences of these. A thinker then is after a set of beliefs and decisions and actions that are defensible and interrelated. In this pursuit thinkers will be making sense of the world as they try to find their way to a better life.

Thinkers will have to make coherent sense:

§ of what situation they are confronted with;

§ of what the significance of that situation is to them;

§ of whether or not this significance and the character of the situation call for inquiry or some different action;

§ of how best to carry out that inquiry or other action—what sources of information and procedures of reasoning are called for and what limits they might impose on the inquiry or other action;

§ of how much time and energy to invest;

§ of when the situation has changed in a way that calls for a change of behavior to another task or to a continuation of the task in another direction; and (throughout)

§ of how to respond to another's inquiries about what the thinker has done and of how to defend what they have done.

In taking all of these measures, even though the thinker might respond quickly and without conscious deliberation, this person need not be responding automatically, without care or self-monitored control of her or his thought. Of course someone might respond that way, but not as a critical thinker.

Critical thought **is an expression of self-controlled endeavors to organize human responses in a way that places thinkers in the world and suits their beliefs, decisions, and actions to the significance of the world.**

Humans cannot do this automatically and without investing their critical responses with their personal and group feeling, as well as shared beliefs and procedures. And people cannot make these feelings, beliefs, and procedures of reasoning their own without being accountable for them and being ready to critically reflect on their acceptability and without being participants in holding others accountable for their understanding and use. All of this requires that critical thinkers be creative in their thought as they conduct inquiry, or as they assemble the evidence for a belief or in favor of a decision.

Reflection Question: Have you ever tried to work with someone who will only follow the script for a job or for a social encounter even though this is not what is most productive or most defensible in the situation? For example, have you ever talked to a customer service person on the phone (usually after a long wait on "hold") who says he or she understands your problem but can do nothing to help since it is not covered in the company rules—"I will bring it to the attention of my supervisor." What were the details of the situation? How did you resolve it or did you? Or have you ever been at a social function where people acted for the most part in a standardized and superficial way—refusing to engage in real conversation or serious observation. Did you have a good time? Conformity and social convention are useful in creating a comfort zone within which strangers might meet. But it is not conducive to critical thought or even to genuine encounters between individuals. This point has become such a cliché that in most movies where significant characters meet up, one of the first things said is "Would you like to get out of here?" In some of those cases, at least, these characters are going off to talk and to really get to know each other, a creative collaboration requiring critical thought.

PERSONAL CONDITION 7

Critical thinkers respect themselves and others as thinkers. Critical thinkers seek to maintain integrity both with respect to their project of seeking well-supported beliefs, decisions, and actions and with respect to the rules and practices of that project. Thus they hold themselves accountable for and take some degree of pleasure or pride in being the best critical thinkers they can be. Striving to be a good critical thinker thus produces a form of self-respect. But part of this self-respect will be respecting others with whom thinkers are engaged in the social practice and institutions of critical thinking. Thus self-respect as a critical thinker will generalize to respect for others as critical thinkers.

This might not sound right since thinkers do not agree in their understanding of problems, assumptions, or procedures with everyone all the time. But still if others proceed in a way based on assumptions and understandings of problems that are themselves defensible by the same sorts of procedures as you would support your conduct as a critical thinker, then they too (at the most general level) are engaged in a common practice of critical thinking with you and you cannot refuse to grant them space to operate as critical thinkers without challenging the credibility of your own basic practices. Respect for critical thinkers as a matter of integrity then has to be combined with charity or respect for other critical thinkers whom we disagree with over particulars, but agree with at the most basic levels. This charity is a form of respect that calls for us to be open to learning from others and to take their views seriously if the occasion arises.

For example, science and religion are supposedly in disagreement over the problems they take seriously, the kinds of assumptions they make about what exists, and how whatever exists can operate. As well science and religion supposedly disagree over procedures practitioners and experts should follow in an inquiry. But suppose, for the sake of argument, that, as some have said, the very foundations of science and religion can be supported ultimately only in the same ways—by relying on those patterns and procedures of inquiry and belief that most effectively serve the freely chosen ends of people who turn to science or religion? Suppose thinking practices in science and religion can claim the same ultimate credentials, namely that they work for their own chosen purposes? Then, even though these two vast human undertakings might differ in particulars at many places and with major consequences, still as critical thinkers, scientists and religious thinkers should respect each other and remain open to interchanges of thought and criticism. Respect both in the form of integrity and charity are expected from critical thinkers.

Reflection Question: Can you give an example or two of when you have had to stick to your guns and continue to think about something in the way that seems best given all you know about the subject? Can you give an example or two of the workings of integrity in your own thinking? Can you remember your response to the viewpoint and thought patterns of the other person involved? Was this a case of your having to say that you see the point of the other and respect it but you just do not agree? If not, can you think of a case where you just disagreed with someone at a fundamental level? What was it— describe the case. How did it all end—did your respect for the other hold up or did the need for integrity dominate and lead to your rejecting or merely putting up with the other person's views?

Mastery Exercises I.3

SELF TEST

How do the following cases show an absence of personal conditions for critical thinking? Answers in Appendix II. Please explain the answers.

1. "No, I don't think so. I'm just going to stick with what I know. My parents voted Republican/Democrat, and I see no reason to change."

2. "Yes, it has a lot of miles on it but these are all road miles and it was well maintained." (Of course what is not said is that those road miles were ones from road racing.)

3. "Yeah, well it sounds ok to me. I think I had heard that sort of thing before about how tires develop bubbles sometimes. Just sell me a new one."

4. "Mr. President, other reporters are now saying that you are keeping the Department of Homeland Security under funded even while you are allowing huge contracts to go to the company formally run by your Vice President. Could you tell us whether that is true?"

5. "Yes, he said he was with the Federal Bureau of Standards and wanted to check out our kitchen to see if it complied. And the next thing we know we are poisoning our customers."

6. "I am not going to discuss this with that heathen. She is one of those who do not even believe in the literal truth of the Bible."

7. "Well, I asked about whether they had a search warrant, and they said yes. What was I supposed to do?"

8. "Well, sure, now I see that I could have made certain that they were selling tickets that each had a 1/1500 chance of winning the Corvette, instead of a 1/1500 chance of being picked to try to draw out a key that would start the Corvette and then signify that I won it. But it seemed so easy—so I bought 100 tickets at $100 a piece thinking I would stand a good chance of getting the winning ticket. I guess that was a mistake."

9. "Well, I tried to tell them about the termites and I knew they were going to have an inspection even though they said they would use the one I recommended—my buddy Herb."

10. "No, I didn't go to all the trouble to ask whether they would take away the scrap material and the old kitchen cabinets after the job was over. I just assumed they would."

Mastery Exercises I.4

ASSESSMENT CHECKUP

> **OBJECTIVES:** To reflect upon an opportunity for critical thinking to see if you exercised the personal conditions of critical thinking discussed above.

INSTRUCTIONS: Review the seven personal conditions for critical thinking and reflect upon the last major purchase you made—computer, car, house, or whatever. Discuss whether each and every one of the personal conditions were fully met appropriately in your conduct during that purchase. Explain why they were or were not. And explain what you could have done better. Write no more than five paragraphs or a standard page and one-half for your discussion.

SECTION 5

Some of the Elements of Critical Thinking

Along the way, the discussion has noted that critical thinkers gather evidence in the examination of what is supportable as true or acceptable as opposed to false or unacceptable. Sometimes this does not work out and the best that can be done is to withhold judgment. And, it was mentioned that this endeavor occurs according to methods and against assumptions and understandings that are shared with others in a group of like-minded people. All of this suggests the need for a list of the elements making up the tools and concerns of critical thinking. There is not any commonly agreed upon list—though some items show up on everybody's lists. One researcher on critical thinking in education, Richard Paul, has constructed his list as follows[4]:

1. The problem or question at issue
2. The purpose or goal of thinking
3. The frame of reference or points of view involved
4. Assumptions made
5. Central concepts and ideas involved
6. Principles or theories used
7. Evidence, data, or reasons advanced
8. Interpretations and claims made
9. Inference, reasoning, and lines of formulated thought
10. Implications and consequences.

Paul certainly has identified many of the factors involved in critical thinking. The elements of critical thinking examined in this book will not be organized in exactly the same way; however, all of the factors Paul mentions will play a part in the discussion, along with still other factors such as the social conditions discussed above. To indicate a bit more clearly what sorts of "elements" will be explored here and why, consider two other case studies drawn from literature. These cases, like that of Antigone, come from tragedies written for the stage. One of these is ancient and related to Antigone. The other is modern, drawn from the previous century.

Oedipus the King: The basic story of Oedipus was set out earlier. Born under the cloud of a prophesy that he would grow up to kill his father and marry his mother, Oedipus, who was of royal lineage, was turned out for the cruelty of starvation. But the servant given the task of ensuring this could not bring himself to do it and Oedipus was saved only to grow up and fulfill the prophesy bringing about terrible results. His story is a classic tragedy. On three separate occasions in the unfolding events, Oedipus lost his head to his blind emotions and brought about tragic results. The first occasion was when he crossed the path of Laius, King of Thebes. The road seemed too narrow for both, but neither would yield. As Oedipus went on, Laius struck him. The young man slew all but one in his father's company. Later, that one would confirm the first disaster; the killing of the father and the widowing of the one that bore him, the very one whom, in ignorance, the killer would soon marry. Later, a seer laid the destruction of Thebes at the feet of Oedipus, attributing the city's problems to the injustice in its being ruled by the unpunished killer of the former king. Creon, brother to Jocasta, Oedipus's wife and long lost mother, took up this accusation. Oedipus responded with a rage and indignation that could be satisfied only by pressing through to the truth; the truth which he heard from that one of Laius's company who escaped the hero's sword. Once again, Oedipus's heart led past his head. This time disaster fell in the revelation that Oedipus was indeed the unpunished culprit. That revelation led Jocasta to hang herself. Oedipus was overcome yet a third time. His final destruction took the form of self-imposed blindness and separation from his city and children, a combination sure in the times to cost him great suffering and probably death. Such were the consequences of Oedipus's passion, and therein lies their tragic dimension.

Now Oedipus could have done otherwise. The story makes that clear when Oedipus is considering whether to go on with his inquiry into the murder of the king of Thebes and Jocasta prevails upon him to follow reason in forming his belief about whether or not he did or could have killed his father. At that point he was willing enough to critically examine the credentials of a claim on his credulity. Oedipus followed her close reasoning to doubt the dread prophecy that Laius would be killed by his son. He followed and agreed with it. This is something he was capable of, all right, even in spite of his hot-headedness. Thus the options open to Oedipus are clear enough. One is the critical use of reason, that is, making the appropriate investigations and then on the basis gained in those inquiries to form well-supported beliefs, decisions, and actions. The other is the subjugation of reason to the sway of current unexamined opinions, preferences, and their associated goals. One lesson of a tragedy such as *Oedipus the King* is that the critical examination of current opinions and even current standards of belief about what is or should be can turn aside terrible problems.

As the discussion will take up in later chapters, such a turn to reason will not always prevail if the thinker is not open to it, not ready for it, but is, for example, caught up instead in prejudice or bias. But the turn to reason can be there waiting, if the thinker makes ready for it. And then the rewards for living well can be great. Clearly, what one believes often makes a difference to the goals that person has and the plans he or she undertakes in pursuit of these goals. Where these beliefs can be reached through a critical examination of their basis, there one stands to gain a lot by drawing upon and applying the skills of critical thinking. If people do not reason critically in such cases, then whether their goals are defensible and rewarding, and whether they can rely on beliefs about how to reach those goals, will be just a matter of chance.

Much of human freedom of action lies in:

- following reasoning in understanding the world,
- determining on the basis of that understanding what options there are,
- evaluating those options,
- forming plans to pursue the options preferred on the basis of reasons,
- and then enacting that plan.

In other words, what people are free to do is, to a great extent, what they make of the world through their reasoned thought. To give up on critical thinking is to give up on that freedom. It is to turn over one's life to the luck of the draw one makes in uncritically forming beliefs, values, preferences, and plans. Or perhaps it is simply to resign oneself to reacting to the world in the ways one happens to at the moment—subjecting oneself, in short, to the caprice or the whim of the moment. Most likely, it is to turn your life over to those who will envision and arrange the world for you. In any event, like Oedipus, without critical thinking, you expose yourself to whatever comes along—often with disastrous results.

Yerma: Undertaking life according to critical reason is not a solitary enterprise, as discussed above in connection with the social conditions of critical thinking. Another story is worth a mention in this connection. Federico Garcia Lorca's play *Yerma* makes quite clear other elements of critical thinking. The story is elegant in its simplicity, yet awesome in the complexity of the difficulties facing its characters. Yerma, as her name suggests, is barren. Although she is the wife of Juan, and although she is driven by the idea of having a son, still the woman has no children. For her this is an intolerable situation. The only role she allows herself is that given all women of her culture, that of a mother. Being a wife is the (only) acceptable context of being a mother. Marriage is not to legitimate sexual relations. Indeed, the relations themselves have point only as a means of reaching fulfillment as a mother, not as a female. In this set of beliefs, one finds the core of a perspective or a point of view on what should be done by members of the culture. Individual variance of style and timing in reaching those goals is tolerated, of course. Still the goals or purposes of that community specify a rigid ethic for its members. As beings that count ethically, women are mothers or potential mothers. Why this is so, the play does not explain. This is just the way of the world and Yerma accepts that completely. She offers the following confidence[5]:

> How can I help complaining when I see you and the other women full of flowers from within, and then see myself useless in the midst of so much beauty!
>
> **MARIA.** But you have other things. If you'd listen to me you'd be happy.
>
> **YERMA.** A farm woman who bears no children is useless—like a handful of thorns—and even bad—even though I may be a part of this wasteland abandoned by the hand of God.

Problems arise for Yerma because of other expectations upon her, both from within her community and from her husband. Part of the rules she has come to embrace require of Yerma both fidelity and submission to her husband in the supposedly joint venture of procreation. But as the story unfolds it turns out that the only creation Juan is interested in is in the fields where he seeks to grow his crops. After a struggle of wills for the duration of the play over the question of having children, Juan finally confronts Yerma with the denial of her one hope of fulfillment. In the face of this she seems to see that the only way in which she can continue to act within the ethic and expectations on her is to kill Juan. In choking him to death, she perhaps asserts that after all the procreation issue is really within her choice, or up to her. Neither Yerma nor Juan could see beyond their own perspective or point of view concerning what is right and worthwhile. Neither could seriously consider the other's viewpoint. The modern/economic and the traditional/familial perspectives could only clash. Standing within their respective viewpoints, Yerma and Juan could not understand nor respect, let alone sympathize, with the other's viewpoint. It was as if they saw the only role of reason as one of working out the applications of a particular perspective, applying it to the world in standard ways with predictable results.

To be sure, they were both right, *from within their individual narrow and exclusionary view of things.* What they lacked was the capacity to use reason and to value a life lived according to reason as a means to find common ground and critique their individual points of view. Thus critical thinking is not just about the application of a perspective or point of view on things. It is not just about seeing the world in terms of the expectations for thinking and deciding and acting coming from those in a group who share an approach to problems, a community of discussion or inquiry, if you will. It is all about the valuing of a life led by reason itself, and lived from a point of view held in common by all thinkers that can serve as the starting point for those seeking to examine, modify, and perhaps reconcile conflicting points of view or reasoned approaches to problems.

Thus this discussion will agree to some extent with Richard Paul's list of the elements of critical thinking. Perhaps the best thing to do is just summarize the elements as this discussion will develop them in later chapters:

Critical thinking does begin in a **problem** that is understood in a shared way by members of a group. Those in that group also agree upon what to **assume** as background knowledge and as **methods for interpreting** the specific forms of the problems of interest that individuals have to cope with. And they also agree on **methods to address those problems by reason.** These assumptions and methods of reasoning and common understanding of the problems of interest all come together to form a **perspective or viewpoint that is shared** on those problems and how to approach them. Thinking within that perspective, no matter how creatively, is an expectation of those in the group or the community conducting the inquiry. At the same time, there is **common ground shared by all critical thinkers** and this includes a value of living well according to reason. This common ground holds out the hope of some way to reconcile differences over how to see and examine and think about the world and the place of humans and others in it. This common ground is the subject of this book. Of course in any community of thinkers there will be **organizing concepts and basic or central beliefs and values,** even if nothing as grand as principles and theories. And, for any occasion of critical thought there will be **implications** that will have to be traced out and used as further tests of those beliefs, and decisions, and actions that led the thinkers to these implications. (If the implications are not good or acceptable, then what led to them is questionable.) Finally, while it is convenient to speak of the work of reason as addressing problems, this is not meant to be restrictive since "problems" here covers:

- problem solving in specific instances;

- examination and analysis of nature or the operation of things or systems;

- the assessment of reasoning;

- the clarification of terms or of a thought's conceptual apparatus;

- reflection on how to formulate a question;

- creating an interpretation;

- working out a translation;

- making plans;

- formulating strategies and goals;

- seeking to articulate or to represent a view or an individual's stands;

- giving, and supporting as best, an explanation of some event;

and on and on, across a wide range and large number of the uses thinkers make of reason. Critical thinking is **multi-purposeful and will benefit** from clarity, honesty, freedom, and the other **personal and social conditions discussed above.**

Conclusion and a Look Ahead

The discussion so far has concentrated on the definition of critical thinking and on some of the (related) social and personal conditions needed for critical thinking to be present, as well as on the elements of critical thinking, some of which will be studied in what follows. Worth special emphasis is the point that there are common elements in all critical thinking. There are problems one needs to get clear on, reasoning procedures one needs to be aware of, information sources one needs to understand and pay careful attention to as he or she proceeds, consequences of thought holding implications for what one believes and decides and does—for how one lives and what one believes, and so on. This common ground is the work of what is to come. The next three chapters are devoted to preparation for critical thinking suggesting in more detail all that needs to be set aside and avoided if one is to seriously and responsibly undertake critical thinking and inquiry. After that the discussion turns to a look at the sources of the support one seeks to provide for beliefs, decisions, or actions in thinking critically. Following an orienting look at the roles of science and the humanities, the discussion then proceeds to take up a study of good and bad techniques of inductive and deductive reasoning before going on to attempt to pull together some considerations important to assessing explanations and arguments in support of a claim. The final chapter is offered as a case study in some of the general features of critical thinking. It is devoted to the reintegration of beliefs, decisions, and actions, and to the support of views on the basis of arguments, all in the area of critical reasoning in ethics.

Notes:

[1] Sophocles. (1962). *Antigone* (ed. by Robinson, Jr., C. A.). *An anthology of greek drama, first series.* New York: Holt, Rinehart and Winston, pages as listed at quotations.

[2] Mere personal preference would be different from that of an expert—say a wine or coffee taster who can articulate what it is about the liquid that is appealing and others can follow her or his lead to see if they agree. In the end one may only be able to say that if you like bitter coffee, that blend is for you, but this is still one step up from saying "I like mocha-almond-fudge and that is the end of it—that is the best ice-cream." The expert can bring us to see or appreciate the liquid for its qualities and then give us a critical reference point. The person who knows what he or she likes, but not why, cannot do that. So one can distinguish informed or reasoned preference from mere personal preference where the former but not the latter lends itself to being an object of critical thought.

[3] See Moore, B. N., and Parker, R. (2003). *Critical thinking.* Boston: McGraw Hill Higher Education, p. 4.

[4] Paul, R. (1993). *Critical thinking, what every person needs to survive in a rapidly changing world* (ed. by Willsen, J. and Binker, A. J. A.). Santa Rosa, CA: Foundation for Critical Thinking, p. 139.

[5] Garcia Lorca, F. (1947). *Yerma.* Garcia Lorca, F. *Three tragedies, blood wedding, yerma, bernarda alba* (trans. by Graham-Lujan, J. and O'Connell, R. L.). New York: New Directions Publishing Corporation, p. 132.

CHAPTER II

Taking Ourselves Seriously: The Uptake of Critical Reasoning

SECTION 1

Becoming a Critical Thinker and Other Rites of Passage

Almost every culture has some rite of passage marking the member's arriving at a new and advanced stage of life where he or she is expected to take on the roles, the attitudes, and the practices of an adult in that culture. Part of coming of age is moving under the full expectations of critical thought as this is understood and practiced in the culture in question. Of course, thinkers are always moving toward full realization of those expectations if they are trying to live within their culture's ways. They never complete this task. And, they do not start down this path doing everything overnight. Instead, they start in little ways, from a very early age, within the influence of their culture. This is so no matter whether that culture is the large framework of a people's life together, or whether it is the subject matter and patterns of inquiry in a field of study or an intellectual discipline like philosophy, or even whether it is the culture of a job or a social organization or a new university class a thinker is joining.

Regardless of the size or the character of that culture, the taking on of the full weight of these expectations is often marked by some ceremony, by some sharp criticism or special remark from a relative or tutor, or yet some other outward sign. What is signaled is that the thinker is now facing the expectations of maturity of thought, attitude, and action found in that group.

Just one expression of this point can be seen (with no intention of any endorsement of any particular religion) by considering the words of the Apostle Paul who spoke of moving beyond thinking and talking as a child, putting behind him the things of childhood. (See 1 Cor. 13:11.)

Thus one way to think systematically about putting to good use the elements of critical thinking is by asking: In general, what do persons need to do in order to come of age as critical thinkers, or, just what sorts of basic expectations of readiness face would-be critical thinkers?

Critical thinking is so familiar and often so close to hand when people choose to engage in it that individuals might forget or else take for granted and neglect the fact that the use of **critical thinking is an option** they have open to them in running their lives. And, it is by no means the only such option. *Alternatives are* **the use of force,** the **use of cunning and various forms of manipulation,** or **simple unthinking conformity** to the ways others believe, decide, and act. That critical thinking is one choice among several is one reason why the definition given earlier marked it as an *undertaking,* suggesting that it is something that people do deliberately, and do not have to do. Critical thinking is something that has to be taken up, not just in outward practice, but in one's inward attitudes and feelings that energize and make significant that practice. And this recognition, that thinking critically is an option not an automatic thing in human life, suggests the place to look first for expectations facing thinkers when they shoulder the full weight of critical reasoning in whatever cultural context they find themselves.

Looking at mistakes in practice or failings of the bearing and attitudes that people might bring to the undertaking of thinking critically gives a clear picture of some of the expectations these thinkers face. The mistakes or failings will pair off against one or more of the expectations thinkers face in their culture. Mistakes in the attitudes with which a person takes up thinking, and in the practice and processes of thinking themselves, fit the term "fallacy." Thus the discussion will turn to some (but not all) of these mistakes in the following explanation of fallacies in the *uptake* of critical reasoning.

SECTION 2

Fallacies of Openness

To engage in critical thinking is to undertake to separate better from worse beliefs, decisions, and actions, by finding those which are well-supported by evidence or reasons and those that are not. Thinkers cannot do this if they bring to the undertaking a distortion in their way of seeing things, or assumptions that skew what they are considering and so predetermine how they are going to view the beliefs (and so on), or sources of belief, or their circumstances. Evidence and reasons cannot be seen as worth considering or as credible, let alone taken seriously, unless thinkers are open to considering them. Thus if bias or prejudice or disregard of another leads a thinker to not consider someone or her beliefs, then this other person might as well say nothing. For example, the person who believes that all lawyers and all politicians are somehow crooked or only act to do what they find to their personal advantage will not trust what such individuals have to say and might thereby miss out on important insights. The same is true of those who are disposed to disbelieve published histories of important events, thinking that if they are published then the authors had to say what was popular or would sell, and so should not be trusted. These are some of the sorts of mistakes in procedure or attitude that would-be critical thinkers might find in their way. They are problems of the thinker not being open to what he or she should be and so being unable to think well or even to think at all. A more complete sampling of some of these mistakes is found in the following:

Fallacies of Openness _____

Bias, prejudice, and **bigotry** are related forms of **failings of openness.** A bias is a leaning people have in favor of or against someone and their thoughts or views, or some institution and their pronouncements, or some belief or line of action, and so on. A bias does not compel someone to think or decide one way or another. But it can be seen as a force pushing in one or another direction; it is an inclination to believe, decide, or act in some way that favors or disfavors someone or some idea. And this push might prevent the thinker from seeing evidence in favor of or against a belief or decision, or it might lead the thinker to ignore some of the relevant facts or circumstances as he or she mentally settles the matter. Prejudice, however, as the name suggests, is present in the form of a judgment expressing the thinker's settled frame of mind or settled belief, decision, or resolve to act. The prejudiced individual, when presented with circumstances activating the prejudice will see these circumstances in a way that is favorable or unfavorable toward someone or something, in the direction of the prejudice. Thus a police officer who is prejudiced against one group of people or another will be likely to suspect someone in that group when a crime occurs and possible perpetrators are being considered. Or the person with a prejudice in favor of one of her or his children will look at circumstances possibly favoring or faulting the child with a mind that is already made up in a way really favoring or not faulting the child. Prejudices, like bias, can be guarded against or overcome. Thinkers can catch themselves exercising a prejudice just as they can be aware that they are biased and take special measures to neutralize the bias. In both cases the distortion of thought can be blocked or overcome. The prejudice can be blocked by correcting the judgments the thinker finds herself with, and the bias can be corrected by the thinker making sure that he considers the available evidence and viewpoints not immediately clear to him. Bigotry is a condition of a thinker (and agent) who has not, or who is unable to, overcome a bias or prejudice and holds this against all the members of a group. The bigot acts these feelings out to the detriment of her or his thinking and is unable to overcome them at the moment (or chooses not to). This is a person who might not be able to avoid the distortion without assistance in changing her or his character. In all of these ways thinkers might be less than open to taking up the project of critical reasoning.

Thus one failing or fallacy of the uptake of critical reasoning is that of bias, another is that of prejudice, and a problem of being stuck in one or the other of these failings is sometimes the result of bigotry.

II.1a. ***The fallacy of bias*** is operating just in case the thinker is unable to consider relevant and available evidence or reasons for a certain belief, decision, or action because he or she is inclined, for no good reason, in a direction running against or in conflict with that certain belief, etc.

> ***For example:*** "Well, I can see why *you* might feel that Brendon is a suspect, but I just find that hard to believe. He seems like a good person to me. So I don't read his presence at the crime scene in the same way. Maybe he really was just taking a long walk that early in the morning."

> ***Or:*** "Well, you can hire her if you want. She does have good test scores. But I am sorry, I just don't trust people with a General Equivalency Diploma (GED) to be able to learn what is needed for this job."

One particular form of the fallacy of bias is what is sometimes called the "Two-Wrongs" or "Two-Wrongs Make a Right" fallacy. Here the thinker suggests it is all right to believe, decide, or act in a direction that would normally be considered wrong, just as a response to a perceived wrong or harm done to her or him. He or she is expressing a bias coming from the perceived wrong or harm and her or his thinking is distorted in a biased way accordingly.

> *For example:* "Of course I'm going to take these pens and printer paper. This will go some of the way to make up for the cheap raise the company gave me last year."

> *Or:* "I cannot really recommend him as a good employee after the way he left here when I would not promote him—just when I really needed his services."

In both of these cases, it is the interpretation of what is said that brings the bias to light. In the first, stealing is claimed as justified because of a poor raise; a claim that hardly seems supportable, and so really looks more like an explanation of the distortion of thinking rather than a justification of the thought pattern. In the second example, the employer refuses to give a recommendation because the employee left after not being promoted. But the employer would have been happy to have the employee's services so there seems to have been nothing wrong with the worker's services. So why not recommend him? This seems to reflect a bias against the employee in the employer's thinking, from all we can tell. That employer is not open to giving the matter proper thought because of an inclination against benefiting the worker who left.

II.1b. *The fallacy of prejudice* is operating just when the thinker forms beliefs, decides, or acts in a way that is favorable or unfavorable toward someone or a group prior to an appropriate consideration of the evidence or the reasons for and against doing so. (Just what is appropriate will differ in ways that are clear, depending upon the context, of course.) Here the problem is not that the thinking is distorted in a way that leads the thinker to ignore or overlook some reasonably accessible features of the circumstances—bias. Rather the thinker has already made up her or his mind on a subject or person and merely brings that judgment to the present circumstances instead of thinking it through at all—prejudice. The distortion comes with the thinker not even seeing the necessity of having to look further than the judgment he or she brings to the circumstances, even though this judgment might be in need of revision or adaptation in the present circumstances (if it was well supportable in any circumstances).

> *For example:* "Judge Haskins was prejudiced against the defendant when she refused to allow the defense attorney to introduce the other security video tape of the robbery clearly showing the defendant being knocked to the floor unconscious by the bank robbers. She had her mind made up all along."

Or: "Surely you don't believe that my child, Johnny/Janey could have walked through your flowers. He/she would just not do something like that."

Or again: "How could he know that I could not do the job well? He had his mind made up already and is just prejudiced against those of German descent because he lost his brother in World War II."

In all of these cases, the thinker had made up her or his mind in a certain direction prior to considering the reasons for and against any judgment, and so cut off the possibility of fully considering all the available evidence. The thinker was closed off to critical thought by prior judgment. Now of course there might be so much resemblance between cases of a certain sort that thinkers would waste their time reconsidering judgments from case to case. Standardization in manufactured products like automobiles should leave critical thinkers indifferent as to whether they receive one or another new auto with the various features they are interested in. (Of course, there are lemons, so quality control on the part of a manufacturer is also important.) But when thinkers add in the differences of driving habits and service treatments that various owners give automobiles, it becomes very important for them to check out, car by car, used autos they might buy. If someone says, "Well, it is an Acme brand automobile, and my family has always owned Acme's so I don't have to check this one out before I buy it. I'm happy with this one," he or she is not open to appropriate critical thinking because of prejudice.

As mentioned above, bigotry is that stamp of character that means that the thinker has lost the capacity to be open to a fair consideration of the evidence and as a result characteristically disfavors all of those in some group. Racism, classism, sexism, for example, if strong, enduring, and expressed in thought and action are forms of bigotry.

There are other ways in which thinkers might fail to be open to evidence or reasons that should be considered. In the cases of bias and prejudice, the failure is in the thinker's own individual thought patterns. In still other cases the thinker seeks to lead others to a bias or prejudice through the abuse the thinker heaps on third parties. One form of such abuse is closely related to prejudice and in fact involves everyone of the members of a group of thinkers in acting like he or she has a prejudice toward all those of a group. This fallacy is sometimes called a mistake of stereotyping.

II.2.

The fallacy of stereotyping occurs just in cases where the thinker has a standard set of beliefs, or other responses to anyone in a certain group and these (often negative) responses are shared by others who, like the thinker, have neither thought to challenge them nor to move beyond them and do not consider members of the typed group as individuals.

For example: "You cannot marry him/her. I mean really, how could you even think about it? After all, she/he is from downstate/from the wrong side of the tracks/is from a bad family/is so unrefined."

Or: "Why would you want to go to that school? It has an open enrollment policy and so you cannot get a good education there."

Thus stereotyping involves a common way of thinking (often or usually negative) that closes off proper investigation of the views expressing the stereotype. Thus it is something like a mass prejudice, a set of beliefs and attitudes held toward multiple others in common by a number of people and carried into a situation of encounter with those victims of the stereotype. So, unlike a prejudice, it is not something individual and it is not directed against solitary individuals. It is a way of lumping individual persons or organizations or even ideas or governments, with others under a set of shared regards of those fitting the stereotype. So it is close to prejudice, but not quite the same.

Another fallacy that is related to bias or prejudice is that of ridicule. Very often a bias or a prejudice will be negative and will be expressed by ridicule of an individual or of a group of persons. But also, ridicule is purposive. The thought of accidental ridicule does not make much sense—accidental denigration, neglect, or maybe even accidental insult, yes, but not ridicule. When we ridicule someone we go after them and with a point—in order to incline another to think less of them, automatically or prior to reflection. Thus ridicule is undertaken to bring about a bias or prejudice another toward a third party.

§ **II.3.**   *The fallacy of ridicule* is the error of seeking to lead another to a bias or prejudice against certain thoughts, beliefs, decisions, or actions of a third party or group of others.

> *For example:* "That is just a stupid idea. How can you even consider some plan like that! Parking should be diagonal, not straight-in."

> *Or:* "Yes, but that kind of price support is communistic and so just plain evil. Surely you don't really support that or any political party that would suggest it?"

> *Or again:* "I have heard people did that, but I never believed it. Why would anyone in their right mind buy a car when you can lease? That's nuts."

In all of these cases the idea is that certain decisions or actions or beliefs are themselves made the object of ridicule. Why would anyone want to seriously consider such a stupid idea or line of action or policy? The impact of the remarks would be to create an inclination against thinking in those ways or a prejudiced judgment running against thinking these ways. And thus this would shut off consideration and stop or close off critical thinking from taking place because of a lack of openness on the part of the would-be thinker.

Some say that we can lump together sarcasm and ridicule but sarcasm is more an emotional tone that speech or writing takes on and it need not block one

from thinking well about something.[1] It seems coincidental that thinkers are often sarcastic when they express bias or prejudice or ridicule. But coincidence is just that. One can ridicule without sarcasm and one can speak or write in a way that is sarcastic without engaging in ridicule, bias, or prejudice: "Well, ok, if you force me to that compromise to get your support for my bill, I guess I have to go along with your suggestion to rescind the tax break," said the Senator sarcastically, but sincerely all the same.

There are still other fallacies that might look like forms of ridicule but need to be kept separate from them. These are three related fallacies that speak against the person who is associated with a belief, action, or decision trying to lead others to reject that act or belief or decision. As they speak against a person and they have a long tradition in rhetorical usage, they are called by the Latin terms *Ad Hominem* (the Latin term for human or man being "hominem"). Some such attacks are personal, some are directed against an individual because of her or his affiliation with a group, and either of these might be spoken in advance of the target person or agency saying or doing something—to lead individuals to disregard what the target person says or does when she or he does it. Each of these is so common that it has its own name. Thus we need to distinguish three fallacies.

II.4.   ***The fallacy of ad hominem abusive*** is the error of speaking against someone with a personal insult or slander or other negative characterization or attribution, in order to present that person's beliefs, decisions or actions as unworthy of consideration or acceptance.

> ***For example:*** "Herman? Herman is the most incompetent person I've run into. Surely you are not going to hire/listen to/follow the example of that pathetic person?"

> ***Or:*** "Well, Carol is just not fully in control of her emotions. You must not take her seriously or you would be hurt yourself. Just ignore her next time she does something like that."

Notice that in the first case, the speaker is using *ridicule* to commit an ad hominem abusive. But this is not so in the second case where the target of the abuse is excused by virtue of emotional distress or disease, but all the same is made the target of abuse to put her actions, beliefs, or decisions out of consideration. Not all ad hominems have to involve ridicule.

> ***Or again:*** "You know I encountered the most stupid sales person today. He urged that I get the more expensive baby stroller even though he admitted that consumer reports favors the less expensive one I went after. Yes, the one costs more and is less useful, but buy it anyway. Go figure!"

Notice that in this third example, there is a single individual that is in question—the speaker just did not know his name. And notice that the reader cannot tell whether the ad hominem, while personal, is a case of ridicule or not. Was the speaker saying the clerk was being inexcusably dense or maybe even conniving and trying to fool the customer? Or was the speaker just saying that even though the clerk could not help it, what was said was not to be considered? The reader cannot tell and yet while the critical thinker will suspend judgment on that question, the larger question of whether the speaker is engaging in critical thinking or closing himself or herself off from it by the fallacy of ad hominem has a clear answer. The speaker is making a mistake.

II.5.   ***The fallacy of ad hominem circumstantial*** is the error of speaking against someone by an insult or slander or other negative representation just because of the target person's group affiliation or professional or economic or other circumstances, in order to present that person's beliefs, decisions, or actions as unworthy of consideration or acceptance.

Thus the insult or other negative representation here "works" by the speaker associating the target person with others in a group and saying that that person is just believing, acting, or deciding as does any in that group and so is not to be taken seriously. Now, of course, there is the unspoken suggestion that the way those in that group believe, decide or act on the relevant issue is not worth following or accepting. So the making of this mistake might reflect bias, prejudice, or stereotyping. But it might not. The speaker might genuinely believe for good reasons that members of a group often are not to be taken seriously as sources of belief or example—consider those in hate groups like Neo-Nazi organizations or terrorists. And also the speaker might just believe that the target person is not to be taken seriously because he or she is just following the crowd of her or his group. But while either of these is better than bias or prejudice, neither is allowing critical thinking to work. Group affiliation by itself does not mean a person's views or actions are worthless—it is only when these views or actions are indefensible that this is so. And conformity is by itself not a clue to the worthlessness of someone's views or actions. Critical thinkers must be open to checking out an individual's beliefs and actions to see if there might be something to them. And if he or she shuts off this possibility by cueing on only group affiliation, then this is the mistake of ad hominem circumstantial.

> ***For example:*** "Well, that is just what a tax and spend liberal democrat would say. Why do you listen to that kind of stuff?"

> ***Or:*** "Yes, but dear, that woman is homeless. What do you expect her to say about the minimum wage?"

> ***Or again:*** "Well, the one was an Eagle Scout and the other was a gang member. Now really, who are you going to believe about why the drugs were found in the gymnasium?"

Both ad hominems can be used to try to block serious attention to another's thoughts or actions. Speakers or writers can try to head off attention to someone's beliefs or decisions or example, *in general and in advance*. In this case it is appropriate to use the phrase "poisoning the well." Of course not every case of poisoning the well has to turn on a personal insult or on an association with others whom the speaker disfavors. Sometimes the reports that poison the well are perfectly accurate and involve well deserved criticism. But still the point is that even if someone has acted, believed, or decided poorly or even criminally in the past, so that such reports are justified, it does not mean that they will do so in the future. And it would be a mistake to offer others the inference that since someone has done badly in the past they are not to be believed or otherwise taken seriously in the future. This is just another way of the speaker closing herself or himself off from that target person in the future or seeking to lead others to do so.

II.6. *The fallacy of poisoning the well* is the error of speaking against someone (or some group) in order to block future consideration and acceptance of her or his (or its) beliefs, decisions, or actions.

> ***For example:*** "Yes, I heard that the *New York Times* was interested in that connection between big business and government. But there is no point in following the story. That is just a liberal newspaper that will play out its particular political line."
>
> ***Or:*** "You're not really going to see Michael Moore's *Fahrenheit 9/11* are you? You know it's just going to be another biased, Moore in-your-face attempt to give an exposé. It will not be worth looking at to get a good idea of what's going on."
>
> ***Or again:*** "Yes I used to read *The Toledo Blade*, but I felt it was so negative on the local university that I stopped. And you know what? I haven't missed it at all. I don't think you would miss it either."
>
> ***Or future bumper sticker:*** "Ignorance is Bliss. Follow Your Bliss"

The spirit of critical thinking is one of openness and taking candidates for a well-supported belief, decision, or action as they come, understood with respect if not sympathy. Critical thinkers will not mistake the belief, decision, or action to be considered with the person or group that puts it forward for consideration—even if at times, and in certain ways, they must "consider the source." And so, critical thinkers will not fail to be open to considering how well supported beliefs, decisions, and actions are, now and in the future, even if they are put forward by those in disagreement with or disliked by the critical thinker.

The critical thinker will work on developing and maintaining the virtue of openness as just explained.

Mastery Exercises II.1

SELF TEST   Bias, prejudice, stereotyping, ridicule, ad hominem abusive, ad hominem circumstantial, poisoning the well

FALLACY IDENTIFICATION PRACTICE.   Following the Tech Tips found at the end of the chapter, identify the fallacies illustrated in the following exercises. Write a sentence explaining your judgment of which fallacy is present in each question. (Answers in Appendix II.)

1. "Well, I don't think we have to consider that applicant very long. He's so recently off the boat, he still has the smell of the old country on him."

2. "I don't know. I've always had a little trouble accepting the possibility of women in the priesthood."

3. "You actually believed him? But he's got all the insight of a gnat—a real nit wit."

4. "Yes, that is what she said. But you do know that she is a lobbyist paid by the tobacco companies? What would you expect her to say about cigarette smoking and cancer?"

5. "Well, I knew the first time I set eyes on her that she would be a wonderful actor. I don't know how, but I could see she had it. We don't need to consider the others. None could hold a candle to her."

6. "Don't take my word for it. Ask around. But you will see that you needn't pay her any mind on that area of medical research. She has the qualifications on paper, but she doesn't cut it in practice."

7. "But don't you see, you went to a two year school at first instead of going right into a four year university. I have always found that people who do that are not the best bets for a loan."

8. "Congressional aides are always easy to influence. Is it any wonder that she took the documents?"

9. "You show me why I shouldn't trust my instincts on this one and let her have the job, and I'll reconsider. But I have a strong leaning in her direction."

10. "You know I don't normally run people down. But here I guess I just can't help it. Jones is not the candidate you want to support. He just doesn't understand the issues. Keep that in mind when you review his record."

11. "Herman, where did you get your diploma, from a mail order catalogue? You need to get your head on straight, guy. I just told you the right way to think about this. What's so hard?"

12. "Yes, well, that's just what a lawyer who works for the public defender's office would say. But do you think we really should plea-bargain this one?"

SECTION 3

Fallacies of Failed Effort in Inquiry

Critical thinkers have to take themselves seriously by remaining open to the consideration of beliefs, decisions, and actions to see if they are well-supported. But in order to check this out, critical thinkers must engage in inquiry into the reasons that might be and have been brought forward as support. If thinkers are unwilling to put forward the effort that inquiry requires, and this is sometimes very great effort, then they will not be taking themselves seriously as critical thinkers. Thus there are a number of mistakes to take notice of whose avoidance pose further conditions for becoming a critical thinker.

The first such mistake that comes to mind is as much as anything a feature of everyday life in northern industrialized countries: **Impatience.** If people are not willing to slow down and take seriously the job of looking for the meaning of and evidence for a claim about some matter, if they are too impatient to inquire, then they have not taken on the role of a critical thinker. Yes, contemporary society in the northern industrialized areas seems to have been accelerated to the point that everyone is supposed to do more, more efficiently, and with great success. Facing that sort of attitude in the workplace and at home, the pace of life sometimes seems relentless and people might be forgiven for making snap judgments and failing to inquire adequately into what they should believe or do. But forgiveness is not the same as endorsement. The critical thinker will resist these pressures and seek to become patient enough to critically sort through options of belief and action in order to separate the well-supported from those that are not. Thus we can identify the fallacy of impatience in reflection. In inquiry this shows up as a lack of the thoroughness that comes from perseverance, a lack of calmness in sorting through the possibilities, and a lack of the readiness to put on hold (for the necessary time of inquiry) those desires that are in conflict with the ones operating in the inquiry.

§ **II.7.** *The fallacy of impatience in reflection, or what could be called "the quick fix fallacy"* is the error of conducting inquiry in a cursory or incomplete and rapid fashion so as to move onto something else or to achieve a rapid resolution of inquiry instead of a deliberately thorough one.

> *For example:* Overheard in the study group: "Oh, come on! How long must we spend on this stupid assignment? I'm out of here."

> *Or:* Television detective to the witness, "Wait, wait, can you tell me only what you saw, not what you think you saw? Just give me the facts, not a bunch of observations I have to sift through."

> *Or again:* Doctor to patient, "Yes, yes, I understand that it was a busy time for you. It must have been exciting for your family. But just tell me where the pain is now and at what level it is. Then I can adjust your medicine. We don't have to consider anything new here."

NOTICE: These are all mistakes whose very expression reinforces the separation from inquiry that they illustrate. The more thinkers talk in a way that tells themselves that they have no time, the more they will tend to think they do not have the time, and the more impatient they will tend to become. And thus these mistakes not only cut off the speaker from good inquiry, they also register or put into words the fact that the speaker is cut off from critical thinking.

A closely related fallacy is found in thinkers turning away from beliefs or decisions or actions they find unpleasant or undesirable. This occurs frequently no matter where thinkers are found, that is no matter their culture or their affluence or job situations. In fact it is so widespread that the mistake has its own name: Wishful Thinking.

§ **II.8.** *The fallacy of wishful thinking* is the error of thinking that one should believe or disbelieve something, choose or reject some option, because to not do so would force one to give up other beliefs or choices you want to hang onto.

> *For example:* "Yes, you must always look on the bright side. So what if your entrance exam scores are mediocre and you have nothing distinctive in your resume? Maybe the medical school admission committee will change their policy and take you anyway. Go ahead and apply."

> *Or:* "Yes, taxes support the federal government and some worthy programs. But if I paid my taxes I would have to give up that vacation. That's a bad choice! Don't ask me to do that!"

Or again: "Well, of course if I go to Hollywood, there is a chance I will not be 'discovered' and become a star. But there is also a chance I will. And if I were to be so 'realistic' I would have nothing to live for, just more months slipping away into years at this rotten diner. I am going to keep my eye on the stars, my own included, and head west."

This problem of wishful thinking is really a way of failing to take part in inquiry because of a personal choice. Just as the quick fix fallacy cuts short inquiry so the thinker can get on to other things, wishful thinking closes it off entirely so the thinker does not even have to bother with these other things that are so unpleasant. A related way of shutting off, or shutting down!, thinking is what is commonly known as magical thinking. In magical thinking the person believes what he or she believes, knowing that it is highly improbable and having no reason to think otherwise, but believing all the same. For example, "I know everyone says I won't get that brand new train set I saw in the window at the hobby shop. But I believe in Santa Claus—he will come through." Well, sometimes yes, but sometimes no. Usually people have to take action to achieve their goals, or else some other person has to do so for them. As the poem goes: "If wishes were horses, beggars would ride."

Wishful thinking looks, on the surface, like another familiar fallacy called slippery slope. But they are different forms of failure to make the proper effort in inquiry. While wishful thinking is a matter of the thinker at some level ignoring the unpleasant consequences of a belief, decision, or action, slippery slope is a case of the thinker counting on the possible, even if improbable, consequences to excuse forgetting about the belief, decision, or action in question.

II.9.   ***The fallacy of slippery slope*** is the error of urging that because a belief, decision, or action could have a string of consequences ending in something bad or even disastrous, we should ignore it and not check out its acceptability.

For example: "Don't you see? If we build the road that far from the village limits, it will be inconvenient for shoppers to come our way. And if that happens, there go our tourist jobs, the restaurants, the antique shops, and then the local services that residents depend upon. And once these jobs and services go so will the people. And then what? This will be another ghost town along a super highway. Don't you people get it? This plan is worthless!"

Or: "Well, at first I thought that if the deal went that way, I would be able to avoid the losses I faced otherwise. But then I got to thinking. What if it didn't? Not only would this mean I would lose out on this particular deal, but the bank would see I am not doing well and would refuse to loan me more to set up the next deal. If they did that I would be out of business and then I would have to go back to school and that means more school loans. My life partner would have to work longer before she went back to school to finish the graduate program. The strain would break us up. It just meant the end of everything. So I went for the conservative play and stayed away from that great opportunity."

Or again: "There is evidence of the government having the materials and the technical know how to make the bomb. And if they had it they would use it. And they seemed morally capable of making it. But if they used it, the attack could paralyze the country and kill hundreds of thousands. And then who would feel safe ever again, and who would vote for me? No, I had no choice but to destroy those who might build that weapon before they did; a preemptive strike was called for."

Slippery slope errors then use the string of possible consequences as a reason for rejecting the belief or decision that could lead to them. And thus this mistake cuts people off from the reasoned examination of the possibilities they might be facing. It takes folks away from inquiry, by providing the excuse that the consequences or implications of what would be inquired into are just too bad to take seriously as part of a well-supported belief, decision, or action. But they might not be—after all that is what disaster planning is partially about, assessing likelihoods of unpleasant outcomes, choosing among them to minimize harm, and then planning how to be ready to take the supported actions.

How then can critical thinkers know that their thinking is taking them in the direction of a mistake of slippery slope as opposed to going along a necessary path of considering grim possibilities? There is not a general formula that would allow thinkers to answer that question. Surely if thinkers have independent evidence for believing that some course of events is likely with or without the action of the thinker, and that these will likely lead through a series of intermediary steps to bad consequences, then these thinkers have the responsibility to determine whether they should allow that realization to stop them from going further in their thinking about that option or whether they should think this through further since it is perhaps the least harmful of the likely options facing them. In other words, thinkers should proceed with inquiry that will allow them to responsibly check on whether the implications of the belief or decision are avoidable (an unlikely, unnecessary risk of action or policy). If they are not avoidable, then they might have to stop the contemplated action or not accept that belief since it would lead to unwarranted problems. Their description of their reasoning might sound like a slippery slope mistake, but it would be the result of inquiry, not of the interference with inquiry, and so would be different from the fallacy.

If thinkers have evidence that there is a good chance a course of action or belief will lead to significant errors or troubles, then, if they can, they should avoid that belief, decision, or action. If not, and there is good reason to go ahead, then they may proceed; perhaps it would even be wrong not to proceed. But these are bits of guidance we cannot find outside of inquiry. The slippery slope fallacy would cut thinkers off from that inquiry.

II.10. *The fallacy of misplaced abstraction* is the error of conducting an inquiry into some singular or individual matter while only considering as relevant those characteristics which the event, person, or options under investigation might share with others.

> *For example:* "When considering which van to buy, Margo and Paul looked at one of those consumer reports rating magazines, at the cost of cars of the recommended sorts available in their state-wide area and at colors of cars their family has always favored." "Really? What about what the two of them want and what their own personal family situation was likely to evolve into? What about the look of that top rated van—do *they* really like that? This is a decision they also have to suit to their own lives."

> *Or:* "Well, of course most married people, and many others your age, are planning a family. But what you have to consider is whether that is right for you, and you will not be able to discover that by looking at what other people do or have done. You must examine and come to know your own mind and heart. You are talking about opening a whole new dimension to your life, not to say that of another as well. Don't be hasty to just go along with what your friends are doing or with what is even right for others. It might not be for you."

> *Or again:* "The crime scene evidence points to Lee Harvey Oswald not acting alone in killing President Kennedy. Of course a couple of important commissions studying the assassination concluded that he acted alone. But that just does not explain the facts of the crime scene and the wound patterns. Don't you see, we have to come up with a coherent view that puts all the details of the situation into a relation that would generate the unique moment of the President's wounding and subsequent death. And for that we might have to follow the trail in some unorthodox directions."

What these examples show is that in the matter of certain important decisions, and in fixing certain beliefs about unique circumstances, the important thing to find out is not only the most general facts about the options. Thinkers must sometimes look for the singular or individual facts or constellation of facts or values in order to explain or to move forward toward a decision or action. Paying attention to only the common features, the recurring, and the repeatable patterns of things and occurrences will not always do the job of explaining or fixing a particular belief or course of action. Sometimes, thinkers just want to know about singular events in all their uniqueness and then it would be a mistake of misplaced abstraction to feature only general features or general laws or habits of behavior in inquiry. To be sure, a thinker can take things too far in the other direction. In fact, if a thinker cannot bring an event under general concepts he or she ultimately cannot understand it in a way that is open to being shared with others. But still, it may be that the feature we want to understand is how a number of features or patterns flowed together to give rise to a situation in which the whole is greater than the sum of its parts, in the sense that no set of concepts could capture the full character or dynamic of the object of inquiry. Hence, the fallacy of misplaced abstraction.

The fallacy of misplaced abstraction takes a couple of forms that are familiar enough to have warranted their own names. On the one hand, *a thinker might refuse to inquire into some phenomenon or what brought it about*—such as a complex emotional state unfelt before—*because he or she cannot find just the right concept or descriptive terms to bring the state under*. This refusal to inquire, or the readiness to cut off inquiry when this point is reached, could be considered an expression of an undue perfectionism on the part of the thinker. And when the expression of this tendency has been found in a thinker's considering a policy or plan, others have referred to it aptly as **the perfectionist fallacy.**[2]

A further form of the fallacy of misplaced abstraction has been called **the line drawing fallacy** and *is found whenever someone refuses to inquire or go further in inquiry because this person is unable to precisely separate out what is of interest from what is not.*[3]

> ***For example:*** "What is the point in trying to understand it, it's just the way I felt at the time and there is no name for that feeling."—a case of the perfectionist fallacy broadly construed

> ***Or:*** "No, I am not going to support that policy. It does not make clear what exactly is to be done if we catch someone failing to uphold it. And I'm not buying a pig in a poke."—a case of the perfectionist fallacy of avoiding inquiry in order to wait until all the detailed objectives can be conveyed in abstract general concepts for all to see

> ***Or:*** "No, I won't sign your petition. Exactly when does the subsidy go to a trucker according to your idea? What if the trucker would have taken the turnpike anyway and you wouldn't have had to pay the subsidy of turnpike fees in that case? You'd pay it for nothing. I'm not signing it until you can draw a nice bright line between those cases of truckers who use the turnpike anyway, and the ones we want to get off of secondary roads onto the turnpikes."—a case of the line drawing fallacy

> ***Or again:*** I understand what you are saying doctor, but I want to know exactly when we should intervene with surgery in my case and every other. Until you can draw that line for me I'm going to keep my internal parts to myself, thank you!"—another case of the line drawing fallacy of avoiding inquiry in the name of seeking abstract general rules for guidance

Mistakes of misplaced abstraction are particularly dangerous for they tend to provide ways for thinkers to wriggle out of taking responsibility for their thoughts and for paying appropriate attention to the situation they are in. And they also tend to lead thinkers to impatience with the messy details of life either leading to ignoring these details or to a kind of paralysis with the hopelessness of coping with these details. An example of this last problem shows up in a recent piece of literature as one of the chief characters tries to figure out where things went wrong for her and where she went wrong[4]:

> The mopping and humming had moved farther down the hallway, and I could hear the deputy on duty clear his throat, turn the pages of a magazine or newspaper. I got up and turned off the light switch near the door. The nurse's button glowed white at the head of my bed, and I made my way back to the chair at the window, the vinyl upholstery sticking to the backs of my bare legs, and I remembered Mrs. Behrani bringing tea and kiwi fruit to her sons' room for me; her brown eyes full of compassion as she looked down at my bruised arms, as if her husband doing that had been the only reason I showed up at her doorstep drunk with Lester's gun.
>
> But it was everything: it was talking to my brother, Frank, and hearing that same old patronizing tone; it was the Mexican boy flicking his tongue out at me, his eyes on my crotch like it was something he'd already seen a hundred times before; it was wearing stolen clothes; it was the bright sun on the day after I had drunk too much with Lester the night before; it was my dry mouth and the deep hangover fear I had that Lester had used me up already and was going back to his wife; it was driving through his neighborhood of one-story ranch homes in the heat looking for what I hoped I wouldn't find—it was all of these things and none of them; it was Lester [showing] . . . what I was sure was a sudden change of heart; it was me letting Lester finish what we'd both started, letting all this happen so I could put off facing my mother and brother with the news that somehow Dad's house had slipped through my fingers: I'd been willing for Lester to do anything so I could put off that moment of judgment.
>
> I looked out over the empty parking lot, at the shadowed wooden fence and the black trees behind it, and for a while I tried to tell myself it was the colonel who had brought all this down on us. It was him not doing the right thing with my father's house. It was his greed, and it was his pride. I remembered him on his new roof deck with his wife and daughter and friends, his expensive suit, a flute of champagne in his hand, potted flowers set in the corners of the railing and on the floor, laughing at something one of the fat rich women had said, the way he looked at me as we drove by, his eyes narrowed, all the muscles of his face still with some kind of concentration that scared me.

Kathy, the character who is speaking here, has lost it all—her house, her freedom (she is going to go to jail) and, most importantly, her capacity as a thinker trying to be critical. She is just bewildered and beaten, cut off from critical thinking and the inquiry as well as openness to considering other possibilities that it demands. And she is paralyzed by all that has happened and that she set in motion. She has lost her agency as a critical thinker because she cannot approach the details of her life in this way and because approaching her life through general rules or general concepts of the society she lived in did not work for her at all.

Mastery Exercises II.2

SELF TEST

Impatience/quick fix fallacy, wishful thinking, slippery slope, misplaced abstraction, perfectionist fallacy, line drawing fallacy

FALLACY IDENTIFICATION PRACTICE. Following the Tech Tips found at the end of the chapter, identify the fallacies illustrated in the following exercises. Write a sentence explaining your judgment of which fallacy is present in each question. (Answers in Appendix II.)

1. "You can do what you want. I'm not budging until I get a completely clear picture of what the new mall will look like."

2. "Yeah, well, that is easy for you to say. But I hope to get the concrete work on that mall and my banker is just like you—won't back me so I can make a good bid until he/she knows exactly whether the owners are going to separate staff from customer parking. I know that there is going to be limited parking. But thinking like this is killing my business."

3. "Come on, Chloe, it's not like you have to invent all of the right answers here. There are rules. It's a simple matter of just applying the right rule. You don't have to agonize over all of the details."

4. "Herb, can't we just forget about all of that genetic work-up and lab work? You can see the guy came off the building roof and is smashed to pulp. Anyone can see that would kill him. And anyone can see that he was working up there painting the trim on the front of the building hanging over the edge. The guy fell off and that's that. Let's get lunch."

5. "No, I don't listen to the news anymore. That is just all negative and if I listen to that stuff too much then I start to wonder what the government is up to and when I do that I get angry. And when that happens, I get depressed. That takes me to the psychologist and that's more than I can afford. I cannot afford to listen to the news anymore."

6. "No, I don't go to hospitals either—no matter who is in there. This is just an immediate downer and I want not to have to feel bad. So I'm staying away."

7. "No I'm not going to take that stuff seriously. Why, if I did I would have to quit driving my new Behemoth SUV because I would know that it is totally irresponsible. So I'm not following all that talk about running out of oil in the next decade."

8. "So then the dam will fill with silt and will eventually either break open or just overflow and flood the downstream communities. And when that happens we will have to rebuild them with long term cheap government loans and that will further add to our tax burden. And then the taxes will become prohibitive and

will lead to businesses and individuals moving out. It will ruin the state—we cannot put in those flood control dams."

9. "But sir, wouldn't it be faster to just paint them all the same color and wouldn't that be cheaper also? Do we really know that customers will not buy our cars if they can't get but one color?"

10. "No, that's not the way I see it. When I look at the class all I see is students. They all hear the same lecture and take the same tests and have the same text. That is fairness in the class. I can't make special accommodations for anyone for any reason."

SECTION 4

Fallacies of Unmerited Credibility

Even for those who are open to inquiry and ready to put forth the effort it demands, there are pitfalls of not taking oneself seriously enough. Sometimes thinkers are too ready to accept beliefs, decisions, or actions as acceptable, as correct to believe, or reasonable to act upon. People get tripped up by putting too much faith in high profile sources, in supposed experts, in unsubstantiated views, in popular opinion, and in the media. All of these mistakes come together under the idea of unmerited credibility or unmerited readiness to accept the views or decisions presented. Some of the fallacies to be identified here are so familiar that they are commonly recognized under standard names. Others are mistakes people encounter frequently enough that they deserve to be recognized with their own name. In all cases the basic idea is that of the thinker being too ready to extend belief or acceptance without checking up on where the claim comes from or what might be said for or against it. The tendency to check first, if one is not sure, to express a kind of weak skepticism or hesitancy to accord acceptance without checking, is a normal expression of taking on the responsibility to find and believe or act on well-supported beliefs or decisions. It is not a form of arrogance, nor should it be taken as offensive or as showing a lack of trust. It is what should be expected of those who take themselves seriously as critical thinkers.

II.11. *The fallacy of appeal to the **status** of a source* is the error of being ready to rely on sources, without checking, just because of their status.

> ***For example:*** "But the EPA *has suggested* that the burning of fossil fuels is not as responsible for atmospheric warming as first thought." "Really, and did that happen about the time that the new pro-business President appointed a new EPA director? Might there be a connection?"

Or: "The *police officer who made the arrest* said she saw the suspect reach for a weapon. That's why she beat the defendant senseless with her baton. That's good enough for me." "Oh really, and I suppose that police officers have never been wrong or never been known to cover up prejudices with such stories about resisting arrest? Was all that force really necessary? Once the person is on the ground with her hands behind her back, what more is necessary by way of force?"

In short, just because a source is respected or usually reliable, thinkers cannot rest complacent with that status and accept anything that comes from that source. After all, a general reputation of reliability is compatible with occasional breakdowns, just as a reputation of unreliability is compatible with occasionally or even frequently "getting it right." Remember critical thinkers are taking personal responsibility for what they endorse. "It's 12:01 A.M.; do you know who your sources are and what they are saying?"

A closely related mistake is found in being too accepting of claims to professional credentials. Some physicians are not to be trusted. Some scientists operate with their own religious prejudices. Some clergy wander from the path. So a critical thinker will be alert to checking the claimed expertise of a source of a claim. As someone once said, "It takes only two people and some printed stationery to make an institute."

II.12. *The fallacy of appeal to unexamined expertise* is the error of being ready to rely on someone's claimed expertise on a subject, without checking.

For example: "Dr. Vision has a degree from Perfection University and says that with proper training anyone can become able to see the aura surrounding the head or body of another person." "Really, and what is Perfection University? Is it accredited? Is there really expertise about that subject?"

Or: "In scientific studies paid for by the tobacco companies, it was found that there is not a close connection that could be called causal between smoking and heart disease." "Ok. But are there studies that are done by sources independent of the tobacco companies that have the same conclusion? Might money have something to do with the findings you report?"

Later (in chapter V) the subjects of just how to recognize an authority and just when to trust an appeal to someone's expertise are explored. For now the point is simply the familiar one that if critical thinkers take personal responsibility for the believability or advisability of what they claim or endorse, then they must tend to check that the expert sources they rely on are ok. If they do not do this, they can be faulted as appealing to unexamined experts.

Going hand in glove with this last point but deserving mention by itself is the mistake of accepting unsubstantiated evidence. Of course one way to do this is to make a mistaken appeal to an unexamined expert. But the thinker cannot assume that just by checking her sources she will avoid relying on unsubstantiated evidence. Many myths are taken as background beliefs by experts of the day. Or prejudice might be working in the recognized experts at a time. For example, for a long time it was thought that women were not physically or emotionally strong enough to fly jet-propelled fighter planes in the military. But then some started asking about the credentials of the evidence for these claims. The claims were found to be unsubstantiated and, if resting on evidence at all, on only anecdotal evidence, or unscientific personal stories. We will talk more about anecdotal evidence later in chapter VII, but here you should take note of the need of critical thinkers to require what is called backing or a clear indication of the kinds and qualifications of evidence that might be brought forward for a claim. Thus one needs to recognize:

II.13. ***The fallacy of appeal to unsubstantiated evidence claims*** is the error of being ready to rely on claims that some assertions support a conclusion without checking on the backing for that evidence or without checking on the reliability of the sources and methods of gaining that evidence.

> ***For example:*** "You know, all people are selfish. What can you expect? Why are you surprised when someone treats you like that?" "Well, not to cause trouble, but how do you know that all people are selfish and just what does that mean? Are there psychological studies or other experimental evidence you can point to as reliable sources? Or is there some way we could check up on that claim, find its backing somehow?"

> ***Or:*** "Well, you might not like it, but that is the way it has to be. This is what doctors have done for some time now to treat prostrate cancer." "Yes, I know that, but what sorts of procedures and sources led physicians to believe the thing to do is always operate or use hormonal therapy? Is there a clear source of substantiation of the claim that this is the way to go—perhaps in physiological studies or long term comparative studies of those who had and those who did not have the treatment? Isn't there some debate about this now-a-days?"

> ***Or again:*** (taken from the movie *Twelve Angry Men*) "Sure, the kid had a knife just like this and the old man said he heard the kid and his father arguing and then a thump and saw the kid tearing down the stairs, and the neighbor saw the whole thing from her bed. But there are lots of knives like this one available in the neighborhood, the old man could not have gotten to the door when he said with his bad hip, and the lady who was in bed was not wearing her glasses to sleep in—nobody does, so how did she see the killing? Is there any evidence that has a clean bill of health? Did the prosecutor give us any evidence that made sense? Is there any evidence here that we can say has a clear backing as being substantiated? No."

Just as thinkers should be unwilling to accept evidence that has a questionable pedigree (if any), they should be unwilling to accept what is just taken as common knowledge by some number of people. This has been recognized in the naming of a family of fallacies all of which are, in one way or another, **appeals to popular opinion.** The general idea here is that just because a group of people believe or accept some claim or decision, it does not mean that that claim or decision is worth acceptance or has credibility. For credibility, let alone for an acceptable degree of credibility, evidence or support is needed; just because someone says it is ok, does not make it so. Thus:

§ **II.14.** *The fallacy of appeal to popular opinion* is the error of being ready to rely on claims or to accept decisions just because others in a group of people (with no particular claim to expertise) do so.

> *For example:* "Come on Harry, everyone is doing it! Put your hair in dreads. It's cool." Here is the characteristic trouble with this kind of appeal—"Come on, everyone thinks so/is doing it." Any appeal set in this characteristic form is often just called an *appeal to popularity.*

> *Or:* "Should it surprise us that he thought the Internet was a place to look for a life partner? That is a pretty common thing you know, and it is becoming more and more common. What's the problem?"

> *Or again:* "Yes, we can rest assured that is the correct diagnosis. It is common practice for doctors to diagnose dementia in cases like this—where the patient is older, forgetful, and acting totally out of character while being depressed."

In all of these cases what is taken as the reason for credibility is the ordinariness or commonness of the beliefs or decisions in question within a certain group of individuals—friends, associates, or even professionals. The claim is that credibility flows from the commonality of belief or decision. But this is not correct, as is known from any number of mistaken beliefs held by almost everyone, including experts, for example the belief that the earth is flat, or that the sun rotates around the earth. Depending upon whether the issue is one of what to believe or what to do, the present discussion can follow the lead of others and name this version of the fallacy of appeal to popularity the fallacy either of *common belief* or *common practice.*

Another version of the fallacy of appeal to popular opinion is commonly known as *peer pressure.* Mothers often teach this fallacy when trying to give children good advice about when not to follow the crowd of their friends:

> *For example:* "No, you may not put your hair in dreadlocks. It is false that everyone is doing it. In fact, it's only your friends who want you to do this; and if they all

jumped off the Tallahatchie Bridge, would you also? Of course not!" (Here is an attempt to help someone avoid the mistake of succumbing to peer pressure.)

Or: "Come on Jill, take a puff, you want to be one of us, don't you?"

Or again: "Hey Jack, what's going on?" "Nothing." "You want to come out with us? We're going to sneak onto the golf course and see if we can get in a few holes before dark." "Naw." "Come on Jack, it's ok. We're all going"

Just as an appeal to popularity can take the form of peer pressure, "Well, but that's just what we all believe in this party, abortion is murder! You are one of us aren't you? You do see it don't you?", it can also take the form of a call to join a group just so as to not be left out, a call that is more general than peer pressure. Peer pressure works by appealing to the target's desire to be accepted by the members of a particular group. The mistake in question now works by appealing to the target's desire to not be left out of a potentially good thing, regardless of group loyalties. This mistake is called the **bandwagon appeal,** and it is very familiar during election campaigns. The idea is to call on the targets to jump onboard the campaign wagon so as not to be left out or left behind in the growing swell of popularity of a cause or a candidate. This mistake does not require any particular group affiliations to get carried away. But it does play on insecurities and the general human desire to be accepted as well as not miss out on something good. This mistake can be hard to resist, but critical thinkers need to do so—granting credibility to beliefs or decisions only when warranted by evidence and not just because the wave of public acceptance is washing over them.

For example: "Well, Congresswoman Sprite, you really should consider co-sponsoring this bill. The congress is coming around to our view and you will want to be prominently associated with it when it comes to the floor."

Or: "Dick, I have one word for you . . . oil. That's where the future is." Remember the famous line from the movie, *The Graduate*, where at a graduation party Dustin Hoffman is told the one word is "plastics"? Well this was really, among other things, a case of a bandwagon appeal.

Or again: "The country is now at war. We need to gather behind our troops and come forward with the kind of support these brave men and women need. Now is the time." Sometimes the bandwagon appeal is very useful for good ends, sometimes for bad ends. But in either case, it is what it is and not the providing of evidence. Instead, the bandwagon appeal is the attempt to move people to grant their credibility to a belief or a decision without proper support; it is just another case of the basic problem of appealing to popular opinion instead of appealing to properly substantiated evidence.

One place where thinkers have to be very careful to avoid the mistakes of granting unmerited credibility is in using the media as sources of information. Remember that all news services have sponsors they are beholden to, and often because of that they have a particular agenda they are seeking to fulfill. Values come into thinking critically, both as sources of motivation and guidance, as well as sources of trouble—when they lead to prejudice, manipulation, or other difficulties. Because of this, it might be worthwhile to round out this survey of possible failings of personal conditions for critical thinking by looking at three ways a thinker's values can get her or him in trouble.

Mastery Exercises II.3

SELF TEST

Appeal to the status of a source, unexamined expertise, unsubstantiated evidence, appeal to popular opinion/appeal to popularity, common practice/common belief, peer pressure, bandwagon appeal

FALLACY IDENTIFICATION PRACTICE. Following the Tech Tips found at the end of the chapter, identify the fallacies illustrated in the following exercises. Write a sentence explaining your judgment of which fallacy is present in each question. (Answers in Appendix II.)

1. "But it was released in the company's annual report. That's good enough for me. I believe they are doing well and we should invest further."

2. "Byron is with the Institute for Inter-Galactic Studies. Of course one can take seriously that press release. The recently received strange transmissions from a million years ago are indeed from another life form."

3. "Well, other people sure think so. What more do you need?"

4. "Yeah, you can count yourself in. But that means you'll want to change your political affiliations. The rest of your new buds wouldn't get caught dead voting the way you are talking about."

5. "Oh, come on. Everybody does that. You mean you've never cheated on your income tax? Really, it's ok. Everybody really does that at least a little."

6. "Nobody believes that any more. Everyone thinks it's ok to live with someone before you marry them. It's only common sense."

7. "Most doctors today will use staples instead of stitches. It must be the best way to go. That's what doctors do."

8. "Well, that's what I heard. Aliens have no teeth since they can vaporize their food with their brain waves and then inhale it. So that is the explanation for their fascination with teeth and that's why they always drill teeth when they abduct earthlings. That is the best explanation I have heard for that fact of alien tooth drilling."

9. "Bush and Kerry are running neck and neck. But during the debates when one starts to pull ahead in the polls, you're going to want to join his supporters quickly so you can say you have been backing a winner!"

10. "All the doctors say that Bill Clinton is doing just fine after his heart operation. That's good enough for me. I'm going to not worry about that one anymore," said Senator Clinton.

SECTION 5

Fallacies of Misplaced Values

Pinpointing what might be the source of the trouble in fallacious reasoning requires a certain distinction. There is a difference between what might be called *background values* in thinking and *foreground values*. Background values are those that motivate and guide thinkers in carrying out the process of thinking. They include, first, the value the thinker assigns to inquiry itself—is it valuable in itself, just as an expression of critical thinking, or is it valuable only as a means to power or to status and recognition? Second, they include the value the thinker assigns to getting at the truth or some other appropriate aim of a stopping place in inquiry. And third, they include the value of using the form of evidence gathering and proof appropriate to the situation and the aim of critical thinking the person should have taken to heart in the inquiry he or she is engaged in. These values operate regardless of what the subject matter of inquiry is, no matter what the inquiry is about. Foreground values are not values motivating or guiding the very occurrence and process of critical thinking regardless of what the thinker is thinking about. They are the values at stake in the particular situation where the thinking is needed—values like determining the guilt or innocence of a defendant, like designing a bridge safe for use in the circumstances of the situation, like conducting a particular scientific inquiry with a particular focus.

Thus as critical thinkers engaged in inquiry try to separate well-supported beliefs, decisions, and actions from those that are not, people will succeed or fail depending in part upon whether they are motivated and guided by the *appropriate* background values. If someone is pursuing inquiry only seeking status, not in order to be able to think well about the subject matter, then it would not be unexpected for this person to be susceptible to impatience or to taking shortcuts that compromise the inquiry. If a thinker is seeking the absolute truth in some matter and not what is most reasonably indicated by the evidence, then this person might never reach a conclusion and this would paralyze, for example, the United States justice system. And if the thinker is going to demand that the only form of proof that is acceptable is that provided in mathematical demonstration that is formalized, this person is condemning the inquiry process to giving up many forms of procedure such as generalizing from a sample, arguing from analogy, or appealing to facts that will influence attitudes in order to move toward an ethical decision. In recognition of these points, three possible failings of the thinker's values need to be mentioned and illustrated.

II.15.

The fallacy of false values in inquiry is the error of proceeding in inquiry while being motivated and guided by a set of background values that does not include a strong element favoring the seeking of well-supported beliefs, decisions, or actions through inquiry.

The problem here is that critical thinking is dedicated to not just calculating what is well-supported, but also taking this to heart. If the thinker is not motivated and guided by a background value of living according to critical inquiry, then her or his critical thought will be in the service of and then limited by some other value. In that case, "critical thought" will amount to no more than calculation of the means to the ends under that other value. There will be no basis moving the thinker to take to heart, as important in itself, the discrimination between the good and the bad. Such a thinker is not taking personal responsibility for thinking critically and then is not a true critical thinker.

> *For example:* Reporter to her editor asking for more time in which to research the story: "But don't you care what the truth/best solution/most defensible decision is?" Editor: "No, not really. I care about getting out the story before my competitors and in a way that will sell newspapers."

> *Or:* "Look, politics is not about what is really right or best for the country. It is about what has the appearance of truth and the appearance of serving the good of the country."

> *Or again:* "Go on and ignore those data. They are surely irrelevant to your overall conclusion and no one will know anyway. If you do not, we might lose the new grant funding."

It is safe to say that in all these cases the intellectual honesty needed by critical thinkers has fallen by the wayside. And it is beyond question that this was avoidable, resulting from a breakdown in the background values moving and guiding the thinking involved. The thinkers are not taking responsibility for getting at the appropriate result from the standpoint of a thinker. They have compromised their efforts in favor of some foreground value like beating the competition, getting elected, or getting the next grant award. This serious problem is a case of a fallacy of false values in inquiry.

§ II.16. ***The fallacy of improper ambitions in inquiry*** is the error of proceeding in inquiry toward a degree of certainty that is unachievable in the sort of inquiry in question.

Aristotle, in his *Nicomachean Ethics,* urged that we should not look for more precision than is appropriate to the task of inquiry at hand. That is the point here.[5]

> Our discussion will be adequate if it has as much clearness as the subject-matter admits of, for precision is not to be sought for alike in all discussions, any more than in all the products of the crafts. . . . it is the mark of an educated man to look for precision in each class of things just so far as the nature of the subject admits; it is evidently equally foolish to accept probable reasoning from a mathematician and to demand from a rhetorician scientific proofs.

Should the pollster demand the certainty that seems to be present in a mathematical proof? Of course not. Should the arresting officer demand the degree of certainty that is asked of the jury in a death-sentence trial? No. Similarly, the mathematician should not be allowed to settle a claim with the degree of certainty that is part of a personal anecdote. Different inquiries bring with them different degrees of rigor and different degrees of certainty of outcome that should not be confused if critical thinkers are to proceed responsibly.

> ***For example:*** Henrietta decided she had had enough. She had looked at three different dealerships (Lincoln, Lexus, and Hummer) for a comfortable economy car. She thought that that was plenty and she could feel good about her research and about settling for a Lexus.

> ***Or:*** Bernie went on from text to text determined to prove beyond doubt that her thesis was entirely new on the subject. She aimed at looking through all the vast literature before she would feel comfortable that she had a thesis worth doing.

> ***Or again:*** "Well, of course, a basic physical examination suggests a tumor. But before we can justify an operation or decide on another course of action we need to carry out several other tests." "But the patient's insurance won't pay for all of that, Doctor. Let's just operate and be done with it. I've never seen a clearer case." "It may be clear to you, Doctor, but I will not take part without the added tests, even if that means we do nothing."

In the first two cases there are clearly mistakes of improper ambitions in inquiry. Henrietta did not look nearly far enough nor in nearly an efficient enough way. And while Bernie's dedication to originality might be laudable, the objective of an entirely new thesis might be a bit over-reaching. Is there any subject that has no history or relatives in research? How could this be understood? In the last example things are not so clear. Here the thinker would have to weigh the demands of what is proper given the dangers to the patient if the doctors do not operate because of the unwillingness of the insurance company to pay, against the dangers to all concerned (physical, legal, and economic) if the doctors do not look further and go ahead to operate. Where do you think the line should be drawn separating proper from improper ambitions in inquiry in such a case?

To pick up on the second of Aristotle's points, that thinkers should not seek a form and standard of proof that is appropriate in one area to be applied in another area or an area with a different subject matter, set of problems, and aims, the work of John Stuart Mill in ethics comes to mind. In Mill's treatise, *Utilitarianism,* he pointed out the tendency of theorists of his day to try to reduce ethical decision making to the fewest possible fundamental principles. From these principles, a number of general rules could be deduced or proven and these rules could guide agents in the everyday situations they face. But what is the proof for the one or more basic principles the ethicist works with? Mill claimed that these could not be proven the way they could be used to prove other general rules. No logical proof would serve as a procedure to support basic ethical principles. Still[6]:

> We are not, however, to infer that its acceptance or rejection must depend on blind impulse or arbitrary choice. There is a larger meaning of the word "proof," in which this question is as amenable to it as any other of the disputed questions of philosophy. The subject is within the cognizance of the rational faculty; and neither does that faculty deal with it solely in the way of intuition. Considerations may be presented capable of determining the intellect either to give or withhold its assent to the doctrine [considerations suited to convince us somehow]; and this is equivalent to proof.

So Mill was saying that there is a form of proof that was rational but not like a familiar logical argument. He went on to suggest that this "proof" worked by making the basic principle (he thought that there was only one) self-evident or clearly appealing to thinkers by showing that this principle served to direct us toward what we really favored anyway. Whether this "proof" worked is one question, but it is not the point here. Mill just gives us one more illustration of Aristotle's point that critical thinking demands different processes of thinking by different thinkers operating in different subject areas or with different problems. So:

§ II.17. *The fallacy of improper processes of reason* is the error of seeking to proceed in critical thought using a form of reasoning or proof that is inappropriate to the problem or subject area in which the thinker is operating.

> ***For example:*** "But that is not the correct way to proceed. You cannot decide a question of what best explains the fossil record by an appeal to faith or by an appeal to what you can or cannot imagine. 'There are more things in heaven and earth,

Horatio, than in your philosophy.' Understanding the appearance of diversity among life forms requires a careful knitting together of the geological and biological records we have."

Or: "Your experimental results, as interesting as they are, are not enough. You must show the expression of the equation or other mathematical statement describing the events so that we have some baseline against which to see if future attempts to reproduce your results really do duplicate them. You cannot just describe a procedure and claim that it shows nature does not operate as we all think it does."

Mastery Exercises II.4

SELF TEST   False values in inquiry, improper ambitions in inquiry, improper processes of reason

FALLACY IDENTIFICATION PRACTICE. Following the Tech Tips found at the end of the chapter, identify the fallacies illustrated or hinted at in the following exercises. Write a sentence explaining your judgment of which fallacy is present in each question. (Answers in Appendix II.)

1. "Yes, if you are the first to clone a human, you will win all sorts of recognition. And you might even get a Nobel prize with lots of money. But is that the reason you are doing this?"
2. "You can try it, but I really don't think that consulting your horoscope is the best way to make business decisions. Do you?"
3. "Don't get your hopes so high would be my advice. You cannot be sure that your choice of a life partner will work out for the best. Concerning something so complex, there are no guarantees in life."
4. "What do you mean, you just want to end the war early? Aren't you aware of what you are unleashing on the future in terms of the struggle for nuclear supremacy?"
5. "Professor Smith indicated in her grant application that funding this research is likely to give the answer to the key problem of the riddle of aging."
6. "Did you know that among the Dogon, what they plant where is decided by a Shaman interpreting the hyena tracks in a grid work they lay out for the animals to walk through? Who needs agricultural science?"
7. "Did you know that head hunters in South America believed that by taking the heads of their enemies and then shrinking them and keeping them they gained the power—strength, cunning, health, and so on, of those whose heads they took?"

Wrap-Up _____

Thus there are several sets of developmental concerns the person needs to take on when becoming a critical thinker. The critical thinker will be concerned about openness, exerting proper effort in inquiry, assigning only merited credibility, and approaching inquiry with the proper background values. This chapter has presented several fallacies that fall under these categories of personal concerns appropriate to the critical thinker.

FALLACIES OF OPENNESS
- **1a.** bias
- **1b.** prejudice
- **2.** stereotyping
- **3.** ridicule
- **4.** ad hominem abusive
- **5.** ad hominem circumstantial
- **6.** poisoning the well

FALLACIES OF FAILED EFFORT IN INQUIRY
- **7.** impatience/quick fix fallacy
- **8.** wishful thinking
- **9.** slippery slope
- **10.** misplaced abstraction
    - **a.** perfectionist fallacy
    - **b.** line drawing fallacy

FALLACIES OF UNMERITED CREDIBILITY
- **11.** appeal to the status of a source
- **12.** unexamined expertise
- **13.** unsubstantiated evidence
- **14.** appeal to popular opinion
    - **a.** appeal to popularity
    - **b.** common practice/common belief
    - **c.** peer pressure
    - **d.** bandwagon appeal

FALLACIES OF MISPLACED VALUES
- **15.** fallacy of false values in inquiry
- **16.** fallacy of improper ambitions in inquiry
- **17.** fallacy of improper process of reason

And that is quite a bit to take in! But if you practice the exercises of the chapter and take your time as you approach reasoning, you will find that the points discussed in this chapter come to be second nature in your assessing reasoning. In order to help practice, consider the following Tech Tips for checking on fallacies.

How do thinkers apply these concepts of fallacy to real cases? The first thing to do is to make sure that you understand the fallacies themselves and how they are different from each other. Gaining that understanding is a matter of reading and perhaps re-reading the text and definitions and going over the examples. Then you need to sensitize yourself by looking for these fallacies, a few at a time, trying to find them in what other people or you yourself do and say. You will make mistakes because this involves interpreting what is said or done and that is sometimes a tricky task. But that is ok—as long as you are not offensive or too hard on yourself Beyond this sensitization study and trial period, you will need to practice the application of these ideas by looking at the exercise examples and trying these out. In order to do this, a general set of procedures might be useful. Consider the following:

1. Read the statements or pieces of conversation carefully, and get clear about what you think is being said, by whom and to whom.
2. Identify and write out for yourself what the focal point of the statement is. What are the people involved talking or arguing about or discussing? This focal point can be specified by asking what it is that the parties involved are trying to decide? That will be the focal point of their conversation. (***For further study:*** compare the idea of the focal point with the question of what is the issue of some thinking. See, for example, Brooke Noel Moore and Richard Parker, *Critical Thinking*. Boston: McGraw Hill, 2003.)
3. Ask yourself what you think is the context of the conversation—who is talking, what are their interests, what are they trying to do in the conversation, what do they assume—where are they coming from?
4. Ask yourself what is happening, what is the speaker trying to do with language— mislead, threaten, convince by appealing to relevant facts, play on the sympathies of those listening, get the listener off the track, make something bad appear to be better than it is, and so on?
5. Once you have figured out what the speaker is trying to do, you can see if any of the fallacies discussed are committed in the way the speaker is proceeding and in what is said.
6. If you think the answer is yes, write a sentence or so explaining what the fallacy is and how it is committed in the case you are considering.

   SO: Review the fallacies covered in this chapter, either in the Quick Reference and Summary or the text above, and review or work through the exercises given above after each section. Also consider the comprehension questions and the application exercises on page 74.

Mastery Exercises II.5

SELF TEST   *Comprehension Questions*

1. What is the difference between background and foreground values in inquiry?

2. What are common background values in inquiry?

3. What other options besides critical thinking do humans have for getting along in the world and with each other?

4. Distinguish bias, prejudice, and bigotry.

5. Explain why ad hominem fallacies and the problem of poisoning the well are fallacies.

6. Wishful thinking and slippery slope might look a lot alike. What is the difference?

7. Why is being "treated like a number" an example of misplaced abstraction?

8. Should you believe whatever is printed and published? What three things should you do to protect yourself against mistakes in taking for granted whatever is printed and published?

9. Why shouldn't you follow common practice and not have to think anymore about what is commonly done or commonly thought?

10. When should you join someone's political followers?

Applications and Everyday Uses _____

REFLECTION QUESTIONS

1. How well do you feel you have taken up the responsibilities of critical thinking in terms spelled out by the fallacies of this chapter? Can you now identify areas where you have some room for improvement? What are those?

2. Think about those you work with, about our public leaders and others in your life who have some degree of authority. Can you say in terms of the fallacies or focal points of the chapter just how these individuals would rate in their openness and efforts in inquiry?

3. How many of your friends or co-workers rely on critical thinking rather than the other alternatives mentioned in this chapter? Explain.

4. Have you made any resolution about what you would do as a parent or a boss to make things better for others than they were for you? Do any of these fit with the personal responsibilities of critical thinkers set out above? Which ones and how so?

APPLICATION EXERCISES

A. Write a training manual page for a company where you have worked or would like to work having to do with developing critical thinkers among your workers. What would you do to put into practice the points of this chapter if you were the boss?

B. Write classroom rules that will enhance critical thinking in your course by helping class members come of age as critical thinkers as this is understood in this chapter.

Notes

[1] See, for example, Moore, B. N., and Parker, R. (2003). *Critical thinking.* Boston: McGraw Hill Higher Education, p. 138.

[2] See Moore and Parker. (2003). Pp. 191, 199, G-5.

[3] See Moore and Parker. (2003). Pp. 191, 192, 199–200, G-4.

[4] Dubus III, A. (2000). *House of sand and fog.* New York: Knopf Publishing Group, pp. 355–56.

[5] Aristotle. (2004). *Nichomachean ethics* (trans. by W. D. Ross). [classics.mit.edu/Aristotle/nicomachaen.1.i.html] Book I Chapter 3.

[6] Mill, J. S. (1957). *Utilitarianism* (ed. by Oskar Piest). Indianapolis: The Liberal Arts Press, Inc., p. 7.

CHAPTER III

Reason Versus Manipulation and Power

SECTION 1

Choosing Your Path

Each person has a choice of how to conduct her or his life. Freedom and the means to carry out one's choice do not always follow it, even if the choice is taken to heart as the central commitment of the individual. Still the individual can undertake to live by her or his power or wits or by being reasonable, guided by critical thinking. Those who choose to live by their wits have committed to moving through the world, by the manipulation of others (and maybe even the manipulation of her- or himself). Those who have chosen power will rely on reason not to trick or maneuver others to where the agent wants them, but to calculate how to most efficiently and effectively take and keep what they want. The previous chapter taught us that reason brings people together in a spirit of openness and impartiality with the intention to create a harmonious and well-supported understanding and shared space in which to live. That chapter sought to characterize what sorts of developmental concerns persons take on in passage to the standing of critical thinkers. The present chapter flows naturally from that study to look at some of the modes of interaction between critical thinkers. In particular, this chapter reviews a number of ways in which one person might substitute a technique of manipulation or the exercise of power for the appropriate technique of critical thinking.

The mistakes in question here have to do with the speaker or writer:

§ evading the subject or focal point,

§ misfiguring or mischaracterizing the focal issue by faulty comparisons or over-simplifications,

§ seducing the target person into thinking in a way that he or she likely would not have otherwise,

§ seeking to force another to believe or decide in some particular way.

Each of these sorts of problems deserves its own section.

SECTION 2

Fallacies of Evasion

Instead of meeting a focal point of discussion squarely and honestly, thinkers will sometimes seek to serve their own well-being by evading the issue. At certain times, for example when the parties to discussion are enemies, extra consideration is important to even keep the door open to joint critical thinking. Here diplomacy is needed instead of bluntness; gentle and mutually sensitive forms of expression are called for. But in ordinary circumstances, while politeness and respect are called for, directness is needed to achieve mutual understanding of the issues on the table. In such normal cases, evasion will side-step or even throw critical thinking off the tracks all together. Four fallacies seem to be particularly well-known forms of evasion.

The first of these takes its (fifteenth century) name from the use of a salted and smoked herring (processes that turned the fish a rich brown color), dragged across the trail of a hunted animal, to divert the dogs and get them off the scent.

III.1. ***The fallacy of red herring*** is a matter of introducing into the discussion or even into the characterization of the focal point of discussion something that is irrelevant and takes the discussion off subject.

When a speaker or writer does this and gets away with it he or she will have evaded the burden of taking a critical part in the discussion of the focal point at issue. But for this reason the use of a red herring (also called a "smoke screen" in discussions of the fallacy) is a manipulation of others in the discussion when they are drawn off target. If this evasion is fully effective, it will involve changing the subject.

> ***For example:*** "Yes, of course, we should pay our taxes on time. But you should remember that there are a couple of traditions on paying taxes. Think of the great Americans who protested at Boston Harbor as the American Revolution was heating up."

Or: "Yes, there is a tradition of bad blood on both sides of the feud and the situation is dangerous. But remember that in ancient times people in the region were able to overcome that and live peacefully. I'm not sure why we should intervene."

Or again: "Well, yes, the Vice President uses coarse language and has thereby brought the office down in prestige, if not into disrepute. But he is a defender of the causes that many wealthy supporters applaud. Let's keep that foremost in our minds as we look to the convention."

Another form of evasion is found *when speakers or writers minimize the importance of some event, statement, or decision. In doing so, people are trying to manipulate those others in the conversation to ignore or disregard the problem that event or statement represents.* One form of this fallacy has been called the "downplayer" by Moore and Parker and is associated with terms like "merely" and "only." (For example: "Well, yes, it looks like a famous person has recently been caught up in insider trading. But the offense involved *only* a few tens of thousands of dollars." "But Herb, the deluxe model was a *mere* $5100 more.") However, this form of manipulation does not require the use of terms such as "only" and "merely." (For example, "Yes, we have been concerned about that dam bursting. Daily inspections have led us to believe that the danger was not great. Failure and collapse would come as a great surprise." How complete were these inspections anyway? What is danger that is not great? Is that less than one in a million? So collapse would be surprising—does that mean anymore than that the speaker does not think the danger is high?) Furthermore, the same sort of *problem of minimizing the importance of something arises even though the speaker or writer is not downplaying the danger or significance of some event or statement.* Sometimes we hear others and their views and decisions simply dismissed as having no importance. This does not require ridicule or bias or an argumentum ad hominem either. In fact, it might involve a characterization of another person or her views as being those of someone who does not count because of their age or economic group or area of residence and might be said with no personal malice at all.

For example: "Horace is just a child. He never grew up. You can't blame him. But you can't take him seriously either. You had better ignore his advice on this one."

Or: "Betty is indeed a beautiful person, inside and out. And she knows the product line perfectly. But she has had trouble closing sales. We cannot send someone like that to set up this account even if she did do the basic groundwork. I think we should send Suregrip. Something this big you don't want to have any problems."

Or again: "Adrianna, my dear, what can I say? What we had was wonderful. But it is not the stuff that two people build a life on. We both need to move on. There is really nothing to discuss."

Perhaps Horace is a child, that is, emotionally immature in some or even many ways. Still he might be the best in his field and his advice might be worth a tremendous amount. The speaker is dismissing Horace and his beliefs without good reason. *Betty's case* might reveal the work of prejudice if the description of the parties involved were more complete. However, regardless of that, there is not any clear reason for setting aside Betty as the person to close the deal. Perhaps she has gotten as far as she has because her personality is just right for the client involved. *Adrianna might not agree* that there is nothing to talk about. Surely one person's dismissing the significance of a relationship requires more than one of the parties saying that there was nothing of substantive significance there. Relationships change lives and should not be tossed aside merely on the say-so of one of the parties.

Thus, in addition to what others have called downplayers, there are problems of dismissing someone or their views through remarks that are patronizing or condescending. These cases of dismissing others are, like the cases of downplayers, attempts to direct attention away from the views or decisions of others. The term "the fallacy of casual dismissal" captures both of these.

III.2. *The fallacy of casual dismissal* is the error of setting aside the potentially significant views or decisions of someone or the significance of an event or occurrence for no reason that challenges their significance, but rather in order to evade the responsibility of seriously considering them.

> *For example:* "Well, yes, Simpson did inflate her expense account report. But it was only by about 5% as far as I can tell."

> *Or:* "Bartholomew did win the Queen's Cup at the Royal Cat Show last year, to be sure. Since then some new competitors have come forward with his features. I think we can safely move on to consider them."

Yet another form of evasion takes place through the use of language to cover up the faults or assets of a person or of that person's views or decisions. In some cases this might amount to a detailed redescription featuring the good or bad aspects of the person or the views in question. In other cases the cover-up does not have to be so elaborate, but might operate through the choice of a single term that does the job. The words for an expression that puts a better face on things and for the practice of choosing such a word are **euphemism** and **euphemize.** For example, "President Clinton has taken a *strong interest* in some of his office staff, over the years." Here "strong interest" does the job of putting a better face on what was clearly sexual misconduct, at least in the White House. The word for an expression that puts a negative or perhaps the worst face on someone or some belief or decision is **dysphemism,** a term that interestingly came into use much later than "euphemism." The use of dysphemisms could serve to cover up assets thinkers should pay attention to. For example, "President Clinton, through the use of NATO, bullied his way to a peace in the Serbo-Croatian-Bosnian conflict." Whatever one thinks of the Balkan conflict, it was a human disaster; and Clinton's work through the Dayton accords and the NATO peacekeeping work were both needed and moderate. So keeping in mind euphemism and dysphemism as well as descriptions and characterizations that are more elaborate but have the same effect, one can speak of a fallacy of "cover-up" or, to go along with present habits of speech, "spin."

III.3. *The fallacy of cover-up or spin* is the error of redescribing or re-presenting someone or her/his beliefs, decisions, or actions as less faulty or less good than they are, by putting a better or worse face on them without good reason and to influence reasoning.

> *For example:* The instructor's habit of braiding his greasy hair as he spoke was an *endearing personal touch* in an otherwise impersonal situation. (Euphemism)
>
> *Or:* "Yes, I've studied his work over the last several years and noticed a decided *turn toward greater efficiency and hopeful signs of real achievement in his professional roles.*" "Really? In other words, he is still befuddled and incompetent, though less so?" (A positive cover-up/spin)
>
> *Or again:* "Herbert Hoover was a man of many accomplishments. He really did have *several personal accomplishments.*" (A paraphrase of a positive cover-up expressed to lighten the negative spin of earlier references to President Hoover. Original statement made by Senator John Kerry in a campaign speech in the Midwest July 4, 2004.)

One of the most direct forms of evasion is in using language in such a way that the speaker or writer does not tell the truth. Forms of this are: outright lying, prevaricating or withholding a clearly important part of the truth, obfuscating or speaking or writing so as to confuse those concerned with the issue, and simply not being forthcoming by volunteering what is clearly relevant and important. *A generally recognized rule of normal conversation is that people will offer up what they know on a subject and believe to be of interest and relevance to the subject.* This rule is especially in play where the discussion is "serious," that is, purposeful and aimed at securing some information or agreement. In such a context, to deceive or fail to be forthcoming in any of the familiar ways mentioned is to be evasive and then to set aside one's responsibility for the mutual inquiry that is critical thinking. While it is not a problem in playful or casual circumstances, such evasion is a serious problem in contexts of critical thinking and is usually put in the service of manipulating or exerting power over one or more others. Thus, speaking of all of these problems, notice should be taken of the very basic mistake of deception. Unfortunately, since discovery of deception requires knowledge of what is kept from view, this fallacy is often difficult to spot. Still, contextual clues can make its presence clear.

III.4. ***The fallacy of deception*** is the error of evading full participation in critical thinking by withholding or misstating information thought to be pertinent to the subject or inquiry at hand.

> ***For example:*** President Clinton said he had never had sexual relations with that woman.
>
> ***Or:*** The White House staff said it had no idea what had happened to the 18 minutes missing from President Nixon's taped meetings concerning the Watergate break-in.
>
> ***Or again:*** At first, the President and the Vice President said they would not supply all of the documents called for by the 9-11 Commission.

Mastery Exercises III.1

SELF TEST

Fallacies of Evasion: red herring; casual dismissal—minimizing the importance of persons or views; euphemism; dysphemism; cover-up or spin; deception

FALLACY IDENTIFICATION PRACTICE. Following the Tech Tips found at the end of chapter II, identify the fallacies illustrated in the following exercises. Write a sentence explaining your judgment of which fallacy is present in each question. (Answers in Appendix II.)

1. Vice President Cheney said that if people in the United States do not vote properly in November 2004, there will be major terrorist attacks—not that he would be responsible of course, but that they would come.
2. When discussing the budget and the country's present economic condition and outlook, President Bush states that Senator Kerry would be a spendthrift in office, increasing the size of government in the bargain.
3. The crimes against prisoners at the Abu Ghraib prison complex in Iraq have been marked as the work of a few misguided and low-level soldiers.
4. Senator Zell Miller (D-GA) has been marked as a "disaffected democrat." After the attack on the democratic candidate for president, this seems a bit soft—it is a _____ applied to this apparently angry man.
5. The worries over the future of energy supplies because oil production is peaking have been labeled by some as "alarmist."
6. According to some, the mining of western Bureau of Land Management Lands to extract a small amount of natural gas has been another environmental disaster. Others have said that such actions have to be placed in the context of the limited supply of natural gas and the general growing shortage of fossil fuel energy. In that larger context, these energy extraction implications for the environment lose any appearance of real significance.
7. President Nixon said he had no involvement in the break-in at the Democratic headquarters in the Watergate Hotel.
8. "Yes, but if you look at it as an opportunity to develop a new shopping center that is wanted by the people, the destruction of that rare natural area is justified."
9. The Enron officials indicated that their practice was just a matter of reinvesting in the company by moving assets to off-shore sites.
10. "You call that an investment opportunity? I'll tell you what it is—it is a real scam. It is just another pyramid scheme."
11. "You might think that someone with that kind of an education had something to say. But in fact that is not so. Look at the person's career. He did not go to the right schools, or study with the right people, he has squandered his career on administration as opposed to excellence in teaching and writing books, and he is close to the mandatory retirement age. I doubt that his views are ones you really need to review here."

SECTION 3

Fallacies of Misfiguration

Figurative language uses emotional suggestions, and various sorts of comparisons or other associations, to give a figurative impression of what the speaker or writer is getting at. So figurative language is used in a non-literal way to figure or sketch out a sense or meaning of what the speaker or writer is getting at. The phrase, "as light as a feather," used to characterize a suitcase, is not to be taken literally. Indeed, as applied to a suitcase, it might be no more than a polite reassurance that it is no trouble for the speaker to carry the bag. "As dry as late October leaves," "as dry as sand," "as dumb—no, dumber than, dirt," are all characterizations that when applied to a person paint a rather unflattering picture. "Dead as a doornail (a stout nail with a big head)" might have suggested something being carefully planned or executed so as to be solidly fixed, "not going anywhere." And so it goes. Roughly, there is an expression which in one field of endeavor (rough as a cob—a dried corn cob), or absolutely ("dumber than dirt", "a true Venus/Adonis") suggests a certain image with certain more or less literal information contained in it and certain positive or negative emotional associations attached. Then, this expression is borrowed and applied to some other kind of object or person or belief or event falling outside its normal range of application. "His was a crazy view, one that is just not open to a sane individual." This creates a picture of the newly characterized thing or person as similar in important ways to what is mentioned, and it sets up a bridge across to the emotional connotations of the original comparison (rough to the touch, coarse and unrefined, uncrafted, for "rough as a cob," and so abrasive and offensive, unpleasant to be exposed to, the "crazy view" is one no one who considered herself or himself sane would want to be associated with—it would be likely to bring on disapproval). These emotional associations can then influence the person who is the speaker's or writer's target: "Well, if that lawyer is rough as a cob, he/she is not for me. That is not my style and why expose myself to the grief?"

"If the worker is dumber than dirt, why would I hire her/him? I don't need to supervise every hour the worker is on the job. And what would it do if I did? It sounds like a headache to me." "That's a crazy view." "Yeah, now that you point that out I don't want any part of it."

Thus in the way thinkers create images of the persons, beliefs, decisions, and actions they encounter, they can influence others. They manipulate them by positive or negative emotional associations into believing or deciding as the thinker wants the target to, or manipulating the others into agreement in attitude with the speaker/writer, and then into agreement in belief or decision where the target's attitude brings that person along to the uptake of the belief or decision.[1] When such influence is undertaken, there is a fallacy of what can be called "mis-figuration." The term should remind the reader of the role of either the figuration or figurative language in these fallacies. There are three such fallacies that deserve special notice.

The first of these mistakes points to what have been called persuasive definitions as the tool of influence as opposed to argumentation.[2] Thus we might seek to offer what looks like a definition—"God is love," which supplies not so much clarification of terms or analysis of their meaning, as emotional association that will open another's thinking and attitudes toward the possibility that there is a God, or that the deity is of a certain sort—loving, as opposed to angry and vengeful. If thinkers were interested in turning the attitudes of those with whom they speak toward or against some belief or decision, then such a tool as an emotionally laden definition would be quite useful. But in critical thinking the aim is different. Instead the basic idea is to provide reasons for or against beliefs, decisions, and actions, evidence that such possibilities are or are not well-supported.

III.5. *The fallacy of persuasive definition* is the error of defining a term in such as way as to seek to manipulate others to approve or disapprove of what is being defined.

> ***For example:*** "A fishing rod is a pole with a hook at one end and a *fool at the other.*"

> ***Or:*** "A terrorist is a *freedom fighter* for a government out of power."

> ***Or again:*** "A sale is any offering of merchandise the price of which has been marked down to what it *should normally sell for.*"

The italicized portions carry the emotional tone that the thinker offering the definition hopes to transfer to the defined term so as to manipulate another into endorsing or rejecting what the defined term applied to. Thus the anonymous author of the first definition is presumably against fishing and wants the reader to be also. (Or perhaps it is just a joke at the expense of fishers.) The author of the second example would be trying to gain the approval of terrorists by associating them with a struggle for freedom—an obscene manipulation, given what terrorism is. The third definition seeks to explode the appeal of special sales offerings as themselves forms of manipulation.

Similar attempts at influence are offered up in *comparisons* where there is a manipulative transference of both emotional tone and credibility from one of the objects or beliefs being compared to the other.[3]

III.6. *The fallacy of persuasive comparison* is the error of offering a comparison so as to manipulate others to approve or disapprove of the target belief, decision, action, or person in the comparison.

> *For example:* "Fallacies in one's reasoning are about as welcome as a summer cold."

> *Or:* "A rich man can get to heaven about as easily as a camel can get through the eye of a needle."

> *Or again:* "Rodney is as reliable as Big Ben/Old Faithful/the Sun."

> *Or yet again:* "Accepting that view of things about your illness and your physician is like splashing cold water on your face on a really hot day. It will feel good for a while, but in the end it will not help your condition. You might as well just accept the truth and not deny it."

III.7. *The fallacy of oversimplification of the alternatives* is the error of presenting the plausible or reasonable options of belief, decision, or action as fewer in number, or less complete, than they really are. This allows the speaker/writer to focus the target reasoner's attention away from attractive possibilities (or from one to be avoided) and on to the alternatives the speaker or writer wants to receive consideration.

The most familiar name for this problem is that of **false-dilemma** (here, a lemma is an argument or value or possibility to be considered, and so a di-lemma is a "two lemma" where both of the two possibilities are usually unpleasant or undesirable). But a false dilemma is important for critical thinking as a form of misfiguration since it is one of the many ways in which the situation might be miscast as oversimplified.

For example, on July 12, 2004, in a speech at the U.S. Nuclear Arsenal, referring to Saddam Hussein and defending his decision to invade Iraq, President Bush said "If I had the choice of defending America and trusting the word of a madman, I'll defend America every time." Several others, such as European critics, urged that there were other options besides these two.

In addition to leaving out alternatives, a speaker or writer might fail to report important features of the alternatives mentioned, or present one of the competing explanations or sets of reasons for or against an alternative belief in a weakened fashion or even present the considerations on behalf of one of the alternatives in an exaggerated or over-blown way that is not truly representative of the alternatives as they present themselves.

To present only a weakened or incomplete form of one of the alternatives, and in particular a weakened version of one of the alternative sets of reasons or views in question, may be called the **straw figure fallacy** (usually called the straw man argument). The name comes from the fact that such a move gives just a caricature of the target position, making one of the alternative arguments or views in question very weak, easily knocked over, and so subject to disapproval held out for clearly inferior candidates for belief or action.

The forms of persuasion and oversimplification noted here are all tied to manipulating others to believe or accept what the speaker/writer wants them to by the emotional associations involved with the persuasion or dilemma or straw figures involved. Because of this it is appropriate to collect them together as mistakes of misfiguration.

For example: "So, really, you can take *this* raise and promotion at our company, or you can look forward to *never* advancing in the profession." Or maybe the person spoken to can just leave and make a better career elsewhere, or change career paths altogether or make it impossible for the boss to not give the disputed small raise—clearly a false dilemma.

Or: "I can see it now. Either I capitulate to you and you rule our marriage for the duration, or you give in to me and I am in control. I don't see any other way. So what's it going to be?" Well it might be neither. They might divorce sooner rather than later. Or both speakers might both find that they are approaching things in a confrontational rather than a productive way that might prolong and strengthen the relationship. Or again, both might give in and apologize. And no doubt many other possibilities are present in the situation as well—counseling, intervention by a relative, etc.—clearly a false dilemma.

Or again: A speaker conveying the sense of an hour and half long meeting in which the details of the situation and several alternatives were gone over and assessed: "Yes, that's what she/he said, the reason we need to do it this way is so the government won't fine the company." This is certainly a straw figure trading on the usual business disapproval of leadership giving in to anyone or to any force.

Or yet again: "Well, I think I know why the U.S. invaded Iraq. It was for the oil. That's what our leadership was really thinking about and all it was thinking about." Whatever the leadership was thinking about, it was not just oil. That seems safe to say. This must be counted a straw figure.

There is much that is going on in any of these misfigurations. This is true of the straw figure problem just as it is true of the others. But in the case of straw figure, since this mistake can be carried off so deftly as to be very hard to spot, it is particularly important to notice that this problem is not just one of manipulation. It is also a problem of real unfairness to the position or views of others (unlike the false dilemma where the speaker/writer might just miss some important alternatives wanting to influence the other thinker, but just not being fully aware of all the positions). Thus "straw figure" could be located with other forms of unfairness toward others in a situation of interactive reasoning about some problem. However, since the straw figure "works" by leading the other to seek to embrace the stronger position or to reject the weakened position, it really depends upon the emotional charge that is conveyed by the weakening involved. Straw figures look bad, and so disreputable, or they do not work well as forms of influence. The critical thinker can see through this attempted manipulation because he or she is interested in the support possible for the position in question, not the way the other puts the position. If the thinker takes the easy way out and buys into what the speaker/writer says about the position, then he or she will be open to the influence offered. It will be no one's fault but that of the person manipulated.

Mastery Exercises III.2

SELF TEST   **Fallacies of Misfiguration:** persuasive comparison, persuasive definition, oversimplification, false dilemma, straw figure fallacy

FALLACY IDENTIFICATION PRACTICE. Following the Tech Tips found at the end of chapter II, identify the fallacies illustrated in the following exercises. Write a sentence explaining your judgment of which fallacy is present in each question. (Answers in Appendix II.)

1. "That textbook is like a great doorway at the gate of a huge city—it is heavy as lead, hard to open, and squeaks instead of sings."
2. "All that proposal really amounts to is the attempt to balance the budget. Yes, to be sure it was several years in the making and its statement takes about 1500 pages, but that is all it really is, that's all you really need to know about it."
3. "What those people really want is for us to be hurt. They don't like us and that's basically what they want."
4. "Look, you can either seek a career in plastics, or you can be left behind in business for the next thirty years. I've got one word for you—plastics."
5. "Loves me, loves me not. Loves me, loves me not. Loves me."
6. "The woman is a veritable work horse. If you want it done, give the job to her."
7. "Taxes are nothing more than legalized theft by the government."
8. "A well-organized militia is a band of revolutionaries or else vigilantes."
9. "The argument of Jessica Mitford's book, *The American Way of Death*, was that we in the United States spend too much on funerals because we are vulnerable when we have to arrange for the services."
10. "Secretary of State Colin Powell made an argument before the United Nations to the effect that Saddam Hussein had weapons of mass destruction. The argument consisted basically of aerial pictures of trucks and factories, and a bunch of charts that no one understood."

SECTION 4

Fallacies of Seduction

A similar situation arises in the cases of what might be called fallacies of seduction. The seduction comes when the speaker/writer manipulates the other thinker by bringing into play feelings that other already has and allowing these to lead to a belief, decision, or action. The person doing the manipulation is not putting the feelings in the thinker and in that way leading the thinker to some belief, decision, or action. Each of the fallacies of misfiguration present the world in a certain light that brings a certain feeling with it. The manipulation there works through leading that thinker to have that feeling. *By contrast, the fallacies of seduction trade on the other thinker already having the relevant feelings and bringing them into play herself/himself, in light of something the speaker/writer says, or does not say, about something.* A perfect example of this is in the case of the fallacy of innuendo or false suggestion. Here the speaker/writer says something about another or about a position or a decision and omits saying anything directly negative, but leaves the other thinker to draw that negative inference herself or himself. Once that inference is drawn, it brings with it the negative emotional feeling that will lead the other thinker to reject that view or person.

> ***For example:*** "Well, now I've never actually seen her take office supplies out of the building. But she sure did stay and work late the nights when they were taken. That I know." The office worker in question is possibly in trouble if the other thinker is suspicious of the worker, takes the path of the suggestion, and infers that she is the culprit. Clearly this would be a mistake, for how did the informant know she worked late? Was she/he there? If so then is he/she not a suspect? And if not, then what is the evidence the worker was there? Who else was there? Did the office worker named have a motive to steal? Is there any basis to the thinker's suspicions in the first place? The critical thinker should at least check out the evidence and its source before buying into the suggestion.

Or: "Why do you say she has a grudge against you? Herbert, you know that Beatrice is your best friend. She wouldn't have failed to invite you to the party; unless . . . Well, no, I can't imagine that, can you?"

Or again: "We here at Acme Widgets have engineered this product from its first appearance on the sales floor. We, not our only competitor, have made it what it is today. You are not going to let a little glitter in advertising fool you about quality, are you? I'm sure you know which one to buy."

Or yet again: "So for that reason cold fusion violates some of the fundamental laws of physics as we know it. Knowing that as they must have, why do you think the authors of these papers supporting cold fusion wrote them? With that question in mind, can you take their conclusions seriously?"

In the first case, the innuendo plays on a readiness to *suspect* people of theft from the office and especially those who seem to have had a clear shot by working off hours. In the second case, the speaker knows what Herbert thinks already and is using innuendo to stimulate that view. He or she is suggesting without saying so that the only explanation for the lack of the invitation is the one Herbert already seems willing enough to believe. And tapping into Herbert's *worry and hurt* she leads him on to his solidifying disapproval of Beatrice. The speaker for Acme is suggesting that the other company has done nothing to develop and improve the product and so could not have a high quality version of the product. If this history were so, then the advertising glitz would appear to be a cover-up just as the Acme speaker suggested and the product to buy would be Acme's. But this history does not mean that the competitor has not improved the product by going beyond Acme's designs. The appeal is to the *traditionalism* of the listener who hears the history and might be inclined by that to reject the competitor as a newcomer with nothing to offer. And, finally, the appeal in the last example is to a kind of elitism tied to traditional physics. In light of this elitist appeal, the only reason the cold fusion supporters might have written what they did would be the discreditable motives of wanting to upset the apple-cart and gain personal benefit, or wanting to threaten the foundations of the field. For someone who buys into *the bias* of approving the traditional views, this suggestion then turns the tendency toward disbelief of the challenger views. Thus:

III.8.   *The fallacy of innuendo/false suggestion* is the error of leading another to reject or not take seriously a belief, decision, action, or person by tapping into a pre-existing emotionally charged view that runs counter to that belief, decision, action, or positive assessment of the person in question.

Another form of seduction, as it is understood here, is the fallacy of appeals to flattery or the thinker's vanity, or what is sometimes called apple-polishing—among other things. Here the appeal is very straightforward: butter-up the thinker and he or she will agree with what you want her or him to agree with. It is interesting that this way of manipulating plays very effectively into what is known about persuasion. In particular when someone is given something positive, like a compliment tapping into her or his vanity or feelings about self and reinforcing good feelings, there is a greater tendency to reciprocate or give back in kind something that is positive. The recipient feels indebted and also feels a certain amount of loyalty. This psychology of persuasion is all very familiar so there is no point in going on about it. Instead consider the following definition and examples.

III.9. *The fallacy of appealing to flattery or vanity* is the error of leading another to accept or to take seriously a belief, decision, action, or person by tapping into a pre-existing positively emotionally charged view of her- or himself that the other feels, so that he or she feels indebted or for other reasons eager to reciprocate by accepting the belief, decision, action, or positive assessment in question.

> *For example:* "Senator, you are the quickest and most well-informed member of the appropriations committee. I am sure that you see the merits of this bill and I hope we can count on your support."

> *Or:* "But Professor, I have heard that you are one of the most fair people on campus so I was sure that you would take into account how hard I worked and give me a few more points on that basis. Isn't one supposed to be rewarded for effort in this country?"

> *Or again:* "But the claim of the defendant is not going to make it on the basis of this flimsy excuse of being home alone asleep in front of the TV at the time of the crime. You members of the jury are intelligent and have excellent judgment. You have heard the facts. You are morally upright and not afraid to do what needs to be done. I know you will do your duty and find the defendant guilty."

The last of the fallacies of seduction to be considered here is that of *appeal to pity*. Like the others in this group, this fallacy appeals to pre-existing emotions found in the other who is the target of the manipulation. The emotion is pity or sympathy for those in trouble or hurt or having a hard time. Thus a speaker/writer might try to influence another's opinion in favor of a certain view, decision, action, or a certain person by saying what will give rise to sympathy for that view, decision, action, or person.

> *For example:* "Of course, it's an old plan that has proven unworkable. But the President needs a rallying point after that close election—vote for the missile defense system!"

> *Or:* Heard in the sentencing phase at a trial: "Yes, your honor, my client has three prior felony convictions, but he was raised in the most harsh conditions the United

States has to offer a young child: abandoned to the streets, not encouraged to go to school let alone helped when there, running with gangs for his own protection and in and out of jail for a variety of problems. Surely you can take this to heart and give a light sentence?"

Or yet again: "Yes, the position is silly, just not well thought out. But he needs the publication to secure tenure. Can't you find it in your heart to review the paper with a sympathetic eye this time? If you do, I'm sure you will find sufficient merit to warrant publishing it."

Thus:

III.10.   ***The fallacy of appealing to pity or sympathy*** is the error of leading another to accept or to take seriously a belief, decision, action, or person by tapping into a pre-existing sympathy with or pity for it, pointing out how the pity or sympathy is deserved, but not giving any reasons for the belief, decision, action, or assessment itself.

Notice, however, that the following is not a case of a fallacy of appealing to sympathy or pity.

Non-example: "Sure, I think you should give to this charity. If we don't all get involved, even in this small way, we will be part of the cause of great suffering. Let's not be part of the problem, but instead part of the solution."

Here the speaker is seeking to point out that there is a need that can be met only by action and that people should be sympathetic with that because it is a real need. The sympathy the speaker is seeking to arouse should move people to act because it allows them to perceive a real fact relevant to whether to give or not—the real need of the people or other beings in question.

Non-example: "Sure, it is true that Galileo's late views are all the more remarkable than the earlier ones in some ways. Later in his life he lived under house arrest, he was forbidden to continue his work, yet he did so and it had to be smuggled out of the country to be published, he was going blind, and suffered from some such disease as arthritis in much of his body."

This is not to say that his views are acceptable because of the circumstances of his writing them. But it is to say that they are all the more remarkable because of those circumstances. The conditions arousing pity or sympathy should favor this assessment of Galileo and his late accomplishments since the factors mentioned were added obstacles in the way of his work.

Mastery Exercises III.3

SELF TEST

Fallacies of Seduction: innuendo/false suggestion, appealing to flattery or vanity, appealing to pity or sympathy

FALLACY IDENTIFICATION PRACTICE. Following the Tech Tips found at the end of chapter II, identify the fallacies illustrated in the following exercises. Write a sentence explaining your judgment of which fallacy is present in each question. (Answers in Appendix II.)

1. "Well, I don't know. I have a friend who had an operation by that surgeon. And he said that she did an ok job, but he would not say any more about it. You know, it wasn't what he said so much as what he didn't say."

2. "Algon, I know that you had a better system than that. I can't imagine our having trouble with our heating and cooling if you do the work. Of course, your bid was a little high. And while we know you are more than worth it—nobody better in the business—still, do you think you could reconsider your bottom line?"

3. Richard thought that he would try something else since all the flowers and candy did not do the trick. So he cooked up this idea to take Regina to the nursing home where a friend of his worked and show her how good he was with a grandmotherly type—not his grandmother of course since she had already passed away. Rather his friend would fix him up with a grandmother who has Alzheimer's and who will not know that he is not related. What's the harm, right? The grandmother gets a visit and Richard gets the chance to show his better side. Well, we know that this is a deception and that's the harm—in part. But that aside, what kind of appeal is Richard trying to make?

4. The owner of the barber shop said to one of her regular customers: "Herb, you know I don't mess in other people's business. But if I were you, I would just stay away from Clyde. There is just something about him. I can't put my finger on it but it doesn't seem right."

5. "Oh, Pastor Martin, welcome to our little gathering. You can't know how happy you have made us by coming. We have heard so many good things about you. And your membership has done nothing but praise you to the heavens—no really! So hearing all of that, we thought you would be the perfect one to give the benediction at the opening of our fundraiser for homeless pets. Here, let me get you some more coffee!"

6. "True, Bernie has fallen on hard times. But he would never tell you that in order to get some financial assistance. It's just that we knew he had worked for you in the 1990s, and if his side of the business goes under, ours does as well and seventeen people will lose their jobs. Can't you reconsider that loan application?"

7. "Ah, Mr. Hendricks, I know you had wanted to go home early this evening, but I need these reports for the meeting first thing tomorrow morning. I want you to get them out for me before you leave. You know how the Board is so dependent upon you in these matters. Without you they would forget their own names—some do even in spite of your efforts. And we need to get them to move on this by 10:00 in the morning."

SECTION 5

Fallacies of Shock and Awe

There is a big reach to the next category of fallacies of manipulation and power. Here the discussion moves away from appealing to feelings already present in the other thinker. Instead the mistakes in question are ones that rely on bringing into being motivations and emotions the target thinker does not already have. And the influence is not meant to be subtle as in misfiguration. Rather, it is meant to be overwhelming. In another way, there is not such a big difference from those fallacies already considered. The speaker/writer is still trying to manipulate by the appeal to emotion in some way. In the cases in question now, acceptance of a belief, decision, or action is sought through upsetting the other thinker in such a way, and to such a degree, as to lead her or him to that acceptance. Fear, or destabilizing shock, or emphasis, is used to throw the other thinker off balance and to make her or him open to accept what comes next, as a way to find some stability or security in the circumstances. So, these failures of critical thinking might be called **fallacies of shock and awe** to use a name reminiscent of the character intended for the early parts of the second U.S. invasion of Iraq. The most famous of these is known as the scare tactic:

§ **III.11.** *The fallacy of scare tactics* is the error of leading another to accept or to take seriously a belief, decision, action, or person by causing fear in that other person of the consequences of non-acceptance.

> *For example:* "Well you can disagree if you want. Maybe you can get someone to donate money for your car payments after you lose your job."

> *Or:* "No, you don't have to go in there and lie to the investigating committee. But if you don't you will be ridiculed by the rest of the party and never re-elected."

Or again: "Surely you see the merits of that interpretation of the events, do you not? That is, after all, the view we are taking into court and you do want to live to see your children grow up, don't you?"

Here the idea is simple: accept some view, believe, or choose some option, or else suffer the consequences in the (supposed) control of the manipulator. So those who commit this fallacy are trying to move you to believe or decide or act some way in order to avoid some negative consequences they are threatening you with. Fallacies of this sort hardly ever really work to change beliefs or real choices, though they all too often work to change behavior.

Note, however, that the fallacy of appeal to force or scare tactics is different from a warning where someone points out impending negative consequences if you do not take care or change course. And they are different from orders or clarifications of orders in circumstances where the person giving the orders is in a position to ensure that noncompliance is followed by negative consequences. Of course, in the case of warnings and orders, the negative consequences are not ones that are pending because of the desire to manipulate.

Non-example: "You had better watch out. If you put that answer on the test you will be marked down for it and it's not because the instructor has no sense of humor. It's just the wrong answer."—a warning

Or: "The court finds you guilty and your sentence is three years' probation during which time you must report regularly to your probation officer. Failure to do so will lead to your arrest and possible incarceration."—an order and the consequences of not following it

Or again: "Well, of course I want you to take that hill. I just gave you a direct order." (Spoken by a commanding officer, this is not a scare tactic—even though the field officer could be punished severely for disobedience. It is just a clarification of an order where there are serious consequences if the field officer does not comply.)

III.12.

The fallacy of appealing to anger or indignation is the error of leading another to accept or to take seriously (or reject) a belief, decision, action, or person by displaying anger or indignation over the possible or real rejection of that belief, decision, action, or person. The expression of anger is intended to be destabilizing to others since this generally makes humans uncomfortable. The idea is that quieting the anger or indignation by accepting (or rejecting) the belief, or decision, or action in question will achieve a restoration of desired stability in the situation.

For example: "It makes me so angry when I see those people on the street corners begging for what they claim will feed their family. There they stand in their nice clothing with their well-written signs. Why don't they just get a real job like the rest of have to? I am offended by that sort of behavior and I can't take their appeal seriously—can you?"

Or: "First he was willing enough to go, in fact he re-upped for another tour. And then when he got back what does he do? He protests the war and even burns his draft card. What's the matter with someone like that. It makes me so mad to see him doing that. How could you even think about agreeing with him about war?" (This example also suggests another problem which is discussed in the following chapter, IV, namely the problem of having one's beliefs faulted for changing one's mind. See that discussion under fallacy IV.4.)

Or again: "Well, you can listen to her if you wish. But I cannot assign any credibility to a minister who had an extra-marital affair that led to a divorce. I am indignant (morally disapproving) over that incident and would accept nothing she says. Surely you feel the same way?"—moral indignation

III.13.

The fallacy of hyperbole is the error of leading another to accept or to take seriously a belief, decision, action, or person by tapping into a pre-existing readiness to follow someone who displays certitude by inappropriately exaggerated emphasis.

For example: "That is really cool dude! Unbelievable! It's like positively awesome that you think that is the right way to go in your investments. Now what about your friend here? Do you also want to get in on this outta-sight opportunity?"

Or: Overheard at the executive staff meeting: "I thought about it very carefully. But the more I considered it, the more clearly I realized that offering peanut butter and jelly sandwiches at McDonald's is the worst—not about the worst, but really the worst—idea I have ever heard. I have been in the fast-food business for approximately thirty years now. And I have never encountered an idea this bad. I mean never, in thirty years with four different companies. What do the rest of you think?"

Or again: "That is really a preposterous story, Private. Have you listened to yourself? You were captured, put under threat of death, then you end up safe and sound on your relatives' doorstep two countries away. Do you know that sounds just nuts? You can't really expect us to believe it and you cannot believe it yourself. What do you say to that?"

Thus in all three of the shock and awe mistakes a speaker or writer is seeking to unsettle another thinker and, while the person is off balance, to move them to the acceptance of a belief, decision, or action that the thinker might not otherwise have taken up. In the case of scare tactics it is fear that is the working emotion that leads to the acceptance (or at least to behavior as if there were acceptance). In the case of anger or indignation the show of either of these emotionally charged conditions is enough to be unsettling and to move the (now uncomfortable) other thinker to capitulate in acceptance of the belief, decision, or action in question. In the case of an appeal to indignation the anger has the apparent blessing of being on the side of what is morally or legally called for. But of course, this might be only apparent since everyone has run into self-righteous indignation. In the case of exaggeration or emphasis the other thinker is manipulated by the speaker's/writer's strong words and perhaps gestures. If the other feels that strongly and the thinker sympathizers, he or she will be moved to the same view. Enthusiasm is infectious and can draw humans along just as anger can repel them and fear can drive them.

Mastery Exercises III.4

SELF TEST

Fallacies of Shock and Awe: scare tactics, appeal to anger or indignation, hyperbole

FALLACY IDENTIFICATION PRACTICE. Following the Tech Tips found at the end of chapter II, identify the fallacies illustrated in the following exercises. Write a sentence explaining your judgment of which fallacy is present in each question. (Answers in Appendix II.)

1. "Yeah right. That's just the person I want to talk to. Last time I tried to, she said I should make an appointment. Who does she think she is? That's just not right. She is going to have to come to me this time if she wants that bill to be considered. And that's just the way you should feel too."

2. "You can take it or leave it. That is my last offer. I've got the car on the lot and if you think you can find it and get a better price somewhere else, then you should go there."

3. "No, doggone it. I am not going to send it with that inferior courier service again and I don't want you to either. This has been every other day for a week they have delayed getting to us, or so it seems. I've had it!"

4. "You know this is just the best there is. You can look high and low and talk to anyone you want to. Even test drive other brands. There is not a better car made in the world than this Geo. It is superb, just superior in every way. Now do you want to make an offer I can take to my manager?"

5. "No, you don't have to give me your endorsement. But then I don't have to keep quiet about the kick-back from the construction of the new high school either. I'm sure you'd like to explain that to the city government and to the tax collectors."

6. "I cannot believe my good luck! I have finally found you! And now you can make me the happiest man on the block. There is nothing, and I mean nothing, that would please me more than to have your agreement on our petition to recall the Mayor. Yours could be the best, the most influential signature I could collect. Will you sign?"

7. "You are not going to associate yourself with that liar are you? I cannot tell you when I have been so disgusted as when I found out what she had said about the new gym teacher. And I know that what she said is untrue."

Wrap-Up

The bottom line, of course, is that might does not make right and neither does clever manipulation; nor do they make truth. The responsibility of the critical thinker is to see through such attempts to manipulate and always look for credible sources and strong support. Short of those, the critical thinker will reject the belief, or decision, if there is reason to do so, or will suspend judgment until inquiry, even the shared inquiry of argumentation, can produce reasons sufficient for accepting or rejecting the focal claims or views. Just as there are several dimensions of taking oneself seriously as a critical thinker, there are several commitments one makes when taking up reason as opposed to manipulation or the reliance upon power to find one's place and way in the world. Having come of age as a critical thinker and having committed to reason as opposed to guile or power, there are still other general guideposts the critical thinker will follow in inquiry. The following chapter (chapter IV) is devoted to identifying and clarifying some of these further mistakes the critical thinker will avoid.

It might be useful to close out this chapter with a listing of the mistakes and leading concepts covered here. The numbering picks up that from of the previous chapter:

FALLACIES OF EVASION

18. red herring
19. casual dismissal
20. euphemism
21. dysphemism
22. cover-up or spin
23. deception

FALLACIES OF MISFIGURATION

24. persuasive comparison
25. persuasive definition
26. oversimplification
27. false dilemma
28. straw figure fallacy

FALLACIES OF SEDUCTION

29. innuendo/false suggestion
30. appealing to flattery or vanity
31. pity or sympathy

FALLACIES OF SHOCK AND AWE

33. scare tactics

34. appeal to anger or indignation

35. hyperbole

SO: Review the fallacies covered in this chapter, either in the Quick Reference and Summary or the text above and consider the Mastery Exercises given after each of the relevant sections. Also consider the comprehension and the application questions below.

Self Test III-ST1

Comprehension Questions

1. Why would someone want to choose the path of critical thinking as opposed to that of power and manipulation?

2. Is every case of a cover-up or of spin a case of deception? What might be the differences?

3. If a thinker minimizes the importance of a person or a view, what are the dangers?

4. Are euphemism and dysphemism both forms of deception? How do they differ?

5. Could there be a rule by which to tell when a characterization or discussion is an oversimplification or does that have to depend upon context?

6. Since you cannot consider every possible option every time you think about something, is it possible to pick out a false dilemma? *Hint:* how could you know which options to leave out of consideration? By saying how you would know that and some of what to leave out can you come around to the beginnings of a view of when a dilemma is false?

7. Is appealing to pity ever acceptable, or rather, are considerations that raise pity or sympathy ever relevant to the critical thinker?

8. When is pointing out to someone that if they do not do or believe something they are in for hard times not a scare tactic?

9. Hyperbole (like *over*simplification) is clearly one of those things that is an excess of something that is not bad in itself. Discuss whether you think what counts as hyperbole is something that could vary between individuals or groups of people.

10. Is anger or is indignation ever allowed as a consideration for why to believe or decide in a certain way? Is there a place in critical thinking for passionate feelings?

11. Can you think of other ways of manipulating or of playing the power card instead of reasoning with another? What about what lobbyists do? Or what about salespeople? Is their work manipulative and not captured here in the list of fallacies in this chapter?

Applications and Everyday Uses _____

REFLECTION QUESTIONS

1. Have you ever relied on manipulation instead of critical thinking? Did you need to? Discuss the specifics.

2. Think about those you work with, about our public leaders and others in your life who have some degree of authority. Can you say in terms of the fallacies or focal points of the chapter just how these individuals have done in their use and furthering of critical thinking? Discuss.

3. Can political campaigns benefit from moving away from power and manipulation toward critical thinking? What rules would you form for campaigns that would have that beneficial effect?

4. Are there relationships in which critical thinking is out of place and power or manipulation are in place? Can you name five such relationships? What about: i) the military, ii) the police in dealing with criminals or criminal suspects, (iii) _____, (iv) _____, (v) _____.

5. Avoiding the straw figure fallacy requires a good deal of judgment on how much of an opponent's argument or reasoning to give and how strongly to put it. Can you give any rules of thumb for doing this? John Stuart Mill, an important 19th century philosopher, thought that you should put opposing views and reasoning in the strongest possible form. Only then is the truth likely to come out. Do you agree or disagree? Why?

6. Is it necessary to live your life through always putting the best, or some kind of, spin on what you say? Is there a difference between spin and personal or group interpretation?

Notes

[1] For a glimpse of how the psychology works here see: Bower, G. H., and Forgas, J. P. (2000). Affect, memory, and social cognition. In Eric Eich, John F. Kihlstrom, Gordon H. Bower, Joseph P. Forgas and Paula M. Niedenthal (Eds.) *Cognition and emotion*, pp. 87–168. Oxford and New York: Oxford University Press.

[2] See Charles L. Stevenson, whose work in ethics did much to introduce the present understanding of this notion of a persuasive definition used in effect to secure an agreement in attitude. See Stevenson, C. L. (1963). *Facts and values, studies in ethical analysis.* New Haven and London: Yale University Press, especially Chapter III. Also see Copi, I. M. and Cohen, C. (2004). *Essentials of logic.* Upper Saddle River, New Jersey:

Pearson/Prentice Hall. And see Moore, B. N., and Parker, R. (2003). *Critical thinking.* Boston: McGraw-Hill Higher Education, for example.

[3] Cf. Moore and Parker. *Critical Thinking* in this extension of Stevenson's idea, and see Copi and Cohen. *Essentials of Logic*—both cited just above.

CHAPTER IV

Reason and Responsibility: Taking Inquiry Seriously

SECTION 1

The Culture of Responsible Reasoning

> Critical thinking is the careful attempt to arrive at well-supported beliefs, decisions, and plans of action, and to take these to heart so that we live accordingly and well.

The definition above is the definition discussed and adopted in chapter I. An important part of that discussion highlights the social, interactive, and participatory aspects of the critical thinking undertaking. If persons are to take up and engage in that activity, they must walk a fine line between integrity and respect or charity to other thinkers with whom they interact. Like participants in every social activity, critical thinkers have certain contributions to make according to certain rules or standards they take responsibility for following. But thinkers cannot do this unless they allow each other to act. That is the basis of autonomy: to act under the direction of one's own reason and, then, according to one's own rules and aims, each must defer to and respect others doing the same. Of course people can try to overpower or manipulate others so as to gain the tolerance needed to act and be taken seriously. But for the critical thinker, as discussed in the previous chapter (III), this is out of the question.

The critical thinker seeks to proceed by reason, and then to be recognized and judged and tolerated by the reason of others. The thinker approaches these others deliberately, through her own or his own reason so as to be judged by those others. Look at it this way: driving can work only if there are roads whose construction and use is shared with others. No one goes by car from town to town and from place of business to place of business without taking part in a large and complex social system shared among many, many participants. And that participation involves granting others the right of way so that the system can exist and then so that each person can herself or himself be granted the right of way by those others in the system. They cannot grant the right of way if they are not participating and they are not participating if the others do not grant them the right of way. By analogy, the same can be said for critical thinking as a joint undertaking where many thinkers participate. To take part in a system where thinking takes place and people recognize this allowing each other to proceed according to appropriate rules and standards requires not just mere tolerance where they stay out of each other's way, but mutual respect where, as much as possible, all respect each other's rules and standards.

Not all rules and standards are the same in all respects, however. The critical thinker writing history does not support her claims in the same ways or even in the same senses as does the thinker in physics. What is relevant in ethical decision making is not entirely the same as what is relevant in solving problems in auto mechanics. What counts as the pursuit of truth in the deliberately adversarial argumentative interaction of the trial courtroom would not count as such in the laboratory or in the religious council. How then might critical thinking be understood as a unified endeavor uniting all thinkers in the undertaking of living well through the use of reason? How can it be that all critical thinkers are on the same page?

The clearest and simplest answer is that critical thinkers share, at some level, the same rules and standards and so face the same expectations—those bridging the gaps between individuals and between fields of study or special arenas of reasoning. The previous two chapters explore some of these expectations common to critical thinkers just as the first chapter discusses a common concept of critical thinking and common elements of critical thinking. Thus all critical thinkers take to their particular problems or focal issues the same expectations about taking themselves seriously and replacing both manipulation and power with reason. Chapter V and beyond will explore the surface contours of common standards holding for all sources of defensible belief, decisions, and actions, and the common rules of procedure for availing oneself of these sources. Thus what holds everybody together as critical thinkers will not be the differences imposed by the problems or purposes they approach by reason, but rather the basic shared features of critical thinkers, as well as the common standards of sources, and rules of procedure they might avail themselves of.

Still, there is another area of concern common to critical thinkers as such. Each thinker is not only answerable to the common expectations on her but also to the particular standards of sources and rules of procedure and interaction for the field of study or the arena of interaction she takes part in. At the same time, as just noted above, the critical thinker is subject to certain rules and expectations of respect and cooperation with others who are outside her particular arena of thought or discussion. Integrity matters to the critical thinker just as does charity or respect of others not sharing the same particular concerns. How are these two, integrity and charity, put together—what are the expectations every critical thinker needs to meet which, in effect, make them all engaged in the practice of that same inquiry? How do the demands of integrity and charity shape the social pursuit of well-supported beliefs, decisions, and actions focused on particular points; the practice of critical thinking? Some of the answer is developed for consideration in the remainder of this chapter. Once again the format of presentation will offer these concerns as fallacies or mistakes to be avoided in reasoning. First charity and then integrity will be investigated alone and in their overlaps, then the discussion turns to more general concerns of all inquiry.

SECTION 2

Fallacies of Charity/Fairness

A tongue-in-cheek characterization of philosophy, that most reason-giving and reason-studying of all fields, has called it the practice of studied mis-understanding.[1] While this is supposed to be a joke, trading on the extent to which philosophers have gone at times to find fault with the views and reasoning of each other, it would not work as a joke unless it had to it the sharp edge of criticism based in reality. Philosophers do seem to want to hold each other to extraordinarily high standards of clarity and rigor. And at times even this much seems not enough—especially if the other's views conflict with the critic's own designs. What this probably shows is that even for philosophers it is hard not to see the other's thought in terms of one's own beliefs and visions. Be that as it may, to indulge in such a practice as studied misunderstanding, purposely mis-reading another's views in a way that makes them open to criticism or apparently weak by contrast with the critic's, is a mistake. This might amount to the problem of oversimplification in the form of the straw figure fallacy—a problem discussed in the previous chapter. Or it might amount to the failure of fairness in argumentation, the give and take of interactive critical inquiry, the unfairness coming in by virtue of the speaker/writer violating the general concern of taking the other seriously and meeting that person's arguments where they are or in the form in which they are given. Straw figure is a misstatement of another's marshalling of evidence. The fallacy of studied misunderstanding is just that, a failure to extend the respect required to understand the other's views correctly.

IV.1. ***The fallacy of studied misunderstanding*** is the error of intentionally misinterpreting or of failing to expend the effort needed to correctly understand another thinker's belief, decision, or action before critically considering and replying to it.

For example: Imagined to have been spoken by an agent of the Pope who was supposedly representing the Court of Inquisition, "Galileo, you have taught doctrines that were forbidden and now must recant these teachings in order to demonstrate your faith. Should you not do so you will be shown the tools of persuasion (tortured) and thereby brought to your senses." (The point is that whether Galileo did violate this prohibition was very much open to dispute, apparently. And this was known to the Pope and apparently to the court, as the story goes. But the studied misunderstanding was put in place instead. See, for example, Redondi, P. (1987). *Galileo heretic* (R. Rosenthal, Trans.). Princeton, New Jersey: Princeton University Press. pp. 258 and ff.)

Or: "You say that all U.S. citizens are deserving of an explicit charge in an arrest warrant and are entitled to legal representation. But these men, while citizens, are being held as prisoners of war and so are not subject to the usual rights of the arrested." The Supreme Court seems to have decided, against the Bush government, that this was a studied misunderstanding of the status of certain imprisoned U.S. citizens and others.

Or again: "The wall being erected by Israel in the West Bank is illegal and must come down, says the international court in a recently issued advisory. But Israel urges that indeed it is just a defensive measure and so the erection and patrolling of the wall are within the prerogative of the State of Israel." As a member of the international community, might Israel be committing the mistake of a studied misunderstanding?

Studied misunderstandings are cases of thinkers not going the distance to understand the others they are critically engaged with, even though they could have done better and did know better. This is clearly a case of not playing fair, or not extending the respect that is due another thinker as critical practice proceeds. Another instance of such unfairness is found in a widely recognized fallacy in which the speaker/writer seeks to shift the burden of proof.

IV.2. *The fallacy of shifting the burden of proof* is the error of trying to avoid having to give reasons for a belief, decision, or action by misassigning to someone else the requirement of giving that proof or evidence.

For example: "Mr. and Ms. Jones claim they were there and saw the UFO land. As a representative of the U.S. Air Force, charged with investigating these events, I can tell you there are no such things as UFO's. But perhaps Mr. and Ms. Jones would like to tell you how they know there are?"

Or: "There are no eye witnesses, no smoking gun, of course. No one can be in someone else's mind. But however circumstantial the evidence is, there is that much and it is up to Martha Stewart to prove her innocence in this affair."

Or again: "Look, I've done my bit in the conversation here. I have tried to show you why we should buy as much house as we can possibly afford. You don't agree. Ok. Then you convince me we should be more careful with our money."

As the last example shows, just who is expected to carry the burden of collecting evidence to convince the others in the interaction of thinking critically, sometimes depends upon the risks involved. So for assigning the burden of proof several rules can be stated: **R1** *The riskier the outcome of the belief, decision, or action he or she wants to accept, the greater part of the burden of proof a thinker has. If the risk is low or relatively low, then the burden of proof can rest upon the person who accepts or is ready to accept the most implausible claim.* A case in point concerns the proof that there were weapons of mass destruction or the activity to make them going on in Iraq before our last invasion. This burden rested on the government and particularly on the executive branch that was trying to take us to war and needed the legislative branch's approval, in particular the Senate's approval. The risks were very high, the facts unclear, at least to many. At times, however, the message went out that it was Iraq's job and in particular Saddam Hussein's job to prove that there were not weapons. Records were demanded and rejected as incomplete. Teams of inspectors were sent in but suspicions were raised about whether they were allowed to talk to all whom they needed to interview and the quality of the inspectors' work was challenged. Historians will debate for some time just whether the burden of proof was shifted fallaciously to Iraqis and dissenters in the American legislative branch as well as to dissenting governments across the world.

R2 *If claims and counter-claims are mutually implausible across the interacting viewpoints or fields of study, then both sides have a serious burden of proof* and slipping that off to one side or the other would involve the mistake of shifting the burden of proof.

Sometimes social practices and institutions make clear divisions of the burden of proof. For example, in a U.S. courtroom it is the prosecution who has the job. But in other cases there are no conventional or institutionalized lines dividing those with different jobs of proof. **R3** *Without such institutions or conventions, the way of respect or fairness is to shoulder the burden of proof for the view that one is putting forward.*

Signals that someone is shifting the burden of proof are occasionally found in the speaker/writer using qualifiers instead of giving evidence. *Qualifiers are terms or phrases used to limit a speaker/writer's commitment to some claim or assertion that he or she has just made.* They are perfectly legitimate in the right circumstances as indicators or as terms of recognition that the case is not settled or does not seem to be as strong as needed in the eyes of the person using the qualifier. Other times, however, someone might use a qualifier in order to avoid or even shift the burden of proof. Those are the cases that are of interest here. Qualifying terms can include "perhaps," "maybe," or a phrase like "if I am not mistaken," "it seems to me," "in all likelihood," "it seems." Fallacious uses of qualifiers to shift the burden of proof would be present in cases like the following:

> ***For example:*** Superintendent speaking to her Board of Education: "Well, yes of course we need to close the schools to avoid the transmission of that disease, or so it seems to me." Or: "Well, of course we have to close the schools to avoid the transmission of that disease, don't you think?"

> ***Or:*** Spoken by the district manager to the store manager who asked for the best policy to follow: "If I am not mistaken, you will find that the best way to handle such an employee is to just fire her or him immediately." (A piece of advice—get that one in writing!)

> ***Or again:*** The graduate director speaking to the graduate student: "Even though it is hardly mainstream, you can certainly interpret that passage in that manner, it seems to me, at least if you want."

Thinkers might be accused of moving away from their responsibility to take a fair share of the work in inquiry when they shift the burden of proof. And that same refusal to take responsibility might appear to be present when speakers or writers accuse others of changing their views in a way that contradicts or is practically incompatible with what they used to believe or do. Senator Kerry was accused frequently of changing his mind on important matters of state like the justifiability of war. These changes of mind have been taken as failings of critical thinking, if not also failings of character, so the assumption seems to have been that Kerry was guilty of some sort of inconsistency that is to be avoided by critical thinkers. Should Kerry have been more careful about being consistent and, so to speak, sticking to his guns? If the answer is yes, then clearly critical thinkers cannot go over the question again in light of new evidence or new experiences and change their mind. But this review and revision is a normal part of critical thinking. And, only those who think people can reach the truth once and for all, or know certain things like foundational principles with complete certainty, would say they should strive to do that all the time and thinkers should never change their mind. Only if certainty were the standard aim of critical thinking and so once a critical thinker reached her goal she would never have to reconsider her views, would it be irresponsible to reconsider. This then marks the territory of another mistake of charity or fairness.

IV.3.

The fallacy of denying reconsideration (or the "flip-flop" fallacy) is the error of faulting someone for inconsistency in her or his thought or actions when that person changes views or decisions after reasoned reconsideration.[2]

There is nothing wrong with accusing someone of making a mistake in changing her or his views, *if* such changes followed no reconsideration or had no good reason behind them. Such changes would be whimsical, arbitrary, or capricious, and changes like that are not the outcome of critical thought, or the provenance of critical thinkers. But if one does reconsider or learns more that is relevant to the same focal issue and on that basis sees it is proper to change her or his views, it would be irresponsible in inquiry not to make that change.

> ***For example:*** "Well, isn't that great, Kerry voted to approve the invasion of Iraq and is now criticizing how the situation is going. But that's just what he does, backtracks and contradicts himself; look at what he did after he returned from Viet Nam."

> ***Or:*** "Do you believe that the ball was caught in bounds or not, ref? You can't make a call and then watch a replay and change your mind!" "Oh yeah. That's exactly what I can do if the play is important enough and I am asked to do so. You don't want me to reconsider after I get more evidence from the replay?"

> ***Or again:*** "Look, we can't give up now. Consider the investment we have in the anti-missile system—it would be simple inconsistency to stop development now." "But now that we have tested it and seen that it does not work in even ideal circumstances in a simple test, we don't want to throw good money after bad! What's inconsistent about that?"

There *is* a form of inconsistency that is a matter of concern as we think about respect for or charity toward other thinkers. This is an inconsistency of not allowing those with a different viewpoint the same sort of basis for their views as a thinker claims for her or his own. So suppose, for example, that an accountant finds that a certain procedure allows previously hidden costs of manufacturing a product to be revealed and taken into account thereby serving the purposes of the business and earning this technique a place in the company's accounting system. But suppose that firm complained when other companies tried to do the same thing to help understand and improve their own accounting needs. This complaint would be foolish and not accepted as appropriate to critical thinking. A good *rule of thumb:* ***What is an acceptable critical thinking procedure for one thinker also should be for others in similar circumstances.*** The basic justification for the new accounting procedure is that it works better than the old methods. And this line of justification works as well for one company as for another.

Now suppose that the same sort of procedure for justification were denied to other thinkers who did not share the same problems or the same aims as the accountants just in question. Suppose instead that the thinkers now in question were concerned with theological or sports medicine issues and found that a certain way of gathering evidence for revelation or miraculous occurrences, or for improvement in an athlete's condition or performance, *served their ends most efficiently.* But suppose the accountants denied any credibility or justifying force from such a pragmatic consideration in the theological and sports medicine cases while holding onto their justification for the new accounting procedure. Would this be good critical thinking? It certainly would not be good thinking to believe that the difference in ends and aims itself justified an acceptance of new techniques of thinking in one field but not in others. In other words, the difference of ends and aims gives no reason to reject the appeal to usefulness in the different cases. But does it allow for the thinkers in the other fields to ask the accountants to agree that they are justified by usefulness in their fields just as are the accountants? It would seem so, yes. The reason is that what the accountants are claiming is that it is the usefulness of the accounting procedures for their ends that justifies them. And the other thinkers can make the same claim. So the accountants would seem to be committed to granting that the others are *as justified as the accountants are.* If the accountants disagreed, they would be making a mistake of inconsistency that fails to respect the others as thinkers when they, the others, have everything going for them that the accountants do, but just have very different ends and aims. The aims and the ends of the others might be mistaken or crazy. But that is a very different matter. So, here is another fallacy of inconsistent, and so unfair, treatment that critical thinkers should avoid.

IV.4.   *The fallacy of denying parity of reasons* is the error of some thinkers refusing to allow those with differing aims and ends of reasoning to use the same general sorts of procedures to support principles or conclusions as those critics do themselves.

> *For example:* "The native medicine men applied herbs when we would use chemotherapeutic agents of a highly refined nature. Theirs is a primitive and pathetically incredible form of medical treatment." "But, for centuries it has worked well for them in the absence of something else. And given the price of Western technology, it is all they can do and all they will have for some time to come. Can it be all that pathetic and incredible in light of that record?"

> *Or:* "Everyone knows that the only way to do serious research is in terms of quantitative studies of the relationships between changes in the values of variables of interest, and changes in the values of other variables. So-called qualitative research involving studies of narratives and oral histories of social events are not credible paths to understanding people and their ways." "But in order to do quantitative studies you have to treat people as objects and measure their various properties

when history is about seeing people as actors on life's stage who follow their values and act deliberately. These differences are all the justification the qualitative methods should need, just as the need to measure the presence of properties in co-occurrence is all the justification needed for the quantitative methods of natural science."

Or again: "Theology has to rely on sources of revealed texts at some point in the chain of justification. Since this cannot be checked out for reliability by experience, it has to be supported by tracing back the interpretations of those revelations through history and the succession of authorities. Science left all that behind long ago. Shouldn't we just throw out all those theological claims?" "But some would say that revelation is a form of experience that has as much claim to trustworthiness as sense experience, and science still has its authorities, they happen to be the ones holding the latest theories that are getting the grant funding as opposed to those running the religious institutions. What's the difference? Can we really throw out religion as being weaker in its methods than science?"

Here, we are on controversial ground and many would take issue with the claim that there is a fallacy of denying parity of reasons in one or another of the examples given. This is not the place to settle the issue. If one or another of the examples generates nervousness, go back and re-read the explanation before the definition of the fallacy. Beyond that the disputes would be about the details, for example, about whether revelation is a form of experience comparable to sense experience as we understand these forms of awareness.

Can thinkers be fair to all concerned, extend respect that is due and deny there is such a fallacy or deny the details that would allow parity of reasons across opposed fields of study and centers of human meaning? Part of the problem that might tempt thinkers to deny such a fallacy is that they tend to see things from within their own perspective or community of discussion or discourse. In Chapter V the discussion will turn to what this means in detail in terms of the perspective of a community of thinkers. But for now the concept of a perspective of thought can be left to our informed imagination. It is clear enough what the perspective of natural science is, as opposed to that of theology, or of self-interested business, as opposed to that of other-sensitive morality. And with that much taken for granted, it is easy to see how a thinker might become caught up in trying to maintain integrity of thought by following the standards and procedures of his or her community of thinkers. And from within such a community, the goings on in other communities where people are addressing other problems through other uses of reason seem very strange indeed. The Catholic Church seems not to have trusted Galileo's uses of the telescope to study the surface of the moon or to observe some of the moons of Jupiter. But the same Church had no trouble with his applying the telescope to the problems of war and commerce. The moon and planets were the domain of the Church and they believed at the time that these bodies did not obey the same laws as physical things on earth did. They were unwilling to make their views accountable to outside methods of reasoning and the theories built on that. Such a failure of external accountability or accountability to external or foreign uses of reason would make the fallacy of the parity of reasons appear to be unsupportable, not a fallacy at all. But surely part of respect between persons and across methods of reasoning and problem sets *is* the requirement of external accountability. A good *rule of thumb:* ***Each thinker must remain open to the possibility that her or his own methods of inquiry and thought need to be revised in light of those used by others.*** A colleague in The College of Pharmacy, who is an excellent and highly recognized researcher, has a special place to look for new ideas to try out in his work in pharmacy. He looks just about anywhere besides pharmacy or the chemical sciences. In fact, one of his best sources is literature, another is history. Ideas from other groups of thinkers outside one's field of study, even if these ideas need to be (carefully!) cast in a figurative form to be used in one's own field, are something to be taken account of, something to which a thinker's thought remains accountable.

§ IV.5.

The fallacy of rejecting external accountability is the error of thinkers refusing to hold themselves and their ideas accountable to the reasoning of others in fields of study using methods different in detail from their own.

> ***For example:*** "I do natural science. What has history to teach me of relevance to my field?" "Well as it turns out and as made clear in the History of Science, quite a bit."

> ***Or:*** "I am just a simple mechanic. Why do I have to worry about chemistry and physics?" "Why, because unless you want to work at Midas switching out mufflers, these other fields of study will help you understand the principles by which the cars you are working on work. And so that knowledge will make you a better analyst of mechanical problems—even with computer diagnostics."

> ***Or again:*** "What does the study of blood chemistry and physiology have to do with bicycle racing?" "Ask Lance Armstrong."

Just how thinkers are accountable to patterns of reasoning and ideas outside their own field of study or their own set of problems is a large question. More is said about this in chapters V and VI. For now, it is clear that *respect for, or charity toward other reasoners makes it incumbent upon thinkers to not casually dismiss the others' standards and expectations of thought even when these differ from their own.* Rather they should remain open to the possibility of learning from the others and correcting their own views. Still, thinkers must maintain some degree of methodological integrity, they must stick to their own guns to some extent, their own methods of approaching and dealing with the problems they take up. To fail to do so is the mistake of the fallacy of rejecting *internal accountability*.

Mastery Exercises IV.1

SELF TEST

Fallacies of Charity/Fairness: studied misunderstanding, shifting the burden of proof, denying reconsideration, denying parity of reasons, rejecting external accountability

FALLACY IDENTIFICATION PRACTICE. Following the Tech Tips found at the end of Chapter II, identify the fallacies illustrated in the following exercises. Write a sentence explaining your judgment of which fallacy is present in each question. (Answers in Appendix II.)

1. "Well, but they are concerned with creation science and not ordinary empirical science. Why should I take that seriously?" "Regardless of whether you should take creation science seriously, the issue is whether their procedures can claim support in ways that your own can. If that is true, then you can hardly just reject what they claim. Maybe you are dealing with different problems and that is the real issue between you. But if their methods are supportable, you cannot just say their thought is worthless." The fallacy the second speaker is explaining here is _____.

2. "No, I don't want to think about the issue in your way. And why should I? I am a police investigator, not a psychic!" "Oh really, what if I can find the perp? Will you pay attention then?" The fallacy the second speaker is hinting at here is _____.

3. "Yes, I see your point and the way you got there. But that is not the way I approach things. Why do I have to reconsider my conclusions just because of your results—no matter how promising they are?"

4. "Of course, you cannot expect anything more from her. But isn't that claim what she just rejected about two weeks ago? What's the point of giving that a second thought?"

5. "Herman said that the reason why he took the money was to be able to get his daughter needed medical attention. Oh that's great. Let's not lock him up. Let's give him a reward for treating his daughter like a princess at someone else's expense."

6. "Look, I know that it is weird, but you know what? Sometimes the world is just weird. And I defy you to prove that I did not see the blob out in a crater on Mt. Parker."

7. "The police report said that you thought Smithson was a likely candidate for this job since it matched his *modus operandi*. Now, here on the stand, you say you are not so sure because of evidence you uncovered since the original arrest. Well, that just doesn't wash officer. We have your report right in front of us and that official word was never changed."

8. "I am sorry I said anything. I really regret it. All I get whenever I bring up any problem is a verbal attack from you. Why is my job to prove everything to you? Don't you have any responsibility here?" The fallacy the second speaker is trying to articulate here is _____.

9. "What do you mean you did what you thought would be best for the company now and in the long run here? Don't you really mean that you did what you thought would make the company and you the most money here? And did you think about the fact that that might come back to haunt us? No, you seem to have been so caught up in your quest for the money that you overlooked the possibility of lawsuits and now you tell me that you did the best for the company? You're fired—that's what's best for the company."

10. "Yes, I guess, now that you point it out, it does look like my methodology of sampling only by phone and computer among the television audience would overlook voters who had no phones, no televisions, or who were not looking at that program, and so could mess up the results of the poll. But that's what I had the money for—a telephone poll advertised on that one program. You weren't offering more money so why should I worry about your criticism?"

SECTION 3

Fallacies of Integrity

§ **IV.6.** *The fallacy of rejecting internal accountability* is the error of thinkers refusing to hold themselves and their ideas accountable to the principles, standards, and general expectations of reasoning facing all in their field of study or all who deal with problems of the sort they are dealing with.

The basic idea here is that within fields of study or problem solving, or within communities of thinkers addressing the same problems, standard principles, background knowledge, and patterns of reasoning for identifying and addressing questions arise and are adopted by the group. Individuals are then expected to follow in these patterns. For example, engineers building bridges must understand and apply the principles of stress bearing on the life and behavior of the materials they will use. Ecologists must see life systems in part in terms of food and energy cycles and interrelationships. Visual artists must be aware of form and structure and their impact upon viewers. These are examples of knowledge and procedures that groups of individuals share as constraints upon the freedom of their thought even as they are empowered by this knowledge. (And, of course, these in-house constraints are in addition to the basic shared procedures of knowledge and reasoning that are investigated elsewhere in this book.) To violate these is to lose one's way in proper thinking about some subject, unless one has very good reasons for doing so and is ready (if not able) to change patterns of thought. It is a central way of behaving *irrationally* to fail to maintain accountability to these central points of thought.

> *For example:* Jean-Baptiste Lamarck held the view that acquired traits of behavior could be inherited by the next generation of an organism type. This, for most of normal biology, contradicts a central tenet separating the acquired and the inherited traits of a being. Lamarckians were failing to maintain proper integrity of biological theory.

> *Or:* Among the Amish, just what counts as appropriate clothing is something that is a serious matter since one religious aim of the group is to avoid pride and

outward competition for attention as is seen elsewhere in connection with styles of dress. One man and his father were excommunicated from a local Amish community because of their insistence that the son should be allowed to put tool pockets on his welding apron. This young man was not displaying the proper sense of respect in the form of integrity and internal accountability.

Or again: Galileo was threatened with excommunication for wanting to retain the views he was developing within the new physics and astronomy. He was not showing proper accountability to principles internal to the framework views of the Catholic Church at the time.

Or yet again: For some time psychologists sought to study human behavior without considering the processes of thought and emotion. Those who ignored these behaviorist limitations were relegated to groups and alliances that were not the recipients of the greatest funding or prestige in most American universities. By not being behaviorists, they had failed in the regard of appropriate internal accountability. This did not make them wrong, necessarily. But it did put them outside the practices that were counted as best and most rational at the time.

The line between what is rational and sensible as opposed to what is myth or conjecture is sometimes a very fine one. All the same, scholars and other thinkers draw this line and with that distinction are able to identify another failure of integrity or respect for the central views and patterns of thought in one's group or reasoning community. This is recognized in so far as speakers or writers sometimes dismiss the thoughts and claims of others as merely myth, not to be taken seriously as scholarly or defensible views. In fact some individuals do sometimes use myths as a way to reassure themselves and as a way to avoid the hard work of honestly meeting a problem in critical thought. Historians have often pointed out that a myth common to and flawing the thought of many Americans such as planners is that of the **limitless frontier.** The myth says: We can continue to build on prime farm land using up what is convenient because it is already relatively level and well-drained. The thought is that people can grow food, or find the peace they gain from open spaces, elsewhere. Hydroponic tomatoes are the product of this attitude as are the latest subdivision in your home area. Some even say that humans must continue to work toward the "conquest of space" because people will need to move to other planets to find natural resources and food growing capabilities when the Earth is used up. Of course there is another way to think about it—maybe the frontier is not limitless. Not everyone in the world accepts the myth of limitless frontiers. Another current myth comes from the economists: Humans are all naturally competitive, greedy, or self-interested and bent on acquiring and using up all they can. This is another myth since many cultures do not now and have not in the past operated or brought up their children to live that way. Finally, in the United States there seems to be the myth that violence is a way to settle problems (even if it is said to be a way of last resort). Violence is celebrated and exploited in television programming, commercial messages, cinema, books, comics, governmental budgets, recorded music, and so on. In spite of hard-won lessons that violence is typically followed by more violence and sometimes by escalated violence (8,000,000 killed in World War I and that did not correct the conditions leading to World War II), this view continues and heroes who settle things with a gun or a lance are revered, as opposed to those who seek to settle problems over the long-term through education, justice, and building close relationships.

The reliance upon such myths or images reflecting such myths can take one away from clear and defensible thought when engaged in inquiry. In doing so it can lead a thinker to fail to remain accountable to the standards and practices comprising rationality in her or his reasoning group(s). Thus another mistake to recognize under the fallacies of integrity is that of the mythic image replacing clear-headed analysis and reflection.

§ IV.7.

The fallacy of mythic images is the error on the part of thinkers interpreting and thinking through the questions/problems they address in terms of the images of myths that seem relevant, rather than trying to meet the problems/questions in a clear and reflective way on their own terms.

> ***For example:*** When asked if there is a case that Iraq had weapons of mass destruction and connections with terrorists, George Tennet allegedly said to President Bush, "It's a slam dunk." Thus the chief of the Central Intelligence Agency availed himself of the myth that intelligence collection and its application to strategic military and defense questions was a game played against enemies and political foes alike. This would count as a case of the mistake of mythic images. (This example also illustrates the basic fallacy of misfiguration discussed in Chapter III.)

> ***Or:*** The followers of Darwin have for years sought to see the operations of evolution in terms of a battle for fitness and competition to be represented in the breeding pool of a species. It might be said that this anthropomorphizes (or treats as if it is intentional human behavior) the adaptive self-organization that suits individuals (and, through genetic inheritance, whole species) for survival. This talk of the competition between organisms and the relation of this to species survival is a mistake of mythic images.

> ***Or again:*** Those who believe they can support the present form of economic development operating in the United States talk of Adam Smith's reference to the operation of the economic system as if guided by a hidden hand to produce, most efficiently, what society's members need, and to do so at the best price. Consumers are reassured that if "markets are left free or unregulated" the hidden hand will benefit them. They should not be reassured since this is another example of the

fallacy of a mythic image. Adam Smith, the author of *The Wealth of Nations* published in 1776, recognized this when he spoke in terms of the market operating as if guided by a hidden hand but added that people can destroy the market's beneficial aspect if they give in to greed.

Nothing in market economics or in evolution guarantees or even promises that things will get better and better if the market is left alone to evolve and work its ways. Yet people are led to believe that this is so by the language of some economists and reporters and politicians, and these people think this way because of this misleading influence. This seems contrary to the spirit of critical thinking, no matter how reassuring it might be.

When challenged on this point, someone making use of the mistake of mythic images might well claim that he or she was just using a way of speaking, a convenience of images to suggest a possibility. Thus someone might commit something like a fallacy of trying to shift the burden of proof by trying to avoid responsibility for using a mythic image. This individual would seek to introduce qualifications suggesting that he or she was not to be taken literally when using such images and the associated thoughts that go with them. But if they were not to be taken seriously, how were they to be taken? Critical thinkers should be on the lookout for what might be called the **fallacy of evading integrity by qualifications** of one's thought. Such qualifications—"only a way of speaking," "just an image used for its suggestive powers," "just an image," "merely a thought"—have their place. But this place is not as a way to wriggle out of responsibility for the clarity and implications of one's thought. As Shakespeare pointed out, one can protest too much—and that includes protesting by too much reliance on qualifications.

On the other hand, one might insist too much. Sometimes thinkers refuse to consider possible opposition to or flaws within their views. One example of this is in the casual version of this error found in sloganeering. A view is distilled into its most succinct form and then paraded out in the form of a slogan, as a standard answer to a question or a problem, allowing the speaker/writer a wall to hide behind and cutting her or himself off from critical appraisal of the views in question. The more harsh or strident version of the problem occurs when someone has a view that he or she insists presents the truth, and so will not entertain the possibility of critical reflection on this view. In this case the appropriate term is that of *dogma*. The problem in either case is that the speaker/writer is no longer holding views with some critical integrity to them, but instead is holding on to fighting points. He or she has put these views out of the reach of critical consideration.

IV.8. *The fallacy of fighting points* is the error committed when thinkers protect their views or their principles or even their patterns of reasoning from critical review, insisting instead on their correctness and then holding them as slogans or dogmas.

For example: "No, that is not open for discussion. In this business organization we know that God exists and is guiding the economic fortunes of Americans in their competition with others in the world." All this might be true, but an organization that protects its basic beliefs from challenge in this way, as opposed to opening them to rational thought, is founding its activities on dogma. Even reasonable faith seems to rest at least on a reasoned free choice about what questions are important and how to approach them.

Or: "They hate us because of our freedom and our way of life. They don't like freedom," some say of terrorists, without any perceived need to explore this view by analysis and empirical evidence. It has become a slogan in a political camp.

Or again: Not without their own slogans, opposing political camps suggest that the way of life in the United States is without religious merit or sanction in its reckless profligacy.

The third leg of the stool of integrity in critical thinking is illustrated by *the problem of not protesting nearly enough.* Just as dogmatism can put a view beyond critical challenge by insisting on its correctness no matter what, *relativism and in particular the view that the speaker/writer can endorse a view as his or hers alone and hold it beyond challenge, is a violation of the integrity of critical thought.* The critical thinker takes responsibility for holding beliefs, making decisions, and undertaking actions on the basis of reasons which separate the better from the worse. To say that this view might be considered wrong by others or it might not be held by many cultures but it is "ok for me" or it is "our way of believing," is an abdication of this responsibility. This is not to deny that there might be honest and even in some ways defensible differences between thinkers and groups of thinkers on what appears to be the very same claim— for example that there is a supernatural deity, or that atoms are made up of strings of energy. Of course there can be such differences. But the claim is that it is sometimes acceptable for critical thinkers to hold beliefs or make decisions that are idiosyncratic or capricious and treated as beyond challenge for that reason, or beyond criticism just because they are idiosyncratic or capricious. Perhaps those who think this way are confusing whether it is correct for them to believe as they wish and the view that what they believe is correct itself—which is what they also often claim. However, in either event, whether just demanding the allowance of holding and acting upon what they want to believe, or thinking that their believing makes it so, there is something basically wrong here. Either practice is surely outside of the workings of critical thinking and individuals or groups who make claims in either of these ways are rejecting their responsibilities as critical thinkers. Thus it is appropriate to recognize the fallacy of relativism. (A separation can and is sometimes made between subjectivism or individualistic relativism and relativism more generally. Unless clarity demands it here, this account will forego that distinction while not denying its usefulness.)

IV.9. *The fallacy of relativism* is the error of thinkers (individuals or groups) adopting or holding views that are idiosyncratic to them, or else, capricious—that is without having reasons for them, holding these views to be true or correct or worth holding just because they hold them. In proceeding this way, these thinkers deny any responsibility to defend these views before accepting them or in the face of challenges. One of the mistakes occurring under this heading is subjectivism or holding that some belief, decision, or action is fine for the thinker even though others in the individual's reasoning group reject or question it.

> *For example:* "Well, the evidence for a connection between smoking cigarettes and cancer is quite well developed. But I don't find that relevant to my decision. I'm going to continue smoking if I want to."

> *Or:* "Freedom is just the chance to do what you want to do. That's what I believe and I see no reason to defend it to you or anybody else."

> *Or again:* "Our Take-The-Sting-Out-Of-Nature Society is dedicated to the eradication of the honeybee." "But bees provide all sorts of important environmental services not the least of which is making honey while making apples and other forms of fruit trees be productive. Why would you want to eradicate them?" "This is our view. Others might not have held stranger ones. But that is our group view and that is the end of the matter, it is clearly correct for us." (Perhaps no one has held a stranger view, but this pattern of belief has been seen all too often in the world history of genocide and of environmental irresponsibility.)

Mastery Exercises IV.2

SELF TEST

Fallacies of Integrity: rejecting internal accountability, mythic images, fallacy of evading integrity by qualifications, fighting points, relativism

FALLACY IDENTIFICATION PRACTICE. Following the Tech Tips found at the end of Chapter II, identify the fallacies illustrated in the following exercises. Write a sentence explaining your judgment of which fallacy is present in each question. (Answers in Appendix II.)

1. "There you have my report. This was a serious breakdown of the company security. My recommendation? We need to hire a professional security company to come in and review our procedures and then set up a new state of the art system of procedures and staff the system with their employees. I think. Don't you agree?"

2. "But what you fail to realize is that this is just the way the world is. It is competitive and directed at defeating the competition in the most devastating terms possible. And if we are to survive in that framework, we must have the largest army and the most advanced weaponry systems possible. That's just the way it is. You either see it or not. Do you get it?"

3. "Look we need to be ready to respond in the name of what is right at a moment's notice. We need to be like the old-time marshalls who knew trouble when they saw it and did something about it without any waiting around. In this regard we need to regain the code of the Old West."

4. "Well, that is what all the latest research says in our field, but I am not going to just follow the fads. I am going to stick with what I know and have done my entire career."

5. "Well, that is what all the latest research says in our field. But you know what? I am going off on my own now and I do not feel the need to ask your permission to do so!"

6. "Yes, that violates my principles and all that you and I and the rest of the community believe is right. But we must not be held back by our basic beliefs. Sometimes it just feels good to shed those for a while and do something a little different."

7. "Well, you go your way and I'll go my way on this matter. I see the point of approaching it in common ways. But for me, right now, the best procedure is to follow my heart."

8. "We must dare to push the envelope of human survivability. A trip to the moon is not just a daring adventure, it is also a great experiment for a new way of life for humans. We must undertake it."

9. "No, I do not want to see it your way. You are just wrong—wrong in your approach, wrong in your calculations, wrong in your conclusions. I've got the right idea and you either see it or you don't."

10. "I have studied it from every angle. It looks like if we are to avoid a collision with that asteroid we will have to send missiles up there and blast it from the sky. Yes, that means we will have a debris field around our earth and bits of the asteroid falling to earth from time to time. But that is the best we can do. Probably. But this is new territory, don't blame me if it doesn't work."

SECTION 4

Fallacies of Evidence Collection

If thinkers do avoid the dangers of relativism, they still might fail to move inquiry ahead because they make one of several very general mistakes in evidence collection. What might go wrong here? Well, the succeeding chapter will discuss the variety of sources of evidence and more specific dangers in using them. But to move into what is of concern here, recall the fallacy of red herring. The fallacy of red herring made its appearance in the previous chapter. Advertising often functions to introduce red herrings by calling a thinker's attention to something that has some visual or other appeal that turns the thinker's attention toward the product or service being advertised ("adverto" in Latin would be a term for turning something toward something else). The important thing here and what makes such ads red herrings is not just their intrusiveness—though that is annoying. It is that what they say or present does not fit into the flow of inquiry that they interrupt, in any of the usual ways of being a source of information or another contribution to inquiry.

Possible Problems with Advertisements

§ They are not observations that are relevant.

§ They do not add a belief to a body of belief or knowledge in a way that makes the thinker's thought more coherent or well organized.

§ They do not clarify or further the analysis that is relevant to the inquiry at hand.

§ The ads do not further, and indeed hinder, accountability for thought.

§ They are designed to be free of the perspectives of thought in which thinkers operate and so they must make appeals through the bias or prejudice of status and through the consumer's fear of falling behind or missing out on appealing things or moments, thus playing on the most unfocused and least critical of emotions and perceptions.

§ They are not engaging the thinker in a relevant narrative which either makes intelligible some aspect of living or moves the flow of reasoning toward a productive vision of the outcome of critical thought.

§ And then, they are beyond the requirements of charity or fairness and integrity discussed earlier in this chapter.

For present purposes, however, the idea is not to reflect further on advertising and red herrings, or on sources of well-supported beliefs or decisions for that matter. The concern is to note that there are a few very general pitfalls to avoid in inquiry. *These are general in so far as the commission of any one of these errors will undermine all appeals to evidence of any sort.* Thus they are problems to avoid in any sort of evidence collection in any sort of inquiry.

The first of these is the very familiar mistake of arguing from or appealing to ignorance. It is, in effect, the "Can too" playground reply of children when they are challenged by other children over whether they may do or say something. Here the basic idea is this:

§ IV.10.   *The fallacy of arguing from ignorance* is the error of thinkers—individuals or groups, arguing that since no one has shown the belief, decision, or action in question to be faulty, then it must be considered critically acceptable; or, since no one has shown that it is not faulty, then it must be considered critically flawed.

> *For example:* "No one, including Saddam Hussein, has shown that Iraq does not have weapons of mass destruction, so we can proceed as though it does."

Notice that this case is one where thinkers need to be careful to remember the situation in context. What is said here is that we can take it that there are weapons and act on that belief as though it is true. This is different from making the more complex claim that the risk is so great *if* there are weapons there, that we must proceed, even though we have no good reason for believing there are weapons and we have no good reason for believing there are not. There were UN inspectors in the country up until the invasion and they were skeptical but coming up empty-handed while Saddam Hussein looked to be obstructionist. But in that context with inspections going on, and no evidence that there were weapons of mass destruction in Iraq, it seems as though the appeal was a case of arguing from ignorance as it is defined here.

Why is this a mistake? Because it involves basically assuming that since something cannot be proven false/true it is true/false. But there are often claims that cannot be shown to be acceptable and yet are perfectly acceptable. And, every time a thinker discovers an "honest" mistake, he or she has found a case where a belief or decision could not be shown to be unacceptable and yet turned out to be so. There is no guarantee that the lack of contrary evidence goes with the acceptability of what that evidence would be contrary to.

> *Or:* "Well, we don't know that Herman did tell the judges about our team's use of steroids." "That's right. But we don't know that he didn't either. And if not Herman, then who? He did it all right."

Here someone ratted-out the team. Was it Herman? Well, here caution is in order also. If the speaker had been saying that the best explanation of the judges finding out is that Herman told them, then this would not be a case of arguing from ignorance. It would be a clumsy appeal to the results of an argument to the best explanation. But that is not what is said here. The talk is that, while there is not evidence for Herman being the informant, there is none against, and that is significant. The addition of "if not Herman then who" seems a rhetorical challenge to shift the burden of proof to the others to challenge the appeal to ignorance involved and so the fallacy of arguing from ignorance has been committed.

> ***Or again:*** "It certainly seems to me like it was her. After all, she could not account for her whereabouts at the time of the murder—and no one else seems to be able to account for her whereabouts either; she has no alibi. Yes, she's the one."

She couldn't prove she was not at the crime scene and no one else could either, so she was there—that is the pitch here, it seems. Here the way the argument is stated almost seems to make it a case of innuendo—hinting that she did it and inviting the audience to conclude that by virtue of their suspicions. But the argument is really that she has no proof she didn't do it so she did it. And that is supposedly a bit of inquiry rather than persuasion. But really it is the counterfeit of inquiry—the speaker is saying that she did it and the reason is that she can't show she did not. But, once again, the absence of reasons for or against acceptability of a belief or decision is not a reason against or for it.

Having mentioned innuendo, it is important to note another mistake in what might look like the collection or presentation of evidence. The air which thinkers breathe is filled with sound-bites these days. These are small, usually isolated bits of claims or information that are put forward as though they told the whole story or were mere reminders of the whole story on some matter. To get one's fill of these one only needs to tune into CNN's Headline News and read the banner streaming across the bottom of the television screen, or go to the home page of MSN and see the feature story leads that set up expectations as to what the reader will learn as well as summarize what MSN finds to be the most important or salient point of the story. In all fairness, there is no claim that in these cases there is not more to the story than is presented. But still, like all news services, these sources are spinning or even slanting the news in a certain way. And this way of setting up the reader or listener is going to lead that person to make inferences to conclusions that may be inaccurate or even biased or prejudiced. The fallacy of conducting inquiry in terms of sound-bites is like innuendo in that it plays into the present state of the person listening or reading, trying to move him or her in a certain direction. But here the appeal is not to an emotion already in place, but to a pattern of thought associations already in place.

> ***For example:*** "So, Martha Stewart, the home fashion guru, has drawn a five-month sentence. Gee, that doesn't seem like a lot. I guess once again the rich and famous are able to beat out the wrath of the judicial system."

But what is not said is that there is a fine assessed, another five month house arrest, and two years probation for someone with a business to run and employees' pay to meet. This is not to say that the sentence for Martha Stewart was just or not. It is to say that there was more to it than met the eye in the July 17, 2004 MSNBC leader. And if someone's collection of information on the case got no further than that sound-bite, then inquiry would have been undermined.

> *Or:* "The American woman who was convicted in Oman of ordering the death of her husband has received the death sentence."

This is a story lead from MSNBC on July 17, 2004. The reader is in danger of leaping to the conclusion that this is some sort of anti-American conspiracy. The story itself does nothing to dispel that inference tendency since it gives only the bare particulars of the story saying that the woman married two years apparently conspired with her 14 year old son (sentenced to 3 years—suspended and slated for immediate deportation), and two Omani men (sentenced to 10 years each). The brief story complicates the situation by introducing another sound bite saying that the American Ambassador was not available for comment.

Both the story lead and the story itself provide no information to put the events into context and to make sense of them, leaving all that up to the inference tendencies of the reader, or not—just serving as one more *body-count story* in which another tragedy is presented in terms of its worst details and nothing more.

Contrast this last example with the MSNBC story that starts off as a body-count story and then shifts to provide the details of why the latest attack on an Iraqi official might have taken place and who might have been involved. July 17 was the anniversary of the Baath Party's rise to power in Iraq, and it provided the natural occasion for yet another attack and failure of civil order in the newly re-established country.

Critical thinkers need to be aware of the information management version of the innuendo, namely the sound bite.

⸘ IV.11.

The fallacy of appealing to a sound-bite is the error of thinkers—individuals or groups—providing information in such a form that (a) it lacks context and sufficient richness to guide interpretation and to understand the main point of the story, and (b) lacks sufficient richness to warrant or support inferences to conclusions it suggests.

Another general failing in evidence collection needs to be noted here. And this follows naturally on the heels of the sound-bite fallacy. In the sound-bite problem, the listener or reader is expected to be able to pick up and fill in the story on her or his own. If this mistake is combined with the fallacy of spin or of innuendo, it will throw the thinker's reflection in a certain direction, and if not it will leave the results up to the fortunes of the thinker's associations of thought on the subject that seems to be in question. A related problem comes along when the thinker makes an appeal to others to go along because doing that is the thing that those others should know is appropriate. For example, sometimes a speaker/writer will say that something is *obvious* or that it is something that *everyone knows,* or that it is something that is *certain,* or *sure, you know?* These phrases call upon the force of supposed common knowledge to carry the point that is brought into prominence by them. "The war in Iraq is about oil? Well, everybody knows that; tell me something I don't know; no kidding." But maybe it is not about oil so much as other sorts of economic opportunities or about the ideals of freedom, or something else entirely? Saying that something is known by everybody is not providing evidence; it is invoking the assumption of evidence, or worse it is dismissing the need to take evidence collection seriously for the claim in question. This is a mistake that has been called the fallacy of "proof surrogate" by some, but will be labeled here as *the fallacy of the insider appeal.* The point is that instead of seeking and providing evidence the thinker acts as though an appeal to others that are supposed to share the same views can settle the matter—whatever that matter is. So a further mistake in collecting evidence is:

§ IV.12. *The fallacy of the insider appeal* is the error of thinkers who substitute for evidence an appeal to the other reasoners who share acceptance or knowledge of the belief or decision in question.

> ***For example:*** "Those physicians who perform abortions are murderers, *everyone knows that.* If we don't allow Kevorkian to assist in euthanasia, then why do we allow abortions?"
>
> ***Or:*** "Those who oppose income taxes for schools are just out of touch. It is *obvious* that this is the way to begin to get school financing on a sound and predictable footing." This *may be obvious* to certain individuals, but that does not make it true or count as adequate evidence for the acceptability of that view.
>
> ***Or again:*** "*We* here at Whispering Pines Country Club *all know* that the club needs membership policies that serve a high-quality collective experience and the well-being of the membership. *It should be no surprise to anyone* that this requires the exclusion of certain sorts of individuals even if they could afford to join and maintain a membership." The speaker is not above a couple of insider appeals, the first to the club membership and the second to anyone who will listen. But neither makes the case.

§ IV.13. *The fallacy of begging the question* amounts to a thinker having as reasons for believing or deciding in some way, something he or she would have no reason to accept if he or she did not already accept the claim or decision he or she is trying to support. In other words, it amounts to a thinker assuming the acceptability of the conclusion he or she is out to support, as part of the reasons for the evidence in support of accepting that conclusion.

This is not exactly the same as **arguing in a circle** though arguing in a circle (at least a very narrow circle) is a matter of begging the question. To argue in a circle is to explicitly use the conclusion as part of the evidence. For example, I think that smoking causes lung cancer because of the fact of lung cancer resulting from smoking. That is a very narrow circle and is of course a mistake—in fact it is one form of the mistake of begging the question. But it is not the only form of this fallacy. For example, suppose that as a physician I said, "Well, I have seen lots of these cases and they always have that subtle symptom of the patient disliking the taste of green vegetables. That is a sure sign of this disease in my experience and so in the presence of that symptom, I think that I am on firm ground to go ahead to diagnose another case of this disease." Here, notice, the doctor is saying that in her or his experience that dislike of vegetables is a sign of the disease. Well where is it said that the physician interpreted her or his experience correctly or was not just picking up on something that is wholly co-incidental like the fact that the patients were not nudists!? This is a case in which the conclusion—"this is a case of that disease," is based upon the assumption that this disease has these symptoms and that they are reliable symptoms of this disease. But why would the thinker accept those symptoms as sure signs of that disease unless he or she was just assuming they were because he or she believes the patient had that disease? Suppose that this patient had those symptoms but that they were caused by some other related but different disease? In begging the question the thinker is mistaken in accepting that something is evidence when taking that as evidence really involves assuming the conclusion is true.

> *For example:* "Well, look, the thing has to be a genetic disease because it is in the children and in both parents. And that sort of distribution always shows a genetic disease." Well, why would you believe that that distribution always showed a genetic basis of a disease unless you already believed the conclusion or the claim at issue—that in this case the assumed connection of the conclusion holds good? And, of course, what the thinker is referring to does not always show a genetic basis—a common cold might be present in the children and in both parents and is not genetically based.

> *Or:* "Gee, I would have to say it is true that there are aliens. Just the other day I saw what clearly was an alien in the meadow out back by the manure pile." How in this world would you think that that was an alien out back by the manure pile— as opposed to steam in the cool evening or methane gas on fire, unless you already believed there were aliens? So you cannot just point to this as the reason for there being aliens.

> *Or again:* "Clinton always had a weakness when it came to making sexual advances to women he worked with. I have seen him many times smile at the females in his office and it was not any ordinary, nice guy smile." Well how would

anyone know it was not an ordinary smile or even a licentious looking smile with no such intent behind it unless one already believed that Clinton was guilty of sexual harassment? Only if one had his or her mind made up about the conclusion would the evidence necessarily or surely seem to support the conclusion.

Or yet again: "Tom Ridge was just caught up in a power grab and was not sincerely interested in the interests of the country when he recently floated a trial balloon of getting the power to cancel or postpone the fall 2004 federal election." Well maybe, and then again maybe not. How would one know without being able to feel Tom Ridge's feelings and thinking his thoughts? Or is it that this is the way that story reads if we assume that Ridge is part of a government trying to grab power by any means? Assume the conclusion and the evidence looks plausible. Hold your judgment on the conclusion so as to remain open to independent evidence and things are not so clear about what was going on.

This last example shows some of what is wrong with conspiracy theories which, by the way, usually beg the question. A good *rule of thumb* is: ***Critical thinkers should seek evidence whose credentials are independent of the acceptance of the conclusion. If this restriction on evidence is not respected, then begging the question is allowed and in effect that permits thinkers to assume the very thing that they are trying to prove in marshalling the proof.*** But if thinkers might assume what they are trying to prove, then they do not need critical thinking at all. They can just believe or choose or do whatever they want and there would be no way to show it was irrational or not well-supported. All the thinker would need to do is believe in what he or she did or decided. That, however, has nothing to do with critical thinking except to help show why begging the question is wrong.

Begging the question is not always easy to spot unless you are reading or listening critically, remembering what assertions a speaker/writer has made and holding that person to them. *Basically the fallacy amounts to failing to give evidence that is acceptable to the thinker independently of her or his accepting the claim or conclusion in question.* This happens more than might be imagined. Watch for it in political speeches, or trial lawyers' summaries, for example.

Lately more and more people who have heard the phrase, "beg the question," have tried to speak that language themselves. What has happened is that the meaning has changed from that described just above to something or someone's actions or beliefs inviting a question. To beg a question in this sense is to do or say what leads to that question. For example, a newscaster might say the following: "The candidate urged that we think of how to attain and keep peace and then went to the campaign bus where she was heard arguing with her husband. The candidate's behavior begs the question of just what does she want in her heart—peace or conflict?" Here begging the question is not what is identified as fallacy IV.12). And this more recent popular usage is one the language would be better off without, for the sake of clarity—or maybe, the fallacy of begging the question is one that logicians and critical thinkers should call the **fallacy of conclusion dependent evidence?** Whatever. Clarity could be served either way. And here the discussion will go with the tradition and use the term as defined above.

Begging the question would allow thinkers to prove whatever they wanted simply by assuming the conclusion in locating evidence for it. There is another fallacy of evidence collection that would allow thinkers to prove whatever they wished to. This is the mistake of appealing to inconsistent premises or evidence statements that cannot be true or acceptable together. *Two statements are inconsistent in this way just in case one is true or acceptable, the other has to be false or unacceptable.* "This ball is blue all over." "This ball is red all over." These must be two different balls. How does a thinker know this? The answer lies in the fact that having a surface color completely of blue is inconsistent with having one that is red. "We need the death penalty in this state. It alone will give us justice for cases of murder and so on." "What this state needs is the abolishment of the death penalty. This alone would give us justice." These are two different conceptions of justice. How does a thinker know this? The answer lies in the contradictory character of these policies. Not only could they not be carried out together, they could not even be considered acceptable together by the same person thinking about the options from the standpoint of a single set of values and reasons. These policy statements are inconsistent.

Well what is so bad about a thinker holding inconsistent beliefs or views of what is acceptable policy? The problem is if a thinker did indulge in inconsistency in this way, then he or she could prove whatever, *both that some conclusion is true or acceptable, and that it is not.* For example, suppose your employer says that she is for fair wages—meaning the same wage or salary for the same job description. And then she hires two people for the very same job but says to one (Person 1) that the salary is $40,000 per year and to the other (Person 2) that the salary is $35,000 per year. Person 1 and Person 2 meet and talk about their new jobs, discovering that they are not being paid the same for the work they do even though this goes against what was said by the boss. Person 1 says this is not fair and decides to go to the boss about it. The boss says that Person 2 is an immigrant/woman/minority/member of a different religion/etc. and does not need the extra $5,000 which can then be pumped back into the business. Now the boss—regardless of her claim that Person 2 does not need the money—is operating on a second basic principle: that she is for fair wages or salary and fair is not equal pay for equal job but is equal pay for equal job *along with* equal need. Let's name that first principle: **Job Only Fairness;** the second can be named **Job and Need Fairness.**

Now let us think about the boss's reasoning. For Person 1 she thinks as follows:

Person 1 is doing job XYZ. The salary for job XYZ is $40,000. It's fair to pay *all the holders of the same job the same salary or wage. (The Job Only Principle)*

So, Person 1 should be paid $40,000.

For Person 2 the boss thinks as follows:

Person 2 is Doing Job XYZ. The salary for job XYZ is $40,000 (normally). It's fair to pay the holders of the same job with the same need the same wage or *salary. (The Job and Need Fairness Principle). Person 2 needs only $35,000.*

So Person 2 should be paid $35,000.

Ok, so now here is a proof for paying the two differently and this policy is right by one principle and wrong by the other principle. But if the thinker, in this case the boss, is allowed to hold *both* of these principles as correct or acceptable, then she can prove both conclusions are acceptable. It is right to pay the holders of the same job the same and not to do so. Now this means that it is right to pay Person 1 at one rate and Person 2 at another, and it is not right to do so.

Probably at this point a critical thinker is saying, "Wait a minute! Which is it? Right or wrong?" This means that the critical thinker would not want to allow inconsistent premises or evidence statements in the support for a conclusion.

Just as begging the question allows thinkers to prove whatever they want to by just assuming the conclusion in collecting the evidence, the fallacy of inconsistent premises allows the thinker to prove too much by allowing the evidence statements to include inconsistencies which will make it possible to prove both that some statement or policy is correct and that it is not. (In fact, chapter VIII will offer a formal illustration of the point that inconsistent premises allow a thinker to prove anything.) The critical thinker then wants to avoid inconsistency in the collection of evidence. Thus the next fallacy to note is that of inconsistent evidence statements or premises.

IV.14. *The fallacy of inconsistent premises* amounts to a thinker proceeding in a way that allows in inconsistent statements of evidence or support for a conclusion.

Examples of cases where inconsistent premises have been held (examples besides ones of job pay, school funding, and corporate/individual taxation, for example) are as follows:

For example: "President Bush has urged the protection of the environment as a high priority, and yet the White House has ordered the EPA to leave out of their recent report information on the dangers of global warming and climate change. No wonder they can call for cleaning up the environment while also endorsing policies that dirty it up."

Or: "Henry Ford said that those who bought the Model T could have any color they wanted as long as it was black. So they could have any color they wanted. And the color they would get is black. So they could not have any color they wanted. No wonder he could claim he was responding to his customers' wants and that he could keep costs down on paint jobs as well."

Or again: "Presidents since Ronald Reagan have urged the importance of supporting our troops and they have reduced spending in Veterans' Administration Medical Centers and for veterans' dependents' health care as well as passed on to soldiers and their families costs formerly paid by the government as an essential part of supporting our troops. Maybe the definition of "supporting our troops" has changed. Or is there just an inconsistency that would allow us to justify, for example, both saying that we are supporting our troops and that we need to empty VA hospitals of many vets who continue to suffer mentally and to be unable to live an ordinary life at work and home?"

Mastery Exercises IV.3

SELF TEST

Fallacies of Evidence Collection: arguing from ignorance, appealing to or relying on the sound-bite, insider appeal, begging the question, arguing in a circle, inconsistent premises

FALLACY IDENTIFICATION PRACTICE. Following the Tech Tips found at the end of Chapter II, identify the fallacies illustrated in the following exercises. Write a sentence explaining your judgment of which fallacy is present in each question. (Answers in Appendix II.)

1. "Well of course there are moonbeams. I'm not going to appeal to all the songs about moonbeams and so on—which presumably there would not be if there weren't moonbeams. But I will just ask you this. What is the proof that there are no moonbeams? Just as I thought—none. So of course there are moonbeams."

2. "I was sure you would understand why I had to do it. Of course it is obvious, but not everyone sees as clearly as you and I."

3. "Why is it going to work? Well, I'll tell you why it is going to work. It will work because the results are guaranteed. That's why."

4. "The enemy must be defeated here. That should be obvious to all of our citizens."

5. "We must hire affirmatively extending every advantage to the physically challenged. That is only fair. At the same time, we must realize the greatest productivity possible and that will require not having to put in any special accessibility measures throughout the plant. That is only fair. The challenge to you managers is to put this all into practice. Remember there is one standard of fairness here—fairness for all. You must hire with fairness in mind. You will know what to do!"

6. "I know that was an alien contact. It had all the earmarks of such a thing. It was at an odd time of day. It was made through a new technology we just discovered. It contained a very cryptic message. 'You will all be better off.' And it was covered up by the government for about a week until some news reporter got hold of it through a government leak."

7. "Yes, yes. There are bits of circumstantial evidence against the man. But that is not at all proof as yet. And until you come up with clear proof of guilt we may believe he is innocent."

8. "Now Mr. Smith has a wonderful background in just the right areas. But it is obvious to those of us who have met him that he is not the person we want representing the company. You will see what we mean when you meet him."

9. "Trance music is so wonderful to listen to. Why? Well, it is because of the way it can just space you out and take you to another level of consciousness."

10. "The police officer said that I was going over eighty. And the evidence? Well, that is his perception—that I was going over eighty. Training or not, that's no good."

11. "All encyclopedias are good places to start your research. There are some that are written by scholars in the fields of the entries reported. And then there are those which are written by committees or by single authors who are very knowledgeable but do not have expertise in all the fields covered. The last are not really good sources to begin your research with. So my suggestion is that an encyclopedia is the place to start."

Wrap-Up

This chapter explores some of what it means to be responsible as a critical thinker. One must act in a way that is guided by and expresses respect for the views of others. This, of course, is different from just accepting whatever they say. Always it means holding them to the common practices and standards of critical thinking while also being ready to be challenged by their particular views and methods. Thus responsibility here involves a careful balance between crediting and challenging others, between being challenged by and critically assessing what others think. Critical thinkers must meet others where these others are and on the basis they present to us. Others must not be misconstrued, if possible. They must not be made to bear the burden of proof unjustifiably. They must be encouraged to reconsider their beliefs on the basis of good reasons—not rejected for doing so. Others must be allowed patterns of reasoning justifiable in the same ways as those of their critics. And critical thinkers must make themselves accountable to others for their own thought patterns and claims.

In addition, the responsible thinker will seek to maintain integrity by holding herself or himself accountable to others who are concerned with the same problems and approach these in the same ways. The critical thinker will avoid the pitfalls of mythic thinking and its trappings of various figurations of problems, beliefs, and options. Inquiry must rest in credible belief and defensible understanding. And the critical thinker will not turn her or his beliefs and methods into fighting points or resort to relativism in the disregard of the challenges of others.

Finally, critical thinkers who are responsible will look for evidence and not take the lack of disproof as proof. This evidence must be rich and adequate to the task at hand, not sound bites or appeals to an in-group already geared to believe or decide in a certain way. The responsible thinker cannot assume the conclusion in collecting her or his evidence for that conclusion and cannot draw a conclusion from inconsistent premises. To do either of these things is to give up on the project of discriminating the good from the bad belief, decision, or action.

Critical thinking is a difficult and engrossing undertaking. It requires the maturity to balance charity with integrity and the self-control to demand of oneself that real inquiry is undertaken so as to put the thinker in a position to create a good explanation or argument for what is of interest at a time. As discussed in chapters IX and X, the thinker must also be open to a continuing examination and reintegration of her or his beliefs, decisions, and actions. Living well is a continuing journey and critical thinking is the global positioning device that can orient one and keep her or him on course. But it also can assist in getting clear in ways that help articulate and determine a destination for that journey. If all of this is to work, however, the thinker must be responsible as well as skilled. The fallacies studied in this and the two previous chapters are the necessary first steps of a thinker taking on that kind of responsibility.

It might be useful to close out this chapter with a listing of the mistakes and leading concepts covered here. The numbers follow the sequence of the fallacies in chapters II and III:

FALLACIES OF CHARITY/FAIRNESS
36. studied misunderstanding
37. shifting the burden of proof
38. denying reconsideration
39. denying parity of reasons
40. rejecting external accountability

FALLACIES OF INTEGRITY
41. rejecting internal accountability
42. mythic images
    a. fallacy of evading integrity by qualifications
43. fighting points
44. relativism

FALLACIES OF EVIDENCE COLLECTION
45. arguing from ignorance
46. appealing to or relying on the sound-bite
47. insider appeal
48. begging the question
    a. arguing in a circle
49. inconsistent premises

SO: Review the fallacies covered in this chapter, either in the Quick Reference and Summary or the text above, and make sure you understand the Mastery Exercises.

Self Test IV-ST1

Comprehension Questions

1. Why is begging the question different from arguing in a circle?

2. Why are cases of denying parity of reasons matters of lack of charity or fairness on the part of a thinker?

3. What is the difference between rejecting internal and rejecting external accountability?

4. What is wrong with inconsistent premises?

5. Contrast a sound-bite fallacy and insider appeal and the fallacy of common practice.

6. How is studied mis-understanding different from the straw figure fallacy?

7. When are mythic images useful and allowed in critical thinking?

8. What do you do when you encounter someone who conflicts with your way of approaching a problem, and yet agrees with your understanding of the problem? After you have checked for whether the person is maintaining internal accountability and you have found that she is, but still reasons differently from you in the matter, what do you do?

9. Why shouldn't we deny parity of reasons?

10. When is a criticism of flip-flopping a fallacy?

11. What is the difference between arguing from ignorance and begging the question?

Self Test IV-ST2

Fallacy Identification Practice

1. According to the Tories, Thomas Jefferson's Declaration of Independence went out of its way to state the policies of King George in a way that showed him as prejudicial toward the colonists. If this is so, this is a case of the fallacy of _____.

2. It was important in stating the Declaration of Independence to counter the divine right of Kings (the supposedly God given right to rule) with an equally divine legitimacy for the needs and desires of the individual colonists. Thus they were all said to be endowed by their Creator with inalienable rights to life, liberty and the pursuit of happiness. This reliance on claims of divine blessing for political rights is a case of the fallacy of _____.

3. The U.S. Air Force colonel in charge of the Roswell investigation pointed out that there was no final evidence that aliens had been in the area, so he concluded that none had been in the area. This involves the fallacy of _____.

4. Sebastian, the local shoemaker who had always lived inland until a day or so ago, said that he was sure the ship coming into harbor was registered under the Finnish flag. It was too far out at sea to make out the flag and this was at a time before radios, planes, and other means of making a direct identification. So Sebastian was making his judgment on the basis of ship shape. But he was sure that it was Finnish because that is exactly the shape that Finnish ships would have.

5. This bottle of wine is very expensive for wine of that type. Just look at the price. No bottle of wine of that type would have that price.

6. Clyde Harmon, the local sheriff, said to Ben Tillman, "Well ok Ben, have it your way. But you know I have you at the scene of the crime that day. It is up to you to provide an alibi for the time of the crime. Speak up or I'm going to have to arrest you. Where were you all afternoon and evening on the 27th of June?"

7. "Yes, you are the head of the department, but I am tenured and I don't have to answer to you about why I cancelled that class."

8. Senator Kerry came home and soon afterward started protesting the war. So first he was for the war and then he was against the war in Vietnam. Why should we take him seriously? He's undependable in his thinking.

9. They are from a different order of Amish. Yes they allow pockets on aprons, but that is proud and we know that and that is all there is to it. We do not have to think it through.

10. The priest wanted to offer the parish guidance on the proposal to allow gambling in the town limits. But he wanted to not lose any more parishioners. So he said that the church's view was that gambling should not be allowed here, not unless you really think it should be. He was guilty of the fallacy of _____.

11. "Easy for you to say. But I have four children to support. And if I think I need to cheat a little on the fireworks I deliver to the customers and then sell the excess later for myself, that's what I'll do. It's right for me."

12. The Bishop agreed that it was right to allow milk coolers because it was necessary for business. But they would not allow in-shop wall or desk phones because they were necessary for business. So the church members used cell phones.

13. Phyllis said to Beatrice, "Susan wanted to release the tapes of the trial, but she was afraid of what the newspapers would do with them. As a result she hung on to them to protect the Governor. But the Governor said that when she found out, she instructed Susan to release the tapes. After all she too knew what the press would do with them and the tapes would make the opposition look worse than the Governor and her party. They all knew how the press would play it and it was obvious that it would hurt the opposition. After hearing that, Susan agreed with the Governor."

14. The boss said a new policy was now in effect. She would pay for no overtime to any worker, under any circumstances. Shortly after she told Herman that she would allow him to work overtime since he had to pay back a loan to her.

15. "They do not want us to have freedom. They are against freedom. That is why they hate us," the politician said in explaining why it was necessary to invade the home of the terrorists.

16. "No, you may not trust that I will reconsider. Divorce is wrong in any circumstances and that is the end of the matter."

Applications and Everyday Uses _____

REFLECTION AND APPLICATION QUESTIONS

1. How well do you feel you have taken up the aim of charity or fairness in critical thinking spelled out by the relevant fallacies of this chapter? Can you give examples of your respect for others' views and say why this was or was not deserved?

2. When you conduct an inquiry with a friend, do you ever catch yourself relying on sound-bites? Write out an account of an example of this or an example of someone doing this to you in a serious conversation.

3. Jones says that he has found a connection between a terrorist group and an in-power head of a foreign state. Smith says that Jones seems to be just stirring up trouble saying that a certain foreign head of state is working with terrorists and that Jones has no clear evidence of this. Smith says that since Jones has no clear evidence besides her interpretation of the behavior of that head of state as consorting with a terrorist, Jones is begging the question. Jones says that since Smith has claimed Jones said the head of state and the terrorist are working together, and since that is not exactly what Jones said, Smith is guilty of a studied mis-understanding. Can you tell the difference between begging the question and a studied mis-understanding? Please explain how you would settle this dispute between Jones and Smith.

4. Have you ever been the victim of someone shifting the burden of proof in a fallacious way? Can you explain what happened and why it was not correct for it to have happened?

5. How would you design a grievance procedure that makes clear the appropriate burdens of proof and avoids all the other fallacies of failure of charity? Sketch the rules of this procedure and explain how they avoid those fallacies.

6. How can you conduct discussions on how to make policy without relying on insider appeals? One method that some have tried to use in this situation is to rely on focus groups bringing in outside members and fresh perspectives. How can these outsiders be used to the best effect? Design rules of discussion for a focus group which is concerned with making policy for a company and involves outsiders as well as insiders from all ranks.

7. Write a grade appeal policy for your university concerning instances of the grade of "F" being assigned for academic dishonesty. Be sure to show who has to prove what to establish his or her case. Also explain what might be presented by each side as proof of its case.

Notes

[1] Personal observation by Professor Charles L. Stevenson.

[2] This fallacy also seems to be what Moore and Parker have in mind when they speak of "pseudo-refutation." However, Moore and Parker do not explain that why the accusation of inconsistency is not a legitimate criticism is that the person criticized has rethought the matter. As pointed out, if one changes her or his mind without rethinking things, then that merits question and perhaps criticism. See Moore, B. N., and Parker, R. (2001). *Critical thinking*. Mountain View, California: Mayfield Publishing Company, p. 177.

CHAPTER V

Sources and Patterns of Appeals to Evidence

There used to be a bittersweet situation comedy television program centered on the life of a family in project housing located in New York. One day, the father in the family was explaining to one of his children about the need to understand each other if you are in a discussion. What was said holds good as a kind of guiding question for this stage of the present discussion of thinking critically: "How you going to know where you're going if you don't know where you're coming from?" In the sit-com, the point was that one needs to know one's own identity and what one is willing to stand up for before he or she tries to become critically involved in a complex world with many cross-currents of temptation and danger. Knowing one's values and identity will help an agent to articulate ends and means that are appropriate and then to look for ways to make these real in one's life. For present purposes the point is not far different. Only by being aware of the sources of their beliefs and information, only by knowing where, as well as how, they can find relevant information from which to draw their beliefs and decisions, will critical thinkers know where they might responsibly head in forming and supporting their beliefs and decisions and in undertaking their actions. Critical thinking demands that thinkers have a good grasp of sources of evidence and a good sense of how to avail themselves of these sources, as well as an understanding of what to do with what they derive from these sources, if they are going to be able to separate the acceptable from the unacceptable. The purpose of this chapter is to investigate what are common sources of evidence, and how critical thinkers might make some good use of these sources.

The subject was raised in earnest in the previous chapter where the text took up how what a speaker/writer contributes to a discussion might not serve to further inquiry. Bullying and manipulation work against critical thinking. In such cases, what is said does not come from any of the ordinary sources the critical thinker needs to pay attention to. For example, if something is put forward that is not the result of observation, or not something that fits coherently into the experience or beliefs or plans of a thinker, or does not reflect the thinker's perspective, then what is the thinker to do with this information? In fact, by what standard could it even be called information for the thinker to work with? Putting the point positively, the thinker is in place, trying to make sense of a world. He or she first encounters this world in experience and might not know just what to make of that experience—might not know what he or she is looking at, what categories or concepts to use to classify what is going on or what is being observed. And the thinker might not know what significance to assign the object of observation in her or his life. "Well, that is a special kind of X-ray machine—just what we need to get the most revealing views of your neck injury. This machine produces what is called a CAT scan." With that information, the thinker can build the observation into a narrative that hangs together and has an order that makes sense of what is going on in the world as the thinker encounters it. "Ok. Now I understand. This is part of what we need to do to diagnose the injury to my neck and then decide on the right thing to do to help me? Ok. It isn't some strange machine that might hurt when it is used on me. It will take something like a picture of my neck." At this point the thinker can articulate her/his feelings and define the proper terms to use to make sense of her/his experience. The thinker now has a new concept with which to interpret the world. And then the thinker can also understand the situation in the official story told by the physicians and other authorities in her/his life of neck injury treatment. So he/she can understand the doctor's perspective a bit better when it comes to grasping the nature of this particular diagnostic tool and its role in forming a plan of care. In fact the thinker is now equipped to bring into play the results of the CAT scan in reasoning to what needs to be done next—neck surgery, physical therapy, or rest. And finally, the thinker might even be able to review her/his previous thinking to modify or update her/his perspective on the character of medical care and how that relates to her/his values. Perhaps the thinker previously thought that the only thing to do with injuries to bones was to cast them until they healed. And now the thinker has a new understanding of the possible kinds of injury and possible forms of treatment for bone injuries—a neck injury might require surgery to fuse bones or to insert metal pins or other reinforcement to strengthen the bones involved. Thus, from observation and making one's experience intelligible in one's own life, to naming it for others to think about, to analyzing it and placing it within the viewpoint of a perspective, critical thinking can identify several different common sources of information in inquiry. This chapter seeks to introduce each of these three—**observation, interpretation,** and **perspective**—and to identify some of the pitfalls and guideposts of using such influences in reasoning.

Observation, Coherence, and Understanding

Interpretation and Personal Intelligibility: Working on Mysteries without Any Clue (Almost)

One of the great tragedies of the previous century was the assassination of President John F. Kennedy, an event that has been preserved on film. As one watches the film with the commentary running in the voice-over background, pops like firecrackers are heard, and the President is filmed as he is knocked backward by the bullets that killed him. This is one of those moments that at first makes no sense—what happened? Why is the President slumping over? Where are the cars going? What is all of the confusion? And then the horror sets in. The President has been shot. Is he all right; will he be all right? Was the first lady hurt? Was anyone else hurt? Who did this? Where did the shots come from? Did they (the authorities) see? Did they get them/him/her? Disbelief is the carpet upon which a jumble of questions are thrown like so many dice or fortune-telling sticks gambling with the future of the world. One cannot look at that film, no matter how many times, even knowing what had happened, without experiencing that moment of confusion. The scene is so incongruous it requires the observer to stop and reinterpret, in order to find a meaning that makes sense of what is observed without meaning and so in the form of bits and pieces. This is not a strange or unusual phenomenon, it is just striking because of its monumental significance. In fact it happens to thinkers each and every time they change the direction of their gaze or read a paragraph. It happens, but with less of a need for a pause and adjustment since for the most part what they encounter is predictable and expected. The meaning they just gave the previous sentence sets up the interpretation of the next sentence, expectations work out. And it all hangs together. In this way the Kennedy assassination images are no different from the little story above of walking into the room with the CAT scan machine, hurting and afraid and wondering "what in the world is this?"

The same sort of thing goes on when one sees a magic show. Someone makes a large coin disappear and reappear in the hair of someone across the room. How did it get over there? What am I seeing? Is there a trick? How does it work? What really went on before my eyes? The magician comes onto the stage for a final trick and disappears along with an elephant, only to ride out for the finale from some door at the back of the studio where the broadcast is coming from. What has happened? What did I see?

Or one is standing in the middle of a stream close to the last step of a large cascade enjoying the feel of the spray on a hot summer's day, and the play of the water in the sunlight coming from off to the right. And then the sound of the water falling morphs into what surely sounds like a human voice. "What is that—am I losing my mind? Is there someone on the bank calling to me? I look and there is no one, at least no one to be seen. What do I make of that?"

It is well known that the senses can "play tricks" on observers and that the emotions as well as expectations that observers bring to a situation cause troubles of misinterpretation or misunderstanding. The discussion of the fallacies of openness in chapter II covered bias; and this is only one way in which expectations can color experiences so that observers see or hear or smell or even feel something that is not really there. Another is the lack of previous experience or the lack of concepts with which to grasp what is being seen. Because the senses "play tricks," so-called eyewitness reports are often challenged in courtrooms, and there are experts hired to taste wines or other products for quality and to smell perfumes before they are marketed. Observation is probably the most basic and common source of beliefs, decisions, and actions, but it is a source that is not trouble free and not something that thinkers can take for granted. In fact, some research suggests that what comes first in an observer is a sense of the whole before her or him. This whole is then divided up by distinctions and conceptual labels that give an analysis of the whole or highlight some aspect of the whole as the most important or most prominent feature.[1] If these accounts are to be believed, then the character of observation is very much influenced by the distinctions and forms of analysis that thinkers are taught in learning a language and in learning specialized bodies of belief.

Here the job is not to enter into a study of these specialized bodies of belief and special techniques of observation—for example those learned by wine tasters or by botanists who can make some distinctions between plants by feeling the leaves. Rather the job is one of reviewing what is much more common and general knowledge about observation and its pitfalls. It is well-known but bears emphasizing that:

§ **Observation should be made in circumstances as close to ideal as possible for the mode of sense and for the sorts of properties to be experienced.** (Do not try to give a taste test of anything if one has a cold, for example. Or if one is trying to discern what a fabric looks like in daylight, take the fabric to the daylight, do not observe it under florescent showroom lights.)

§ **If one *is* seeking a sensuous experience of a certain kind, for its own sake, for example an experience of some sound or tonal quality, try to limit the impact of the other senses**—close your eyes, sit in a comfortable but forgettable chair, use earphones if you have them, and so on, to listen for what you are trying to hear.

§ **Recognize that emotional associations and conceptual distinctions are part of virtually all experiences even if they are not articulated.** So when one thinks of the quality of the experience in order to try to articulate it, be prepared to recognize the influences of the emotions that were prominent as well as the conceptual influences working at the time of the experience. In seeking to minimize these influences, try to avoid judgments pronouncing finally what one saw or heard or tasted, and so on. To adapt what we all are told in art class, draw out, be alert to what one sees, or feels, or hears, or tastes, not what one thinks one sees (or feels, hears, or tastes and so on).

§ **If one *is* seeking to observe in order to form a judgment about the character of some event or the features of some object or process, identify an expert in the field where the judgment is called for and learn what that individual would suggest about *how to observe* and what the experts have said about *what is to be observed*.** For example, when trying to figure out the workings of some piece of computer hardware, compare one's observations with a wiring or other design diagram, or if one is seeking to observe art in a sensitive way, learn some art history and read art criticism so as to find out what those who pay close attention to art interpretation say about it.

§ **Remember that articulating one's experiences will bring out only part of what one has observed, which amounts to paying special attention to a feature of the observed.** In fact, this is an area where particular cultural biases show up, influencing which aspects observers pay particular attention to. For example, in psychological studies, Japanese observers of an aquatic scene were much more likely to pay special attention to the context (i.e., the observation was of a water scene), than were American observers, who were much more likely to pay particular attention to the most prominent objects in the scene (i.e., what was observed was that there was a big fish swimming close to the front of the scene).[2] So if one is looking for "objective" observations, there are personal and cultural biases that need to be guarded against. Some such biases might have to do with purposes and values—one possible explanation given for the Japanese bias for context had to do with the awareness of others and of context so as to be able to orient oneself in an ethically proper way. Other biases might be technological rather than cultural, for example, a distortion of a face portrayed might be due to tricks of the camera. Other oddities in observations that might show up in articulating one's experiences might simply reflect the physical needs of the observer—for example, visual impairments that show up in paintings by some of the great masters and more recent artists.

Regardless of the source of distortion or of departure from the norm, observation as a source of information to support or to inform beliefs, decisions, and actions is basic and pervasive. Critical thinkers need observation as much as they need intellectual understanding. Indeed some would say that observation is not to be separated from understanding. After all, as thinkers proceed through life they keep some sort of running tally of where they are and what they are up to. This personal, working narrative of their life need not be fully articulated or explicit. It is something that can be seen in the regularity and coherence of activities, or else for those thinkers with language, can be articulated to some extent upon reflection (even if only with some prompting by others). If there were no such ongoing narrative sense of one's life, no understanding of where one is and why, and where one is going from there, the events of the world would seem foreign and one would not know how to take them, or even know what one was experiencing. The world for anyone lacking that personal narrative sense of life would be beyond observation in that the thinker could not even place her or himself in that world and pay attention to it in some way that provides results of interest and significance (other than merely classificatory) for that person. Perhaps the person knows the name of what is observed, but still does not know what to do with it, or what difference it makes. (In fact, since a person's understanding of the features of the world is arguably tied to that person's placing those features within the frame of the person's projected and current actions, it is not clear that the person could even classify that world's contents. How does a person classify an object: by following a rule to assign a term to a thing that meets certain criteria or by following a rule to group that thing with others that look or seem similar to it? But without any personal narrative sense of presence in the world, what would it be to follow rules or make comparisons?)

Observation as a source of thought about the world that can yield beliefs, decisions, and actions thus seems to involve a running personal narrative sense of the world on the part of the observer. "What are these things I encounter? What do they mean to me? How do they fit in with what I am doing—or do they? What must I do about them in my doing what I am already doing?" The observer's answer to these questions would be the heart of that narrative. Observation then involves that person keeping an ongoing understanding of where he or she is in the world and what he or she is up to. This, in turn, brings with it a sense of what has gone before and what might well happen next, a set of expectations then, about what the individual will experience next, if and when he or she does certain things. If these expectations are relatively well met, then the individual can feel that he or she has understood the world. And if not, then there has been some misunderstanding to be corrected. The present needs to fit with the past and with the future in expected ways, forming a consistent and coherent whole; background beliefs will need to fit with those of present circumstances now and in the future, both of them within the framework of the thinker's personal narrative. And since this personal narrative takes up and uses commonly held beliefs about what the world is like and how it works, then the observer's personal narrative sense of things must fit also with the framework of more general and widely held beliefs of how things work and of what is possible. Without those fits with other beliefs (and also with the thinker's values), then revision of the beliefs (or decisions) will seem necessary. Lack of fit indicates a real problem to be sorted through and some beliefs (or decision and actions), those that do not fit well, will have to go. So the suggestion is that:

Experience + interpretation → observation + understanding of what is going on and expectations of what is coming next

Expectations of what is coming next + failure to have those expectations met → confusion and lack of understanding → checking and correction of interpretation, or exploration for a new interpretation

This point should receive special clarification. Not all of a person's beliefs can be trusted. Some cannot because they are **inconsistent** with others which have good support. Others must be rejected because they do not form a coherent set with beliefs that have some form of good support. Each of these points needs a little more explanation.

Historians report that people believed one could sail off the edge of the earth, that worms and flies spontaneously generated in manure piles, and that disease was caused by evil spirits and spells. Science has progressed past these beliefs and thinkers now have a new set of commonly held beliefs to work with. The world is spherical; blue flies come from eggs laid in manure piles and elsewhere; disease is caused by bacteria or viruses. Systematic observations and their interpretations have led to this point. But notice that it is not just by observing and articulating the character of the facts that thinkers have come to change their beliefs. Sometimes they find that they can no longer hold beliefs because they are inconsistent with others that are well-founded. So they cannot believe that worms and flies spontaneously generate, because they believe that nothing comes from nothing, and nothing is self-caused—unless it is God. So since worms spontaneously generating would be inconsistent with or would run against the truth of the belief that nothing comes from nothing and the belief that nothing is self-caused, they throw out the assertion about spontaneous generation. *This belief of nothing coming from nothing is more central to the set of common beliefs— many more beliefs fit with this belief than with the view that there is such a thing as spontaneous generation. And this centrality gives it priority since in seeking knowledge people are conservative and seek the most well-integrated set of beliefs possible.* Or consider the humble self-observation that you are now reading this. This is inconsistent— cannot be true along with the belief that you are on a space ship having your teeth drilled by aliens. (I hope that your reading this is a lot less painful!!) So since thinkers trust observation as a method of getting at the truth, they will throw out the alien abduction belief, and trust that they are reading as they seem to be.

Consistency is pretty clear. *When two statements are related so that if one is true then the other is false, then they are inconsistent.* So suppose that a thinker takes a belief as true because of its centrality to a whole set of beliefs, or a belief is taken to be true because it seems to serve as the explanation of a large number of observed events (because of its power to explain a lot of what is taken to be true), or it is taken as true because it seems to record what has been observed in excellent conditions. Then, a good *rule of thumb is:* **If another belief is inconsistent with such central or powerful beliefs, then that other belief should be rejected as false.**

Coherence is a different but related matter. All coherent beliefs are consistent, they can be true at the same time. And a coherent set of beliefs does not contain any inconsistent beliefs. Inconsistency would be a reliable indicator of incoherence, but coherence goes beyond consistency. Not all consistent beliefs are coherent. So what is this coherence? Well, think about the following example.

Jane is wandering through an apparently abandoned house in the country after her car broke down in a snowstorm. The house is run down on the outside, but it is neat, clean, and warm inside. No one is around, that she can see, and there is a broken down "For Sale" sign outside with the sign part dangling from the post part and blowing in the wind. So she looks around after warming up a bit in front of the fire, and she then sees an old dial telephone. She goes over and calls Acme Towing who then sends a truck, picks her up at the door and takes her to her car, which they then tow into town. Warm and safe in her apartment, Jane thinks over the things the tow truck driver said. "Wow, it is lucky you were able to find the telephone booth to make your call and lucky you passed by the old Grimley place. You could have frozen if you were outside much longer, and you certainly would have frozen inside that old house if you had gone in and tried to stay the night there. No one has been in there to even fix the roof since the murder and fire." But Jane doesn't remember a phone call except one made from the old house! And she got warm after going into the house.

So what is going on? (1) The driver is misinformed. Someone has taken over the Grimley place as a squatter and has tapped into the phone line unknown to the telephone company. (2) There are such things as ghosts and they are doing well in the old Grimley place. (3) She was dreaming—but her car is not in her parking space and a call to the garage confirms that they have it and will get it ready by the end of the week for her trip home.

We can make several stories out of this set of observations. Jane has got to wonder what to believe. But notice, some of the stories fit together and some do not. Jane cannot very well believe that the house had been abandoned since the murder and the fire and that she got warm and made a call there, unless she believes in ghosts— and ghostly fires in cold fireplaces. Otherwise she faces some inconsistencies. She could believe that the driver was misinformed, someone is squatting at the Grimley place and the phone company is being ripped off, and there are not ghosts. That is not inconsistent. Now what fits best with her experiences and the common beliefs she shares with others as background assumptions about the way the world is? She could believe that she was dreaming and she got up in her sleep and called the tow truck to come get her car or someone stole her car and took it to the garage, or something like that. But then she could not believe she was on the road, broken down, and the rest.

She *is* warm and safe. She knows that by first hand experience, observation in the best of conditions (and after pinching herself to be sure). But how did she get that way? What best fits together with her other commonly held beliefs about the way the world is and works—(1) that no one lives after death in any form that would allow them to take over and make an old house cozy and convenient, (2) that she really did not dream having car trouble, and (3) that what explains her boots being still wet and cold sitting in a puddle in the front hall, as well as the call to the towing garage, is that she did break down and that somehow she made it to the phone booth two miles up the road, called the tow truck and then all but blacked out until now when she finally warmed up? Her fitting the pieces together in the best way possible: (1) with no inconsistencies, (2) in a way that fits what she has to take as fact—her wet boots, her car being in the garage, and (3) best explains what she can now observe, that is what is meant by the term "coherent" here.

Coherence is the property of a collection of beliefs (or beliefs and values) that:

 consistently fits together what the thinker is considering—background beliefs and other independently credible beliefs such as those held after observation;

 and this consistent set of beliefs provides the material for a story or an account that makes overall sense—that is, is a story that is comprehensible to the thinker (and perhaps to others to whom the thinker is accountable for her or his thinking); and

best explains relevant portions of what the thinker has observed. (See the discussion in chapter IX, on the work of explanations.)

So coherence goes beyond consistency to what saves appearances and what explains the best, and fits the set together intelligibly into one consistent body of belief. When beliefs do fit together coherently, their credibility or "believability" is strengthened—one and all, by this fitting together. This does not mean they are true. Many nicely fitting stories have been shown to be false. But it does raise the credibility of the beliefs in question.

Coherence is often said to be important in ethics. Here judgments assessing particular actions or decisions or even judgments of what principles to accept are made to rest upon finding a coherent mix of such things as *personal feelings* of what is right/wrong or good/bad, *philosophical principles* of ethics, and *common beliefs* about what is right/wrong or good/bad. Writers speak of such a form of coherence in terms of judgments of reflective equilibrium ("wide" or else more restricted equilibrium) where these factors of feeling, principle, and social expectations are brought into harmony. This is a topic the present discussion takes up briefly in the ninth and tenth chapters.

So, here is a good *rule of thumb:*   ***In checking unsupported claims, if a belief fits coherently, and so consistently with our background beliefs as well as our observations, while explaining best what we seem to have to take as fact, all of that together is some reason for accepting it.*** Perhaps later discoveries will give thinkers reason to change their background beliefs, to reformulate or even give up their beliefs based on observation, or give them new and better ways to explain events. For example, it is discovered that flies do come from eggs, diseases from germs. With changes of any one of these sorts, thinkers might well change what they find to be coherent. But that is fine. Coherence is no guarantee of the absolute truth or of finality in claims to know something. *It is just relied upon along with observation as one good source of support for beliefs, or, when values are brought into consideration, even for decisions or actions.* Coherence and observation are not something critical thinkers could do without. But these are not the whole story by any means.

Finally, notice that coherence works hand in hand with observation at the heart of interpretation. They are what allow thinkers to come to make sense of something that is not readily or even after effort able to be classified. The strangeness of the world to the hero of the little story above calls for her to make sense of what happened the night of the big snow storm. And that calls for her to make sense of her experience of being in the abandoned house—dream or strange new reality. Similarly, when a thinker encounters a new form of artistic expression, or finds himself surrounded by persons speaking a foreign language—whether in a foreign land or in a new class!—interpretation is called for, and observation combined with reliance upon coherence is often key to finding some workable view of what is going on or what is being said. Thinkers, like the song lyric says, sometimes find themselves working on mysteries without any clue—or at least without very many clues. At this point the next move should be to observation and coherence even if one cannot articulate what it is that one is experiencing or thinking. A true artist or craftsperson can proceed along getting remarkable results making a hundred adjustments in what he or she is doing and not be able to tell anyone else how or even what he or she was doing. Other persons can proceed along, understanding artistic or political or other sorts of images after a hundred interpretative adjustments to observation, even if they cannot tell anyone else just how they are making those adjustments to what they see. Others, for example conductors of orchestras and art critics or other interpreters, make a living making articulate and explicit what is going on and how to do things. In order to bring interpretation to thought and then to make public that thought, it is important that thinkers have at their disposal means for putting their feelings into thought and their thought into words. The next section takes up aspects of this need. Still, one lesson remains important here—keep an open mind, be observant, learn what there is time to learn, and then remain ready to fit as much together as is possible, coherently. Following that advice, thinkers will be closer to the goal of thinking critically than otherwise.

Mastery Exercises V.1

Exercises on Observation and Coherence

1. Mother to child returning from the birthday party: "Well, now, tell me all about it. Tell me everything you saw and don't leave out a thing." Does this allow the child to respect the general knowledge of making and avoiding the pitfalls in the way of making, good observations? Explain.

2. Consistency is enough for giving a good, coherent story. True or False? Explain.

3. The definition of inconsistency is: _____ . Which of the following are inconsistent: (a) the world is round, but flat; (b) bachelors have never been married and some have been divorced; (c) the stage was uniformly red and green all over—what a show; (d) "I'll tell you, at that moment, time just stood still"; (e) "all at once, I was both very, very angry and incredibly sad!"

4. "The story that he was captured by aliens and had his teeth drilled is a good explanation of why he has so many cavities and it is certainly consistent. So it must be ok—right?"

5. "If your expectations in observations are disappointed, then you should just put up with it. After all, that's life."

6. If you form a belief that is inconsistent with highly central beliefs, then you should review your observations and thinking and work to eliminate the inconsistency.

7. Bias is never a problem tainting observation. True or False? If you think it is false then how do you keep bias out of observation?

8. All bias is personal and shows a faulty character. True or False? Explain.

9. When observing anything we want to be able to take as much in from as many different sensory modes as possible. True or False? Discuss.

10. "Eliminating emotional content from experience as much as possible is a good thing. Right?"

SOURCE 2

Clarification, Definition and Articulation

Personal Narrative Reaching for Public Meaning: Speaking the World with Others

Thinkers need a *personal* narrative focused on intentions and informed by both memory and awareness to take them through the world of their actions and experiences. But just as much, they need a *public* narrative so they can take part in recording and exchanging experiences, views, and claims so as to fully engage in the social process of critical thinking. If thinkers are unable to articulate, or put into words, that portion of their experience that they wish to remember symbolically, and to relate symbolically to others of their beliefs or decisions, and then share with others, they are not just condemned to silence. They are shut off from *deliberate reflection* on the meanings of their past and its relation to their present. (They might remember in some important sense, but they will be unable to say or explain what the previous experience meant to them.) Emotions and feelings, except in their mute, remembered associations with action, would mean no more than mere sensations like the uneasiness of anxiety or the rejuvenating feeling of euphoria. They could not be the complex nuanced windows on the world that they might be. And then persons could not be thinkers who reflect and act upon, or share with others, what their life means in shared terms. Further, thinkers would be cut off from sharing what provides recognition by others, namely their understanding of their thought and the presence in the world that it gives them. And then, thinkers would be left out of one of the most important ways that critical thinkers are social, namely in the exchange of reasons for and against beliefs, decisions, and actions.

Many scholars of various sorts now say that thinking which is important to belief, decision, and action in significant senses does *not* require a language of public exchange and common meanings.[3] Still, there is no doubt that *much* of what is critical thinking requires precisely this. In fact, much of a critical thinker's grasp of the world is provided by language and the concepts and relationships expressed within language. Without a shared language, individuals cannot experience many of the small parts of the variety of things they think about or the relationships within which they understand those things. Consequently, thinkers must come to terms with what they mean by their utterances. They must find ways to articulate and sort through possible interpretations of what they encounter—either through the senses directly or in linguistic or other representations. And, as discussed just above, they then must seek the understandings that are possible and find those that are most coherent with what else they believe or have decided.

These necessities demand that *the critical thinker strive for clarity of thought and expression.* And to understand a bit about the sources and failings of this clarity is the purpose of this section. Spoken and written communications are notorious for sometimes needing expansion and restatement to reach clarity. Sometimes one does not figure out what is being said or what the author means until reaching the end of a paragraph or even a page. And sometimes even that much does not clear things up. Terms and whole sentences might have more than one meaning or, that is, might be *ambiguous.* And they might lack precision in ways that make what is being said unclear in the sense of being *vague.*

Clarification of what is ambiguous or vague might be out of reach of the thinker who is trying to understand. What is the meaning of the assertion that William Howard Taft was an enormous public figure—he was very important in civic life, or he was very large in body size, or both? Both are true, and short of asking the author which was intended, something that is not possible, there is no way to clear up the unclarity. "The right side panel should be connected to the feet of the cabinet before the seams are glued" would not be a very good instruction for building a piece of furniture if there is not more precision about *just when* the cabinet side is to be attached to the cabinet feet. If that is not in the instructions, then the builder is on her or his own. Still, thinkers can take steps toward clarity by *first understanding what to look for when trying to clarify individual terms* and *secondly by becoming sensitized to spotting ambiguity and vagueness so as to avoid them herself or himself.* With this in mind the discussion turns to some remarks first on definition, and then on ambiguity and vagueness.

The use of terms to convey ideas changes over time. Thus terms often have meanings they have brought along from earlier centuries as well as meanings they have only recently come to have. For example, the term "like" used as a conjunction in place of "as" or "as if" has a long history going back to the *14th century!* It is used that way now when someone says something such as "It was like he went off, man—way over the top." This would amount to saying it was as if the other exploded or lost control of her or his emotions. But the term "like" also is used currently (in what might be a derivative way) to announce or introduce an opinion, or an impression—"It was like *soooo*, way awesome, dude." And this seems to be an extension of the conjunctive use. In fact both are listed as meanings of the term "like" used as a conjunction. (See the *Merriam-Webster's collegiate dictionary* (10th ed.). (1993). Springfield, MA: Merriam-Webster, Incorporated, p. 674.)

Further, new technology, new situations or information, or else new interpretations of old situations, call for new terminology. Thus the terms "biochemistry," "string theory," "virus" (computer or otherwise), and "meme" all have come along recently as terms to express new outlooks, fields of study, or phenomena that thinkers wish to discuss. Also, as illustrated by the new use of the term "string" in physics as a field of ordered energy that goes into making up particles, *old terms are given new meanings because of their figurative powers to express an idea.* Or again, some talk of "dissing" an individual or of being "dissed." Here the idea is one of expressing disrespect of someone, and the term disrespect is turned into a term of action and then converted to a form that allows someone to say what is done to a person when he or she is made the object of disrespect—he or she has been dissed or "put down."

Finally (for present purposes), *terms take on new emotional overtones having been given emotive definitions in terms that already carry the lasting or new overtones.* An example from an earlier chapter is "God is love." Another example would be that of "sketchy," which in one use now seems to bring with it the overtones of being suspicious or not to be trusted because of not being forthright or forthcoming—hence not fully clear or explained or worked out—sketchy.

These dimensions of the living character of language present several problems which definitions of individual terms serve to address. First, there is *the problem of making clear just what is the current common meaning of a term—when the term would be used correctly and when not.* Second, there is *the need to clarify which of several current meanings of a term is being employed by a speaker or writer.* Third, and related to the second problem, is *the issue of introducing new terms or new uses of old terms to serve purposes that have just emerged.* And fourth, is *the problem of creating or revealing the emotional overtones speakers and writers sometimes have in the terms they use.* Each of these problems has given rise to a form of definition that has been widely recognized as a device for clarifying the language thinkers use.

Definitions

DEFINITION V.1

Reportive definitions attempt to state or to report the rules or the conditions for the correct use of a term in a language group.

For example: Consider the conditions fulfilled by all and only those persons we would call bachelors in the marital sense. The lexical or dictionary definition is roughly: Adult males who have never been married (as opposed to children who do not yet qualify for being bachelors and as opposed to adults whose spouse has died or who have been divorced).

By the way, if you have not noticed, this definition as a report on how English-speaking people in industrialized countries correctly use the term "bachelor" is out of date. The term now also applies to adult women who have never been married. So here in the definition is a rule that it is correct to apply the term to any man or woman who has never been married and it is incorrect to apply the term to anyone who does not fit these conditions of never having been married. *Another way to put this is that reportive definitions seek to give the conditions met by all and only cases of what the term correctly applies to.* (The point could also be put in terms of what are called necessary and sufficient conditions. But that terminology will not be introduced until the eighth chapter. Those who are interested might turn ahead to find that terminology in the quick reference and summary or in chapter VIII.) Notice that this particular example also illustrates the stress reportive definitions are under. Some would loosely speak even of those who are divorced as bachelors. In a living language, reportive definitions have to be updated from time to time.

Reportive definitions are not always just arbitrary rules for the use of a term. Such definitions are not just records of speech patterns. They are like mini-documentaries showing how a language group understands a part of the world. The term bachelor shows that a language group divides the world into those that are married, divorced, survivors of a spouse, or children. Someone who is adult and does not support the institution of marriage or the traditions of ordering the world in terms of married and unmarried people might resist being called a bachelor even though he or she is adult and has never been married. Instead that person might prefer being spoken of as being alone, or single, or on their own, or by herself/himself.

In some cases the reportive definitions of terms give an account of what a thing or an animal is that conveys information that is part of a group's outlook, and there is nothing to dispute. For example, the lexical definition of the term "horse" in *Merriam-Webster's Collegiate Dictionary* (10th ed.) describes the general size, shape, and eating habits of horses, gives the biological classification, and gives some of the history and some of the uses of horses. There is a lot of information in that definition and probably a committee of English users in the United States would trim some of it out. Still, the definition does a decent job of bringing into focus the conditions under which it is correct to use the term horse in the group of English language users. Again, the term "thermostat," might be defined as any device for automatically regulating temperature through switching on or off heating and cooling machines so as to keep the ambient temperature in some area within a certain range, and, an instrument operating by some sort of sensing device which closes a heating or cooling switch when the thermostat changes condition in response to changes in ambient air temperature. Here there is a whole explanation of how a thermostat works and what it does or what is its function. This is hardly the stuff of great legends and contains nothing most would dispute or restate. But, all the same, such definitions are an important source of information about what the term applies to and an important revelation of what technology is available (to some) within the language group.

So reportive definitions can explain, they can give the genus and species or other biological groupings of things, they can give rules of a game by defining the legitimate moves of the pieces of the game—like the king and queen pieces in chess or the cards made trump in a game of bridge. ***Thus definitions can convey information that can settle disputes and move forward inquiry itself as a source of information.*** This is one reason why the definitions of some terms are so hotly contested in various societies. Currently in the United States, some examples that stand out are the terms: "marriage," "life," "person," "privacy," "rights," and "genocide." Were there reportive definitions of these terms agreed upon among all English speakers in the United States, many crimes, court cases, and political battles would be avoided. So reportive definitions are very important sources of evidence for beliefs, decisions, and the planning as well as assessment of actions. Shortly, the discussion will turn to deciding whether reportive definitions are good or bad.

Clearly there are many terms that have two or more meanings which could be given reportive definitions. Consider the term "grip," which is used for one's manual grasp, for a psychological state of self-control ("get a grip!"), and for a small suitcase taken on short trips. Or in some cases there are terms that cover a family of different kinds of things; for example, the term "barn" which covers hay barns, horse barns, calving barns (for livestock births), milking/dairy barns, and barns for storage of machinery.

Further there are terms that are vague and whose lack of precision is troublesome since what the term is a term for is important in some way to a group of speakers and writers. For example consider the term "intelligence." What is intelligence exactly—all know it is important, but there is no settled reportive definition that conveys just what one has when one is intelligent other than intellectual abilities. What is needed perhaps is a definition like that for "thermostat" given above which explains what intelligence is. But there is no accepted theory of what accounts for intellectual ability—maybe the task is too broad or too vague in itself to have a precise or clear answer.

In any event, *there needs to be a form of definition which clarifies language by picking out which of many meanings is intended by the speaker or writer, or which of many sorts of things covered by the term is intended, or finally which gives some indication of a test or an operation by which the correct application of a term could be made.* The form of definition appropriate to these tasks will be called **stipulative definition.** This term could be restricted to only one or more of these functions, however, for present purposes the author will stipulate that:

DEFINITION V.2

"Stipulative definition" will cover definitions which indicate which of many possible meanings a term will be used with, a definition that picks out as the class of things referred to one from among the many the term might cover, or which makes more precise the application of some vague term.

Stipulative definitions will also include specifications of the technical or new meaning given to a term in order to convey some new or technical information or idea—in order to articulate the world to others. For example, a speaker might say that he or she will mean by the term "underemployed," any case of working at a job requiring competencies and preparation less than those of the employed person. Or again, a writer might indicate that the term "trial balloon" will indicate any idea or proposal that an official circulates to the public to find reaction before deciding whether to formally propose the idea. Equally importantly, a speaker/writer might specify a test or operation to perform in order to see if a term like "intelligence" applies. Thus the intelligence of children is measured by a variety of tests and whether or not the person is considered intelligent at all or very much so is simply a matter of the results of these examinations. The tests are then taken as indicators of abilities at problem solving, or expressing oneself, or of other forms or understandings of intelligence. **Operational definitions,** as these stipulations are usually called, are of fundamental importance in science in so far as they allow for a standardization of meaning and then of conditions for testing hypotheses and reporting the results of these tests. Temperature and pressure, for example, are then no longer vague but made precise to a degree needed for exact testing and scientific communication.

DEFINITION V.3

The third sort of definition in question is the persuasive or emotive definition in which a speaker/writer seeks to attach some emotional tone to a term and thereby persuade the users of the term to share some value or attitude.

For example: (an example given earlier in this book): "God is love" in which the term "God"—a term that has been given so many meanings as to have become imprecise or vague is given a new meaning, that of love or of caring, and then there is a shift away from any notions of God as angry, vengeful, and dominating toward a view of the Deity as caring, concerned, and supportive if not empowering. The authority and majesty of God—those emotional dimensions of the meaning of the term "God"—are then attached to the caring and concern of love directing the interests of users of the term toward that concern and care. In this case, there is a second transfer of emotion for the term "love" brings with it its own positive associations of acceptance and warmth. Thus the majesty and authority of the Deity is now associated with the acceptance and warmth of love. So the emotional dimensions of the term emotively or persuasively defined are themselves changed. (Perhaps another example of this would be "war is hell.")

Not all persuasive definitions have this double redirection of emotional overtones.

For example: "justice is helping your friends and hurting your enemies," or "peace of mind is keeping your investments safe," or "children are the future of communities."

Here there is nothing particularly positive or negative emotionally about the future of communities or keeping one's investments safe. But when used to define children or peace of mind, respectively, these not only change the meaning of the terms but redirect attitudes or interests associated with the term defined. The case of justice amounting to helping one's friends and hurting one's enemies might seem to carry emotional overtones in both directions, but it need not. One might be neutral about helping one's friends believing that this should be done only when deserved, and about hurting one's enemies believing that this also should be done only when deserved. But it is clear that speakers are raised to have positive emotional associations with justice and these become redirected (for many speakers) in having the vague content of the meaning of "justice" précised in this way.

So then as one philosopher defined the term, "*persuasive definition*":

"gives a new conceptual meaning to a familiar word without substantially changing the emotive meaning, and . . . is used with the conscious or unconscious purpose of changing, by this means, the direction of people's interests."[4]

Clearly, persuasive definitions can exert an important influence in determining a language-user group's understanding and values. They can shift the meaning that would be given in a reportive definition of a term or serve as stipulative definitions making that shift. And all the while the approval or disapproval tendencies that run with the emotional dimension of the term's meaning are redirected.

These three forms of definitions then clearly demonstrate how definitions themselves can be sources of evidence or support for beliefs, decisions, and actions. So the *rule of thumb* here is: ***The very anchor pins of informational and value-laden outlooks are found in definitions.*** Change the definition of the terms "person" and "life" so as to include a beginning point in the womb and society and its relationships would be changed dramatically in the United States. But how is one to know if such definitions are good or meet the standards of a critical thinker? In every case the answer seems to lie in whether the purposes of the definition are served well.

Consider reportive definitions. If a reportive definition does the job of reporting when and only when it is correct to apply the term defined to what it applies to—correct according to a certain language user group, then great. But if it is stated so as to include or cover more than it should it is **too broad**—for example, defining a bachelor as any adult who is not now married, and so allowing in the divorced, the widowed, and those who had marriages annulled. If a reportive definition rules out or fails to cover or include cases of what the term defined should apply to, then it is **too narrow.** For example, defining a bachelor as an adult who has never been married and is over 45 makes the term too restrictive. The definition is **too narrow.** But if the reportive term gets it just right so that the term so defined fits all and only the things it is supposed to, then it is a good reportive definition. So for example:

1. A whale is any creature living in salt water and that grows to larger than ten feet in length. This is **too broad** since it would include many sea creatures like giant squid and octopuses as well as some large sea lions.

2. A fir tree is any evergreen that has needles that are flat. This is **too broad** since not only firs have needles that are flat.

3. A professional baseball player is anyone who is paid for playing ball with a glove and bat and ball. This is **too broad** since it also includes cricket.

4. A journal is any collection of papers that records personal thoughts on some matter. This is **too broad** since it might also include notes on a book, shopping lists, and love letters.

5. A medicine is any substance that someone takes to alleviate the symptoms of a disease. This is **too broad** since it might include alcohol in whiskey or other drinks, illegal drugs, diet supplements, coffee or soft drinks with caffeine, and so on.

6. A book is any collection of printed or written pages on some topic of scholarly interest. This is **too narrow** since lots of books are not scholarly and so would be ruled out by this definition. Also some books are on topics that *should* be of scholarly interest but are not. So it also fails to include those and is **too narrow** also on that count.

7. A passenger car is any self-propelled vehicle capable of carrying passengers and that consumes fuel at more than 35 miles per gallon. Unfortunately this excludes too many cars that do not get good mileage. It is **too narrow.**

8. A model is anyone who tries on and shows off clothes for New York designer shows. Well, a lot of models never see the ramps in New York designer shows and so this is **too narrow.**

9. A polygon is a closed plane figure bounded by no more than eight sides. Well, what about all those many sided figures that have more than eight sides? This is **too narrow.**

10. A queen is the wife of a king. Well, what about those queens who never marry? This is **too narrow.**

11. A newspaper is any periodical printed on paper that seeks to report all the latest developments. This is **too narrow** since it excludes online newspapers and journals, and since it excludes those specialty newspapers like the *Wall Street Journal.* And it is **too broad** since it includes professional society newsletters, journals with conference proceedings, and so on.

If a ***stipulative definition*** *does its job of clarifying by précising or coining a new word, then it is a good one; if it does not then it is not. Thus a stipulative definition might end up so complex that it does not really clear things up.* This would happen when the author is trying to coin a new word for a complex phenomenon and ends up with a definition no one can follow. Unfortunately, some say philosophy and literary criticism are full of such stipulations. A stipulative definition can also go wrong when the author is trying to give an operational definition for something that leaves a good deal to one's judgment—for example, stylistic excellence in athletic performance might be defined in a workshop for Olympic judges of gymnastic floor exercises. But the operational definition might be so complex that the judges have to rely on their personal experience and sense of artistic merit. Such a stipulative definition is perhaps worse than none in such circumstances.

If a ***persuasive definition*** *is effective it will introduce a shift in what is understood by a term without shifting the emotional overtones of the term so that interests or attitudes are redirected, or even values changed.* Two things can go wrong. The shift in content of conceptual meaning might not be accepted, or the defined terms can bring with them emotional overtones of their own that overpower the overtones the author was trying to shift to other things. For example, "Religion is the opium of the people," said Karl Marx. And yet many reject Marx because of this, rather than shift their disapproval of opium over to religion. Clearly here is a case in which the author sought to define a term in other terms that had their own heavy overlay of emotion and disapproval so as to carry off a shift of attitude *against* religion—"Opium? Why would I want to take religion seriously then?" But the conceptual content did not shift with the figurative use of defining language for a dependency creating substance. Now consider an example of the second sort of problem—the defined terms might bring with them emotional overtones that overpower those of the defining term so the shift in attitude does not take place. Take the definition of "freedom" as "the lack of limitations on those playing at life." Here the conceptual content might transfer so that freedom is seen as complete liberty or absence of restraint and then the approval attached to freedom by those in Western industrialized countries might come to lead toward approval of playing at life. But playing at life, at least in the United States, is widely disapproved of and so this persuasive definition might fail to effect a change of attitudes, the approval of freedom being overpowered by the disapproval of devoting one's adult life to play.

Finally, *persuasive definitions might well fail in the conceptual content they offer as the non-emotional meaning of a term.* If it were said that all the world's a stage (as one of Shakespeare's characters did) and this were accepted, then it would indeed lead to a redirection of interest and a shift in attitudes toward seeking approval for appearance and performance rather than substance. (In fact many people believe just that—defense attorneys, civil suit attorneys, and politicians are stereotyped in this way.) But for that very reason some might object that no, not all of the world is a stage. Some of life is, in its substance, deadly serious, and to treat it as just theater is to become alienated from reality. Such an alienation might indeed become a form of pathology. And so *a persuasive definition might be criticized on the basis of the reasonableness or defensibleness of the conceptual shift it suggests as well as on the effectiveness of its attempt to shift the direction of attitudes.* Similarly, *critical thinkers might reject a reportive definition not just as too broad or too narrow, but as **revisonary** in unacceptable ways.* If the information or outlook conveyed in a definition runs counter to accepted doctrine, as it does, according to some, in the definition of personhood beginning at the first union of human sperm and egg, then the definition itself will become not the source to settle disputes but the site of the battle itself. A little below, the question of conflicts between perspectives is taken up and more is said on this topic.

So definitions of the three sorts reviewed above can be better or worse. It is important to remember this and that definitions are important sources of evidence and support for beliefs, decisions, and actions. The point is (1) that many of the basic views of the world are packed into definitions—look at the definitions of the term "God" in different religions, look at the definition of the terms "human being" and "person," and (2) often in reasoning thinkers start off from or end up with definitions—definitions give the unchallengeable rock bottom of thinking in the language groups thinkers use. Thus definitions are important to giving and assessing reasons and reasoning.

AMBIGUITY. Another important element of clarity is ambiguity where a term or phrase, or even a sentence, has more than one meaning and we cannot tell from the context which meaning is intended. The term "grip" refers to a small suitcase people used to think was just right as an overnight case on the train, to the hand grasp of someone, to the grasp of reality one has (get a grip!). Which of these meanings is intended might be very significant as we speak about the parent's decision to treat the child because of her losing her grip. Did the parents make a good decision? Well, are we talking about the child losing a small suitcase, or her physical grasp, or what? Only by clearing up the ambiguity can the reasoning be understood and assessed. Ambiguities can be hard to spot in your own writing—after all, you usually know what you are talking about and trying to say! And they can be hard to fairly spot and deal with in anyone's reasoning, for they might make that reasoning weaker by bringing in the **fallacy of equivocation.**

V.1.   ***The fallacy of equivocation*** is the error of a thinker using a term in one of its meanings in one part of an argument, and in another of its meanings in a separate part of the argument so that the flow from evidence to conclusion is interrupted.

For example: Aristophanes to the boss: "Herman has lost his grip. That's why we cannot allow him to see this new client. If someone deals with a new client then he should have full control over himself." Boss: "So you want me to believe that Herman's arthritis interfering with his handshake is good reason to believe that he lacks the psychological control to deal properly with a client? Come on."

Or: "Those actions during the war were inhuman. That is something everyone agrees with. So there is no reason we should not treat these criminals as though they had no human rights. They showed they were not capable of having them." Here the problem is that "inhuman" means horrible and reprehensible, not the actions of something other than a human. But the person giving the evidence is saying that since the actions were inhuman they were not performed by a human being. The ambiguity lies in the term "inhuman."

Or again: "The contract said I would be a crew leader and you are only paying me for being a crew member. Every day I have been the first in line on the docks to move what needed to be moved as we agreed. And such leadership should be rewarded with the wages that go to leaders of crews." Boss: "Nice try Bozo, but being first in line is not the same as being the one in charge. It might be leading but it isn't leadership. Now get back to work or clean out your locker."

Ambiguity and cases of equivocation can be spotted and straightened out *if the thinkers can communicate with each other*. If we look only at the bare written or spoken language it might be hard to tell what is meant. That is why avoiding ambiguity is so important. This is true in sentences as much as in terms or phrases. One should be careful in the use of pronouns so the reference is clear. Sometimes this requires that writing be read out loud to another as part of proofing it. Or it requires that the author use clear referring expressions or descriptions that pick out just who or what is intended. For example:

> "George and Rudy went to the cashier's office and he just lost it. He grabbed the cash drawer and then the tall man ran out to the parking lot where he was shot to death and was seen clutching the money as he went to the promised land."

Well ok. Now who grabbed the cash drawer? George, Rudy, the cashier? And who was shot? The same person as the one that grabbed the cash drawer? Finally, was he—whoever he was—seen going to the promised land or just grabbing the money as he died? The sentence could mean a number of things depending on reference and the difference between figurative and literal uses of language. Whoever the reporter is needs to work on getting these matters straightened out. The context might show a thinker all of that—suppose you were an eye witness to the crime and the shooting. But often the context is not supplied. In those cases the thinker must depend upon the author for clarity as provided by the writing or speech.

VAGUENESS. Vagueness, or lack of precision in the use of language, is almost always present, and that is a good thing. Speakers and writers cannot give a full description of the events or processes or states of affairs they encounter—even if they had time and others would be patient. Some aspects of a situation or an encounter go unnoticed as irrelevant or unimportant. Some aspects are blocked by personal or even public agendas. Much went unsaid at the 9/11 Commission hearings, in part by people trying to cover their tracks and in part because of the information being classified. As well, vagueness often allows people with views that differ significantly to come together under a single banner to support a single line of action or a single project. Earlier when talking about the social conditions of critical thinking, the need for everyone getting on the same page and getting behind a line of action or a line of thought was discussed. This is possible sometimes *only* because of vagueness. If everyone had to have the same definition of freedom and that definition had to be very precise, there would be serious conflict or the term "freedom" would not bring to mind a widely supported condition of life.

So it is often good news that language is not exact. Very often some degree of vagueness is useful or even necessary. But how much vagueness is good and how often is it necessary? Well, you no doubt get the point: **it all depends.** In addition to the virtues of vagueness mentioned in the previous paragraph, vagueness allows thinkers to speak without doing the detail to death, and boring others out of their minds or out of the conversation. *So how much is too much, and how often is too often? That depends upon the context of thinking, the situation.* What is ok for a Cub Scout merit badge on the physics of the solar system might not get you an "A" on the physics exam in that 3000 college-level course. Demands for precision vary and thinkers need to respond accordingly. However, beyond saying that and the importance of vagueness noted already, it is difficult to be precise about how much precision is needed, and when it is needed, in general.

There is one form of precision that demands further comment, however. Sometimes thinkers might become confused as they negotiate the relationships of parts and wholes. Thus recent coverage of a major French bicycle race showed one team measuring out the weight of each part of their bicycles and noting how new technology has kept that weight low. The person giving commentary went on to point out how light this made the bicycle overall. Now in fact the bikes are very light compared to what most people ride; no question about that. However, the move from the precise measurements of relatively lightweight components to the judgment that the combination of all of these components is lightweight is fallacious. Similarly, it would be a mistake to say that since the truck that brought the bicycles to the race venue was very heavy, then the various components of the truck or of its cargo must be very heavy as well. The fallacies in question here are those of composition and division.

§ **V.2.**   *The fallacy of composition* is the error of attributing to the whole any arbitrarily selected one (or all) of the properties of the parts making up the whole, just because they are properties of what make up the whole.

§ **V.3.**   *The fallacy of division* is the error of attributing to the component parts of a whole any arbitrarily selected one (or all) of the properties of that whole itself, just because they are properties of the whole.

> *For example:* "The bicycle parts are each lighter compared to last year's models, so the bike itself is going to be lighter than last year's model!" **Composition**

> "The bike weighs much less than the one used for the same purpose last year. So this pedal crank will weigh much less than the comparable part from last year's bike." **Division**

> *Or:* "The delegates to the Democratic National Convention were evenly mixed in numbers between men and women. So every state must have an equal number of women and men delegates." **Division**

> "The delegates each believe in the goodness of economic opportunity, so the convention itself could be said to be in favor of economic opportunity." Well, if by "the convention" is meant the gathering of people in a certain place under certain authority, in order for the party to accomplish certain ends, then no, the convention does not believe anything—it is not the kind of thing that has beliefs. So that would be a case of **composition.** If the collection of the delegates is what is meant by the convention—that is, all the people there considered as individuals, then, yes, everyone has the belief that economic opportunity is good. Here it is crucial to avoid the ambiguity of the term "convention."

> *Or again:* "It is the mission of the university to serve the larger community in economic development and higher education. So each instructor must have some obligation to work on projects of economic service to the community as well as teach classes." No. The institution of the university might be dedicated to what is stated in its mission statement, meaning its leadership will strive to arrange things so that those goals are met. But this does not imply that every instructor will be working on both of these goals personally. **Division**

> "I've heard that silk sport jackets have threads that are uneven and even lumpy. That's why I would never wear one. Who wants a jacket that is uneven and lumpy?" In terms of the overall appearance, the whole garment is greater than the sum of

its parts and the lumpy threads provide occasional points of interest and a texture that some find pleasing. The jacket does not look lumpy as a whole. **Composition**

Precision is a desired trait of some writing and speaking, especially that which articulates what thinkers need to be very careful about communicating and agreeing upon in detail. This will sometimes involve comparisons or contrasts between the whole and its parts. In this arena, as elsewhere, it is important to avoid the fallacies of composition and division. Vagueness might be addressed in seeking comparisons or contrasts. But if so, these pitfalls of composition and division would themselves be too high a price to pay.[5]

Thus vagueness can be a resource to thought that provides a way to unite thinkers on certain points. At other times, like ambiguity, it is an impediment to the clarity needed for critical thinking. As the discussion goes on to talk about reasoning processes and assessments, there will be the need to ask if the terms of the reasoning are clear enough for the purposes at hand, and if there are ambiguities which ruin the proper flow of reasoning. What this section does, in part then, is prepare you for later work. But remember the central role definitions play in anchoring thought. Definitions are a way of fixing ideas about what kinds of things there are and how they operate, and even about how they should operate. They are fundamentally important to our thinking. Common meaning and shared public understanding go hand in hand. Without them, common beliefs and a public realm of reason where people operate according to the same standards and procedures of thought would not be possible. And without common definitions there could not be public and widely held beliefs, traditions, and understandings of what there is and the way it all works.

The personal narrative spoken of above is essential to individuals getting along in the world. But a public narrative giving background beliefs and ways of reasoning common to members of groups who then hold each other accountable to use these beliefs and procedures is equally important to critical thinking. Definitions and the careful management of ambiguity and vagueness allow individual thinkers to articulate their own views and experiences in a language accessible to all and so to bring their personal narrative to terms in which it can become part of the public narrative. Thus critical thinkers can be themselves *and* take part in the social enterprise of critical thinking. This will be clearer with this chapter's later talk about perspective as a source of evidence and process in reasoning.

Mastery Exercises V.2

SELF-TEST

Exercises on Definitions, Ambiguity, and Vagueness

1. What is a personal life narrative? What is a public narrative? Briefly, what is the relevance of these narratives to critical thinking?

2. Why are definitions of a reportive sort important to critical thinking?

3. Is the following definition reportive, stipulative, or emotive? How can you tell in this case? "A floppy disk is any removable device for storing electronic data generated on a computer."

4. Is the definition in the previous question a good one? Explain.

5. A reportive definition that is too broad is one that would count as correct the application of the defined term to things to which it should not really be applied. True or False? Is the following definition too broad? Explain. "An evergreen tree is one whose color stays green or bluish all year long."

6. Why is vagueness important? How do we get rid of it? When do we want to get rid of it?

7. "The man said that he was going to get you the money as soon as the check came through from his company. I asked him when that would be. He said he expected it soon." This last statement is ambiguous or vague? What is the difference? Explain.

8. All the smallest component parts of that racing engine are made of aluminum or titanium. Every one of these parts is very light because of the material it is made of. The engine itself must be really light too. This is a case of the fallacy of

   _____.

9. Humans on earth breathe air which has a high concentration of oxygen. Deep sea divers breathe air that has a high concentration of nitrogen. Nitrogen and oxygen are not the same. And the deep seas are on Earth. So deep sea divers are not human! What is the fallacy in this argument? How could you straighten things out so that there is not a problem here?

10. What is a revisionary definition? Is a definition being revisionary always a bad thing?

SOURCE 3

Analysis, Accounts, and Authority

Authoritative or Public Narrative as Official Accounts _____

The role of definitions as sources of evidence raises the question of just how thinkers settle on the common beliefs and procedures of reasoning they come to use. And how is it that thinkers get it right, or is there any way to separate common beliefs and procedures that should be accepted from those that should not? These, of course, are highly complex questions. But in this section part of the answer will come to the fore. ***One answer to these questions is that thinkers rely on experts.*** Courtroom dramas often portray calling in someone to give expert testimony. Federal grants are awarded only after review by experts in the field of the research seeking funding. Conferences of physicians, academics, and other specialists or experts themselves provide important forms of respect to the words and thought of experts recognized by their colleagues. All thinkers go to dictionaries or encyclopedias or other reference sources and these have been compiled by experts. Textbooks are supposedly the distillation of the best thought at a time in a field or at least one defensible and important take on this thought. Popularizers of science and other fields in journal articles and self-help books convey the expertise to other thinkers, the public press reports on the thoughts and accomplishments of experts in science and economic reporting as well as reports on other areas of endeavor like the arts and the humanities. In all of these ways, authorities in the various fields of research or inquiry will help ordinary thinkers to find the best-of-the-best or the thought-to-be-most-defensible-of-the best beliefs and procedures. If these views are effectively disseminated through the various secondary outlets mentioned—outlets like textbooks and national journals like *Scientific American,* then the views will come to be understood and taken up by thinkers whenever they deal with the relevant areas of inquiry. As this process goes along, of course, the views get distorted and watered down so that common beliefs are sometimes only a poor reproduction of the expertise behind them—rather like a fourth or fifth generation copy of a copy of some typed sheet. The public views of expertise are sometimes faded and warped. But still the process goes on. A major source of beliefs and reasoning patterns applied to particular sorts of problems is found in the appeals thinkers make to authorities.

Some texts on critical thinking will identify appeals to authority not as legitimate sources of support for beliefs, decisions, and values, but as fallacies to avoid. To be sure, some appeals to authority are mistakes of reasoning. But not all are. The main purpose of this section is to clarify the process of appealing to authority, to identify the pitfalls in making such appeals, and to say a bit about how authorities might be identified and how they are related to experts in a field.

Appealing to Authority

Appeals to an authority are forms of arguments, not in the sense of quarrels, but in the sense of attempts to provide evidence for some claim or conclusion. They amount to saying that since the authority says it is so, then it is so. Arguments in the sense important in this book are composed of statements with two sorts of functions: some provide evidence and others assert what the evidence is supposed to support. The evidence is stated in what are called *premises* and the supported assertion is the *conclusion or claim*. So in appeals to authority, the assertion that an authority says something is so is the premise, and the assertion that it is so is the conclusion or claim.

Appeals to the authority of others always amount to reasoning that since the authority is an expert and is probably using her or his expertise, what the authority offers as credible or acceptable is so.

Clearly, if the authority did say so and knows what he or she is talking about, then this is good reason for holding to that belief or way of thinking. If the authority did not say that or there is a question about whether he/she knows, then thinkers would be well served by withholding judgment.

So there are a number of rules or constraints that need to be operating in appeals to authority if these appeals are to be defensible.

RULES FOR APPEALING TO AUTHORITY

1. **There must be expertise on the issue in question**—if the topic of discussion is the best flavor of ice cream, or the best batter since Hank Aaron, or the best astrologer to listen to, then appeal to an expert is not going to cut it. These are issues where there is no real expertise, so appealing to a so-called expert is not going to help. (That said, however, Barry Bonds looks like a pretty good candidate to challenge Aaron.)

2. **The person appealed to must have this expertise**—it is no good to appeal to someone who lacks the expertise needed to know about what we are interested in. If a thinker wants a medical opinion he or she should not appeal to the person who plays a physician on a soap opera. If one wants a car fixed, he or she should not take it to a tennis pro who lives and breathes tennis. This is what is so ridiculous about so much advertising. What, for example, do movie stars know about what is a safe and effective diet for all people?

3. **The experts must not disagree**—So you go to court and they bring their experts and you bring yours, and who is the judge or jury to believe? If they were thinking critically, they would believe neither, if their credentials were equal. But then judges and juries need to make decisions in courts, so maybe people cannot be good critical thinkers there? Or maybe there are other considerations that would help decide which experts to accept.

4. **The expertise must have been used in reaching the claim in question**—Unfortunately, lots of people who are experts get big heads and do not think about what they say, or go beyond the reach of their expertise. Why listen to them?

5. **The expertise that was used must not have been compromised** by bias, ill-health, dishonesty, or lack of proper checking on the part of the expert. Unfortunately, lots of people sell out, or become ill or overworked and claim to use their expertise when they are not using it effectively, if at all. Critical thinkers do not need to hear an expert if he/she is not using her/his expertise well. What would be the point in that?

So there are a number of pitfalls to be avoided by thinkers appealing to someone's expertise. Failure to meet the conditions of any of these rules would disqualify the appeal and count as a mistake of fallacious appeal to authority. But if one meets these conditions or does so to the extent possible for him or her, then the appeal is acceptable and counts as good support for the claim attributed to the expert.

Why should thinkers trust experts other than the fact that they often have little choice? Well it is because experts have gone through special training, have partaken of special education, have made careful observations and given state-of-the-art interpretations of them, and so on. Thus thinkers can look to those who have the appropriate education or training, appropriate licensure, a significant record of accomplishments or experiences, a reputation or position among those with recognized expertise, or a recognized track record of success in giving judgments, advice, or opinions on relevant matters. A look at this list indicates that the way thinkers might recognize experts is on the basis of degrees earned, certificates of accreditation, a record of successes, and standing among groups of thinkers in a field of inquiry. Of course, not any degree will do. A degree from any accredited university is better than one from Fly-By-Night University Online. Other qualifications need to be made. Picking a financial adviser might be as important and as difficult as picking a life partner—or so some say. A fit of personality and qualities inspiring confidence are important beyond the basic knowledge any financial adviser should have. A record of success is also important.

Reflection Question: Can you name several experts who qualify on these grounds?

Mastery Exercises V.3

SELF-TEST   *Exercises on Authority*

1. Dr. Phil tells you that you need to regain self-respect through taking steps to become more popular. He suggests getting a nice used car to replace your old clunker. This will improve your image and at least open some doors to being more popular. But you need to get a good quality car. He recommends a Yugo, an economy automobile from the former Yugoslavia—any Yugo will do. Should you take his advice on what car to buy? What rule for appealing to authorities is relevant in answering this question?

2. Britney Spears says that when it comes to the best non-fiction, *The Life of a Teen Age Idol*—her autobiography (not really) is the one to read. Should we trust her opinion? What rule for appealing to authorities is relevant in answering this question?

3. Garrison Keillor, creator and host of *A Prairie Home Companion* radio program, recommends the Sleep-Number Bed for the best night's rest you will ever have. Garrison sleeps like the rest of us, and probably he has tried out the Sleep-Number Bed. Should we go with his recommendation? What rule for appealing to authorities is relevant in answering this question?

4. The lawyer who was hanging around the emergency room when you went in suggests that you sue the company that built the ladder you fell off of. Should you take her up on that? What rule for appealing to authorities is relevant in answering this question?

5. You favor the Funky Wintergreens, and your best friend says that no, The Fundamental Deluxe is the best new band in the area. What is your other friend to believe? Can either recommendation be taken as identifying the best new band? What rule for appealing to authorities is relevant in answering this question?

6. The court-appointed psychiatrist says the defendant is able to stand trial and the psychiatrist the defense attorney hired says that the defendant is not in control of his faculties and could not know right from wrong and so cannot stand trial. Which expert should we listen to? What rule for appealing to authorities is relevant in answering this question?

7. The television ad comes on with a person in a white coat saying that she is not a doctor but she plays one on a daytime drama. This person says that she endorses a certain headache remedy and believes that that is the one to buy. Is this recommendation something to pay attention to? What rule for appealing to authorities is relevant in answering this question?

8. The car company notifies you that the car they sold you is defective and is being recalled since without warning it can fail and cause a serious wreck. The letter says that the car company has designed a way to fix this and wants you to bring in your car to be fixed. Should you believe them and take your car in? What rule for appealing to authorities is relevant in answering this question?

9. One of the leading figures in the astrophysics of black holes says that he got it wrong since energy and so information can escape from the gravitational pull of these collapsed stars. Can you rely on that claim? What rule for appealing to authorities is relevant in answering this question?

10. Dr. Knows, the plastic surgeon who did the faces of a famous singer brother and sister, says that she can make you look like a star attractive beyond your wildest dreams and can get it paid for by hooking the case up with the television program Extremely Made-Over who is willing to pay her a lot of money for this work. Assuming you want to look like a star and be attractive beyond your wildest dreams do you take this person's word for it and agree to the make-over? What rule for appealing to authorities is relevant in answering this question?

Even after meeting all the same qualifications and having roughly equivalent experiences several experts might disagree. This is clear not only because the modes of inquiry in virtually any field are far from unequivocal and their application introduces even more variance. Some of these differences can be reconciled with experts agreeing that either of the conflicting views might have merit or they might have different merits which a consumer of the knowledge needs to choose between. However, some disagreements are not so amiable—constituting real conflicts that provide a moment of growth in inquiry and a moment of pause in critical thinkers seeking to tap into expertise in the field. There are many such unsettled areas in all fields. One, for example, might have been resolved recently when the famous astrophysicist Stephen Hawking conceded that he had probably misunderstood the workings of black holes, or the residue of dead and collapsed stars, and paid off his bet with a colleague for the price of an encyclopedia.

So does appealing to experts, those individuals recognized by appropriate means as having expertise or knowledge on some matter, serve as an incontrovertible source of knowledge, a final source of truth? No, in spite of the fact that some experts and some wannabe experts would say so, it is not so. Knowledge grows and the hard questions, while sometimes answered, sometimes continue unanswered. As noted above, background beliefs can be and are challenged. Definitions and whole conceptual contents change. Expertise is changed with developments in fields of study. Whether death and diamonds are forever is perhaps an open question. But whether expertise is forever is a question that can be answered differently. In the details of theories that are agreed to have credibility, and even in some cases at the foundations of fields of inquiry, in large part, no, *expertise is not forever.*

Still it is the grasp of background knowledge and of the processes of reasoning in fields of inquiry that makes authorities or those recognized as experts invaluable to critical thought. This grasp puts them in the position to be the arbiters of public knowledge, the judges of what is the official received word on this or that subject of inquiry. From a thinker's personal narrative to the public version he or she articulates to share with others, there is not any purple robe of official approval that is warranted. However, when these narratives are found to fit under or perhaps even come to be accepted by the experts as changes in their views, such royal colors may be worn. This does not make the individual's views any the worse to wear. But a conflict with the authoritative word on a subject can make a thinker's beliefs or decisions appear as no more substantial than a birthday suit. At the end of the succeeding section the relationship of authority between experts and the ordinary thinker will be taken up in a bit more detail.

Finally, in these background beliefs, patterns of thinking, and even rules of evidence grasped by experts, there are differences that go with what is suitable to different sets of problems. Experts in one field need feel no need to claim expertise in another. (An old academic cliché characterizes research work in the university as coming to know more and more about less and less.) As discussed in chapter II, the inquiry comprising critical thought is not purposeless but rather focused on problems of varying sorts with which the details of procedure and evidence will vary as well. When an expert has a grasp of a field of inquiry or body of knowledge, what does he or she have? How might this focal point where expertise becomes visible be described? How should the core of the official narrative in any field be characterized in general outline? Certainly part of it has to do with what will be called the perspective of a group of thinkers who share concerns and modes of inquiry. This is the subject of the section to follow.

SOURCE 4

Perspective and Multicultural Critical Thinking

> A perspective of the sort in question here is a view on how, generally, thinkers should reason about some matter while conducting inquiry. And though it might not be surprising that thinkers are always thinking within one perspective or another, the claim is well worth exploring: Critical thinkers reason about what they reason about only from one or another perspective, in fact only within one or another instance of what might be called a community of discussion.

A few examples should introduce the point and suggest an analysis of a community of discussion and of its perspective on reasoning.

THE HUMMINGBIRD EXPERT. Several years ago, there was a story reported through the AP wire service about a hummingbird expert who had returned from the moist tropics of South America, deathly ill. It seems he had come in contact with an animal he should have avoided in the jungle and was now suffering from liver failure. He was being tended by the New York physicians in the hospital where he was, and they thought he had no chance of survival. He also had summoned the shamans or religious figures of the jungle tribe which had adopted him after he spent a great deal of time with them over the years. So, there were the nurses and doctors of modern medicine taking blood and giving IV's, and then there were the shamans giving herbs and doing dances. Representatives of two very different worlds or rather two very different worldviews or perspectives were treating him.

What made their perspectives different? First they had different concepts of health and of the problems of medicine or curing in general. The modern health care providers saw illness as a breakdown in the physical workings of a physical thing—the body. The shamans saw illness as a problem manifested physically, but really based on the imbalance or disharmony of spiritual forces ruling the forests in which they lived and acting out through the animals and other things of the forests. The hummingbird expert had come across an animal, a toad, and had gotten his spiritual forces out of harmony since that animal was forbidden or taboo to him. But the New York physicians were having none of this. The problem was a physical one. If he did encounter a toad before becoming ill, it might have poisoned him and since the liver serves to filter out poisons, it was no wonder then that he was dying of liver failure. But they saw the problem as physical and the cure as drugs or surgery—or would have seen it that way if the scientist had not been so far gone. The shamans were trying to restore harmony and balance of the spiritual forces. The doctors were trying to make a physically dying man comfortable.

- Their outlooks on what was their concern or the set of problems they were to reason about were different.

- Their outlooks about what might exist to cause a problem of interest were different.

- Their outlooks on how thinkers should try to identify exactly which of the possibilities of interest were true or were actualities differed.

- Their outlooks on what was the way to cure or bring back to health this important patient differed also.

GALILEO AND THE INQUISITION. Another story is relevant here, the familiar one of Galileo, the physicist and astronomer. Galileo had been a science and mathematics teacher in Italy for some time. He had improved the "Spy Glass" into a telescope that he used as a tool to observe the heavens. And this led to his publication of works claiming among other things that there were mountains on the moon, there were many moons belonging to Jupiter, and there were spots on the sun. What was so controversial about all of that? Well, according to Aristotle whom the Inquisition authorities followed, these objects are heavenly objects and as such are perfect and eternal, and thus they could not have imperfections like mountains and valleys, spots and unseen moons circling them. Also Galileo had sided with a Polish monk who about 100 years earlier had claimed that the earth moves around the sun, not the other way around. So what? Well, if the Earth is not the center of the universe then man was not either, but had not God placed man in the center to worship and glorify Him? Or so said the church authority behind the Inquisition. Galileo was warned not to teach any of this as the truth, but he claimed to have been told he could teach it as merely theory. When he did that, he was hauled before the Inquisition and found guilty of heresy. Further he was told to recant his views on astronomy and physics. The choice he was given was to take back what he said and never teach it again, or to be introduced to the instruments of torture—in this case the rack where you are tied to an expandable table by wrists and ankles and then pulled apart until you see the error of your ways. (How about that for a scare tactic?) Galileo gave in and spent the rest of his days under house arrest supposedly no longer doing research in physics. In fact, however, not only did he continue his research, but he arranged for it to be smuggled out of the reach of the church and published in Holland.

Galileo thought that thinkers could have both religion and science since these were different in a number of regards. They differed in their purpose or the problems they approached through reason. They did not share the same background beliefs about what exists to frame the possibilities of the problems of interest. Religion and science differed in how to study what exists as a problem of the moment and then also differed in the procedures and methods they used to solve or manage the problems that are of interest. Needless to say, the church disagreed about how harmless these differences were. The one viewpoint conflicts with the other in its implications and so it must be set aside. Galileo died under house arrest and was forgiven by the Roman Catholic Church only a few years ago.

LORCA'S PLAY YERMA.   The playwright Lorca gives another familiar story to work with. Juan and Yerma were characters in a play by the Spanish playwright Federico Garcia Lorca. "Yerma" means "barren" and fits the leading female character that was married for many years but had no children. For someone in rural Spain and of the Catholic faith who saw herself in part defined as a potential mother and who wanted a child very much, this barrenness was maddening. The play is the story of Juan and Yerma's struggle over whether there would be children in their marriage. She very much wanted children, but he wanted to wait to build his farming estate and fortune. She thought about adultery, but this was forbidden and no part of what she could agree to. She was offered a relative's child in adoption, but the definitions of "woman" and "true fulfillment" she was working with from her perspective disallowed that. It had to be a child born of her body or no child. She went to a spring gypsy festival in the hills, and found this turned out to be an orgy. But we will never know what she would have done in her desperation since Juan found her, humiliated her, and dragged her back to the farm. Later, in the village square, she confronted Juan demanding to know whether he intended to have a child with her ever. He said no and to make matters worse he sought to embrace her in that public square, as if to prove his dominance.

She strangled him to death and as the villagers gathered, she held out her arms as if to keep them away and she said, "No, leave me alone. I have killed my son."

What is common to all these stories is a kind of insoluble clash of viewpoints between the members of communities concerned with some issues or set of problems, people who approach these problems in common ways through the use of reason. The conflicts might arise in the nature of the problems as these individuals understand them. But the conflicts deepen and become all but impossible to resolve as the differing methods of approach and the background knowledge drawn upon are developed and come into play.

Communities of Discussion

> **A community of discussion is a group of people who are expected to think in similar ways or according to common guidelines and with common assumptions about matters of common interest and about problems understood in a more or less common way throughout the community.**

The community hangs together because of the members' transmitting and using the same rules and assumptions in dealing with problems of the same sort. And it hangs together by virtue of the members' requiring each other to think this way by holding each other to account if they do not. From the viewpoint of the Inquisition, what they were doing was protecting the true faith from the seeds of Reformation rebellion and fragmentation. They were holding to account those who were supposed to think in the same way about the same things and with the same purposes. Galileo thought that if thinkers could have multiple purposes, then why not, and why not pursue the different ways of thinking appropriate to those different purposes? But no, that was not in the game plan of the Church. The Church, as the supreme authority on matters of faith and understanding, took up the task of keeping in its own control the official narrative of the nature of the world. It needed to place its problems and ways of thinking above all others, and Galileo did not want to bend to that. He had his own priorities beyond those of saving his immortal soul.

So let us review: A community of discussion is a group of people who share an interest in a common set of problems and approach those problems through reason in the same ways and with the same background assumptions. They also seek to enforce commonality of reasoning and assumptions and maybe even the priority of problems by accountability and possibly punishment.

Thus the perspective of a community of discussion includes several aspects or common patterns of thinking:

1. common ways of looking at the set of problems of special interest to members of the group;
2. common background assumptions and bodies of belief as well as values relevant to understanding the world in so far as the problems of interest are concerned—touchstones of belief and value any narrative must fit with coherently;
3. common procedures for diagnosing what particular problems of interest there are (if any) in a particular set of circumstances—common ways to conduct inquiry so as to identify and formulate the particular problems of interest in particular contexts; and
4. common procedures to arrive at and reflect upon the character of solutions to identified problems, or common procedures to think of how to conclude the inquiry in a particular case.

For example: Galileo, as a scientist, saw the world as made up of only physical things. He wanted to study the regularities of behavior of these things and to express them mathematically. The church, and Galileo as a Christian and a Catholic, saw the world as made up of physical things and spirits and the main problem for any human is to figure out how to live so as to rejoin her or his immortal soul with God for eternity. All else was subservient to that. The things that existed for Galileo the scientist were physical substances in motion and extended in space. For the church there were also spirits, or souls, and God. For the scientist, the problems are explaining and predicting the movements and occurrences of physical things. For the church the problem was to find our way to Heaven, so any particular situation was of interest only in so far as it was a challenge or threat against or opportunity to further that project. So for each situation the scientist or faithful needed procedures of thinking that would clarify just what problems of interest lurk in these circumstances. And then community members need procedures of thought that tell just how they are to deal with those problems so as to serve the general interests they have as a member of the group— either to be able to explain or predict this particular occurrence, or to be able to avoid the pitfalls of this circumstance and continue in their faith in God, and in their movement toward Heaven. Thus beliefs and values shared by the group in shared official or authoritative public narratives guide individuals as they inter-weave their personal narrative of life with the public account of the world, always subject to the scrutiny and always accountable to the other members of the group or at least to the authorities of the group. Perhaps a highly schematic summary would be useful to present these different perspectives.

Illustration of the Elements of a Perspective of a Community of Discussion Reviewing the Case of Galileo and the Church

CHURCH   **SCIENCE**

(1) Problem: How to go to heaven
(How to live so as to reach beatitude.)

How heaven goes.
(How to gain real knowledge of the rules of classical mechanics.)

(2) Background Knowledge:
(What exists, how does it work, what does it matter for problems of interest or what values are at work in dealing with the problems of interest.)

What Exists:

Immortal Souls
Deity
Physical Things
Persons

Physical Objects and Their Properties and Processes

How Do Existing Things Operate?

Persons—by Free Choice and
Responsible Thinking

Deterministic Causation,
No Responsibility—All beliefs and choices, every event is caused.
All occurrences are the same, physical and blind.

God by Creation *Ex Nihilo*
And by Judging Omnisciently

Why Does It Matter?

We have a certain potential as a mark of creation and we need to live up to that to be fully real.

It doesn't. Nature is value free. All that matters is the truth in understanding the world according to the procedures of empirical science.

(3) Procedures of Assessing Present Circumstances Relative to Problems of Interest

Assumptions of the Faith
Prayer and Counsel with Clergy
Appeals to Authority and Tradition

Study of Revealed Sacred Texts
Mystical Experience of Revelation

Appeals to Experience and Mathematical Description
Controlled Experiments and Observations and Their Careful Repetition in Controlled Conditions

(4) Procedures of Dealing with Problems or Opportunities of Interest

Prayer for Guidance and Praise

Study of Texts

Right Decision Making
Confession of Sins and Penance

Reflection Toward Grasping Patterns or the Best Explanation, and Conduct of Experiments
Checking of Other Studies and Repetition of Experiments
Hypothesis, Testing, and Generalizations,
Independent Checking of Experiments and Reflections

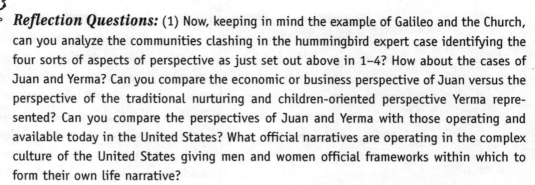

Reflection Questions: (1) Now, keeping in mind the example of Galileo and the Church, can you analyze the communities clashing in the hummingbird expert case identifying the four sorts of aspects of perspective as just set out above in 1–4? How about the cases of Juan and Yerma? Can you compare the economic or business perspective of Juan versus the perspective of the traditional nurturing and children-oriented perspective Yerma represented? Can you compare the perspectives of Juan and Yerma with those operating and available today in the United States? What official narratives are operating in the complex culture of the United States giving men and women official frameworks within which to form their own life narrative?

(2) Identify and, in the manner illustrated in the case of Galileo and the Church, give an analysis of any community of discussion of which you are a member. Can you identify a community whose perspective clashes with that of your own?

Importance of the Concepts of Community of Discussion and Perspective

Now what has this to do with critical reasoning? Well the answer to that question is "A LOT—A WHOLE LOT!!" In the first place remember that very often reasoning begins in definitions and appeals to expert authority. Where are these definitions enshrined and who comes up with them? How are they protected and modified and by whom? Where do authorities come from? How are they recognized? Who is the authority in a position to give stipulative definitions? Very often the answer to all of these questions goes back to the way the community of discussion is structured and how it works to credit views as correct, and people as experts. This becomes clear especially in cases of conflicts between perspectives of different communities, a point discussed further below. *But the point for now is that what counts as a common sense assumption, and who is an authority, and what is an acceptable procedure to follow to identify and solve or manage problems of interest, all are spelled out for thinkers by the operations and the operating rules of the communities of discussion they belong to. So what counts as good critical thinking about some problem or questions of interest, even what counts concerning whether someone formulates a question correctly or productively depends on what community of discussion that individual belongs to.*

Appeals to authority that are legitimate will identify and hear the views of an expert who is recognized as such in a community of discussion. And within that community, if the authority speaks and is using her or his expertise and is not sick, or fatigued, or otherwise indisposed, and is not bribed or otherwise compromised, then thinkers may accept what the authority says is so. But in another community that authority might have no standing and then thinkers would not successfully appeal to that same individual as a source of belief or decisions or support for beliefs or decisions. Many communities might share concepts and definitions of terms, but not necessarily. *Should a thinker seek to use terms in ways that are inappropriate or simply* *incorrect within her or his community of discussion, this will be a reason for criticism, a fault in her or his thinking. Thus communities not only sanction beliefs and values and procedures of thought through a system of authoritative narrative making. They also sanction the very use of terms and so the very terms in which an individual member of the community might articulate her or his personal life narrative and fit it under the public narratives of the group. **That is, <u>what thinkers mean to themselves is to some large extent dependent upon the thinking of the groups they belong to.</u>** So what com-*munities a thinker belongs to has a lot to do with what counts as critical thinking—from the way he or she understands the problems to be dealt with, to the taken-for-granted knowledge used in confronting a problem of interest, to the procedures available to spot and deal with the particular real problems encountered in living within the thought of those communities.

Reflection Question: Have you ever thought of the courses you are taking as introducing you to or taking you deeper into the thinking of a new and different community of discussion? Try out this thought next time you try to shift gears in changing classes, or in going from task to task at your work place, or in leaving the work place and in going home to be with your family or friends.[6]

So let us review: The perspective of a community of discussion has several aspects or elements:

1. A set of problems or concerns that are of interest to all those within the community of discussion—a set of problems to approach and deal with by reasoning in a certain way. For example, a desire to be healthy in so far as health is defined in some way such as physical or spiritual health or well-being.

2. A set of background assumptions or a body of background knowledge that tells members of the community what there is, generally how it can act or be acted upon, and why or how it is important. Thus, a set of beliefs about what kinds of things exist and how they act, and their significance in so far as these matters might be important to the members or might pose specific problems or opportunities of the sorts of interest to the members of the community. For example, a set of beliefs constituting a body of knowledge about how people get sick, what can make them well, what a healer has to do to bring about what can make patients well, and so on.

3. A set of procedures of reasoning for the members to use to interpret and analyze their surroundings and circumstances to see where they stand in those circumstances in relation to the problems of interest—"are we now facing a problem of the sort of interest in the community? Are we now facing an opportunity to accomplish something of value within the viewpoint of community?" For example, a set of procedures for diagnosing an illness in a particular patient at a particular time.

4. A set of procedures of reasoning for the members to use in addressing any actual particular problems or opportunities of interest as they find these while using the methods of (3) above. Thus each perspective will have a set of procedures for figuring out how to solve or manage or take advantage of the opportunity or problem of interest in these circumstances. For example, a set of procedures of treatment for say a bad heart—rest, operation, change of diet, right exercise program, regular check-ups, medications.

Reasoning Within and Reasoning About the Perspective of a Community of Discussion

Notice it is one thing to talk about what is real or right within the framework of a community's perspective. For Galileo as a Catholic, what was real was God, his immortal soul, the possibility of beatitude or perdition, and so on. For him as a scientist what was real was what he studied—physical things and the patterns of their behavior and their mathematical expression. He knew what to do and how to do it in general and in particular cases—although as far as what to do in scientific research he was formulating methods and standards as he himself went about his novel work

Things are very different if the problem is how to decide between the perspectives of the two communities, science and Catholicism, as guides to living and basic beliefs about what there is and what it matters. How do thinkers decide between these two perspectives and the communities they inform if they come in conflict? How do they decide between science and religion? This is a question that is still a matter of considerable discussion (and disagreement!). Basically, Galileo's approach was to decide between them on the basis of his purposes. For the purpose of going to heaven, Catholicism seemed to be the path to travel, and perhaps in his view it would have been better than alternative paths such as Protestantism, Buddhism, Taoism, or Hinduism, and so on. But for purposes of understanding the universe and its workings as a physical thing, his new science was best. But how do thinkers choose between these two or give one priority over the other if they conflict? How do they choose between the different purposes and the assumptions the perspectives bring along with them? Perhaps all that can be done is:

 continue to speak about the issues involved and the nature of the disagreements— what is really at stake, what can be handled by vagueness, what is something where no compromise is possible; and

 recognize that critical thinkers are very complex individuals approaching the world through a number of partially conflicting perspectives and not all of what is important to making sense of life is found within any one perspective.

On this approach, what is truth according to critical thinking is a matter that belongs within and is settled within a perspective, not in the gap between perspectives. *Truth is something thinkers can reach as they think **within** a community's perspective, even if they cannot reach it when they think **about** different perspectives.* That may seem unsatisfying. But how could a critical thinker show that what a perspective says is real, really is real or true; how can thinkers answer these questions without begging the question? One view, and the view of this book (while it is only one among other views) is that thinkers cannot do this. Thinkers can only try to proceed critically and in the spirit of open, impartial thought seek to arrive at a community perspective, which is functional for the many varied things they need and want to do. Of course, if thinkers must be uncharitable or fail to show respect to other thinkers or must commit one or more of the fallacies reviewed above, or must use reasoning patterns shown below to be fallacious, then their perspective cannot be credible. But if proceeding in the spirit of critical thinking as set out in the discussion throughout this book, conflicting perspectives emerge as guiding narratives about inquiry and the world, then as critical thinkers they would seek to address these differences with the combination of respect and integrity suggested in the procedures just above.

This will put critical thinking into a world of multiple and conflicting perspectives. But this seems to be the human condition and the best that can be done without giving up reason in favor of force or power or guile. Critical thinking must work *within* perspectives and yet it also must seek consistency and coherence and effectiveness along with both integrity and respect in thinking *about* when communities are defensible in how their perspectives are structured. Perhaps that is the best that thinkers can do without violating the spirit or the letter of critical thinking. Human action and striving is basic—necessary and irrepressible. Humans must seek to think consistently, efficiently, effectively, and coherently and with mutual respect in order to serve their needs and their undertakings. Perhaps that is all that thinkers can strive for in choosing between communities of discussion and critically assessing and even modifying their own perspectives.

So, then, in dealing with conflicts between communities of discussion and perspectives, like dealing with conflicts between authorities, thinkers can do several things:

1. Thinkers can seek a higher authority or a more inclusive community and perspective to bring the conflicting ones together and resolve their conflicts. Perhaps vagueness could serve as a refuge in this tactic—for example, the appeal to the values of freedom, or decency, or the general spread of critical thinking.
2. Thinkers can try to separate out the conflicting authorities, definitions, or community perspectives and avoid the conflict—Galileo's strategy.
3. Thinkers can agree to disagree and go about their separate ways. This was something Yerma and Juan could not do. One had to win over the other—both were guilty of making their perspectives fighting points. And, as a result, they both lost all of what they sought.

4. Thinkers can continue the conversation between the conflicting parties trying to find common ground or a way to be apart. That is, they can continue the engagement of critical conversation while agreeing to disagree. This can be the way among members of a pluralistic society or among intellectuals. But the temptation to politicize disputes or to take up "thought-bites" or else sound-bites as fighting points is often too great.

Mastery Exercises V.4

SELF-TEST *Exercises on Communities of Discussion*

1. Can critical thinkers decide a conflict between their perspective and that of others who disagree with them by simply insisting on the correctness of their views? Why not? What fallacies discussed in earlier chapters might be involved in that move?

2. What are the kinds of beliefs and procedures that make up the perspective of a community of discussion? Can you give an example of such a community and its perspective—one coming from your own life?

3. On the views of this text, are questions of truth and falsehood settled within or outside of the perspective of a community of discussion?

4. What is the relation between authority and the perspective of a community of discussion?

5. What is the relation between integrity and the perspective of a community of discussion?

6. What is the relation between charity or respect and the perspective of a community of discussion?

7. Can critical thinkers belong to more than one community of discussion even if these have potentially conflicting perspectives?

8. Can or must a critical thinker take as fighting points the views that serve as background assumptions in one of her or his communities of discussion?

9. Do the background assumptions of a community of discussion limit what one can observe in the world?

10. Is there anything that unites critical thinkers who belong to different and conflicting communities of discussion?

Wrap Up

Which of these strategies thinkers, individuals, or even societies use to deal with conflicting perspectives can serve as a measure of their ethical thinking and fiber. Chapter X will touch on this theme. In closing this chapter there are two points to emphasize. First, as members of communities of discussion who are accountable to its perspectives as discussed above, an important concern of any thinker is maintaining critical integrity or staying accountable to the definitions, concepts, and procedures of those perspectives he or she lives under. Not only will these frame her or his articulation and shape the effort of turning that articulation of a personal life narrative into a public narrative, but also they will specify the terms in which he or she must defend her/his thoughts and actions. It will be important then to the thinker's very understanding of herself/himself, and so her/his identity, that he or she seeks to live by, to defend, and even to hold up as true or most acceptable those perspectives. This puts individuals in conflict if they do not also proceed with charity or respect by being open both (1) *to granting others (who are accountable to different perspectives) credibility by parity of reasoning,* and (2) *to challenging their own views by taking seriously the views of others in conflict—external accountability.*

Thus in this chapter several sources of beliefs, decision, action, or the support they need among critical thinkers have come to the fore. Observation and the thought needed to render it intelligible by getting a coherent sense of what one is experiencing or what one has lived through fit the world into a personal life narrative—and through that, fit persons into the world. Definitions and the common language they support allow for thinkers to articulate important portions of their experience into an account of things to share with others making possible a presentation and defense of one's beliefs, decisions, and actions to others who do the same. These articulations and accounts must fit within the frame of authoritative views if they are to have credibility, even as they might marshal agreement and challenge existing authority in order to replace it. Out of such challenges and fittings-in comes enough commonality across persons that authorities can state the official or the received commonly accepted views in a group. These can then become the perspectives of groups in which thinkers function.

The statement of the group's official narrative on the problems it concerns itself with will give views embodying the community's perspective. The presence of such perspectives both allows for integrity and standards of critical thought, and conflicts among these allow for charity or mutual respect within the limits of good thinking shared by all. Knowing and credibility can then be found within, *and even between,* different and conflicting communities. Living by that knowing, and conducting themselves within the spirit of its generation, is the aspiration of critical thinkers.

Informed by the distinction between thinking within and about the perspectives of communities of discussion, the text now turns to an introductory look at various patterns of reasoning common to (and underlying the effective functioning of) different communities. At points the discussion will come back to thinking about communities and their perspectives. But, for the most part, the next few chapters will address general issues of thinking within communities. The first task is to say a bit more about how critical thought might be organized into arguments. Here the discussion will consider both arguments in science and in the humanities. Then the discussion turns to patterns of inductive and deductive argumentation.

Notes

[1] For more on this subject, see Hurley, S. L. (1998). *Consciousness in action.* Cambridge, MA: Harvard University Press, on "access"; and Thelen, E. and Smith, L. B. (2002). *A dynamic systems approach to the development of cognition and action.* Cambridge, MA: A Bradford Book, The MIT Press, p. 320.

[2] See Nisbett, R. E. (2003). *The geography of thought, how Asians and Westerners think differently . . . and why.* New York: The Free Press.

[3] See, Bermudez, J. L. (2003). *Thinking without words.* Oxford and New York: Oxford University Press.

[4] Stevenson, C. L. (1993). *Facts and values, studies in ethical analysis.* New Haven and London: Yale University Press, p. 32.

[5] Because not all cases of these fallacies involve confusing properties of individuals with those of groups—not all wholes are groups or collectivities, it seems best to treat these problems in connection with vagueness and the need for precision rather than ambiguity. This departs from the treatment of others, for example, Moore and Parker, pp. 52–54 of the 6th edition, pp. 56–57 of the 7th edition cited previously.

[6] The question of approaching reasoning in terms of communities of discussion tied to an understanding of the problems of interest is also related to the question of studying reasoning in terms of domain specificity. On the latter topic see Gigerenzer, G. (2000). *Adaptive thinking, rationality in the real world.* New York: Oxford University Press, chapters 10 and 11.

CHAPTER VI

Inquiry in Science and the Humanities: Understanding the Work and Progress of Arguments

SECTION 1

The Culture of Inquiry

Since Socrates, the author(s) of the Tao Te Ching, the ancient Chinese book of wisdom, and Siddhartha Gautama, the Indian thinker who was responsible for Buddhism (all 6th and 5th century B.C. thinkers), there have been those who have asked questions and stated the extraordinary, stirring things up. These figures and others have forced people to examine or rethink and perhaps bring more coherence, system, or consistency to their thought. That is one thing philosophers do for anyone who will listen. Of course they also try to give coherent, systematic, and consistent views on the nature and significance of various matters. But most likely (and no matter how fervently the author believes them) these accounts are offered in the spirit of a reply and a suggestion for further discussion in an ongoing conversation, coterminous with humans living the examined life. So what follows here is offered in that spirit and constitutes just a few remarks on inquiry in the humanities and the sciences. These remarks are not meant to be final, but rather more as suggestions to think about in the context of reflecting on the nature and point of critical thinking. In that light, they would best serve if they provoke as many questions as they seem to settle.

Living and the Life of Inquiry

What then is inquiry, and why do we engage in it? In chapter IV this question was opened on the way to discussing some elements of personal responsibility of the critical thinker undertaking inquiry. Here the discussion takes a different direction considering first what inquiry gives us in the sciences and the humanities and some of the important forms that inquiry takes in those divisions of intellectual labor. Then the discussion turns to very general remarks about the tools of critical inquiry, arguments. The point, operations, and functions of the elements of arguments come to the fore. This sets the stage for the discussion of the next two chapters where inductive and deductive arguments are considered in more detail. In order to maintain continuity with what has gone before, Galileo's struggle with the Roman Catholic Church provides a nice case study for the understanding of the point of inquiry in the humanities and the sciences and a review of the sources of inquiry in those contexts.

The endeavor of inquiry seems so familiar, so much a part of everyday life, that these questions seem almost needless. Human beings are active. Activity for humans involves inquiry. Inquiry arises out of a problem or question which presents itself in the course of ongoing human endeavors. Inquiry is natural to the members of the species. Everyone knows what it is by first hand experience! So what is all the fuss about?

Humans *are* active beings who are limited in their powers and who must depend upon their minds to meet their needs. Also, they are creatures of curiosity who are capable of feeling both fascination and inspiration. As such, humans are dependent upon investigation to satisfy their searching and to quell the fears always lurking on the dark side of awe. Further, they are creatures who make meaning and thereby artic-ulate, for everything they know of, what significance it has. In the processes of this articulation, humans can be said to record the importance of the parts of our world, making them for all to know, useful, threatening, uplifting, distressing, pleasurable, distasteful, sacred, secular, and so on.[1] And yet further, they are system builders who find it useful and reassuring to organize their world into kinds of things which behave, or look, or otherwise share similarities of significance to them. Humans depend upon their intellect to articulate these similarities and to interrelate them so that the parts of our world are understood as coming from or leading to each other, or else as giving meaning and significance to what came before or afterward. What could be more nat-ural than humans involved in inquiry?

And yet, the nature and rules of success in inquiry are not clear. They are some-thing people have to struggle to grasp, and work hard to practice. As is clear from the preceding discussion of perspective, it is hard to say just what best practice is in these matters, and it is harder to follow through. Why?

Part of the problem comes in with the complexity of what human agents under-take and achieve. They do not just engage in discrete actions resulting from the choices they make on isolated occasions. They are whole beings. It is the same person who takes out your garbage, teaches your classes or performs some other job you hold, plans your career, delights and agonizes over nurturing your children, pays your bills, decides and carries out a strategy for economic survival or progress, articulates, exer-cises, and expresses your spirituality, and so on. That is you doing all those things. Humans weave their actions together to form the fabric of extended and complex activities which are combined to make up a life. The apparently isolated actions they engage in, like taking out the garbage this Thursday, are less the warp and woof of the fabric of their lives and more interruptions of their extended projects like being a teacher, or running a business, or governing a nation, all while nurturing children. Human agents are amazing in all the things they do at one time, in their ability to inte-grate these into more or less one life, and in the exercise of judgment and choice which is needed for success at doing these many things at one time over the course of a life-time. They are amazing because this integration is difficult and complex resulting in a set of beliefs, decisions, and commitments in which any change calls for many adjustments. And this connectedness of activity complicates the understanding of inquiry. Consider some indication of the complexity of this problem of personal integration.

Multiple projects in life, serving different needs, expressing different dimensions and talents, all integrated into one person, over the course of a lifetime, even as individual persons change in their physical and mental capabilities, even as the world changes around them, this is the truly amazing work of human beings. As people travel through life, they are **critical beings** selecting from the various cognitive and decision paths open to them and assessing the choices of others. They are **economic beings** seeking to provide for the necessities and wants of their journey. They are **cultural beings** seeking to attire themselves in or to express the religious, artistic, technological, and other aspects of the cultures within which they seek to live. They are **moral agents**, trying to orient themselves by impartial and defensible standards of right, wrong, good, and bad while respecting others doing the same. And, they are **legal agents** maintaining order by obeying a set of laws and regulations enabling or constraining their behavior in a multitude of ways. In these dimensions of life, humans engage in science, the arts, the humanities, engineering, and personal as well as collective decision making not in isolated and clearly delineated moments, but all at once and all of a piece. Can inquiry be the same, either in detail or even in general in all these different sorts of agency? Can it be a single thing as people both practice these different forms of agency and keep them tied together into one person, responsible for her or his accomplishments and undertakings?

A Case in Point

Galileo was a typical agent in the regards just mentioned. If it were possible to drop in on him one would find him facing the same sorts of stresses and strains as anyone else now faces. The "spyglass," or telescope, had been developed in Holland as a tool of war and commerce. Galileo improved upon this first crude instrument and through this technological improvement sought monetary support for his research. He was a mathematician and on that basis sought a university post where he might find the beginnings of security and peace for his inquiries. He was a religious man, and for that he appears to have kept a secure place in his heart for the faith of a Roman Catholic. And, he was a scientist, seeking to discover and understand regularities in the behavior of things in the world, and then to express these mathematically in general statements backed up by controlled experiments testing what we would now call models of what he was studying. How could he keep all of these life projects together and flourishing in one person? That was one of the major problems he faced. In Galileo's case, however, this was no low stakes game, for as discussed already he was being watched by the inquisition, that political arm of the church protecting the true faith (as they saw it).

In fact, to review what was stated in the previous chapter, Galileo was brought to recant the more troublesome of his beliefs about the way the world worked. He thought, so he said, that he had gained permission to teach his physical and astronomical science as theory, even though some of his claims seemed to challenge the literal truth of the Bible. But, apparently (so certain church officials said), he was mistaken in this. When the time came and the chips were down, he was shown to be holding a weak hand. He recanted, and lived the rest of his life under house arrest. Nevertheless, even under house arrest, he continued his scientific studies, and even published some of them in the more progressive climate of Holland.

At the time of his first being accused and then during the time of his trial and imprisonment, Galileo was asked to choose between his professional life and his religious life. But he refused, saying that the choice was unnecessary since his religious beliefs served him in only a part of his person, while his science served him in another part. The beliefs of faith taught him "how to go to heaven," while his scientific work taught him "how heaven goes" (as he quoted from a cleric). In other words, Galileo took the view that he could integrate the apparently conflicting parts of his life by simply compartmentalizing them and keeping them separate. As a scientist, he would not think about his immortal soul and the challenges facing him as a religious man. As one of the faithful, he would not think about and speculate on the mechanics and dynamics of physical phenomena. [See Galileo's Letter to the Grand Duchess Christina. In S. Drake (Trans. & Ed.) (1957), *Discoveries and opinions of Galileo.* Garden City, NY: Doubleday & Company, Inc., Doubleday Anchor.]

Was that an acceptable strategy? It clearly did not satisfy the church. And this is not surprising. After all, one of the founding fathers of that institution was Augustine who said in a treatise on freewill that no learning should be allowed if it might challenge faith and take a person off the path to heaven. Dividing sets of beliefs and modes of inquiry into nice, neat but separate compartments would not be allowed. As a member of the church, each of the faithful must take full responsibility for who he or she is and what her or his beliefs are, in their entirety. Integration of beliefs and our ways of knowing had to result in one whole person, not a complex of persons who happen to share the same bodily history. The church seemed to require the very same person to accept responsibility for her scientific beliefs as accepted responsibility for her religious beliefs, and if the two are in conflict logically or in what they tell one to do, then the single person must accept responsibility for holding heretical beliefs, both as a scientist and as a church member. There is no avoiding responsibility for heresy by just switching hats. [For an interesting and clear discussion of the issues here see E. McMullin. (1998). Galileo on science and scripture. In P. Machamer (Ed.), *The Cambridge companion to Galileo.* Cambridge, UK: Cambridge University Press.] And surely the church had a point here.

People do not allow each other to espouse a respect for the environment and then litter while continuing to drive in ways wasting gas, or otherwise consume in ways that are not environmentally responsible. It seems not acceptable to claim that as a member of a democratic society you are pro-choice, but when it comes to legislation allowing abortions you are against all of it on religious grounds. It is not acceptable to say that as a business person you are allowed to cheat—for all is fair in love and war, but as a parent or a spouse, or a church official, you are not allowed to cheat for there morality should take precedence over economics. The requirement is that persons who are responsible ethical and critical agents be whole, not compartmentalized according to what is to their convenience.

Science Separate from the Humanities

To be sure, it can be said on Galileo's behalf that science *is a special sort of enterprise,* seeking generally to solve problems of how to explain and control events in the world by reference to hypotheses which can be tested and supported in experience. And in the abstract, science even can be seen as using some of the same kinds of methods as the humanities such as appealing to authority, and organizing its interpretative and explanatory narratives into sub-disciplines.

The sciences use these sources of support for beliefs and decisions in the service of learning what can be discovered by controlled experience or observation, and then interpreted and expressed mathematically as regularities of process and connections between events and things of various sorts in our world.

The sciences are not in the business of debating visions of how to live well as are the humanities. Thus the problems served by reason through various methods of inquiry, and then the methods themselves, are somewhat different in the work of the humanities from what they are in the work of the sciences. And then, religion (rather than the critical reflection upon the nature of religion), as well as other aspects of culture such as the actual practice of economics, law, and morality are possibly parts of yet *other* sorts of enterprise, including practical ethics, which have *other* goals and *somewhat other* methods of securing these.

Galileo was right, up to a point; but his plea was unavailing. Groups of the religiously faithful, of researchers studying the same sorts of problems in science, of people subject to the same laws, rules, policies, and so on form communities of inquiry or discussion which differ from each other in their aims or goals, their standards of evidence, and in the details of their methods of fixing belief or making policy. But, at the end of the day, no matter how many different communities of discussion a person belongs to, that individual is responsible for all of the beliefs he or she holds and all the actions he/she undertakes in these different communities. Where there are conflicts, people must either be clear about what these conflicts are and choose to take responsibility for being heretical or hypocritical, or they must reintegrate their beliefs, and the communities in which they live and inquire, into a new or revised order with a new set of beliefs and values where some clearly are given precedence over others so that there is no longer any conflict, and so they can commit themselves to the whole revised set of beliefs—*at least for the moment.* If they cannot fit all of their previous beliefs into the new set, and they do not want to simply give up some of those left out, then they must take a stance of skepticism and maintain a lack of commitment to those remaining beliefs. And they must continue to reflect on and consider or talk about these remaining beliefs. In this second case, people must live *in a creative tension or in a state of what some theorists call "criticality,"* a state of creative tension between chaos and rigidly fixed views and responses.[2] (Recall the discussion in chapter II.)

The Importance of Understanding Inquiry in the Humanities and in Science

Here then, lies the explanation of the nature and importance of the humanities.

> **Study in philosophy, history, literature, cultural anthropology, the claims of ethics, the foundations of law, the justice of the state, and other areas of the humanities are just what humans need to get clear about what beliefs and values they hold, what modes of inquiry they use, what understandings of humans and other beings they assume, in the communities of discussion where they "live and move and have their being."**
>
> **Also, study in the humanities is just what is needed to critically assess, modify, and reintegrate, at least for the moment, various sets of beliefs, value commitments, and assumptions.**

That is the point of the humanities. That is their value. In this way, the humanities sit squarely at the heart of the human attempt to live well and reasonably, understanding both who they are as agents, and how to proceed to make the decisions they must in order to build a coherent and worthwhile life. The humanities have always enabled people to integrate or remake their beliefs, values, and modes of inquiry so as to live responsibly as one person—or as one society.

Caution is needed here to avoid misunderstanding. The claim is that the humanities can and have served humans well in making them more self-conscious about their various commitments in inquiry—both in terms of helping them to understand the nature and significance of the content and method of these inquiries as they try to weave them into a single coherent and consistent view of a world and their life within that world, and in terms of enabling them to form that single viewpoint. This must be kept separate from (at least) four other claims.

(1) This is not the only work of the humanities. It is not the work of poets or historians, or novelists or even philosophers, all of the time. Indeed the main enterprise of the humanities as practiced within and across these disciplines is to explore, and to show the significance of the world in both the sense of the value and the human meaning of its parts and processes of the world. For this reason, people write literature and history as well as write critically about writing it. They practice law as well as reflect on the justice of legal institutions. And so it goes. The idea is only that the humanities are the arena in which, collectively, humans do weave their integrated versions of the results of all inquiry. And the study of the humanities is the endeavor which places humans in that collective enterprise, as well as best equips them to make the most of their individual and social activities as responsible beings creating lives and civilizations.

The humanities can provide a critical theory of living well and the means to apply this theory by integrating its various threads.

And, further, this is work that cannot be done without the work of science.

(2) It is not as though the humanities in their more synthetic collaborations can operate in a scientific vacuum. On the contrary, it seems:

The sciences provide the broad content of living well in that they strive to reveal the limits nature places upon physical and social existence and thus, in effect, show the physical and social possibilities open for realizing or making concrete the life well lived.

Living well calls for impartiality and justice? Fine. Now what can that mean in our world of physical realities, limited resources, and humans acting in contact with others? Science might be said to be about observation and measurement in order to understand why things are as they are. This knowledge enables humans to know what to expect so that they can use and not be hurt by the events in their natural and social worlds. Without this knowledge, the humanities, as concerned with the value and meaning of things, would have nothing to value and interpret! Thus to adapt a statement first made by Immanuel Kant, the eighteenth century Prussian philosopher ("Form without content is empty, content without form is blind." *Critique of Pure Reason*): "Science without the humanities is blind to what should be done, and the humanities without science are empty of the knowledge of how to do what should be done."

Thus the claim is not that the humanities in their disciplinary or cross-disciplinary inquiries are complete without science. That would be foolish. It would be as foolish as to say that science without some incorporation of the study of value and meaning is complete to a life well-lived. The two complement and, it seems, mutually influence each other. One person who has seen this and made much of it said the following[3]:

> Hence, the distinguishing of the two faculties, reason and intellect, coincides with a distinction between two altogether different mental activities, thinking and knowing, and two altogether different concerns, meaning, in the first category, and cognition [knowing the world through the senses and abstractions from observations], in the second. (Arendt, p. 14)

> . . . the assumption must be that thinking and reason are not concerned with what the intellect is concerned with. To anticipate, and put it in a nutshell: the need of reason is not inspired by the quest for truth but by the quest for meaning. And truth and meaning are not the same. The basic fallacy, taking precedence over all specific . . . fallacies [in thinking about the way things are] is to interpret meaning on the model of truth. (Arendt, p. 15)

(3) The third caution is that science and the humanities cannot make real an integrated life well-led apart from engineering and politics. Of course they cannot. If the humanities as communities of inquiry bring possibilities of values and meaning to the journey, and the sciences bring the physical and social possibilities to the journey, engineering and the making of policy and governance bring the possibility of realizing in everyday practice some of the visions of the humanities within some of the physical and social theories of the sciences. Thus engineering and politics make their own particular contributions to the life lived-well.

(4) And finally, one other caution is needed. The humanities, or rather the methods prominent across these communities of inquiry, have enabled humans to integrate the many lives they lead. They do this in two ways. First it is the humanities that concern themselves with understanding the significance of events—both their meaning and their value. But second and more importantly, they concern themselves with the processes of building coherent belief and value systems to guide decisions about what to do about the events and opportunities encountered in the natural and social worlds, all the while adjudicating disputes between contending alternatives. The sciences do form theories or systems of belief, of course. However, in the end they do not seek to tell people either what is the good life or how it is proper to integrate all beliefs and decisions into a collective or individual view of a responsible and properly led life.[4] That seems to be the job of a collaboration of the humanities, using the methods of the humanities. But, of course, and this is the caution, *the humanities cannot do this removed from the influence of the belief systems of the sciences, nor do the sciences and humanities proceed with their work removed from the belief systems of engineers and policy makers. All play a part.* Everyone, no doubt, influences the workings of the others in the endeavor. But, perhaps, at the end of the day, it is the methods of the humanities which exercise most influence in this endeavor to identify a coherent view of a life well-lived in the here and now of our world. Perhaps the sciences provide a

model for the theory of the good life, while it is the humanities which provide that theory and it is engineering and policy studies (broadly construed) which breathe life into this model and theory by connecting them to real practice.

These qualifications concerning the power of the humanities might seem quite enough for present purposes. However, there is one other general reminder. Not all issues *can be resolved* into a single, *stable*, coherent, consistent, and useful system of beliefs and commitments. As illustrated by the examples of Galileo, the ongoing debate about the death penalty, and recent debates about cloning human beings (or "subjects"), the work of the humanities is at best only temporarily done. *"Done temporarily"* because advances in science and technology, increases in population, natural catastrophes, policy changes, and other developments provide humans with new problems whose significance they must seek, and about which they must decide policy. *"At best done"* because some of the conflicts humans face, problems such as the reconciliation of science and religion, and the question of the nature of human life and the legitimacy of abortion, not only are not yet settled, but seem not to be issues humans are likely to settle at all, even temporarily. In other words, there seem to be some conflicts, puzzles, and questions which humans will never settle since there are too many good answers and not enough agreement on methods by which to choose between these answers. Science and religion can be reconciled if humans understand the deity to be the mysterious natural order which scientists discover. Or they can be reconciled if they understand the ultimate explanations of events in the world to involve divine intervention. But neither of these approaches is acceptable to more than one side of the debate. And so the conflict continues. Perhaps the best thing to do in such cases is to appreciate the differences and the stakes of the debate and try to facilitate an uneasy peace as the opposing sides continue to talk in order to resolve their differences or to find a way to live together in peace. Here the humanities can lead us, but the destination is not set, and the discussion is dynamic, not determined.

Scientific and Humanistic Uses of the Sources of Evidence in Inquiry

If all of this is so, it would be of some use to invite reflection on inquiry in science and the humanities. The differences noted between the aims of science and the aims of the humanities might suggest that inquiry in these two areas is quite different. In fact, of course, the sources of evidence are the same in both, but vary in the ways in which they are used, the background knowledge of the communities of inquiry in which they are used and the standards of knowing and acceptability they serve. This is not the place to try to summarize the discussions on these differences. Still, it is appropriate before the discussion proceeds into the specifics of investigating particular patterns of reasoning to quickly raise some questions about these differences.

(A) OBSERVATION AND THE CONSTRUCTION OF A COHERENT PERSONAL NARRATIVE. One of the lessons of the story concerning Galileo's life is how scientific observation is standardized while observation for the creation of a life narrative is individualized. Of course when any particular scientist makes observations the account of these and of how they were made could be told in such a way as to emphasize the individual or idiosyncratic character of them. But that story would not be found in the lab notebooks. The important thing there is what can be described in terms allowing for others to repeat the conditions and operations of the observations so as to be able to test the accuracy and completeness of what the scientific observer said. This is necessary since the claim of the observer is an implicitly general one: When in these circumstances . . . , this change is introduced . . . , then this happens. Only with such observations will the scientist be able to reach the kind of repeatability and regularity that will allow her or him to explain and effectively make general predictions about what goes on in what circumstances. Also, only in the face of such regularity will the patterns of connections in the world that scientists seek to tell others about be open to mathematical or other standardized and efficient expression. Scientific observation is conducted—that is deliberately engaged in, in order to collect data for analysis and later use in formulating or testing hypotheses. Here the world is an object to be studied and figured out. The scientist deliberately takes her or himself out of the observed so as to isolate that and bring it under abstract general concepts. Or at least this has been the model for a long time (at least since Galileo), and remains so in the physical sciences. In the human sciences, some observers place themselves in the world they want to observe by participating in this world so as to get the feel of it and to try to understand it from the inside out, so to speak. Participatory research is present in cultural anthropology as well as ethology and ethnobotany, for example.

Some would complain that participatory research conducted as just described is not really science for it trades the objective-observer-of-the-world viewpoint for the subjective-participant-in-the-world viewpoint. In the end, it is not clear that thinkers need choose so much as be aware of this difference and take up the viewpoint appropriate to the inquiry they engage in. Thus the appropriate viewpoint would be objectifying for the physical sciences, and as will become clear shortly, also for logic, for example. The appropriate viewpoint for the humanities would make subjects of observers in so far as these areas of inquiry study humans operating in the world to make sense or meaning of their lives (or not), and study the practice of good reasoning in the context of living. This distinction does not work just to separate the physical sciences from the humanities, for example. It is also relevant in separating, for example, biology as a biochemical study of life from ecology as a study of life forms in contact and adaptation.

One way to indicate how observation in the humanities is "subjectified" is by reporting some research done on children as they watched *Sesame Street*. Two studies by Dan Anderson and Elizabeth Lorch are reported in the recent book, *The Tipping*

Point, How Little Things Can Make a Big Difference, by Malcolm Gladwell (Boston: Little, Brown and Company, 2000, 2002, see pages 100–101.). The first study provided evidence that the children watching *Sesame Street* were attending to and following meaning rather than the colors, changes of scene, and other visual attractors in the televised images. The second study observed children who played with toys made available where they watched the television program. This second study showed that the children who played with the toys were as effective in picking up the meaning of the program segments as those who were focused on the program alone. Both groups of children, those who played while they watched, and those who only watched, learned an equal amount from and about the program. So what? This seems to suggest that to study the children as program watchers, they should not be objectified but rather observed as meaning makers or as subjects of thought, and apparently discriminating subjects, perhaps even persons engaged in critical thought as they watched. The children, as Gladwell points out, were not reduced to zombies by the television as are adults—who probably use it to "zone out" or to purposely shut down their critical watching and listening.

Observation in the humanities then can be characterized as subjectified or conducted from the standpoint of a subject involved in what is observed, and participatory, rather than objectifying and removed as just described. Observation in the humanities seems to be devoted to trying to enter the world of someone or of some subject of experience, and trying to understand interpretation, conceptualization and so meaning making as thought leading to personal understanding on the part of agents, not as objective observers. In this way feeling and emotional tone are important to observation in the humanities where they would not be in the sciences. And if the sciences are after public or official narratives allowing them to explain and predict things that happen, the humanities are after personal narratives and expressions that allow individuals to put together a coherent, successful, and satisfying life. If that is so, then clearly observation in the sciences must take thinkers toward public accounts of things described in standard ways and conceptualized abstractly. In the humanities, by contrast, observation must take thinkers toward personal accounts of actions and experiences described in ways apt to the individual's understanding of what he/she is doing and where and how he/she is doing it. Abstract concepts are sources of frustration rather than welcome tools. And this would seem to be so even for those practices of the humanities that seek to understand thinking, story making, interpretation, theory making, and so across philosophy, literature, history, drama theory, and the rest. For even there, if the work does not begin with the world as experienced by agents with concerns, it will not be accepted as true to its subject matter.[5] Still, just how do concepts, background assumptions, the expectations of others, and so on work on the observer in science and in the humanities? When Galileo was observing as a scientist, as opposed to an individual trying to relate to the ethical leadership of his time, how did he see things differently beyond what has already been said? This question will be left for reflection.

(B) AUTHORITY AND TRADITION.   The case of Galileo illustrates well the second of the sources which the humanities and science rely on, namely, authority and tradition. The problem with Galileo's science according to the church was that it did not rest on tradition, nor did it respect the authority of Aristotle and other church-approved thinkers. Galileo followed the dictates of his experiments and reason, and blazed his own trails, as well as confirming those scouted by others before him such as Copernicus. In doing so, Galileo challenged the church as the established source of knowledge of the external world. And he became one of the parents of modern science. But by what authority did he proceed? How does modern science establish the authoritativeness of the claims of its members? What role does tradition now play in science and in the humanities? Is it true that tradition within science concerns values about the sorts of goals to pursue and the processes to use? How then is science to be separated from the humanities in general at these points? What, within the rules of critical thinking, are the conditions of proper and legitimate appeals to authority in science and in the humanities? What are the different structures of authority there and the differences in the ways they work? These are also questions for further reflection.

(C) THE MAKING AND PERPETUATION OF COMMUNITY NARRATIVES.   Cultures, societies, and smaller communities tell common stories enshrining and passing on favored accounts of what the world and its inhabitants are like, favored explanations of why things are the ways they are, accounts of what potential humans and other beings have, and of what is worthwhile or not. In doing so, they seek to articulate a coherent account of who they are and what they might hope for. Galileo was happy to contribute to the stories people tell about the physical world and how it works. He was unwilling to try adding to the story told about the nature and possibilities of the spiritual world. According to his beliefs, it was the job of the church figures, interpreting the teaching of the Holy Ghost, to tell "how to go to heaven." Galileo was taking on the job of telling "how the heavens go." (See Galileo, cited above, page 186.) The study of the humanities can teach both what narratives have been told by what people, and when, but also how narratives, personal and communal, come to be. In this work, thinkers might gain a sense of just how a coherent story is formed and how it has to meet various criteria such as accommodating most ordinary beliefs or much of "common sense" before it can be accepted. Of course these stories are value laden and are in flux, slowly evolving as the communities which they serve face changing climatic, technological, economic, cultural, or other conditions. Who was the human in the days of early Christianity, in the Reformation, in the Enlightenment, in the romantic period, and in the modern period of mass destruction in world war? Is there any final way to adjudicate the disputes between the conflicting claims of these perspectives? How is the canonical legitimated? What makes the best, most coherent story for a community? Is the work of science (the physical as well as the social sciences) also value laden? Can the work of science also be seen as work of constructing a common narrative or story, even if it is one whose point in human life will be different from that of the stories of the humanities? Are scientific theories a form of narrative account that organizes and explains experience in some special way? How differently do the narratives of science and those of the humanities impact human life? These are all questions which the practices of creating and critiquing narratives raise for thinkers seeking to understand the methods of the humanities and their relations to the methods of the sciences.

(D) CRITICAL ANALYSIS AND INTERPRETATION OF COMMUNITIES OF INQUIRY OR DISCUSSION. Perspectives, whether scientific or humanistic, need to be maintained. Analysis, assessment, and modification of the parts of perspectives—their background assumptions, and patterns of accepted reasoning—must be ongoing. Galileo sought to revise the procedures of, and to reconstitute the membership of the scientific community of discussion in his time. The community he would have formed was different from that of the church in the kinds of goals its members sought to reach—to figure out how heaven goes, as opposed to figuring out how to go to heaven and then making the trip! His scientific community was different from the community of the church in the basic beliefs it held about what exists and why it does what it does. Also it differed in the way it studied those things and controlled them. The church differed on all of these counts as discussed above. But can science and the humanities be partitioned off into communities of discussion differing along the lines suggested above? How do thinkers move from personal narrative to socially entrenched narrative, to established theory and communities of discussion? That is, how does that work as a matter of critical thinking, not just sociology or history? How can thinkers make sense of critiques of communities of discussion and progress as they modify or change the elements of thinking and perspective making up communities of discussion? How do they adjudicate disputes across such communities, between, for example, astronomy, biology, and geology on the one hand and religion on the other? How do they integrate these differing communities into a coherent viewpoint informing their lives? Or can they? Some of these questions will arise again in chapter VII and chapter X. Most must be left for further study elsewhere.

(E) CONTINUING DIALOGUE AND INTERPRETATION WHEN INTERCOMMUNITY DEBATES CANNOT BE SETTLED. Sometimes there are conflicting perspectives on gaining knowledge and there is no clear, good way to decide between them. This is so in the humanities as well as the sciences. Consider the questions, respectively, on how to decide: What is a person? What is a black hole? Sometimes the dialogue simply continues as thinkers try to reconcile their differences by appeal to common beliefs or goals. Perhaps they will end up with the same more or less coherent system of beliefs and values. But there is no guarantee. Whatever they differed on, Galileo and the church had a common faith in reasoning and in not appearing to ignore or to try to force the other to believe some way. This common faith in reason, in inquiry, can keep the conversation going as thinkers look for common ground with those in conflict. But what exactly is this common faith and how far does it require thinkers to go in tolerating the beliefs and assessments of others with whom we disagree for apparently good reason? Is this common faith one that stands above each of the sciences and each of the humanities and arts and other fields of inquiry? How can appeals to it be understood as available to settle disputes between the sciences and the humanities, for example?

(F) THE ANALYSIS OF RISK AND OF DIFFERENT FORMS OF VALUE IN ISSUES FROM THE MOMENTOUS TO THE MUNDANE.   Every inquiry is motivated and then has some values at its base. But what are these values? Are they objective and real, or are they just preferences or passing interests? How can thinkers support claims of individual or group values being really worthwhile? And if values are really worthwhile do they automatically have a claim on us rationally and in psychological fact, as a means to a certain kind of life—one led by reason? What does it mean for us to bring a value into our lives or to have a value, or to live by a value? And how can we resolve conflicts between values? There is not much to say here in brief. Much ink is spilled on how and whether humans know what is good, right, obligatory, and the rest. There is not even any real agreement on where to begin—preferences and their satisfactions, human interests, duty, contracts and other agreements, and on, and on, and on. Perhaps for present purposes, just exploring what were the values involved can help other thinkers appreciate the conflicts Galileo faced and can help them form an intelligent view on whether or not Galileo could resolve those conflicts. Finding or even searching for what might serve as leading, lifelong values might help prioritize human commitments and help thinkers see how to resolve some of the greatest conflicts between communities of inquiry. And then again. . . . (some of these reflections are addressed in the final chapter.)

(G) THE RESPONSIBLE INTEGRATION OF BELIEFS AND VALUES IN PRACTICAL DECISION MAKING.   One other source and use of evidence that the humanities illustrate in the writing and study of literature and history, for example, is the process of practical reasoning by re-integration of any individual's or a society's aims, values, and beliefs. The first step in the process of practical reasoning involves (1) the review of opportunities and past commitments, (2) the drawing of easy and hidden connections with present values and priorities, and (3) the explorations of the impacts of human options on their own social context and the lives of other people. The second step is seeking to learn which course of action would most fully serve one's multiple priorities and commitments and most completely harmonize these with those of others whose own undertakings should not be disturbed. This "learning" is part prediction, part discovery, part paying attention to the legitimate expectations on individuals, and part an attempt to determine in imagination what it is thinkers really want or are striving for. The "learning" is less acquisition of knowledge than it is forming a tentative and experimental judgment which constructs a possible future. And thus the third step in this practical reasoning involves an attempt to imagine what seems best and trying to imagine one's life and the lives of others shaped by one's judgment with all the compromises, changes, and new commitments this would bring with it. If thinkers can rethink their lives, or reinvent themselves by reintegrating their beliefs, values, and aims to accommodate this possible choice in their life plan, and if they can do this while still making coherent sense of what they stand for, and while still meeting the expectations of others on them, then they can adopt that choice and go about the further experiment of trying to realize it.

Once again, the reintegration of beliefs is not something foreign to science and thinkers would do well to understand how this works in the case of scientific inquiry. However, for science, reintegration seems to be in the service of reaching the best explanation, the most coherent interpretation and inclusive model, the most inclusive and suggestive taxonomy, that allows science to reintegrate its beliefs as it goes from observation to theory. Thus, once again, it seems that science and the humanities differ importantly, while being alike. The aims and the means, though similar at one level of description, are different and complementary at another.

Imagine how life could be if this integrative "use of evidence" were granted a place. Perhaps Galileo failed in this regard. Still, this was no small task in the historical context. It was no small thing for him to apply it. Indeed to thinkers today, even more than to Galileo, this concern with the responsible integration of beliefs and values in decision making must seem daunting. But the techniques and dimensions of this (perhaps culminating) use of reason are surely at the heart of living well. It behooves each thinker to be concerned about and to try to practice this and the other endeavors of the humanities and the sciences, and the arts and techné.

SECTION 2

The Central Tool of Inquiry—Argument

The seven aspects of inquiry just spoken of may be compared to the spokes of a wheel turning on a common axle. That turning point is argument—whether this takes the form of a narrative or a more formally structured attempt to provide evidence for a conclusion.

Soon the discussion will take up separately patterns of reasoning in both inductive and deductive arguments. The remainder of this chapter is preparation for getting the most out of those later discussions. The first order of business is to narrow the focus down to arguments and indeed highly structured arguments as one particular form of the use of language.

Consider the following examples:

1. The dress was a black silk sheath with black sequins at the hem and the cuffs of the three-quarter-length sleeves. It had a modestly high scooped front and a deeply scooped back gathered to the shoulders. That was the dress she was wearing when she shot to death Mrs. McKlanski's husband.
2. "First you take the two side panels and connect them to the top and bottom pieces with the special hook screws—part 3 in the parts illustration. **Do not tighten fully!**"
3. "He was able to get into the apartment because a window was left open by the alley close to the dumpster. The dumpster had been emptied that day and was light enough to push over and then stand on to get access to the window. All this took place right after he saw the Captain leave for the mess hall. The alley was cordoned off for a parade and the housing was close enough to a wall at the back of the army post so that he could not have been seen pushing the dumpster or

climbing on it. After gaining access in that fashion, he was able to plant the incriminating evidence. We found his DNA samples on the dumpster in the form of skin he scraped off getting on it and in the apartment in the form of blood dripped on the floor under the bed and under the chest where he planted the documents. We move that all charges against the Captain be dropped."

4. The reasons why it did not work are that the battery needed to set off the model rocket engine was too low to send the charge needed and the fuel was damp from being in a wet tent overnight at the rally.

5. "Herb went to the farm as is clear from the following. The tread on one of his tires has a distinctive flaw caused by some road hazard someone ran over. That flaw, actually a chunk out of the inside of the left rear tire, is very distinctive. Plaster casts made at the scene fit the tire perfectly. Further, Herb swore that the car was in his possession all day and that he had made a business call in the vicinity of the farm, that day—even though he claims he did not go to the farm or even down the road to the farm. He said in his testimony that he ate in his car and did not leave it for more than three minutes to wash up at a service station. Clearly this is sufficient to establish that Herb was at the farm, the scene of the crime."

6. "Watch out! That crane is tipping!"

Notice that each of the above is a different use of language, the first to give a description of a dress, the second to give a part of a set of instructions, the third to explain how someone could have gotten into the apartment and then to argue that it was someone other than the defendant, the fourth to explain why the model rocket did not fire, and next a longer argument—one devoted to showing that someone was at the scene of the crime presumably on the day the crime took place, and finally the sixth to shout a warning. Description, instruction, explanation reconstructing some event, explanation of some non-occurrence, argument, and warning are the different functions of discourse at work here.

Both of the arguments—that the person in question did enter the room by the dumpster and back window, and that the person in question was at the scene of the crime on the farm, try to present evidence for a conclusion or a claim—he/she got in through the window off the dumpster, this is clear from the DNA evidence; he/she was at the farm, one knows so from the tire track and other circumstances of the car's use. As defined in the previous chapter, *an argument is a set of statements some of which give evidence for one or more others. The evidence bearing statements are the premises while the supported statement(s) is the conclusion(s) or claim(s)*. Explanations can be divided up into statements of what is being explained and what does the explaining. But these are not called "claim" and "premises" because explanations are doing something different in thought than arguments—something to be discussed in chapters VII and IX. Before looking more closely at arguments, a little more might be said on this distinction between explanation and arguments.

Explanations: Notice that when one tries to explain what has happened (or what will happen), he/she is assuming that something has occurred (or will occur) and is trying to understand what brought it about, or is trying to understand why someone decided in a certain way—what made that person decide in that way. Explainers are looking for what in the world produced the thing of interest or for some way to understand or make intelligible what happened, and not for reasons for believing that in fact it did occur or reasons for deciding on a certain option as the best one open. That makes all the difference—even though the language of explanations and deductive arguments might use the same words of "reason for" and "because of" and "why something is so." Perhaps an example will help. "Toledo was elected president of Peru." This really happened a few years ago, but of course it was a person named Toledo who was elected, not the city in Ohio or in Spain!

Now one might ask two things, both using the language of "why was Toledo elected?"

1. "Why was Toledo elected?" meaning what brought it about that Toledo was elected and
2. "Why was Toledo elected?" meaning what reason does anyone have for believing that Toledo was elected?

Question (1) calls for an explanation. He was elected because people did not trust his opponent who had been president once before and really messed things up. It was the lack of trust that made people vote for Toledo, not the phase of the moon, not what the voters had to eat, or did not have, before going to the polls, not their horoscope. These statements would point to **what was present and caused the thing or event** to be explained.

Question (2) calls for an argument providing evidence for the truth of the claim that Toledo was elected. One can ask, why do you think it is true that Toledo was elected? And the proper response would be to refer the listener to such things as: *Toledo's opponent conceded with 60% of the vote counted. Toledo's vote count was significantly in excess of that for his opponent. There was no reason to believe that the election was fraudulent.* These statements would be **evidence for the truth** of the claim that Toledo was elected, but they would not explain why the voters voted as they did or why there was an election only one year after the former President was re-elected through fraud, and so on.

So:

Explanations tell why or how something came about. The why of it is a matter of what brought it about—some physical cause or pattern of the operation of physical things, some set of reasons or motives, or some pattern of practices or institutional operations in society, or some function or goal or purpose served.[6] The explanation tells you how it came to be, not the reasons why it is true to say that it came to be. Truth is a second level or meta-level property of the relations of claims made in language to the world when those claims tell it like it is, or to other claims giving evidence of things being the way one claims them to be. Why or how something comes to pass or is done is a first or same level feature of what came to be. It is a feature of the world that brought about what happened; the being of the explaining thing or event fits crucially into an account of how things came to be as they are.

Usually: "Why explanations" will tell you what happened to bring something about. **And they will focus on something that is of special interest and is understandable to the audience**. "How explanations" will tell you how—what you could do to bring something about yourself, if you have the right tools and so on. **These also will focus on something of interest and that is understandable to the audience.** (The portions in bold are discussed further in chapter VII.) Notice that the detective does not want to know whether the light was on in the room when the painting was stolen, unless this had something to do with the crime—for example, unless it shows the likelihood that the crime was committed with the light off, by a blind person who was familiar with the room. The health inspector does not want to know what brand of refrigerator the restaurant is using unless that has something to do with the reliability of the restaurant's food being preserved safely. And so it goes—interest, the interests of the people asking for the explanation, play a large part in what is the correct explanation for whichever context or situation we are dealing with. This is no surprise since these interests will determine to some extent the problem the explanation is to address and with that, often, the community of inquiry or discussion in which the explanation is to be given, and so the assumptions and procedures to be used in the explanation.

Arguments are reasons for saying or believing that something is a certain way or that a claim is true of the world, or that what is said is correct. Giving reasons why something is true does not in itself bring it about. So if you point out that since Jones is human, Jones will get old and die, that is not to make her die. You are no part of the explanation of Jones dying—Jones is still alive! Rather what is going on is that you are arguing that it is true that Jones will die. But if you put Jones in Dr. Diabolical's time machine and fast forward her through the next seventy years without giving her the elixir so that she travels with the machine as opposed to continuing to age as the time of the machine goes forward, then she will get old and die. You made her do that. You are part of the explanation of her dying.

Or consider a different example: the argument for saying that it is true that George Washington died, would point to the usual length of time people live, when Washington was born, the reports in the newspapers of the time, the DNA of the bones in Washington's grave and so on. All of that would be evidence for, or part of the premises for, an argument to the conclusion that it is true that Washington, George Washington, the first President of the United States, is dead. None of this evidence would have been part of the explanation of Washington dying.

Mastery Exercises VI.1

SELF TEST

Comprehension Questions

1. What are the basic parts of an argument?

2. What terms are common to explanations and arguments?

3. How would you separate explanations from arguments?

4. Will all explanations be of interest to anyone with an interest in the occurrence of an event? Why or why not?

5. Might a narrative serve as an argument? Have you ever been convinced, and for good reason, by a story that something is true? Can you give an example? For example, is Darwin's story of the differences of animals he found in various places on his voyage on the ship *H.M.S. Beagle,* a presentation of evidence for evolution?

Mastery Exercises VI.2

SELF TEST

Distinguishing Arguments and Explanations and Other Uses of Language

INSTRUCTIONS: For each of the following, reflect on whether the language gives an argument, an explanation, or some other form of discourse. Mark your answer down and then check the answers in Appendix II. Briefly explain why the correct answer is correct.

1. "Florence went to the florists" convention and found the most beautiful flowers from Africa. She used these liberally in the arrangement she did for the flower show. That was what earned her the blue ribbon."

2. "Time heals all wounds, but sometimes a bandage helps. The bandage will keep out infection and that is one of the enemies of healing."

3. "The reason why moths fly to light is that it's a good place to meet other moths."

4. "The reason why Smith won the Volkswagen is that she kept her hand on the hood longest in the recent contest at Val's Volkswagens."

5. "Herb said, 'But I couldn't get to work on time—you're not going to believe this, but really I was captured by Russian mob members and held for ransom. But when they found what a nobody I really am, they let me go after beating me up for their trouble.'"

6. "If you wish to get the best cutting results, you should clean the blade platform and sharpen the mower blades every three weeks during the mowing season."

7. "Britten went to Yale. That's why he talks that way—with that funny kind of accent while using those extraordinary words."

8. "The car stopped in the passing lane just flat out of gas. That's why it happened."

9. "The car stopped in the passing lane flat out of gas. I saw it stop and the driver get out, slam the door, get a gas can from the trunk, run across five lanes of traffic, and start walking back to the exit where he had just gotten on. That's how I know it stopped out of gas. Good thing it was 2:30 and traffic was light."

10. "Be careful. That vase is worth $30,000 bucks!"

11. "She did it because she chose to get the money that way. Why do you think anyone robs a bank?"

12. "That's what happened. The reason is that the stock market responded to the rising price of oil and prices of auto stocks went lower. That's why it was the economy that really killed Greene—even though she chose to jump. The woman had everything tied up in a Hummer dealership and in Hummer stock—and those things are gas guzzlers."

13. "One-hundred three nations co-sponsored the censure of polluting nations. That's why the general assembly had to take a vote. The charter says that is the way it is, so that is why."

14. "The new sports car went very fast and it cost a lot of money. That's what I found out when I went to the showroom."

15. "Grayson was guilty, no doubt about it. The jury vote and the judge's acceptance of it are there for all to read in the court record. That's why it is so."

SECTION 3

Framing Arguments,
An Introduction

Arguments are all the same and very much different. They all have some evidentiary component, the premise(s), and a supported component, the claim. That much is characteristic of arguments, though sometimes premises are not stated in setting out an argument and sometimes the conclusion is not stated. What is different is how the arguments flow, how the evidence is brought together, and the way it lends support to the conclusion. In order to become able to assess arguments, critical thinkers must come to be able to understand the premises and the conclusion and the flow of one to another. Thus it would be useful to have some way to make sense of all that.

Several forms of analysis of argument structure and evidentiary flow have been devised. For the purposes of coming to understand the general, functional differences between statements providing evidence in support of a conclusion, there is none that is better, perhaps, than a form of analysis designed by philosopher Stephen Toulmin (published in Toulmin, S., Rieke, R., and Janik, J. (1984). *An introduction to reasoning* (2nd ed.). New York: Macmillan Publishing Co., Inc.). This approach will be discussed and extensively illustrated in a short while. But first it might be good to just mention another way of looking at arguments.

Sometimes arguments function only by virtue of assembling a number of bits of evidence or a number of facts. Other times it seems that a single bit of evidence carries the day. Thus compare:

1. Herman strangled Henrietta's pet chicken.
2. Herman confessed to killing Henrietta's pet chicken.

Both 1 and 2 are premises for the conclusion that Herman is the killer. Neither requires the other.

But now look at the following:

3. Herman was the only one at home on the farm that day. 4. No one else came on the place. 5. The dog cannot use its paws to strangle things and Henrietta's pet chicken was strangled to death. So Herman killed it.

Here a number of circumstantial factors provide sufficient evidence for saying Herman did in the chicken.

Thus one way to see the work of the premises in an argument is to ask *if they do the job by themselves or only with other premises*. Remember that when premises establish a conclusion by themselves, that is, without other statements that are true and false independently of each of those premises, then still they can be brought together to establish the conclusion in a bit of argumentative overkill. Thus arguments can be seen as the convergence of evidence statements sufficient by themselves, or not, to establish a single conclusion.

And, of course there is not any reason why a single statement might not establish two or more different conclusions. Thus "Herman strangled Henrietta's pet chicken" might support not only the conclusion that Herman killed the chicken, but also the conclusion that Herman saddened Henrietta.

Alternatively, in a case like the first one concerning Herman above, arguments that have the same conclusion can be seen as running parallel to each other supporting the same conclusion but in a separate flow of evidence.

Further notice that once a conclusion is established, it can be used in a further argument as a premise. So the terms "premise" and "conclusion" do not apply to only certain statements. Statements do not come to thinkers divided into the camps of premise or conclusion. But then this means that there could be a whole series of arguments in which evidence flows to a conclusion which serves as evidence (with or without other premises) for another conclusion and so on.

All of this is valuable to think about and even to outline the basic structures of arguments as of one of the sorts just described. None of this way of approaching arguments does much to help thinkers understand the different ways in which premises might support conclusions, however. And if thinkers are to become sensitive to the flow of reasoning in an argument, more is needed. Toulmin's approach to understanding the structure of an argument provides an important part of this "more." What it gives is a way to understand the different sorts of evidence that premises can provide; how they play different roles in an argument. Toulmin's method of outlining distinguishes several different kinds of premises by their role in the support for the argument and so gives an indication of the different ways in which pieces of evidence support a conclusion. It also shows how to include statements that are not premises (or claims) of the argument, but instead are limits on the claims of the argument—statements introducing so-called qualifiers, or the reasons qualifiers are needed, namely, rebuttals. The first thing to do is to list the different roles of assertions in arguments according to Toulmin:

CLAIM/CONCLUSION.   This is familiar enough that there is nothing new to report here except that Toulmin prefers "claim."

GROUND.   Statements of particular facts relevant as evidence for the claim of the argument. (See Toulmin, Rieke, and Janik, 1984, p. 38) Thus consider the following arguments: *All glasses containing ice and water condense water vapor on their outside in a hot humid environment.* **This glass has ice and water and is sitting in a hot humid environment.** Therefore <u>this glass has condensed water vapor on its outside</u>. *Glasses with condensed water vapor on their outside are slippery.* **This glass has condensed water vapor on the outside.** So, <u>this glass is slippery</u>.

The conclusions are <u>underlined</u>. The grounds of the arguments are in **bold.** And the statements in *italics* are something else to be discussed in a moment. So the flow of the reasoning goes from the facts that this is a glass in a hot humid environment with ice and water in it, to the claim that the glass is condensing water vapor on its outside, and the fact that this glass has condensed water vapor on it to the claim that the glass is slippery. The facts are the particular evidence given here for those claims. But what about the other assertions—the ones in italics?

WARRANTS.   Warrants are assertions that connect the grounds (or particular facts) to the claim. They are statements that allow one to move in reasoning from the evidence to the claim. They might be further facts stated in generalizations, or they might be rules, or they might be definitions, or they might be equations, or some other connecting link between the facts of the case and claim about the case. For example:

A: (1) *Rain is good for plants.* (2) It is now raining (again!). (3) So this weather is good for plants.

B: (1) You promised Herb that you would pay him back today! (2) *People should always keep their promises* and so (3) you should pay him back today.

C: (1) *All squares are four-sided enclosed figures with sides of equal length.* (2) This is a square. So (3) we know the sides are going to be of equal length. (While this is not of much interest alone, try to build a house with squared areas without it!)

D: (1) 15 times $30.00 equals $450. (2) You pay me $30.00 per hour and I worked 15 hours. (3) *You owe me for what I work, that was our agreement.* So you owe me $450! It's that simple.

E: (1) *15 times $30.00 equals $450.00.* (2) You are indebted to me for the number of hours I work—at that agreed rate. (3) Therefore your total debt to me is $450.00

The warrants are all in *italics*. The first is a generalization of fact. The second is a rule of ethics. The third is a definition or a truth of definition. The fourth is a reminder of an ethically charged relationship between the speaker and employer. And the fifth is a simple arithmetic equation. Notice that if one takes out these warranting statements one is left with a big gap and could not really draw the conclusion in question—or could not do so legitimately. Something would be left out of the argument. If one does not know that rain is good for plants, how would he or she ever move from the fact that it is raining to the conclusion that this weather is good for plants? Or if one did not know that squares have equal sides, how would he or she move from this being a square to the conclusion that the sides of this figure or space are of equal length? And suppose that one knew how much he or she got paid, and how long he/she worked, but did not know how to multiply. How would it be possible to figure out what is owed?

Warrants span the gap between particular facts (singular or general) and the conclusion a thinker draws from them. They conceptually legitimate the inference from grounds to conclusion, from facts or what is taken as such to a claim.

Another important kind of warrant is **a principle of reasoning or of knowledge.** This might sound mysterious, but it is not. Suppose that the two restrictions on thinkers as they move from a sample (for example of voters) to a conclusion (for example, the Republican is going to win) is that (1) the sample is large enough to show the true patterns of the distributions of votes and (2) the sample is not biased so that the people polled are truly representative of the spread of preferences of all voters. Then consider this argument:

Suppose exit polls (the sample that researchers reason from in predicting winners on election day) show a strong and winning preference in favor of Bush. The sample was of a significantly large number of voters and the sample was representative of the patterns of preferences across the voting populace. So it is clear that Bush will win. *This way of putting the argument really concludes that **one can know** from the sample that Bush will win.* And for that conclusion from those facts about the sample results, the warrant has to be that *thinkers can gain knowledge from samples, if the samples are sufficiently large to be significant and if they accurately present, that is, they truly represent the patterns of preferences of the voting populace resulting from the various pressures and choices among that population.*

So warrants (including principles of reasoning and evidence themselves, when the conclusion is about what one can reason to or what one can know) serve as bridges and are needed in the argument to link facts and conclusion.

BACKING.   But these are not the only roles of premises or evidence assertions. **Another is to provide support for the warrant itself!** (Compare this with the concern to avoid the fallacy of unsubstantiated evidence in chapter II.) For example, if one needs to support the warrant about when it is ok to use a sample to gain knowledge about voting preferences and winners, he/she might point to the fact that that is what is meant by the phrase "warranted conclusion from a sample." Or one might say that that is just how thinkers proceed in sampling research that is accepted in the field. Or one might point to the mathematics of such samples and their reliability of predicting what turns out to be true. All of these statements would show support for the warrant.

Statements providing evidence for warrants are called **backing statements** and are said to provide backing for those argument bridges. Consider the following argument: (1) All Italian racing cars are fast. The reasons for this claim are that (2) Italian racecars have won many international competitions and (3) only very fast cars are capable of winning international competitions. (4) Those races are very tough; the competition is very fierce. Here (1) is the claim. (2) gives the grounds. (3) gives the warrant. And (4) is an abbreviated way of saying that research and history show that those races are between very fast cars and are hard fought with fierce competition, so that only very fast cars will win. 4) gives the backing for the warrant in (3).

Two further kinds of statements show up in arguments according to Toulmin:

QUALIFIERS AND REBUTTALS.   These two go together. A rebuttal might challenge the grounds *or* the warrant *or* the backing. If it challenged the grounds then what is needed is a further argument for the grounds—an argument with the grounds statement as the conclusion. If the challenge is to the warrant, then what is needed is backing. And if it is a challenge to the backing, one needs support for saying that the backing gives a proper statement of how reasoning goes or is supposed to go within the group of reasoners where the argument occurs. *That is where reasoning about the acceptability of a perspective on gaining knowledge comes in.* Also a rebuttal might just say that the conclusion is too strong on the basis of the evidence given. In that case what is needed is not more evidence, but a qualifier for the conclusion, a limiting phrase like "probably," or "in all likelihood," or "as far as our reasoning takes us," or something like these. A qualifier just limits the strength of the claim the reasoner is making; instead of concluding the claim is true (period), one can say it seems likely to be true, or there is some reason for thinking it true.

Putting all of this together into a graphic presentation of the argument discussed above the following comes out: (1) All Italian racing cars are fast. The reasons for this claim are that (2) Italian racecars have won many international competitions and (3) only very fast cars are capable of winning international competitions. (4) Those races are very tough; the competition is very fierce. Notice that the kind of function of the premise is named and then the number of the premise or conclusion is placed in the space of that kind of function:

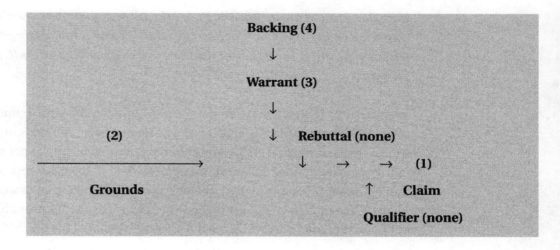

Consider another example or two:

Argument X: (1) Herman went to Carson City and saw fourteen horses hurt in the rodeo. (2) Herman then went on to Cheyenne's rodeo and saw fifteen horses injured in the rodeo there. (3) He then went on to the Calgary Stampede where he saw forty-seven horse injuries in that huge rodeo. (4) Then he went to his little county fair in Pine Bluffs, Nebraska where he saw five horses injured in that small rodeo. (5) He concluded that rodeos are injurious to horses. (6) Of course he only went to four rodeos, even if they did include some of the biggest and oldest in the world. (7) So maybe he should say only that there is some strong evidence for saying that rodeos are injurious to horses. But he can conclude that much. After all (8) if we sample enough cases and these are representative, then we can move from that sample to a generalization asserting the sampled patterns to be true of the entire population we are talking about— here rodeos and rodeo horses. And (9) this is just what is accepted and justified practice among sampling researchers using samples in their reasoning.

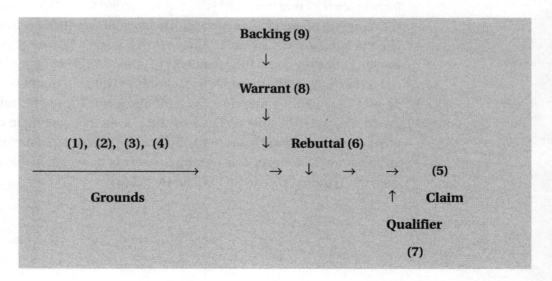

Now this form of outlining allows for the incorporation of a tentative conclusion into the display of the flow before the rebuttal and a rephrasing of the conclusion with the qualifier built in. But that seems like a needless complication for present purposes.

Argument Y: (1) If we get sloppy toward the end, we are sure to make a mistake and mess up all our efforts. (2) That's just a basic fact of human psychology. (3) Herman worked along diligently on his model of the Eiffel Tower, but he got sloppy toward the end. Was it any wonder that (4) Herman messed up all his hard work on the Eiffel Tower model? But now you say (5) that's being too harsh, he had to go to work and he wanted to finish the model. Well, ok. Maybe I should say that he (6) probably got sloppy and (4′) so **he** probably messed up the model—he's probably the one to fault.

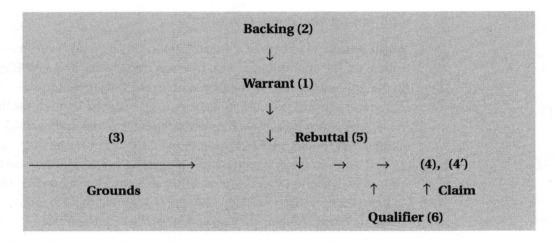

Why is this form of analysis important? The answer is, "for several reasons." In constructing arguments thinkers will benefit from setting out the structure in outline form to see if all that is needed is included. Second the outlining is helpful for spotting the omission of premises (usually grounds), or for clarifying warrants and seeing the need to qualify conclusions. The same is true when a thinker goes about the work of thinking critically about the arguments of others. A side benefit of learning this material is that such outlining analysis techniques will help thinkers to grasp the flow of deductive reasoning presented in symbolic form. These outlining techniques will prove very valuable now and in the future. Even in engaging in critical reading for other courses, they will come in handy. For this reason, several more examples will be given before the self test. These examples will not be set out in the Toulmin form; however, this is a good exercise in itself for the reader.

THE BASIC TOULMIN FORM:

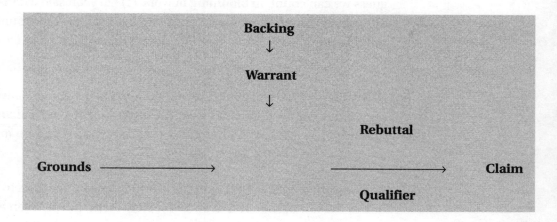

Examples

G = grounds, W = warrant, B = backing, C = claim, R = rebuttal, and Q = qualifier

A. (1) Herb worked hard in every class. (2) He read the assignments. (3) He did the exercises. (4) He took the practice tests. (5) He went in on office hours with questions. (6) So he is sure trying hard to master the material, get a good grade, and get his money's worth. (7) After all, that is what you do to really do well in a class and get the full value out of it. 8) That is what all the counselors say. G = 1, 2, 3, 4, 5; W = 7; B = 8; C = 6

B. (1) Henrietta developed a great network by going to all the right parties, (2) getting to know the friends of the personnel directors, (3) studying hard at the university, and (4) being seen at honorary award presentations, as well as (5) interviewing beginning with her sophomore year. (6) She is going to get a great job. (7) These are all the things that contribute to success in landing a great job. 8) All the best job-hunting books say so. G = 1, 2, 3, 4, 5; C = 6; W = 7; B = 8

C. (1) The president of the company has announced that we are going to introduce this new car in three years. (2) If we are going to do that, we had better get to work since we have a lot of design and prototype tasks to complete. (3) And since these tasks take so much time, we will have to give up vacations and weekends for about a year at least. (4) So I guess you had better cancel those plans for the cruise and sell those tickets. (5) If you can't get away from your desk then you will have to reschedule those plans and recoup your losses as best you can. G = 1, 2, 3; W = 5; C = 4

D. (1) It is raining. (2) If it rains the ground gets wet and the flowers bloom. (3) So I guess we can count on blooming flowers. (4) Oh yeah said a detractor—only if you are not in a desert where the rain dries up before it hits the ground. (5) Well ok with that exception—barring desertification of this area, we can count on the flowers blooming. G = 1, W = 2, C = 3, R = 4, Q = 5

E. (1) Further, we have to go further, (2) we are making good headway. (3) We should see land soon, in maybe a week. [in reply—(4) If your calculations are right, Colombo.] (5) Well, yes, it is not a certainty, but it can be a surety! G = 1, 2; W = X; C = 3; R = 4; Q = 5

F. (1) It was the pitching that won the World Series for Arizona in 2002. (2) You can look at the low earned run average for New York—hardly even a hit in all but one game. (3) The most valuable players were pitchers. (4) The best hitters for New York could do nothing effective on a regular basis in the hitting department—nothing. (5) New York has great pitchers and Arizona has great hitters, (6) but the ones who made it possible were the Arizona pitchers. (7) If you have a combination like this, then you have got a set of victories attributable to the winning pitchers. G = 2, 3, 4; W = 7; C = 1, 6; (5) gives a rhetorical context, setting up the emphasis of the claim in (6). *Notice the repetition of the claim to lead into the argument and then to close the set of particular grounds in an emphatic way.*

G. (1) This is what the experts say—there is global warming. (2) If the experts say something is so, then it is so. (3) So, there is global warming. (4) But not all the experts agree—so (5) maybe I had better say that almost all indications are that there is global warming. (6) Better keep out the shorts and tank tops! G = 1; W = 2; C = 3; R = 4; C + Q = 5; (6) gives another conclusion drawn from the main argument and an assumed warrant about providing weather-appropriate clothing for oneself—it is irrelevant to this argument's structure. *Notice that here the warrant is a principle of knowledge identifying authorities as sources of knowledge or evidence needed for good arguments to support a claim. Of course, earlier discussions have pointed out that one must be careful in appealing to authority. So this warrant could be filled out by listing all the rules for appealing to authority to ensure that it was stated fully.* However, there is no point to that here.

H. (1) Herb and Henrietta both have red hair. (2) A recessive gene controls red hair so that (3) if such a hair color is present, both genes for hair color in a person have to be expressed in red hair color. (4) But if you have both parents with only one type of hair color gene, then the child will have only one type of hair color gene. (5) So this baby is going to have red hair!

Now, this can be analyzed as two linked arguments or as one. Understood as two: the argument is missing a conclusion which then becomes a premise for the second argument: G = 1, 2; W = 3; **C* = Both parents have only one kind of hair color gene.** And with that conclusion you can have G = the assumed claim/premise; W = 4; C = 5. If the passage is taken as containing one argument then the assumed premise/conclusion **C*** is needed as an additional premise and then it goes as follows: G = 1, 2, 3, **and** the assumed premise **C*;** W = 4; C = 5

I. (1) The environment is deteriorating. (2) There is more air pollution as measured by inner city asthma cases. (3) There is more acid rain as measured by lake kills and forest damage. (4) There is more ice melting everywhere in all the glaciers and ice cap areas. (5) There is more desertification everywhere there are humans. (6) All of these things are signs of deterioration if not impending disaster. G = 2, 3, 4, 5; W = 6, C = 1

J. (1) Fine china is really amazing. (2) Just think of the purity of materials and the refinement of processes that are needed to get that thinness and that strength combined with that translucence. (3) Such technological wonders really are works of art and high civilization. (4) Any time you have that sort of technological refinement and purity of materials it marks a real accomplishment of society. G = 2, W = 3, C = 1, B = 4

Mastery Exercises VI.3

SELF TEST

Comprehension Questions

1. What is the function of a warrant?

2. What is the relationship of backing to warrants?

3. What are the sources of backing statements?

4. Can grounds be stated in general assertions about the features of all things of a certain sort?

5. Need all rebuttals be answered in the argument by a qualifier?

6. What kinds of warrants are there? Can you find in some other subject matter some principles of knowledge or reasoning that serve as a warrant?

Mastery Exercises VI.4

SELF TEST

PRACTICE EXERCISES ON THE TOULMIN METHOD OF ARGUMENT OUTLINING. As in the illustrations above, number or put a letter next to each of the premises and conclusions in the following sets of statements and then indicate what are grounds, warrants, claims, and backing, rebuttals, or qualifiers—if there are any. Either put this into the outline form or indicate the results of your work as in the illustrations above. If any crucial items are missing, supply these. (Answers in Appendix II.)

1. Suppose that the President has decided that he will send more troops to the Philippines only if he wants to invade the area held by the rebels. We know he is sending more troops to the Philippines. So on that supposition, he wants to invade the rebels' stronghold.

2. If you want to do well in critical thinking and get as much out of it as possible, then you should do the exercises in the textbook. If you do the exercises in the textbook, then you will need to read the book and ask questions about what you do not understand. So, if you want to do well in critical thinking and get as much out of the course as possible, then you will need to read the book and ask questions about what you do not understand. (Missing a Warrant.)

3. The Pistons are off to a slow start for a former championship team. Either they need to start winning a lot more of their games or they do not have a chance to be champions again. They do not have a prayer of winning a lot more games with their present attitude and personnel, and these do not look like they will change. So they are not going to be champions again.

4. In some places in Russia the pollution from fossil fuels and agricultural chemicals and the health care as well as food quality are so bad that the infant mortality rate is 100+ per thousand live births. In Guatemala, the infant mortality rate is only 30–40 per thousand and in the United States it is much less. So in the United States and in Guatemala, pollution from fossil fuels and agricultural chemicals, health care, and food quality are not as bad as they are in Russia. (Missing a Warrant.)

5. Why don't you try an American car? All successful school principals have tried American cars and I happen to know that you aspire to be a successful high school principal. (Missing an explicit conclusion or claim.)

6. Only if you use your mind and push it like athletes push their physical limits will you grow and become your best mentally. Oedipus did not grow and become his best mentally, nor did Juan and Yerma, so these people did not use their minds and push them like athletes push their physical limits.

7. The world "philosophy" begins with "p". If a name of a discipline begins with a "p" then it is intriguing and rewarding—think of political science and physics. Is it any wonder then that philosophy is intriguing and rewarding?

8. If Jeep closes in Toledo, we should change the base of this city's economy. But we all know that we should change the base of this city's economy regardless. So Jeep is going to close.

9. If you go north from Toledo, Ohio, for five miles, then you will get to Michigan. If you get to Michigan, then you will be in the land of wolverines and other strange beasts. So if you go north five miles, you will be in the land of wolverines and other strange beasts. (Missing a Warrant.)

10. Why bother voting? If your candidate is elected, he or she will only spend her or his time trying to get reelected. And if someone is a good politician she won't spend time trying to get reelected but will tend to the business of the people. So either your candidate is good and will not be reelected or your candidate is bad and is going to get reelected. What's the point? (Missing Grounds and a Warrant.)

SECTION 4

Closing Notes and Transition

This much provides a good introduction to the character of arguments and prepares the ground for the discussion of familiar patterns of reasoning along with an analysis of when they are good and bad. There are two matters to clear up before going on to those matters, however. The first is the problem of missing premises and assessing arguments that, well, are not all there. The second point is a reminder of a topic introduced earlier—the use of qualifiers, and the general lesson attached to it.

Missing Premises

Much of the time, thinkers are so involved in their context that they can anticipate what each other is going to say next. Or they can supply what the other leaves implicit counting on the shared experience and perspective he or she enjoys with the speaker/writer. This often leads to many parts of arguments being left unsaid. Warrants are a frequent omission among those who share a perspective in a community of inquiry. But often grounds and conclusions are left out for the listener or reader to supply. Earlier this was said to be the way in which innuendo works—by the thinker supplying grounds or conclusions and so making the argument her or his own.

The question then arises, how does a thinker know what to supply while interpreting the reasoning of another? How does the thinker distinguish between a case where he or she should supply some element of the argument and one where the person making the argument has just given an argument that is bad because it is not well thought through? Here the requirement of charity will take thinkers some of the way as will their integrity as thinkers who are interested in approaching others through reason and so are inclined to make the best of what the others say in order to find the strongest reasoning to address. But there are no general rules with any degree of particularity greater than this.

Consider an example argument:

> Farmers need less rain at this point. There is a lot of water starting to build up in a lot of fields and many of the seedlings look that yellowish green that plants get when they have too much water.

Notice that there is a lot left out here—for example, the point that farmers want healthy plants, and that too much water is bad for plants seeking to grow to maturity and produce fruit. These are things thinkers take for granted—everybody knows that stuff—so thinkers do not have to explicitly state these points. But they are part of the reasoning, or else the reasoning does not amount to much. Premises are often unstated and when they are left out, thinkers need to supply them to assess the reasoning. Arguments with missing premises are called enthymemes (pronounced "in-tha-meems"). Notice also that lots of times conclusions are unstated. For example, "You are standing on my foot and it hurts." Here there is an argument implied—it is: you are standing on my foot and it hurts. If someone is hurting another, they should stop it. Getting off my foot will stop hurting me. SO, you should get off my foot! Here the conclusion—you should get off my foot—is unstated (as are some of the premises). But thinkers do not have to state all the premises and the conclusion. Everyone has had something fall on a foot and knows that undue pressure hurts.

Now if thinkers want help supplying premises or conclusions in tough cases, there is nothing that will do the job except seeking to understand whom you are reading or speaking with, understanding the perspective of that person, and perhaps understanding where that person is headed in her or his thinking. If one can ask about these matters and clarify them in conversation, then that is the way to proceed. If not and there is a danger of misunderstanding, a good *rule of thumb* is: ***A thinker should proceed so as to supply as little as possible while making the argument as strong as possible.*** Sometimes in doing this one might misinterpret the other's argument. But that is the way it is in exchanging reasons. Sometimes thinkers just get it wrong. In fact, in some cases the speaker or writer is confused or does not know exactly what he/she wants to say. So in some cases there is really nothing to get wrong or get right. *In fact, the lack of clarity in thinking and the selectiveness in articulating one's thoughts both suggest that just what the argument is that one offers is not really settled until an articulation has been tried out and examined by all parties.* Still thinkers have to proceed somehow to assess their own and another's reasoning. *So, if something seems left out, follow "the principle of charity" that suggests that the best thing to do is to interpret and supply missing elements to the reasoning of others so as to make their reasoning as strong as seems warranted in the context.* And then, if possible, ask—"Is that what you are thinking?" This is part of critical thinking in a way that it is not part of logic as will be made clear below in chapter VIII.

The next and final point to mention here is that after looking through the Toulmin analysis pattern, it should be clear why the false use of qualifiers is a way of not expending proper effort in reasoning. Qualifiers could be used to simply duck responsibility for providing the best researched premises from the best sources, with the most well-backed warrants and the best reasoning to reach a conclusion. In any case that fits this problem description, the thinker should not proceed or should make explicit that the evidence is weak, the source could not be trusted fully, the warrant is not well understood or not properly backed, or else the reasoning is weak or flawed in some way. Critical thinkers learn from mistakes that they spot. Knowing any of the things that qualifiers are used irresponsibly to cover up is a good thing. It provides an opportunity to learn things important to reasoning well on some matter.

Wrap Up

ASSESSING ARGUMENTS 101

By now things should be coming together and just how arguments are built is something that should be visible on the horizon. The way evidence flows to the support of the conclusion is something that everyone should be getting the feel of. If so, then a comment or two on assessing arguments should not be out of line. The first thing in assessing arguments is to find the conclusion and then try to get some idea of the line of support offered for that. This line might be of either of two different sorts. **Deductive arguments** seek to provide demonstrations of the truth of their conclusions; they seek to show that the conclusion must be true because the premises are true and the reasoning pattern is such that if the premises are true then the conclusion has to be true. Successful deductive reasoning patterns are *valid* in their process of linking premises and conclusion. Chapter VIII is devoted to some elementary aspects of identifying valid arguments. **Inductive arguments** are those that are intended to give some good *strong* evidence for the conclusion but not evidence that demonstrates the conclusion beyond a shadow of doubt. Inductive premises try to start with true premises all right. But unlike deductive arguments they proceed by a process of reasoning that does not guarantee the truth of the conclusion even if the premises are true. The patterns of inductive reasoning are only going to *make it more or less likely that the conclusion is acceptable if the premises are.* Chapter VII is devoted to looking at some of the elementary aspects of inductive reasoning.

The point to emphasize now is that: (1) once a thinker has identified the premises and conclusion of an argument and (2) has an idea of the structure of the argument, (3) then he or she should check to see if the argument is intended to be deductive or inductive. Once that has been determined the thinker is ready for the next step.

ASSESSING ARGUMENTS 102

The next thing to do is check out whether or not the premises are acceptable. Some of this has been covered—does the premise come from a reliable authority or a commonly accepted definition? And once a thinker has checked out the acceptability of the argument's premises this person will go on to check out the process of reasoning. This can be done after checking to see whether it is a deductive or an inductive argument that is in question.

ASSESSING ARGUMENTS 103

The next step is to actually see if the process of reasoning is reliable to the extent called for by the type of argument. This could be done by learning a long list of patterns of reasoning that are good and bad and then just checking to see where, on which list, the pattern of the argument in question falls. But that is both tedious and unnecessary. Instead there are general processes allowing thinkers to tell good patterns from bad patterns, and then, like the person taught how to fish instead of being given fish to eat, the thinkers can go off and operate on their own. Such ways of separating reasoning well from reasoning poorly are the subject of the following two chapters, VII and VIII.

Notes

[1] See Damasio, A. (1999). *The feeling of what happens, body and emotion in the mmaking of consciousness.* San Diego, New York and London: A Harvest Book, Harcourt, Inc., Chapter One, especially p. 24 and Chapter Two on how thought is practice oriented.

[2] If you are interested in this phenomenon of things being on the brink of chaos or reorganization, you might want to look in, Bak, P. (1995). *How nature works, the science of self-organized criticality.* New York: Copernicus, Springer-Verlag New York Inc.; and Kauffman, S. (1995). *At home in the universe, the search for the laws of self-organization and complexity.* New York and Oxford: Oxford University Press.

[3] Arendt, H. (1978). *The life of the mind.* One Thinking. San Diego: Harcourt, Inc., pp. 14, 15.

[4] Or they no longer do that. See Midgley, M. (2003). *The myths we live by.* London and New York: Routledge, especially chapter 2.

[5] This is a point of criticism that works especially against those who seek to understand the mind fully or predominantly in terms of the work of the brain. See, for example, Ian Hacking's critical review of Damasio's latest book, Hacking, I. *Looking for Spinoza: joy, sorrow, and the feeling brain* by Antonio Damasio. *New York Review of Books,* June 24, 2004, Volume LI, Number 11. Also see Bermudez, J. L. (2003). *Thinking without words.* Oxford and New York: Oxford University Press.

[6] For classical discussions of the nature and types of explanation, see, for example: Nagel, E. (1961). *The structure of science, problems in the logic of scientific explanation.* New York: Harcourt, Brace & World, Inc.; and Achinstein, P. (1983). *The nature of explanation.* New York and Oxford: Oxford University Press.

CHAPTER VII

Getting Along in the World, Some Elementary Concepts and Techniques of Inductive Reasoning

INTRODUCTION

The Culture of Inductive Reasoning

What did you have for breakfast? Many of us had cereal, maybe toast or a muffin or a Pop-Tart. All of these have something in common: they came from or contain mainly grains. And what are these grains essentially? Cereal grains, that is rice, wheat, oats, and even corn, are grasses or rather grass seeds. "But that is crazy—they do not look like grass and they do not taste like grasses." Yes, they really are grasses that have been bred, since agriculture began about 10,000 years ago, to produce the grains we now know. At first individual plants were selected, presumably because they had the largest amounts of the largest seeds and because they went through droughts or disease attacks and met other environmental threats while still producing seeds or grain. Some of these seeds were saved to plant again and to cross pollinate in the gardens or fields and then again were selected in order to pick the individual plants with the greatest yield in the local conditions. And so it went for a long time—individual plants being selected for what served the immediate purposes of food production and resown and crossing in the field again. This crossing and the mechanisms of food plant improvement were unknown to the planters, but eventually they produced the base stock of the plants we have come to know and love to eat today. After the development of genetic theory and learning about the workings of the plant structure itself, planters and breeders were able to become even more deliberately selective, controlling which plants fertilized which plants, and thus were able to physically link the observed traits they were interested in developing in their plants. Even more recently, scientists have partially unraveled the genetic code of cereal grains and can now even identify the genes that produce or control the production of the desired traits like grain size and drought resistance. This allows them to find desirable traits in wild or domesticated plants that can be bred into production crops to improve them even further. Thus humans have moved from the casual association of individual plants and traits they want, to matching kinds of traits in plant stocks, to finding the causes of their desirable traits, all so they know better and better what seed to plant to get greater and more reliable yields. Casual association through generalizations from studied samples, to causal analysis and even genetic manipulation—this progression provides a kind of history of human improvement of food production.

So what? Well, most of those reading this book will be around 65 years of age in 2050. At that time the world will have a population of around 9,000,000,000, yes nine billion. It now has a population of around six billion. So in the span of 46 years the population of the world will have increased by one-half its present size. And what will you eat for breakfast then—assuming the weather cooperates so humans can still grow needed food? Clearly, if humans are eating the same kinds of things, then production has to increase rapidly and tremendously. That makes this little story very, very important to everyone today and all those 3,000,000,000 who will be born and live between now and 2050.

How are humans going to do it? Welcome to the world as seen through inductive reasoning. This chapter will provide an elementary introduction to some aspects of inductive reasoning, that reasoning that reaches beyond the evidence presented to venture a conclusion based on but not guaranteed by that evidence. The order of topics will follow the progress of human seed planters as just sketched above. In approaching a problem like food production, thinkers first must rely on associations and analogies to try to reproduce the features of desired individuals in other desired individuals. Then whole groups of individuals can provide the evidence for making claims about whole populations; thinkers can reason from samples to populations they represent. Finally, with more technique and analysis, humans have gotten at the controlling factors of interest and have seen how they cause the results of interest. As the point might have been put three hundred years ago, thinkers have unlocked the powers of things to bring about specific changes in the world. [This progression of reasoning techniques at work in producing food is, in effect, illustrated well in a recent story on the history of plant breeding: Goff, S. A. and Salmeron, J. M. (2004). Back to the future of cereals. *Scientific American.* August 2004.] Thus this chapter will discuss a bit about arguments from analogy, reasoning from a sample to a generalization, and about causal reasoning.

PATTERNS OF INDUCTIVE REASONING

Arguments from Analogy

This form of reasoning is seen in the early stages of the history of food production. Then, humans did not know much if anything about the mechanisms controlling the inheritance of desirable traits in plants. They only knew they wanted plants that produced seeds like the particular ones they just ate; and they wanted lots of them.

The sort of reasoning used by the first farmers was that of arguing from analogy. This is one, and perhaps the weakest or most unreliable, method of inductive reasoning. In spite of this it is absolutely necessary to thinkers who lack the knowledge of how things work or of what causes what. Not very reliable, but necessary to thinkers when venturing into unknown territory in order to serve some interest—that is the character of this form of reasoning. Now inductive reasoning is a matter of seeking to provide some, but not foolproof or demonstrative, support for a conclusion. The reasoning process of inductive arguments always takes a thinker beyond available evidence and for that reason extends knowledge into the unknown of what exists beyond present experience. Inductive reasoning takes thinkers into the next day, the unexamined case, the unknown behavior of things. But at the same time such reasoning limits knowledge because even if the evidence statements one works with are true, the reasoning patterns themselves are such that there is no guarantee that the conclusion will be true—even if the argument is a good one. Any reasoning with this feature cannot be considered fully reliable. It could go wrong. So inductive reasoning is always less than foolproof. And arguments from analogy are particularly so.

Since thinkers do not always know what specific events or things cause what, they have to rely heavily on analogy when they want to say that since this particular thing or event has two interesting features or processes going together, another specific event or thing which has one of these processes or features will also have the other. (Since this plant has lots of seeds and is good to eat, another like it will also. Since this car is a Yugo and not good, this other car, which is a Yugo, also will not be good.) Analogies proceed on the basis of comparisons of individuals in one regard and seek to extend these comparisons beyond to other features that have not been checked out in experience.

> This shirt is seersucker and very cool on hot days, this other shirt is also seersucker (the observed comparison) and so it will be cool on hot days (the extension of the comparison beyond present experience).

Arguments from analogy are always about specific individuals and proceed by comparing two or more individuals in one or more regards and then thinkers infer that since the individuals compared are alike in some regard they have experienced in both of them, they are also alike in a feature they have experienced in only one of them.

For example: We treated our cut with the herb golden seal before and we got better. This plant looks like that herb. So if we treat our cut with this plant we will get better.

The general form of arguments from analogy is the following:

The warrant is:	Similarities in one regard are generally accompanied by similarities in another regard.
The grounds are:	Object or event 1 has property or process P
	Object or event 2 has property or process P
	Object 1 also has property or process Q
Therefore:	Object or event 2 also has property or process Q

Now, even though reasoning of this sort is extremely risky, there are rules we can follow to find relatively strong arguments from analogy and to separate them out from relatively weak arguments from analogy. There are four of these rules.[1] These and their rationales can be set out as follows:

The first three are rules citing circumstances under which an argument from analogy is stronger than it otherwise would be if it did not meet the condition of the rule. The last or fourth rule is one for noting when and why an argument from analogy is relatively weaker than it might otherwise have been.

1. **The argument is stronger the greater the number of cases there are in which the analogy (or comparison of interest) holds up.**

   For example: "Last week I had a peanut butter, lettuce, and mustard sandwich. This past Tuesday I had a peanut butter, lettuce, and mustard sandwich.

And both times I have felt incredibly relaxed afterwards. In fact, I have eaten over five hundred and fifty such sandwiches over the last two years and each time I got that very relaxed feeling afterwards. I am nervous and going to lunch. I think I'll have a peanut butter, lettuce, and mustard sandwich. And the sandwich I have then will make me feel relaxed again."

This argument from analogy to a particular conclusion about feeling well fits rule one. This business about relaxation might be just so much superstition or self-fulfilling prophecy. But at least by this rule the argument is stronger than it otherwise would be.

Why should this be so? Why should thinkers rely on such a rule for assessing or constructing arguments from analogy? Well, the basic idea is that if events in nature are not causally connected they are just random and it would seem very, very unlikely to have two properties like eating such a sandwich and feeling a certain way going together for over five hundred occurrences if they were not really connected somehow. So in following this rule, the analogy might seem to get at some real connection between features or processes. That is the backing for this rule when it is followed in an argument from analogy.

 2. **The argument is stronger the more ways in which the objects, events, persons, etc. being compared are alike in ways in addition to that of the first comparison.**

For example: This red car is a Ferrari 308 GTS roadster with a V-12 engine and a six-speed transmission. It is very fast. This other red car is also a Ferrari 308 GTS roadster with a V-12 engine and a six-speed transmission. It will also be very fast.

Why should this be so? Why should thinkers rely on this rule? The basic idea here is that the more the similarities between the things being compared, the greater the likelihood that one of the properties in which they are similar will ensure that the comparison of interest holds up. In the example, since the cars were the same brand and had the same engine and transmission and body style, it was more likely that they would both be fast than if they were just the same brand and for example, one had a V-8 and the other a V-12 engine. The more similarities, the more likely it seems that something relevant to the comparison of interest—the cars being fast—would be ensured. This is what people count on when they buy a car after scoping it out in some consumer magazine, and when they buy franchised or name brand food goods. And with cars, that expectation is why there is such a thing as a lemon law.

 3. **The argument is *stronger* the greater the number of cases in which the analogy holds up where the objects, events, or persons are otherwise different.**

For example: "Dora, Darnell, David, Dierrdra, and Daisy all bought cars at Devilish Dan's Dandy Dodges. Dora got a convertible. Darnell got a Caravan (mini-van). David bought a 4-door mid-size Stratus. Dierrdra got the Dodge version of the Neon. Daisy took the Viper. All these Dodges were dependable. I'm going to buy a Dodge Shadow at Devilish Dan's Dandy Dodges because I want a dependable car."

Why should this decision be a good one? Why should thinkers rely on this rule? The basic idea is that the more cases where the connection of interest holds up (buying a Dodge automobile and getting a reliable car) and where the things being compared are otherwise different (in this case different models), then the greater the chance that there is some direct connection between the properties where the comparison holds up—in the example a connection between being a Dodge product from Devilish Dan's and being dependable. Again there are no guarantees here. But in such cases it looks like a good explanation of the comparison holding up, in spite of all these differences, is that there is a real causal or other connection between the properties of interest. And if that is so, that connection will ensure that the comparison holds up again in the next case.

4. **The argument is *weaker* the greater the number of ways the two objects, persons, events, etc. under comparison differ from each other and no reason is given to believe these differences do not make a difference to whether the comparison of interest holds.**

   For example: "Last year Herb had a garden and grew all his own vegetables for the year. Sally raised sheep, sheared them, spun wool, and knitted all the wool clothing she needed for the winter. Lucy cut and barked trees, aged, treated, and notched them, then built her own home. The only thing these three had in common is that they are humans. I'm a human. I think I'll build a battleship this year. Let's see, do I want a Forestall class, a Russian or a Japanese design, or . . ."

Why should thinkers mark an argument from analogy as weaker in cases where there are unexplained differences or differences between the things being compared than when there is no reason given for believing the differences are irrelevant to the comparison? Why should thinkers pay attention to unexplained differences? In the example, there are many unexplained differences between building a battleship and gardening and making wool clothing—from scratch, so to speak. Sure, all those involved were humans, but there is no reason for believing that this comparison gives individuals the ability to do everything, even build a battleship. This case is not like the case for the third rule, for there one sees that a difference in model and all that entails does not make a difference to being Dodges from Devilish Dan's and also being dependable. Here in the battleship example one might well believe that there were lots of reasons for the abilities of these individuals and that they had nothing essential to do with being human. But in the Dodge case, it seems to be beyond coincidence that there is some connection between being a Dodge or being set up by a dealer and being dependable. The standardization of designs and manufacturing procedures usually involved, very likely would make that connection a usual thing. There is no similar standardization among humans and there is no such standardization among the tasks involved in the example, especially between building a battleship and the other less complex tasks. Differences that are unexplained in this way are going to weaken an argument from analogy.

Rule One says: the greater the number of cases where the comparison of interest holds up, the stronger the argument.

Rule Two says: the greater the number of similarities there are between the objects being compared the stronger the argument. (Of course things would be even better if the similarities are known to be relevant to a connection between the properties singled out in the comparison—for example, being a red Ferrari GTS with a V-12 engine and being fast. But, as in the ancient crop breeding example, typically if arguments from analogy are needed it is because the thinkers do not know what is relevant to what, or how it might be relevant.)

Rule Three says: the greater number of case where the comparison of interest holds up and what is compared is otherwise different, the stronger the argument.

Rule Four says: the greater number of unexplained differences there are between the things compared, the weaker the argument.

Mastery Exercises VII.1

SELF TEST

PRACTICE ASSESSING ARGUMENTS FROM ANALOGY. Notice the Tech Tips above. Reflect on the following arguments, finding the conclusion and then the premises. Decide what rule for assessing arguments from analogy the argument is a case of and note whether the argument is stronger or weaker because of that. Write a sentence explaining your assessment. (Answers in Appendix II.)

1. "This hammock looks comfortable, but it hurt my back. That hammock looked comfortable, but hurt my back. In fact all the 53 hammocks I tried out at Herb's Hammock Hut looked very comfortable but hurt my back. Here is another one of those tempting hammocks. It looks so comfortable, but I'll bet it is really going to hurt my back."

2. "This Krost pen was expensive and hard to hold. It was the Elegance model. This other pen is a Krost and in the Elegance line. I'll bet it is just as hard to hold and just as expensive."

3. "The medicine came in a blue bottle, tasted like chalk, and was very potent. This medicine comes in a blue bottle, and tastes like chalk. I'll bet it is very potent also."

4. "Shama's fleece lined jacket came from Richard's and was made by Bolumbia. It was very warm. Wow, look at this great color in a fleece lined jacket on clearance at Richard's! It's a Bolumbia. I'll bet it is really warm."

5. "Caleb's new computer has a 15 GHz speed processor. It was made by NoWay Computers especially for gaming. And it has 500 megs of RDRAM. He says it is really cool in the special effects it gives gamers. I am going to NoWay to get one of their 15 GHz gaming computers with the 500 megs of RDRAM. I can't wait for those wild special effects as I play."

6. "Herb went to the swamp and saw the flying saucers. Henrietta was with him and saw the same thing. Before them Betty, Francine, Henry, Juan, Yerma, and President Grant had all been to that swamp and saw the flying saucers. I'm going tonight. I can't wait to finally see some flying saucers myself."

7. "My buddy's Krell WhizBang computer has Garmon/Kardon speakers. They are great. And I found these great knock-off G/K speakers! I can't wait to hook them up to my PlodAlong word processor. I'm sure the sound will be wonderful."

8. "Stewed okra, or slicks, is disgusting to eat. It's strange because fried okra is a wonderful tasting dish. It's just like, well, seasoned french fried potatoes. I'll bet fried spinach is great too. Stewed it's disgusting but fried, I'll bet it's great. It's what's for supper tonight."

9. "Henrietta's dress is a designer evening gown from Chic of Chantilly; Daisy's dress is a designer sundress from SunnyShoulders. Freda's dress is a designer workplace model from HappyPays. Dierrdra's dress is a designer maternity model from GreatExpectations. They were all expensive dresses. My designer gardening dress from GrowingGreen is going to be expensive also. But I'm going to get it anyway!"

10. "I have the Funky Wintergreen's first album of chamber music. It is great. I also have the Spearmint Twins first CD of folk music, and that is great. The Yankee Chicklets first recorded jazz work was super. Should I get this new CD, the first Ambient-Rock Fusion work by the Big Red? All the other 'chewing gum name' first CDs I have are wonderful. This one will be too."

SECTION 2

Arguments from a Sample to a Generalization

At some point arguments from particular cases to particular cases concerning whether a certain connection of properties will hold up can be left behind in favor of arguing that connections between properties hold in whole populations because they are found in a smaller group taken as a sample of the larger population. This is illustrated by research reported in the grain genetics article mentioned above. The authors of the article discuss the work of a scientist in evolutionary anthropology looking at the development of the corn plant by early farmers. This individual studied corn that was domesticated approximately four and one-half millennia ago in one region of Mexico. He concluded that all the corn in that area had important characteristics that also happen to be features of modern corn. The research was based on looking at corn cobs. But, clearly, the researchers did not look at the cobs of every piece of corn grown there over some period of time. That would have been impossible. Presumably they were not there to be found and studied. The cobs that were found could only constitute a sample or a smaller subset of the actual population of corn cobs generated by the farmers there and then. Such reasoning from a smaller representation of the larger population, to the properties of the whole or some percentage of the population is what this discussion takes as reasoning from a sample to a generalization. What are the properties and pitfalls of such a pattern of reasoning? That is the subject of this sub-section.

The sorts of arguments in question proceed from the properties of the members of a sample to the properties of all or some percentage of the members of an entire group of things. In this reasoning thinkers move past the sample, or past the things examined and taken as representing the whole group, to a claim about all the members of the group—examined or not. This is a fundamentally important sort of argument since it is basically the central form of reasoning used in science and engineering to reach generalizations when thinkers are trying to move from observations of occurrences to general claims about the kinds of things that were observed. (Science also proceeds by (1) forming hypotheses and seeking to refute them, and by (2) arguing that a certain general claim will provide the best explanation of what is observed so it must be true. These are not the present concerns.) *The sort of reasoning of interest here is called various things: inductive generalizations, statistical generalizations, and even inductive enumerations.* The last label is incorrect, or at least misleading, since to enumerate the members of a group involves considering each one and this departs from reaching a generalization on the basis of a sample or a consideration of only a (supposedly) representative subset of the entire group.

So what is the general form of inductive generalizations? And what are the problems one might encounter in reasoning this way? These arguments note a pattern in some portion of a whole group (the sample) and project that pattern over the entire group.

The warrant is:	The sample is representative of the entire group or collection in question, so the patterns of the relationships between properties or events of various sorts seen in the sample are also patterns in the entire group.
The grounds are:	Such arguments are listed in a statement of what is found in the sample:
	Object 1 has properties P and Q
	Object 2 has properties P and Q
	Object 3 has properties P and Q
	Object 4 has properties P and Q
	(And so on to some number of cases N)
	Object N has properties P and Q
Therefore:	All objects with property P also have property Q.

The sample might reveal that only a certain percentage of the cases examined show a co-occurrence of properties P and Q, for example 47%, and the conclusion should be limited to reflect that, so instead of concluding that all objects with property P have property Q, one should conclude that 47% do, or almost half do, or perhaps, "for present purposes a significant number do." In such a case one might want to speak of a *statistical* generalization as opposed to an inductive generalization.

Notice that this sort of an argument—an inductive generalization—does not establish anything more than a **co-occurrence or a correlation** of two or more properties or kinds of events. This is not the same as reasoning to a causal or else to any kind of necessary connection between occurrences of the properties in question. If a thinker samples voting habits among factory workers and finds that 67% vote Democratic and then concludes that 67% of all factory workers vote Democratic, he/she might well have good reason to believe that for two-thirds of factory workers, the kind of work they do or their working conditions, or some other work related factors cause, and so go with voting Democratic. But the thinker has not shown this in coming to the generalization. Co-occurrence or correlations which these arguments give evidence of are not necessarily more than two or more properties going together with some regularity. In a later section the discussion turns to causation and the connection between events or properties occurring together in the world.

Now when is this sort of reasoning good? *When does it give conclusions that critical thinkers can trust or when is it reliable, and how strong is that reliability?* A second look at the warrant for such arguments should make clear the fact that everything turns on getting a sample that really does represent the patterns of connection between the properties of interest as these patterns are found in the entire group under investigation. And there are two general ways that things can go wrong with a sample so that it is not representative of the patterns of the property connection in the entire group. The sample might not be large enough and the sample might be biased.

SOME REMARKS ON SAMPLE SIZE. Take out a quarter from the coins in the piggy bank and flip it in the air, catch it, and turn it over on the table in front of you. Heads or tails (obverse or converse)? Mark down the results. Do it again for a total of thirty-five flips. Suppose the pattern is 12 heads and 23 tails. Is this sufficient to tell us that if you flip a quarter you will get tails about two-thirds of the time and heads the remaining third of the time? Well, probably not. After all, assuming that the coin is not weighted unevenly or there is no other special feature to make it come down one way or the other, there is a fifty-fifty chance that flipping the coin will bring up heads or tails. That is, heads should come up about fifty percent of the time, not 33 percent. What has gone wrong with the reasoning? Well, there might be several things. Maybe one should not infer anything from the fact that quarters have two sides and so, in theory, if there is nothing pushing the coin one way or the other, one can expect it to show up heads about fifty tosses out of one hundred. (Maybe there is no connection between probabilities determined before experience and those determined after experience.) Maybe there is some undiscovered fact of the universe that quarters come up heads about half as often as tails? Well, what would one think of that explanation—perhaps it goes against well-established theory, and is needlessly complex or is just unclear? In fact, if the coin is "fair," that is, there is nothing about it that makes it come down tails more often than heads, then the flips should evenly distribute between heads and tails. So what has gone wrong?

Well, maybe the problem is that the coin has not been flipped enough times to show the real patterns of distribution of heads versus tails in the flip results? This might come under the familiar cliché—"wait long enough and you'll see it all." That could very well be the problem and in fact one can test it, of course. If one flips the coin a sufficient number of times and there is nothing about it that makes it come down on one side more often than the other, then it will come out about fifty-fifty. Flipping it a sufficient number of times would have allowed the true pattern of distribution of heads and tails to show itself. This would be an expression of the Law of Large Numbers saying that what is unlikely to emerge as a pattern in a small number of cases becomes more likely in a larger number of cases.[2]

So the first thing necessary to inductive generalizations being relatively strong is that they must rest on a sample that considers a sufficiently large number of cases of what is under examination. If a sample is not of an acceptable size then the generalization from it is said to commit the *fallacy of being a hasty generalization.*

What is a sufficiently large number of cases? Of course a sample including every item covered by the generalization would be perfect if one wants relative certainty. But that would defeat the purpose of the sampling approach to supporting generalizations. But this also gives a clue to the answer to the question here. Up to a point, the larger the sample, the more confident thinkers can feel about their generalizations, and the less they would have to qualify them by limiting the claim of the conclusion. But this leaves things unsuitably vague. So return to the corn example for a moment. The researchers in evolutionary anthropology found corn cobs in several sites and had them analyzed to determine what sorts of shape the plant they came from might have had, and what sorts of food values they offered. Presumably, these cobs were of the sorts that were being consumed by the people who grew them and there were no others so succulent that the whole ear, cob and all, was consumed leaving no evidence to analyze. That is, presumably what was found was uniform and not special in some way relative to corn crops of the time and region so that it was as if they were **randomly** selected or that these cobs individually had as much of a chance of being selected as any other corn to be treated as they were and to end up on the scientist's bench. If so, then using statistical concepts and tables, a numerically very precise answer could be given as to how many of these cobs should have been found to give the food value patterns and the plant structure patterns of the entire crop from the areas where the samples were collected. Presumably the total harvest was large in number of cobs, and if it was more than 10,000 cobs of corn, then if the sample was really random, it would be sufficient for a high level of confidence if the sample included 1,000 to 1,500 cases. In order to be justified in being almost completely sure of the generalization that all the corn cobs of that era had those properties, the number of the cobs sampled would not have to be larger. If the total population were smaller, then, statistically, the sample size could be adjusted downward and still yield a generalization that deserved the same confidence.[3]

Thus to be justified in being highly confident of a correlation in a whole population, basing one's judgment on a sample:

- One needs to suit sample size to the size of the total population.

- In increasing sample size, there are diminishing returns so that while a sample size of 1000 for a total population of 9,000 will justify a very high confidence level of surety, increasing that to 1,500 or 2,000 will not raise that level greatly.

- Statistical analysis can tell you what the sample size should be if your claim is to come very close to the way things are, or within a certain error margin.

- So there is a mathematical technique for determining appropriate sample size.

However, the solution is not just that statistics can answer the size question, and so for a precise answer to the question "how big should the sample be" all you need is to take a statistics class. That is only part of the story. There are several qualifications to make.

First, if the population of interest for the generalization is truly homogenous and thus a sample really can be randomly made, then the sample might need to be only quite small. Suppose that Pastoral Farms Dairy is processing milk today from cows grazed on the lower forty. The cows are all the same breed, have had all the same health treatments and protections, the equipment was all cleaned before the batch was processed, the processing was the same for all of the milk, the containers are all the same in production source and design and materials, and the milk was all mixed thoroughly in cooling vats before being processed, none of the machinery had a breakdown during the run, there were no power outages, and so on. Suppose that 10,000 quarts of milk are packaged that day. Then should the owners of Pastoral Farms take 1000–1500 quarts off the line and sample them for purity? There seems to be no real need or justification for that. If any one of the quarts has the same stuff put in, in the same way, and put in the same containers, then what would be the point other than to wipe out 10–15% of the production for that day—something a competitor might be interested in, but not the owners of Pastoral Farms! It would seem adequate to pull off a small number of quarts and sample them to certify that the entire batch of milk is pure and marketable. Of course, most of the time thinkers cannot count on such homogeneity.

Second, as is made clear by the previous example, sampling in the real world requires time and money. Both of these factors can limit what one takes to be needed for a strong inductive generalization. The dairy example is one case in point with regard to money. Consider another where things are not so simple. For example, suppose that someone wants to learn about the views of the student body on what changes would be most beneficial for the university (aside from lowering tuition, of course). A thinker might try to take a poll, sampling opinion on the relative merits of

(1) free tailgate parties before every football game, (2) easier access to grades and class schedules, (3) longer hours for the library, (4) more food choices in the student union, and (5) the development of a shopping village on university grounds. Such a survey costs money to construct, money to administer, and money to analyze after the responses are in. Suppose the researcher has money to process a survey of only four items instead of the five listed and he or she has money to poll only 1% of the students instead of 5% or 7.5% of the 20,000 students. Then the researcher must make a choice about what options to consider—in fact, the above list obviously reflects some choices about what to include and what to leave out (free stables and horse feed for all students riding a horse to school are left out, for example). And the researcher must talk to students in numbers that might not give an accurate reading of the student pulse on campus. So if the researcher runs a poll to determine student views on beneficial changes at the university, the results will not necessarily be representative of the real student-body views because he or she can only poll so many students on so many possible changes. The real views on what would be beneficial changes might go unknown. Still the researcher can indicate all of this, pointing out that the results cover only some of the possible options and a sample size that requires the conclusion be qualified. Perhaps the researcher would want to conclude only that of the four items in the poll, 200 students preferred an addition to the student union over all the other options. Of course, such a carefully qualified report would not ring many bells for reader appeal in the campus newspaper.

Third, clearly, sample size can be limited by the time researchers have also, regardless of the funds they have to expend. A thinker might be limited in time because of poor planning, because of a danger he or she is trying to take care of with the information to be collected (for example, a survey on who has had what immunizations and diseases so as to know how best to cope with a terrible bacterium that has made its way onto campus), or because of a schedule that has been imposed by uncontrolled and unpredictable circumstances. Whatever the reason, the ideal of a sample sufficiently large to truly reveal the pattern of connections between properties or occurrences researchers are interested in will sometimes be hard to achieve. And so while good critical thinking in making inductive generalizations should strive for a sufficiently large sample, all things considered, thinkers might have to, and *sometimes should* settle for less. But then they should say so as well. Thus assessing inductive generalizations is complicated by the circumstances of particular situations where samples are sought and used.

In the end then:

1. If dealing with truly homogeneous populations, where there is nothing to distinguish the items in the population, one from another, as far as the correlation of the properties of interest is concerned (the milk packaged at that plant that day and its purity, for example), then samples can be small in number and warrant high levels of confidence. They should be randomly taken, but in the circumstances of this

degree of homogeneity this is a procedural caution not a substantive guarantee of the reliability of the inference.

2. In the case of situations where the populations are large and generally homogeneous, a random sample can be properly sized by statistical procedures. In the case that these are not available, the *rule of thumb* is that ***the larger the sample the stronger the level of confidence that is warranted.***

3. Samples will not always be large enough and yet for any of a variety of reasons that might be the best that can be done. In such cases, qualifications of how a generalization based on a sample is stated should be explicit and appropriate. The school superintendent who must reach a generalization that students with certain symptoms or with certain diseases are a threat to others and must be kept home, often will have to make such determinations even though the generalizations could be marked as hasty. Still they must act, sometimes with tragic results as with the suspension from school of children with HIV/AIDS, before more was learned about its transmission. Thus, though it appears paradoxical, while a hasty generalization is fallacious reasoning, sometimes it is what is best overall for a critical thinker to rely on.

SOME REMARKS ON SAMPLE BIAS. The other sort of problem which can come up in making inductive generalizations is that the sample, whether large enough or not, is biased: the sample cases a thinker chooses to look at are not truly representative of the whole population under consideration. Let us go back to the quarter flipping for a moment. Notice that one reason the quarter might have landed on the reverse more often than on the obverse side is that there is something uneven about the weight distribution of the sides of the quarter so that that ⅓, ⅔ result comes about. Thus selecting this particular coin might give a biased picture of the result one would get if he or she flipped many quarters a sufficient number of times.

Another example will perhaps lock in these ideas. Suppose a thinker wants to find out what fathers have meant in the lives of children and suppose he or she decides to sample a large number of daughters of divorced fathers in order to see what sorts of properties are associated with being a father. Will the thinker be likely to get the entire and unbiased picture? No, of course not. The fact that the person is talking only to daughters and not also sons, and to only divorced fathers as opposed to those who are still married but separated, still married and living with the child's mother, neither divorced nor living with the mother because of the illness or death or other circumstances of the mother, can be expected to make a difference to the results. In other words, there are all sorts of circumstances in which fathers and children come together, or not, and where there is an influence for good or ill exercised by the father in the life of the child. If one were seeking to identify and determine how pervasive these influences are, one would have to look at all sorts of cases showing all the possible relationships between father and child, so as to be able to avoid the bias introduced by looking at only some sorts of cases of the influence of fathers on children.

How does a thinker avoid bias in sampling? Well, the answer in part should be clear from the milk packaging example above. In part it depends upon whether there are a lot of differences in the population that might make a difference to the fact and nature of the connections between the correlated items under study—a heterogeneous population, or whether the population is very much the same throughout—homogeneous. A good *rule of thumb* is: ***If the population is homogeneous, then a thinker need only randomly select cases to sample using some method of picking them out which gives as much of a chance of being selected to any one in the population as to any other.*** And, another good *rule of thumb* is: ***If the population is heterogeneous, then the researcher needs to make the sample reflect the sorts of differences in the population as a whole that might make a difference to the connections of properties that are being studied.***

The milk example is one case of a homogeneous population of study. But many things are so standardized these days that any one might be selected and serve well as part of an unbiased sample. Suppose you need to test screwdrivers for a company known for its quality of product and for its quality control during manufacturing. Then reaching into the bin and pulling out any one or more of the screwdrivers made that day according to usual specifications would serve to get an unbiased sample for you to take to the lab. Unfortunately the world is not always so simple. In fact, what is usual is difference among the things and events of the world, and what is constant is change. Most samples are going to be heterogeneous in ways that might make a difference to the correlation one is interested in studying. For example, maybe 70% of the manufacturing jobs are now held by workers with more than a high school diploma and of that group maybe 35% hold an advanced degree. These differences in years and achievements in education might make a difference to how these persons vote. So if one conducts research on voting behavior of persons holding manufacturing jobs, these differences might be things that have to be reflected in the construction of the sample. How about another example?

Suppose one wants to determine whether or not calling on 4th graders to read aloud in class retards their progress in learning to read (the subject of a highly informal personal reflection by the scholar of education and former elementary school teacher, John Holt). A person could not assume that all 4th graders or all 4th grade classes are the same in important ways. Maybe those children from a home where they have been read to are more confident and more tolerant of criticism when making a mistake in reading. Maybe those from high achieving homes, even if they have been read to, are less tolerant of criticism because they have been sensitized by too much criticism. Maybe some classrooms are more critical and more stressful than others. Maybe being in a private versus public, or a parochial versus secular, school makes a difference. Maybe being in an urban school, an inner-city school, or a suburban school makes a difference. And so it goes. In this sort of case a random selection might not give a true picture of the entire population because it could end up selecting only a portion of the cases representing a portion of the trends of influences in reality. (The sample would have to be random, not just across an entire population, but random for each of the different sub-populations the research has to consider, and representative of the proportion of each of these sub-populations in the entire population.) *Here, instead of relying on a simple random sample across the entire population of 4th graders, researchers would have to carefully identify what they think are influencing differences among students and schools and classrooms and then find what percentage of the total population has these various differentiating features. Then they would have to construct a sample that has the same percentages of the differences that might make a difference, as there are cases of such differences in the total population. This sample, called a* **stratified sample,** *will be much less likely to be biased than one where we do not go to all this trouble.*

   Bias in a sample comes about when one constructs that sample so that it is not representative of the whole population because it overlooks some important influence on the possible correlation being studied. Suppose a thinker only looks at those individuals who go to the best schools with the most favorable student-teacher ratio and come from loving supportive homes where questioning each other is encouraged. Then the results of looking at that group might well indicate that there is no connection between calling on 4th graders to read out loud and difficulties in learning to read. But what about the rest of the children who do not fit that biased profile? If research factors them in then a different result might very well come out. In effect this is what is wrong with **polls** that have self-selected respondents, or are worded in ways that direct the respondent to answer in a way that does not reveal her or his true beliefs or preferences (see the fallacies of chapters II and III above). In either case what is most often revealed is a bias, not a representation of the general populace. (For example, a survey of those attending the Republican and Democratic national conventions might get lots of responses when it is concerned with the reasons why the Republican platform is so strong. But this research would be biased in two ways—it is likely to get only positive *or* negative responses from each of the conventions, and secondly the questions would be loaded by the assumption built into the survey that the Republican platform is quite strong.)

Hasty and Biased Generalizations and Anecdotal Stories _____

So there are two general sorts of problems that inductive generalizations run into—reasoning from a sample that is insufficiently large—called the fallacy of hasty generalization, and reasoning from a biased sample. There is a third sort of problem with some reasoning that looks like generalizing from a sample. This is what is called **relying on an anecdote.** *In this context an anecdote is a story relating the personal experiences of one or more individuals (usually the speaker or acquaintances) which suggests some correlation, and is taken as evidence for the truth of the generalization claiming that correlation.* For example: "When my taxes were audited I worked with the nicest person. This individual was patient, understanding, and kind. I don't know what all the fuss is about. All audits are a piece of cake." Well, some might disagree, but the real point is that this argument to a generalization is not based on a sample at all. To do research with a sample involves selecting some cases of a population to represent the entire population and then to argue that correlations found, or not found, there are in the entire population, or not. However happy one might be for the person who told the story about the tax audit, this story was not the reporting of research involving a sampling of some population.

So this has been a quick and elementary look at the general features and pitfalls of inductive generalizations. In order to fix ideas consider the following examples and decide whether they are acceptable or unacceptable bits of reasoning. Can you say why they are as you think they are?

1. **"For years, I have been rolling the bills of my baseball caps by putting them overnight in Pringles cans. I've done this with approximately 37 baseball caps. And all my friends at school (a high school of 3700 students where I am the most popular student there, and everyone wears baseball caps) do the same. Even the dorks at the school do that and it always works. So all baseball cap bills can be rolled effectively with Pringles cans."**

At first glance, this might strike one as a reasonably good generalization. The sample might well be a large number of the 3700 students at the speaker's high school. Although this number is not precise, since the speaker is the most popular person at the school one might well believe that the speaker would count a very large percentage of the 3700 students as friends and then as people who roll their baseball cap bills with Pringles cans. If this reasoning is not acceptable, then the argument is weak since it could involve only a few, up to maybe a hundred, or ?? friends, and that would make for a hasty generalization since the sample size would be too small to represent the entire school population, let alone the entire country or wherever people wear baseball caps with rolled bills. Pringles cans and baseball caps might be fairly standardized in size, strength, and so on, so there might be no problems of possibly relevant differences weakening the argument here. However, the account tells nothing about the location and student body make-up of the school. It is a large and probably diverse high school. But if the speaker's friendship circle is not very large, or the high school is extraordinary in some way—say by being in a rich suburb of California, then examining a sample from that school only or a sample of her/his friends alone might bias the sample. Finally, since the conclusion is drawn for all baseball cap bills, this should have a qualifier relating the conclusion to the high school in question. Alternatively, the argument needs larger sample numbers and some assurance that the bills on all baseball caps are the same or very similar in relevant respects everywhere. If one had to judge, the argument is definitely hasty if the generalization covers all people and caps everywhere. Maybe it is biased, but that is not clear by any means.

2. **"I sampled three of the 47 aardvark hunters in the world. They all use old Pentax cameras. So all the aardvark hunters in the world use old Pentax cameras."**

There are only a few aardvark hunters in the world according to this claim. But still three is a relatively small percentage of a relatively small number. Maybe there is a direct connection between the sort of person to hunt aardvarks and using an old Pentax camera. But this sample is likely too small to get at such a connection in this way. Further, there is no clear evidence that the three selected are not special in some way. Maybe they all lived in the hometown of the researcher, Aardvarkville, which also happens to have the world's largest and finest outlet and service center for Pentax cameras? So it definitely seems hasty, but maybe it is also biased.

3. **I have sampled 51 of the leading fashion photographers. Some use Pentax cameras. Some use Minoltas. Some use Sony. Some use Panasonic. But these are all single lens reflex cameras. So all the leading fashion photographers use single lens reflex cameras."**

Here one does not know how many leading fashion photographers there are so there is no way of telling whether the sample is too small and so the generalization is hasty, without further work. The statement of the argument is simply too vague. But one can see that the person making the generalization has looked at a number of different brands of cameras used in the fashion photography business. And they all seem to be single lens reflex. So there is no reason to believe the sample was biased. However, because of the lack of information on the total number of leading photographers of this sort, one should withhold judgment since this might be a hasty generalization.

Mastery Exercises VII.2

SELF TEST

PRACTICE ASSESSING ARGUMENTS TO A GENERALIZATION FROM A SAMPLE.
Reflect on the following arguments finding the conclusion and then the premises.
Decide whether the argument is good or bad and select the option that answers that
question. Write a sentence or two explaining why that is the correct answer. (Answers
in Appendix II.)

1. Nutritionists have studied samples of Big Macs, Whoppers, and Wendy's Classics.
   These samples were collected from 10,000 of those restaurants in the best neighborhoods, around the world. In every case, the meat in the burgers was found to
   be properly cooked and meeting all local health regulations. So we can eat with
   confidence at any of these sorts of restaurants, throughout the world, knowing
   that their burgers are going to be properly cooked and meeting all local health
   standards. This generalization is: (a) good, (b) bad because of too small a sample,
   (c) bad because biased, (d) both biased and hasty.

2. AMF was interested in testing the roll of its bowling balls when thrown on different alleys. They wanted to claim that their bowling balls rolled fastest of all bowling balls in all kinds and conditions of alleys. So they went to five lanes in the town
   of their corporate offices. One alley had just resurfaced the lanes and the varnish
   had just dried and hardened enough to use. One alley was old and worn out with
   scuffed and dented lanes. The other three were all somewhere in between. In
   these varied conditions with a standard machine driven roller they tested the
   speed of their bowling balls against three of the nine leading brands of bowling
   balls. The AMF balls were the fastest on all of the different lane conditions. So
   their next ad campaign said that AMF Bowling Balls are the fastest anywhere, any-
   time. This generalization based on that research is: (a) good, (b) biased, (c) hasty,
   (d) both biased and hasty.

3. Bruce and Brenda raised Burgundy wine grapes. They had 1400 acres planted
   with the same variety of these and these were all on the same river valley hillside
   facing the same direction and with the same degree of slope. They needed to know
   just when to pick the grapes and so they tested when it got close to time. But they
   only wanted to test a few spots so as not to waste grapes needlessly. All the grapes
   received the same amount of water and had the same nutrients in the soil. So
   their researchers just picked only 10 vines at random and sampled one bunch
   of grapes from each vine. On this basis they decided all the grapes would be perfect to pick on August 20. The generalization was (a) good, (b) biased, (c) hasty,
   (d) both biased and hasty.

4. George, a professional cigar taster, sampled Cubano Supremos cigars for the manufacturer. The cigar company knew that the cigars are smoked about 60% of the
   time with coffee, about 30% of the time with brandy, and 10% of the time with no
   beverage. George tested the cigars with each of the three outer tobacco wrappers
   being considered—A, B, and C. He tested each of the wrappers with an equal num-

ber of trials with coffee, brandy, and with no beverage—five trials with each of the wrappers with coffee, brandy and no beverage. He concluded that overall the best tasting smoke was with wrapper B. His generalization was (a) good, (b) biased, (c) hasty, (d) both biased and hasty, (e) anecdotal.

5. Henderson was salesperson of the month for 11 months last year. At the award ceremony she was asked what was the secret to good sales records. Her answer? "Selling is easy. It just amounts to stubbornness—being unwilling to take no for an answer from your potential customer. Every sale is like an argument; you have to insist on winning it." Her generalization was: (a) good, (b) biased, (c) hasty, (d) both biased and hasty, (e) anecdotal.

6. Freda Fremont flew kites for fun. She preferred the new plastic stunt kites. She was going to get a new one and wanted the most durable. There were four brands to choose from and Freda sampled each of them twice in different conditions: the Fremont Flyer in rain and snow—it did not last, the Frequent Flyer in sun and near tornado conditions—it did not last, the Faster Flyer in hurricanes and sleet— it did not last, and the Fragile Flyer in sun and light breezes and sun and moderate winds—it was just fine. So the most durable stunt kite is the Fragile Flyer. The generalization is (a) good, (b) biased, (c) hasty, (d) both biased and hasty.

7. Horace wanted to confirm the connection between lightning and ozone (that chemical that makes the air smell funny sometimes after a lightning strike). He took his ozone detector to Kansas in the summer and was able to sample the air within 500 feet of the strike almost immediately after 10,000 lightning strikes. He found very high concentrations of ozone after each strike. Horace concluded that lightning strikes are always accompanied by ozone. The generalization is (a) good, (b) biased, (c) hasty, (d) both biased and hasty.

8. The U.S. government was recently asked by a small beef packer who wanted to get its Japanese business back whether it could test every cow slaughtered for mad cow disease. The government said no, it would be too expensive for larger producers and it is unnecessary. (See the AP story by Kenji Hall, U.S., Japan compromise on mad cow tests. July 22, 2004.) So 6% of the cows slaughtered will be tested. Is that an adequate assurance of safety? (a) No, because it does not ensure that the selection will be random or otherwise unbiased, (b) No, because not enough beef is sampled to have a reasonable assurance against such a dreaded threat, (c) Yes, it is good.

9. I have listened to every recorded piece of music by a famous saxophonist and they all sound the same. Basically, I believe that this person's music is all the same. This generalization is (a) good, (b) biased, (c) hasty, (d) both biased and hasty, (e) anecdotal.

10. All diesels are comparatively dirty to operate—when compared with gasoline engine equipped vehicles used for personal transportation. I know this because the Institute for the Promotion of the Gasoline Engine ran tests on thirty percent of the brands of diesel automobile engines and eighty percent of brands of diesel truck engines and found that on average the particulate pollution coming from a diesel engine is much greater than from the brands of gasoline engines tested. This generalization is (a) good, (b) biased, (c) hasty, (d) both biased and hasty, (e) anecdotal.

Mastery Exercises VII.3

SELF-TEST

EXERCISES ON ANALOGIES AND GENERALIZATIONS. Find the best answer to the questions asked in each of the following sections and record for later comparison with the answers in Appendix II. Please include a sentence along with your answer.

Analogies:

1. "My neighbor's cockatiel has a real liking for pinyon nuts. Herb's bird does also. In fact all the birds owned by the members of my poker club—fifteen of them—like pinyon nuts. If I get a bird and want to keep it happy I guess I had better get some pinyon nuts myself." This analogy is Good/Bad _____ by Rule_____

2. "Herb's new home entertainment center is a BestSound and has fourteen speakers. It sounds great. Beatrice's has fourteen speakers though it is a HardyCardboard system. It sounds great. My new system is a Roomblaster and it has fourteen speakers. I bet it is going to sound great." This analogy is Good/Bad _____ by Rule_____

3. "Beaner's House Blend regular coffee makes me nervous—that is, when I drink it. Gavalia's Costa Rican Peabody regular coffee makes me nervous when I drink it. Choc-Full of Nuts regular coffee makes me nervous when I drink it. In fact I have tried lots of different brands and beans of coffees and the regular ones all make me nervous when I drink them. I guess this new Wiredzone Coffee, the Cheery Morning regular coffee, will make me nervous also. Smells great though." This analogy is Good/Bad _____ by Rule_____

4. "No, no Katy got the black one with the sequined hem from Needless Markup's New Boutique shop. And guess what, it was very, very expensive." "Oh, I know. I got a dress very much like that one you describe, but mine also had sequins on the sleeve hems. It was much too much to pay even though I got it at Needless Markup's new suburban store." "But wait, her dress had that kind of sequin decoration on the sleeves also. I bet it was exactly the same dress—a scooped back gathered to the shoulders?" "Oh you're kidding. That is the same dress! That is such a cool dress. But mine is coming apart already. I am going to take it back." "Really, I'd better tell Katy. I'll bet hers starts to come apart too." This analogy is Good/Bad _____ by Rule_____

5. "You know that '99 Civic EX I saw for sale on the side of road near Oregon? I saw a Hummer body and frame, you know that huge civilian version of the military personnel carrier, which some nut had put that same small four-cylinder engine in. Talk about going the wrong direction! *But I guess that is a great way to get super*

mileage, that '99 got 35 around town." "Well I don't know. There's not much the same between a Hummer and a Civic when it comes to what counts for gas mileage." Which speaker is right? Answer by assessing the italicized as the conclusion of an argument from analogy. This analogy is Good/Bad _____ by Rule _____

Generalizations:

Governor Thompson ordered a study of the connections between children being read to at home and the rate at which those children learn to read in school. He was interested in seeing if those who are read to learn faster than those who are not. His idea was that if he could help children learn to read faster by making available talking books to homes across the state, then he would go after the money to buy them. In order to study this he looked at the families of three schools in California. These were all located in the area of the posh Sonoma Valley region of wine growing. In all, the study lasted for two years and followed the progress of 124 children, 75 of whom were designated as coming from non-reading homes and the rest from homes where they were read to. The findings were that the children who were read to progressed at approximately a 30% more rapid rate of reading skill learning when compared to those in the other group. Gov. Thompson concluded that this was good enough to justify spending the $13,000,000 to provide every first grader's home in Illinois with a variety of talking books that children could read along with. Do you agree with him?

6. The generalization was that: (a) the children of wine growers read better than others, (b) those who are children of wine growers and who the parents read to learn to read more rapidly than those who are not read to, (c) the children who live in affluent California communities and are read to learn to read faster than those who live in affluent communities and are not read to, (d) children everywhere who are read to learn to read faster than do those who are not.

7. The generalization was (a) good, (b) biased, (c) hasty, (d) anecdotal, (e) more than just one of the preceding—list those that apply _____

8. The generalization was biased because (a) it was not looking at all of the children in the Sonoma region, (b) it studied only first graders where the children were trying to learn to read, (c) it studied only children from a wine growing region, (d) it studied only children from one part of the country, (e) more than just one of the preceding—list those that apply _____

9. The generalization could have been made stronger by being based upon a sample that (a) included all of the children in the Sonoma Valley region, (b) included all of the children in California, (c) at least 10,000 to 15,000 first grade students from across the country, (d) concentrated upon only children that are read to by their parents.

10. The generalization's sample should include a representation of all the factors that might affect the connection between being read to and coming to read faster so as to not miss some factor that might make the general population different from the population studied, in a regard that is relevant. In order to do this the sample should have been (a) arbitrary, (b) stratified, (c) random, (d) equal in number to all of the children the conclusion holds for, (e) none of the preceding.

PATTERNS OF INDUCTIVE REASONING

Identifying Causes of Particular Events

Thinkers argue to and analyze the significance of correlations seeking to determine whether the connection observed is accidental or rooted in something about one or both of the associated events or properties. Caused, or perhaps resulting from sharing a common cause like the fever and sniffles of your cold, or just coincidental? That is the question of this section. In the case of *analogies* thinkers seek to extend knowledge of the connection of features *in one particular case to those in another particular case,* by virtue of similarities. In *inductive generalizations,* thinkers seek to extend their knowledge of *the association of features in a sample of examined cases to those in whole groups of cases of those sorts.* The discussion now turns to the next step in this progression from particular cases to groups, turning to identifying *what might give the underlying explanation of the connections between some features of things or between some events.* How are critical thinkers to identify the cause of occurrences such as the appearance of or change in the features of things.

Many discussions of this work of critical reason center on what have become known as Mill's Methods, so named for John Stuart Mill the 19th century English philosopher credited with their collection and clear statement. This discussion will proceed from this point as well. However it might be of interest to notice that in 1739 and 1740 a Scottish philosopher named David Hume published a work called *A Treatise of Human Nature* in which he presented much of this wisdom conveyed 100 years later by Mill. So it is fitting to begin the discussion of Mill's Methods with a quotation from David Hume to present these common ideas which every thinker makes use of.

5. There is another principle which hangs upon this, viz. [namely] that where several different objects produce the same effect, it must be by means of some quality

which we discover to be common amongst them. For as like effects imply like causes, we must always ascribe the causation to the circumstance wherein we discover the resemblance.

6. The following principle is founded on the same reason. The difference in the effects of two resembling objects must proceed from that particular in which they differ. For as like causes always produce like effects, when in any instance we find our expectation to be disappointed, we must conclude that this irregularity proceeds from some difference in the causes.

7. When any object increases or decreases or diminishes with the increase or diminution of its cause, it is to be regarded as a compounded effect, derived from the union of the several different effects which arise from the several different parts of the cause. The absence or presence of one part of the cause is here supposed to be always attended with the absence or presence of a proportional part of the effect. This constant conjunction sufficiently proves that the one part is the cause of the other. We must, however, beware not to draw such a conclusion from a few experiments. A certain degree of heat gives pleasure; if your diminish that heat, the pleasure diminishes; but it does not follow, that if you augment it beyond a certain degree, the pleasure will likewise augment; for we find that it degenerates into pain.[4]

Mill's methods of identifying causes pick up on the three patterns of reasoning Hume spoke of and one other to be introduced in a moment. In addition Mill identifies another that has come to be considered by many as characteristic of the method of science itself. The first of the methods Hume spoke of was what is now called the method of agreement, the second is now called the method of difference, and the third is called the method of concomitant variation. Hume also talked about another method Mill spoke of, the combination of the methods of agreement and difference.

Method of Agreement: **When two or more occurrences of the event in question are compared, the factor(s) that are common are the cause or part of the cause of those events.** So when events of a certain sort occur multiple times and there is a common element in the circumstances of those occurrences, then that is the cause or part of it. (Alternatively, it might be the effect or part of the effect. But presumably the cause is the preceding event and the effect the following event and so the two usually would be easily distinguished. Thus in this discussion the extra-baggage of the terms "or the effect or part of the effect" will not be repeated, though they can be assumed for the first four methods.)

For example: Every time the car sputtered and stopped or died, it was out of gas. So running out of gas was the cause or part of the cause of the car stopping.

Or: Suppose that every term, right before final examinations, you start drinking heavily—you have 13–15 cups of regular coffee per day. And suppose that every time around finals you become very nervous. The method of agreement would say that the cause of your nervousness was drinking the coffee or that was part of the cause (speaking loosely for saying the cause or part of it was the amount of caffeine in the coffee).

This method is the one Hume speaks of in rule 5 above. Notice one has to be cautious here since what is taken as cause and as effect might both have a common source in a third occurrence. For example, maybe you have a super tolerance for caffeine and really what was making you drink a lot of coffee and causing whatever the caffeine was doing to your body, and causing the presumed effect of the nervousness, was that you have a very strong fear of failure and a high achievement motivation so you are always nervous around exam time and that makes you study more and then drink more coffee and then take in all that caffeine with whatever it does to you. So your psychology might be what is behind all of the exam time symptoms you are showing. How might you know? That brings up the next method.

Method of Difference: **When the circumstances of an occurrence(s) of the event in question are compared with those of the nonoccurrence(s) of the event, the factor(s) present in the case of the occurrence and absent in the case of the nonoccurrence is the cause or part of the cause of the event in question.**

> *For example:* The time Aunt Mattie bet on the horses and the jockey had lots of experience, her horse won. But when she bet on a horse with an inexperienced jockey, her horse lost. So the cause of her winning was the horse being ridden by an experienced jockey.
>
> *Or:* Suppose you notice that when you ate that hot food without yogurt it upset your stomach. And then when you went back to the same restaurant for some more of that good tasting food, you had the same dishes but you ate yogurt with your meal and did not get an upset stomach. Well then, the yogurt was the cause or part of the cause of your getting through the meal with no upset stomach.

Notice that the method of agreement can help researchers pick up on the likely ingredients in causes, while the method of difference can help narrow those factors down to those that really make a difference and so are really the cause or part of the cause. And, the method of agreement can help narrow down differences in occurrences from those cases where the occurrence takes place, thus allowing researchers to find those factors that will always be present when the effect occurs. It is always the case that there are lots of agreements between the cases when something of interest takes place. The sun was shining, the time was before noon, the century was the 21st, the occurrence took place on planet Earth, and so on. Most of these will be agreements that are irrelevant. Some of this, researchers will know beforehand as they draw on their own experience and the background assumptions of their community of inquiry's perspective to identify what is a plausible candidate for a causal factor and what is not. But once the researcher gets past that point, he or she will need the method of difference to narrow down to the factors that have to be present for the event of interest to occur. Similarly there are always lots of differences that make no difference to the occurrence and nonoccurrence of the event in question and can be present or not with the occurrence of interest. So the method of agreement can help find those differences that always make a difference and so those factors that always need to be present as opposed to those that do not.

It was this back and forth narrowing down that Hume spoke of in the following passage:

> There is no phenomenon in nature but what is compounded and modified by so many different circumstances, that, in order to arrive at the decisive point, we must carefully separate whatever is superfluous, and inquire, by new experiment, if every particular circumstance of the first experiment is essential to it. These new experiments are liable to a discussion of the same kind; so that the utmost constancy is required to make us persevere in our inquiry, and the utmost sagacity to choose the right way among so many that present themselves.[5]

Thus researchers in effect rely on what Mill called the combined methods of agreement and difference:

 Combined Methods of Agreement and Difference: **When the same factor is identified as the cause or part of the cause by both methods of agreement and difference used together in alternation, then it is the cause or part of the cause of the events in question.** The methods are used together in alternation when the method of difference is used to narrow down causal possibilities as identified by the method of agreement, or when the method of agreement is used to check and confirm the presence in all cases of the occurrence of interest those possible causes identified by the method of difference, and when they are used alternatively to narrow down and confirm some of the possibilities identified by either method.

> ***For example:*** Suppose there was a case of food poisoning in the student union and sales records indicate that all those who got sick had the ginger coated beef surprise, the stewed okra with sour cream and consommé sauce, and the ice-cream-on-a-turkey-drumstick fantasy dessert. These are all possibilities for the cause if the method of agreement is used. But then one might bring in to play the method of difference and find that all those who had the ginger coated beef surprise and the turkey drumstick fantasy dessert got sick even though they did not have the okra. Looking at the cases where there was sickness and there was not,

we see that the relevant differences are the beef and the turkey. They both might be part of the cause or they might be co-occurring but not both causally involved factors. Perhaps one could tell by further uses of the method of difference or perhaps one could ask for volunteers and feed them either the beef or the turkey ice cream or both and see how they fare. If the only ones to get sick were the ones who ate both, this would be further confirmation by the method of agreement that both differences were relevant differences.

Another possibility would be to introduce a new method into the mix at this point. Researchers could check to see if there was any difference in the degree of illness depending upon how much of each, the beef or ice-cream dessert, was eaten. If there was, this would suggest that the food to blame was that one that had this varying association with the degree of illness—the more eaten the worse, the less eaten the less severe the case of the illness. This result could be explained by the consideration Hume introduced in rule 7, quoted above. The reasoning involved has been generalized and is captured in Mill's method of concomitant variation.

Method of Concomitant Variation: When two or more characteristics vary together (either positively or negatively) then one is the cause or part of the cause of the other.

For example: The more blood there was in the water the greater the shark's feeding frenzy. So the blood was the cause or part of the cause of the feeding frenzy.

Or: The more of the turkey fantasy that students ate, the sicker they got, so that dish was the cause or part of the cause of the illness.

Or again: The more Clarence studied, the worse his scores on the quizzes. He concluded that studying was actually hurting his performance. But why? Maybe it is time to check in at the medical center to explore test anxiety and how to cope, or to see the professor, to determine whether he is overcooking the quiz study work.

One last method was recognized by Mill and it is a natural follow-up to the others just considered.

Method of Residues: When background knowledge allows you to eliminate other possible causes and you are sure that the factors you are left with are possible causes, then the factor remaining, the residue, is the cause or part of the cause of the event in question.

For example: On a cool morning, before breakfast, patient Paul was found to have a fever. This elevated body temperature could not have been due to exertion, to eating, or to the ambient temperature being excessively warm. The only other possibility was that he had an infection. So that was decided to be the cause or part of the cause of the fever.

TWO FURTHER CAUTIONS. When one uses the method of agreement one must beware of possible coincidences where what is marked as cause and what is marked as effect do occur together and do follow each other respectively, but where each has some independent cause that is operating in the circumstances. For example, it might be the case that one is impressed by the neatness of the dress of a uniformed police officer and one has a tendency to give such people some respect and deference that one would not accord to others. But the uniform's appearance might be nothing more than the work of the laundry where the officers take their clothing (and they are really slobs or unconcerned about starched and pressed uniforms), and the respect might come from childhood training or the deference from fear on the part of the citizens. It is good not to rely on just the method of agreement, or for that matter the method of difference alone. And, of course researchers in the sciences do not, since they use both and also forms of concomitant variation in controlled experiments, as well as the method of residues, in their reflections.

Sometimes, thinkers will immediately jump to the conclusion that since one thing follows another the first is the cause of the second. This of course is mistaken as any number of counter-examples would show:

For example: (To take a famous philosophical example first) Whenever Big Ben strikes 12:00 noon, across England many, many workers go to lunch. But surely the clock striking did not cause the breaking for lunch.

Or: Every time Tiger Woods wins a golf tournament, it is Sunday or Monday. But Woods' winning did not cause the day of the week to be one of those two! Nor did the day of the week cause him to win!

The mistake is called the fallacy of **post hoc *ergo propter hoc*** which is the mistake of inferring that because one event follows another the second is the cause of the first.

TECH TIPS

1. The method of agreement draws on multiple cases to identify the common features in the circumstances as the cause or part of the cause.

2. The method of difference compares a case where the occurrence of interest is found with one where it is not and looks for differences in the circumstances of the two cases. These are the cause or part of the cause.

3. The combined method uses agreements to find possible causes and narrows these down by the method of difference and then checks differences that are possible causes by the method of agreement, alternating until what is identified as the cause or part of the cause is always present when the effect is present and is such that its absence is always found with the absence of the effect.

4. The method of concomitant variation identifies the cause or part of the cause by spotting positive or negative variations in properties of co-occurrences.

5. The method of residues eliminates possible causes by using prior knowledge of relevant causes and effects, and narrows down to the cause or part of the cause.

Mastery Exercises VII.4

SELF-TEST

IDENTIFICATION OF CAUSES. Identify the form of identification of a cause in each of the following and assess whether the method is well used. Then explain your response. Record your answers and compare them with those in Appendix II.

1. Jason tried to check out all the possibilities. The sound distortion was not coming from a broken humbucker. It was not coming from a loose neck. The strings were all in place and properly tuned. None of the frets was loose or broken. The bridge was properly in place. All the electronics were ok. So it must be that the guitar body is cracked. Rats! Jason used what method to reach his conclusion: (a) agreement, (b) difference, (c) residues, (d) concomitant variation.

2. Gloria tried to fix the motor by first plugging it in and checking the circuit breaker. Next she changed the plug and that made no difference. Then she took the motor apart and cleaned the brushes—still nothing. Next she took it apart again and replaced the brushes and cleaned the whole thing inside and out. She plugged it in and nothing happened. She angrily shook the plug and then the motor took off and ran like a champ. She said, "Well, I wish I had done that shaking thing before!" Assuming that the shaking was the only difference this time, that is during this try, was Gloria right that that caused the motor to run or was part of the cause of the motor running? (a) yes (b) no

3. Under the same assumption as in (2), does Gloria know that the only cause of the motor running was the shaking of the plug in the socket? (a) yes (b) no

4. Aretha bought the new carpet cleaner from Homes 'R Us. This was the new PE Floor Cleaner Complete. She could not wait to have the machine run over the carpets so she asked her neighbor to come in and try it while she dusted and supervised from her wheelchair. Her neighbor Boris had a slight back pain when he started but he was glad to help out. After finishing one room, Boris's back now hurt. The end of the next room's carpet saw Boris crawling over to Aretha's spare wheelchair and climbing in. Boris concluded that running the machine was the cause of the current level of pain. Boris was right of course. What is the name of the method by which he identified the cause? Fill in the blank _____.

5. George was turning into a real couch potato. In fact he was gaining a lot of weight and he was becoming concerned about this. So he started to think about this. He knew that when he watched television before, he could eat four Twinkies and drink five glasses of milk a day and he did not gain any weight. He also knew that he was up to 14 Twinkies a day and about four gallons of milk a day. He concluded that the Twinkies *and* the milk were the cause or part of the cause of his problem. He then decided he wanted to try to cut back a little and so he cut back to only

five glasses a milk a day with the 14 Twinkies but he did not start to lose any weight. So then, still determined, he cut back to only four Twinkies and about four gallons of milk a day. He did not lose any weight that way either. So once again he concluded that it was the combination of Twinkies and milk. So he went back to the four Twinkies and the five glasses of milk per day and he lost weight back to where he had been before he started the milk and Twinkies bingeing. He concluded that the excess milk and Twinkies caused his weight gain. He was right, of course, but what method did he use to figure this out? (a) agreement, (b) difference, (c) agreement and difference, (d) residues, (e) concomitant variation.

6. "I put a new bulb in and the electricity surged through the circuit blowing the bulb and tripping the circuit breaker. Wow! Changing that bulb sure got results." Was he right?

7. "The several times I have washed my new car, no more than a half hour later, it rained. I used to think that this business of washing your car making it rain was just superstition. But now I'm a believer." What do you think of this generalization? This is clearly not going to fly—the sample is too small to generalize to all cars and car washes. Further, this is no doubt a biased sample for the speaker seems to live in a rainy or fairly moist area. What about all those cars and car washes in the desert and in southern California? This goes in the "no pile" on both counts—sample size and bias. Now what about it as a case of identification of a cause?

8. "Every time I dialed that number I got that strange noise until I dialed the area code first. When I dialed the area code first, the call went through. I guess that not dialing the area code was causing my problems." What method of causation identification is this?

9. "The more I tried to explain, the more he shouted that I just did not understand and I should keep my mouth shut! It seemed that I could not say a thing without making him angry and the more I said, the worse his anger. Next time I had better just be quiet!" What method of causation identification is at work here?

10. "During Indian summer the last few years, the soy bugs have come out. I guess the cooler weather followed by the warmer weather causes them to hatch." Method?

11. "Every time I write with a pencil I break the point. But if I use a fountain pen I never bend the point, no matter how fine it is. I guess my pressing hard with the pencil is the cause." Method?

12. "All those who have gotten cancer have worn clothes much of the time during the day. That strongly suggests that clothes cause cancer—I guess we should all become nudists. Anybody have a problem with that?"

13. "Well, I knew a little about cooking and I knew that the flavor was so spicy because of the cayenne pepper in the dish. I have used that recipe before and know how much salt, cumin, and black pepper go into it. None of these is enough to make it spicy like that and there is no taste of excess use of any of these. The only other

ingredient that might make it spicy is the cayenne. Since I'm allergic to cayenne, I had better leave that chili alone!" Method?

14. "All my snapdragons did well this year. But then the more rain followed by bright sunny days there has been in the past the better they did. Since there was so much this year, more than usual, that's why they did so well." Method?

PATTERNS OF INDUCTIVE REASONING

Is Cause More Than Correlation?

Even with careful experimental controls, sophisticated statistical analysis, and repeated testing, causal reasoning will not find some connection of force or power or other "smoking gun" of reality relating events or things in the world. Observation is adequate to noting sequences of events or changes, not actual transformations or the workings of these transformations that underlie and then are identified as causes of what sequences are observed. (And even at that, observation emphasizes one aspect of what is going on over another, that is manifests decisions about what is a possible separation of events in the world, even in picking out which events might be causally connected.) Explanations or accounts of these transformations will always operate at a level, or point to factors, different from actual transformations. It is no good to try to explain some event, say the division of a cell in mitosis by simply describing what is seen under the microscope. "And then the chromosomes divided and the cell became two." That describes part of the sequence all right, but in a way it explains nothing. It would be part of only a circular and so thoroughly unsatisfactory explanation—it happened because it happened. But then, to point to the cause or the explaining factors will always take thinkers beyond what is being explained. So the causes are never observed in observing the sequences of events that are cause and effect related.

If this is so, then, at most, studies of what causes what give thinkers a very well substantiated account of two or more events of certain kinds being reliably connected in their experience so that if one is present, they can predict or retrodict the other. (To retrodict some event is to predict back in time to see what cause was there for the effect that one is now curious about. Think of the corn cob case related above.) And this point requires a bit more attention.

For a long time people seemed to think that causal connections between events in the world were some sorts of power or forces bringing about the changes people experience. But in the 18th century a Scottish empiricist skeptic thought that talk of powers was too mysterious to be helpful in science and even in everyday life. This philosopher and social critic was the very David Hume quoted above. Hume is famous for the view that thinkers should try to understand the concept of cause and effect through an analysis of the psychology of experiencing causal connections. So he asked just what it was that people were really aware of in experiencing a cause and effect connection. Hume's answer was that thinkers never sense any real connection, but only the regular succession of events of two sorts. When the succession is regular, they come to expect the second whenever they experience the first. So when people see lightening, they come to expect thunder, or when they bite into a lemon, they come to expect to have a sour taste sensation in their mouths, and so on. Cause and effect connections between events are nothing more than the fact that events of one sort are regularly succeeded by events of another sort and people have come to form a habit of expecting to experience an event of the second sort whenever they experience an event of the first sort. What is in the world when there is a cause and effect relationship? The answer is, "nothing more than a constant conjunction of events of the two sorts in question, plus a habit of thought associating them."

This fits well with thinkers saying that all they establish in their thinking about the world in cause and effect terms is that there is a reliable correlation between events of the two sorts they call cause and effect. Now in the philosophy of science around the middle of last century, this view was taken up but it was found to be too loose—there must be something to distinguish between events that just happen to be correlated or happen to be found together but are not really causally related, and those which are not only found together but also are really related. For example, thinkers know about the physics of magnetism and can see magnets actually attracting the iron filings close to them. Well, that is, they see what they call the magnets brought close to the filings and at some point the filings moving to the magnet. That is not a coincidence. So what is so special about this case? The answer given at first was that the events which are really causally related were the ones that could be spoken of in a universal hypothetical statement linking cause with effect in certain circumstances, *and* this hypothetical statement was true, *but not as a matter of accident or coincidence.*

A hypothetical statement is just any statement that is expressed in an "if _____ then _____" form: If it rains, then the ground gets wet; If you eat too many blintzes, you will put on weight; If you are reading this, then you are not asleep and dreaming. A universal hypothetical statement is one that speaks of all the things referred to in the "if clause" or the "if" part of the statement—all rain, all blintzes, all readers, in the examples in the previous sentences. Now a universal hypothetical statement linking events of two kinds in certain circumstances is simply a universal hypothetical statement that is asserted to hold true within certain assumed conditions: *So whenever it rains and the relative humidity is not what it is in the desert,* then the ground will get wet (if it is in a desert, the rain evaporates before it hits the ground and you have what they call in the Rocky Mountain West, "virga rain"). *If you eat too many blintzes in the conditions that you are not sick with cancer, or you do not have the metabolism rate of a hummingbird, or you are not living on sugar and working terribly hard at physical labor,* then you are going to put on weight—the conditions of normal metabolism rate and so on are assumed as conditions in which the hypothetical statement is asserted as true. *If you are not a sleep walker* and are a reader, and you are reading this then you are awake. And so it goes. Every universal hypothetical statement about the world is asserted with the assumption that it holds within some given conditions. So what these philosophers of science were saying is that if you have events of two sorts that are referred to in a universal hypothetical statement which is true in the assumed conditions of its assertion, and it is not true by accident or by coincidence, then you have a causal connection of the events of the sorts referred to in the statement.

Well fine, but the whole account turns on the universal hypothetical **not being true by accident.** And just when is that? When the world has that real causal connection? Well yes, but when is that—after all, the true universal hypothetical statement was brought up to explain causal connections, and now it seems that it really does not do the job. How can one distinguish universal hypothetical statements that are not true by accident from those that are?

Some have tried to answer this question by saying that non-accidentally true statements of the sorts *thinkers are after are ones that will support subjunctive conditionals. That is they will still be true even if thinkers turn them from statements about what actually happens into statements of what would happen (in certain assumed conditions) if it were the case that the "if part" of the statement were to come true.* So, for example,

> If it is non-accidentally true that in non-desert environments, if it rains the ground gets wet, then in such environments (that is, assuming those conditions are holding), then if it were to rain, then the ground really would get wet.

And then because such a statement is true, thinkers could say that rain is the cause of the ground getting wet. But universal hypotheticals that are only accidentally true could *not* support such translations into statements about what *would* be the case, *if.* For example, "if something is a Tuesday, then it is a day on which I teach critical thinking." True this term, but short of requiring that the assumed conditions guarantee that everything is just as it happens to be this term, this will not always be true. Sometimes I teach critical thinking on Monday and Wednesday, so "If you were to select any Tuesday, then it would be a day I teach critical thinking" is not a true statement, unless you assume circumstances that make the if/then statement true; that is, unless you assume it is true! In the case of the rain statement the assumption was that one is not in the desert conditions as far as relative humidity goes. But that by itself does not guarantee that the "if/then" statement is true.

Now thinkers could fuss around a lot more with this test of translating universal hypothetical statements of fact into statements of what would happen if we were to do something in certain conditions. (And they have.) There are some real philosophical problems with the test as it is described in the preceding paragraph—they are problems having to do with how one identifies and talks about the assumed conditions and their role in the test. But in the end, the same residual problem comes up—how can one look at a universal hypothetical statement and know that it would support such a translation into what would happen if one were to. . . . ? The short of it seems to be that one cannot tell those statements without finding when one has a reliable causal connection holding between events of the sorts talked about in the statements. So this puts the discussion back where it started.

The problem of how thinkers are to understand causality and be able to spot causal connection decisively has not been solved to the knowledge of the author. Some of those who want to say this is a problem of methods used by thinkers doing the empirical research to single out causal connections are working on statistical analyses of the connections of causes to effects. These researchers still are looking for a way to find cause and effect connections in reality, a test for such real connections. A latter day Hume on the point (Nelson Goodman) suggested another approach—namely that really thinkers identify real or causal connections in terms of the connections between events that become **entrenched** in ordinary or community-of-discussion thinking. So a connection between cause and effect is one that has been confirmed in experience (compare with Mill's Method of agreement), challenged with disconfirmation but so far is still holding up, and a connection that it is still of use to the thinkers accepting it: reliable, not disconfirmed, useful connections thinkers make as they string together features of the world into their accounts or stories of what brings about what—that is what cause and effect amounts to. This is a sophisticated version of Hume's view of things. And it is a view that is compatible with the statistical analyses of causation (the statistics will make precise just how thinkers are to confirm the connections between events of the sorts they find to be causally related).

SECTION 5

So What If Cause Is No More Than a Certain Supported, Unchallenged, and Useful Connection Made by Those in a Community of Discussion?

Well, the "so what" is very important because it suggests that when one gives a causal account of the connection between two events, or when one makes a discovery of cause and effect connections between two events, then that person is not finding any necessary connections or real and mysterious connections between events of certain sorts in the world. Rather the person is finding and articulating what stories or narratives are reliable and useful in their associating events of different sorts in certain ways in certain conditions. One is just giving an account of what things are and how they work, an account that might be supplemented or abandoned as one moves through her or his experimental investigations. The "right" accounts in science and everyday investigation (as people think about what brings about what) are up for revision and are really interpretations of the world given through a narrative for the purposes of explanation and prediction (or at least for these purposes). This has tremendous social consequences. For example, for a long time it was believed that women could not fly fighter jets because they lacked the physical strength and the emotional control to remain calm in combat at high G's in flight. Now that is recognized to be false, indeed prejudiced, and no more thought to be a feature of women generally than it is of men generally. The causal story has changed about how jet fighter pilots work and who qualifies. So too the story has changed about the nature of the atom, about the nature of social behavior (is it all selfish, or is it all cultural in basis), about mental illness, and about any number of other matters where humans thought they had good evidence for causal connections.

The point and suggestion is that perhaps thinkers should believe that there is no way to articulate what in reality makes for a causal connection as opposed to an accidental connection or a coincidence, except by providing an account of the occurrence and associations of events that is defensible, not challenged in spite of attempts to do so, and useful. So an important *rule of thumb* is: ***If this is plausible then researchers should begin to think of causal connections as the connections thinkers settle on when their explanatory and predictive stories of how things are related are defensibly accepted and used within a group of thinkers as part of the group's perspective on the world.*** This does not make them true as grounded somehow in the very nature of the world. But it does allow for thinkers to say how things in the world seem to be connected really, and to say what counts as evidence to that effect.

It is just that thinkers should never get themselves into thinking about the connections they find as though they are features of objects and they have to be that way; they should not allow themselves to think that they are finding connections depending on the hidden natures of things, as opposed to finding the ways thinkers see the nature of things (for good reasons) in their interpretive and predictive and explanatory schemes. On this view, part of the test of claims about what causes what is a set of questions about how humans came to think that way, whether they might be motivated by bias or economics or hatreds or politics, for example. And if it can be shown that there is some such influence, or any wishful thinking, or any other of the fallacies discussed in work on critical thinking, then the claim should be rejected, just as if there is a shortage of what the testing and interpretative procedures of the appropriate community of thinkers would call good evidence for the causal claim. Politics, self-interest, bias, and other such considerations do sometimes come into play in making the stories through which thinkers interpret the world, and in science as well as everyday thinking individuals need to avoid any influence from such factors, or at least they need to admit that there might be such influences making things look the ways people see them and thereby interfering with inquiry.

If thinkers make that admission, it might make them less tolerant of passing off racism, prejudice, self-fulfilling prophecies, and other uncritical reasoning as good thinking about the world. Think how far that would take thinkers in ordering society and in relating to other nations and other peoples. Would the Second World War and Nazi "science" have occurred, or slavery, or colonial, sexual, or inter-species exploitation occur, if causal claims were subject to this understanding and thus subject to the demands for charity or respect as well as integrity of thought, to demands for freedom from bias and an awareness of history of how people have thought about things being causally related? Well, whatever the answer to those "what-if" questions, thinkers should respect the need for an awareness of possible bias and an awareness of the evolving nature of ideas. These put limits on the claim of any idea of a specific causal connection to being the whole truth and nothing but the truth. That much is surely part of thinking critically.

Wrap Up and Look Forward

This chapter has explored aspects of the powers and pitfalls of inductive reasoning. Such reasoning is absolutely irreplaceable if inference is to go beyond the evidence thinkers have on a subject. Such reasoning turned out to not be foolproof. However, it was never intended to be, unlike deductive reasoning. The discussion has only scratched the surface and the discussion to follow of deductive reasoning can do no more itself. In the chapter to come, however, an overview will emerge of some of the patterns of reasoning that are familiar to everyone and used everyday, and of why and how they can be tested all but mechanically. Before heading there, a review test on inductive reasoning might be useful.[6]

Mastery Exercises VII.5

SELF-TEST   *Inductive Reasoning Unit Test*

SECTION I   **IDENTIFICATIONS AND DEFINITIONS:** Match the correct definition or identification from the list on the left with the terms or concepts given in the list on the right and put the letter of the correct match in the appropriate number slot in the answer template at the end of the test. Then check Appendix II to correct your answers.

1. Inferring that since the values of the two variables increase or decrease together in some related way, they are causally related
2. The mistake of reasoning that since this follows that, that causes this
3. Moving to a general conclusion before possessing adequate evidence because your sample is too small
4. A sample which has been constructed to fit with an overly limited number of possible forms of influence on a connection of interest
5. Concluding something is the cause of something else because it is the one possibility left after others have been eliminated
6. Reasoning that since two events always agree in a certain feature, this is the cause of the events in question
7. Patterns of associations which societies come to expect or count upon and in terms of which they see the world are said to be
8. Arguments that are offered to move to conclusions beyond the evidence in the premises
9. Arguing that since this case is like another in one regard it is like that other in another regard also
10. The relationship between any two sorts of events when one changes with the other

A. Hasty generalization

B. Habeas Corpus

C. Hideous Corpus

D. Method of Residues

E. Method of Refuse

F. Valid

G. Analogy

H. Caveat Emperor

I. S-Bend Fallacy

J. Post Hoc, Ergo Propter Hoc

K. Correlation

L. Prejudiced

M. Biased

N. Accident

O. Concomitant Variation

P. The All Star Fallacy

Q. Inductive

R. Entrenched

S. Method of Agreement

ARGUMENTS FROM ANALOGY: In each case indicate whether the argument is good or bad and what rule for arguments from analogy leads you to this conclusion.

11. "Well, she had tried going out with a blond who looked like DiCaprio, a black haired man who looked like Glover, and a red haired man who looked like Red Skelton. In every case it was the same. All they could do was name drop and try to get money out of her for their next picture production. That was enough, she thought, to show her that she shouldn't go out with this brown haired man who looks like Harrison Ford. It would be the same deal all over again—boring name-dropping and the inevitable appeal for funding." Good/Bad (Mark "G" or "B") _____, Rule (Please put in the correct number) _____

12. Rachel thought she would go to The Chef's Sauce Pan. This is a chain restaurant she had been to probably forty times in her recent travels across the country as a driver of an 18-wheel rig. And she had never been disappointed on any of these occasions so she was sure she would not be disappointed in this case either. Good/Bad _____, Rule _____

13. "Well," he thought, "here we go again. This is another professor who is so full of herself that she will not be able to come down to the level of the introductory students in class and communicate effectively." After all he had had the experience at least 12 times before, of a professor coming into a class and immediately using big words to impress, giving huge reading assignments which make sense only if you have read half or more of the material already, and lecturing on and on about everything that the texts have to say. "Well," he thought, "I can get out now or put up with it. But I have to take the course for my major so I guess I'm stuck. I'll just have to make the best of it." Good/Bad _____, Rule _____

14. He was convinced the guy was not to be trusted. After all he had hired repair personnel lots of times before when he had work to do around the house. And every time, they did not do all of what they said they would and they charged him more than they had estimated the job would cost. So he was convinced that if he allowed this person from the neighborhood-volunteer-help-group to assist him free of charge with his taxes, he would be very sorry. He was sure he would prove untrustworthy. Good/Bad _____, Rule _____

15. Norman came to the conclusion that his neighbor's pizza, Heinrich's Pizza, should be very good and so he decided to get one. He reached this conclusion from the following evidence: He had had real good luck with German designed and made food products. He had gotten a Beer Garden frozen stuffed flounder and that product had been tasty. He had had Gertzertrauma Rhine wines and they had always been good. And he had had Greta's Blondies frozen desserts and found them particularly tasty. So he thought that since Adolph and his recipe for pizza were German the pizzas would be enjoyable also. Good/Bad _____, Rule _____

SECTION III

GENERALIZATIONS: Indicate whether the following are good generalizations, bad because of too small a sample, bad because of a biased sample, or bad because of being merely anecdotal.

16. A market researcher had looked at all the leading brands and all their models of American cars—that is all those cars made in America by the big three automakers, Ford, General Motors, and Daimler-Chrysler. After her studies, she concluded that while they are cheaper to maintain and repair, they just do not last beyond 125,000 miles. So, since she was looking for cars to recommend because they last through 200,000 miles, she decided she could not recommend any of those made by an American owned company. None of these was worthy of her recommendation. (a) Good, (b) Bad—too small a sample, (c) Bad—biased sample, (d) Bad—too small a sample and biased, (e) Bad—merely anecdotal

17. "A recent study looked at a random selection of the incoming first grade students in fourteen private schools across the country for the last two years. These students were found to be spoiled brats. Therefore all those entering first grade in schools across the country are spoiled brats. If I were teaching first grade now, at a private or a public school, I would quit!" (a) Good, (b) Bad—too small a sample, (c) Bad—biased sample, (d) Bad—too small a sample and biased, (e) Bad—merely anecdotal

18. She knew that she could ace that exam. She had learned it would be just like the others this professor gives in terms of the kinds of questions and what materials are covered. And a random sample of all this professor's students had shown that since the questions and materials were of the types they were, for every one of the tests from this professor, all a student needed to do was to study hard and pay attention to the notes offered by the professor. This was sufficient for an A in the case of one hundred percent of those students sampled. Further since she had carefully gone over the notes for this class and studied hard the whole term, she was looking forward to the A on this exam. (a) Good, (b) Bad—too small a sample, (c) Bad—biased sample, (d) Bad—too small a sample and biased, (e) Bad—merely anecdotal

19. She had tried (without getting any relief) every aspirin related product on the market, taking far more of some than the labels said she should. She gave up—there was no product that could fix her headache. (a) Good, (b) Bad—too small a sample, (c) Bad—biased sample, (d) Bad—too small a sample and biased, (e) Bad—merely anecdotal

20. Garbage cans come and garbage cans go, but the Enduro Supreme 55-gallon was the exception in terms of durability and capacity. She knew this because she found out that it had been the biggest seller in the southwest United States for over three years—over 5,000 of the 7,000 sold were Enduro Supremes. And she knew that southwesterners were smart shoppers. (a) Good, (b) Bad—too small a sample, (c) Bad—biased sample, (d) Bad—too small a sample and biased, (e) Bad—merely anecdotal

IDENTIFICATIONS OF CAUSES: Consider the following little story and then answer the questions that follow. To answer each question, pick a letter for true or false and then list all the correct numbers of the method or methods by which that answer of true or false would be established.

Twelve thousand eight hundred spectators had food at the last Louisiana Paddlewheels game. Of these, 8,000 had the dill pickle flavored apple chips—a real Louisiana specialty, and 8,000 had the brain and liver spread with crackers. Besides these, 1,300 had the peaches with lemon yogurt surprise with peanuts in it and 4,700 had the roots and berries hot dogs with the sour cream sauce. In addition, 12,000 spectators had bottled milk and cookies with the artichoke sauce. (It was a pretty wholesome crowd.) Also all the players had the frozen Orange Dreamsicle with the creamy ice-cream center. Those who had the roots and berries dogs with the sour cream sauce got sick. And those who had the yogurt surprise got sick. Those 1,200 who had both of these—the dogs and the surprise, got sicker than those 3,600 who had only one of them.

21. Dill pickle flavored apple chips were the cause of the sickness.

   (a) true, (b) false by (i) method of agreement, (ii) method of difference, (iii) method of agreement and difference, (iv) method of residues, (v) method of concomitant variation

22. Peaches with lemon yogurt and peanuts was the cause of the sickness.

   (a) true, (b) false by (i) method of agreement, (ii) method of difference, (iii) method of agreement and difference, (iv) method of residues, (v) method of concomitant variation

23. Brain and liver spread and crackers was the cause of the sickness.

   (a) true, (b) false by (i) method of agreement, (ii) method of difference, (iii) method of agreement and difference, (iv) method of residues, (v) method of concomitant variation

24. Unfrozen cultured milk products like yogurt and sour cream were the cause of the sickness.

   (a) true, (b) false by (i) method of agreement, (ii) method of difference, (iii) method of agreement and difference, (iv) method of residues, (v) method of concomitant variation

25. The sickest 1,200 were made ill by both the hot dogs and sour cream sauce and the yogurt surprise with peanuts.

   (a) true, (b) false by (i) method of agreement, (ii) method of difference, (iii) method of agreement and difference, (iv) method of residues, (v) method of concomitant variation

Answer Template

Name _____

Section I.

1. _____   6. _____
2. _____   7. _____
3. _____   8. _____
4. _____   9. _____
5. _____   10. _____

Section II.

11. Good/Bad _____, Rule _____

12. Good/Bad _____, Rule _____

13. Good/Bad _____, Rule _____

14. Good/Bad _____, Rule _____

15. Good/Bad _____, Rule _____

Section III.

16. _____

17. _____

18. _____

19. _____

20. _____

Section IV.

21. True/False _____, Method(s) _____

22. True/False _____, Method(s) _____

23. True/False _____, Method(s) _____

24. True/False _____, Method(s) _____

25. True/False _____, Method(s) _____

Notes

[1] This discussion of the rules for assessing arguments from analogy is based largely on the discussion of Irving M. Copi. The most recent version of this discussion is found in, Copi, I. M. and Cohen, C. (2004). *Essentials of logic.* Upper Saddle River, New Jersey: Prentice Hall, Pearson Education, Inc. (See pages 278–90.)

[2] See, for example, Shermer, M. Miracle on probability street, the law of large numbers guarantees that one-in-a-million miracles happen 295 times a day in America. *Scientific American.* August 2004, p. 32.

[3] See, for example, the discussion of statistical analysis in, Moore, B. N. and and Parker, R. (2003). *Critical thinking.* Boston: McGraw-Hill Higher Education, pp. 369 and 368.

[4] Hume, D. (1961). Section XV Rules By Which To Judge Of Causes And Effects, Of the Understanding, Part I. In: *A treatise of human nature.* Garden City, New York: Dolphin Books Doubleday & Company, Inc., pp. 159–160.

[5] Hume, D. (1961). Ibid., p. 160.

[6] The patterns showing the general structure of arguments from analogy and arguments to a generalization from a sample are derived partially from: Copi, I. M. (1961). *Introduction to logic* (2nd ed.). New York: The Macmillan Company, pp. 340 and 361, respectively. And see: Copi, I. M. (1986) *Informal logic.* New York: Macmillan Publishing Company, pp. 170 and 202, respectively. The second of these patterns is found in Moore, B. N. and Parker, R. (2003). *Critical Thinking* (7th ed.). Boston: McGraw-Hill Higher Education, p. 358.

CHAPTER VIII

Words to Live By—Some Elementary Concepts and Patterns of Deductive Reasoning

INTRODUCTION

The Culture of Deductive Reasoning

A number of times in the earlier parts of the discussion, there has been reason to speak of the value of simplicity in thought. This will be a theme when talking about good and bad explanations in chapter IX to follow. But it is particularly useful to keep in mind in the discussion of deductive reasoning. And it is not just a concern of efficiency when speaking of deductive reasoning. Rather simplicity here is a reflection of the fact that the concern in addressing deductive arguments is with form not content. An illustration will help. Appeals to authority were seen to fall into a certain pattern:

> The/An authority says that some statement s is true. (Grounds) There is expertise, the authority speaking has that authority and without it being compromised the authority used it in reaching the view in question. (Backing) If the authority says that something is so, then it is so. (Warrant) So, or therefore, the statement s is true or is so.

Put with a little more order the argument would go as follows:

> Authorities can be trusted when there is expertise, they have the needed expertise, they are using the expertise in forming a view and their use has not been compromised.

1. If an authority says s is true then it is true.

   The/An authority says s is true.

   Therefore: s is true.

Now notice that this is not really an argument, but the shell of an argument or the form of an argument into which any number of appeals to authority could be put, regardless of the particular thing said by whatever statement s is standing in for. It would work as well for appealing to authorities about how to cure warts, how to fix your car, or how to select a life partner (at least it could if there was any expertise on how to select a life partner!). This concept of an argument form is quite important. It allows thinkers to understand the workings and the possible pitfalls of any number of arguments. The backing gives an idea of where appeals to authority can go wrong in ways that undermine the authority of the expert or would-be expert in question. The warrant shows that the appeal rests on the trustworthiness of the authority covered in the backing. The second premise shows that trouble might come in the form of an authority being misquoted or lied about. And the final line or the statement of the claim—s is true (separated off by the line above it drawn under the statement of the grounds) shows another aspect of how things might go wrong. *There might be something that goes wrong in the reasoning involved, regardless of the truth of the premises and of whether the person of whom the warrant is supposed to hold, does fit the conditions of the backing.* To tease out that other element of the worth of the reasoning, consider another couple of examples:

2. If it rains the ground gets wet.

    It is raining. _____

Therefore: The ground is getting wet.

3. If the oven timer does not work, then the supper will be burned.

    The timer did not work this time. _____

Therefore: The supper burned.

Notice that in all of these arguments, (1), (2), and (3), the premises and conclusion have a similar form even though their subject matter is quite different. In every case the argument is of the following sort:

X. If s then t.

    s _____

Therefore: t

Noticing this, a thinker has another question to ask about arguments of this form—is it the case that any statements one might substitute consistently for the letters "s" and "t" will yield an argument that is as good as the appeal to authority argument seems to be, at least in the basic reasoning involved? And how would one tell this? If there is some way to check the worth of the reasoning process itself involved in arguments of this form, regardless of their content, then there would be a powerful and efficient method to check up on reasoning. And maybe there are other forms of arguments that are equally good and can be checked just for their reasoning process, regardless of their content? This will not tell critical thinkers everything they want to know about the worth of arguments, but it would be an important contribution to that knowledge. And what a gift it would be to be able to conduct this assessment of the argument forms and thus of all instances of those forms. This would mean you could check the reasoning process in all instances of that form, and then not have to check each single argument's reasoning process!

As it turns out, such a form of reasoning checking has been developed and is there for the asking. That method of checking arguments is what this chapter is about. However, this procedure has only been developed for one large and important kind of argument—deductive arguments, where the author of the argument intends to demonstrate beyond a doubt that the conclusion is true or acceptable. (For inductive arguments, you saw several sets of rules or other concerns that must be addressed in checking the various reasoning processes of arguing by analogy and so on.) ***In deductive arguments the idea is that if the evidence statements are true, then the reasoning process should be such that it allows in no possibility of error.*** If deductive argument is good it should preserve the truth thinkers strive for in the premises as the thinkers draw conclusions from those premises. That is, the idea is to find forms of reasoning that are such that: *if the premises are true the conclusion has to be true.* Such arguments are called **valid,** and if such arguments really do have true premises then they are called **sound.**

> So valid arguments have reasoning processes that preserve truth—if the premises are true then the conclusion will have to be also, and sound arguments are valid arguments with true premises.

So the objective is to try to find a way to check arguments for their validity, some process that looks at the form of arguments not at the content of the arguments so that whole kinds of reasoning patterns can be checked, rather than checking the single instances one at a time. Aristotle and others in ancient Greece and logicians in the middle ages sought such an approach to deductive reasoning about claims expressed in general and singular statements about kinds of things and instances of these kinds. For present purposes this approach will not be pursued. This quick introduction will focus on individual statements about particular things in the world and combinations of these into complex wholes. The focus will be on what is sometimes called propositional logic. Even so this will serve the purpose of introducing the study of formal ways of expressing and checking for the validity of arguments. And it will provide a very powerful tool to check a number of arguments used frequently in everyday thinking, including those deductive argument patterns found in planning a course of action.

Thus the aims of the chapter are two: (1) To give a brief introduction to checking the validity of certain deductive arguments, (2) To provide some sense of the workings of several basic patterns of deductive inference and combinations of them. This is not a basic introduction to formal logic—the discussion will not go that far into these matters, and it will look at only a very small portion of the argument forms for which symbolization and mechanical validity checking techniques have been worked out.

SECTION 1

Understanding Validity

The object is to find a way to check whether or not the reasoning involved in an argument is truth preserving. Is the argument valid? Notice that this is a special sense of "valid." Critical thinkers do not mean that a valid argument is a case of an argument that is strong or is trustworthy or is plausible—all of which "valid" means in ordinary speech. No, this is a technical use which is stipulatively defined. The technical notion of validity is that according to which only arguments are valid, and those that are, are so because of a relation between the premises and conclusion so that (you guessed it) if the premises are true the conclusion has to be true.

Remember that validity is not the same as truth—arguments are not true or false, only the statements making them up are. And remember that the feature of validity is a *hypothetical* feature—that is, it is a property that the argument has *under assumed certain conditions,* namely that the premises are true, so that *if* they are true (and they might not be) the conclusion has to be true. So when checking for validity, thinkers are not really interested in whether the premises are true. That question is set aside. Rather the focus is on whether the premises are related to the conclusion in such a way that if they are true, then the conclusion has to be true.

If it rains on Mars, and the temperatures and humidity are like they are around Toledo, Ohio, then the ground gets wet. It does rain on Mars and the temperatures and humidity are like they are around here. So, on Mars the ground gets wet. Now these premises are not both true. As far as is known it does not rain on Mars and the temperatures and humidity are a good deal different from around Toledo. Still, if things are as they are said to be in the premises, then the conclusion has to be true also.

If the moon is made of green cheese, it smells.

_____The moon is made of green cheese._____

Therefore (thf.) The moon smells.

The premises are hardly what one would call true, but the argument is valid all the same. If the moon really were made of green cheese, it would smell since things made of green cheese smell.

Either the Distance Learning (DL) office will never have another problem with its computers, or elephants can fly.

_____Elephants cannot fly._____

thf. The DL office will sometime have another problem.

Now the first premise here is not true. Remember false dilemmas from the discussion of fallacies? This is one. Still the argument is valid. The first premise says that one of two things is true—DL trouble never again or elephants can fly. And the second premise says that one of these things is not true—elephants cannot fly. So then what has to be the case, if one assumes the premises are true (as one would do if one were checking for validity)? Well the other alternative besides the elephant one has to be true. The pattern of reasoning is valid.

So what is desired is a simple way to look at an argument and check for validity. It turns out that this desire can be satisfied since there are several methods for checking validity of the arguments of the sort in question. This discussion will bring out two of them—the short truth table method, and the method of natural deduction.

SECTION 2

Understanding Basic Propositional Forms

The methods to be discussed deal with arguments formulated in what can be treated as *basic propositional forms and what are called truth functional compounds of these basic statements*. They concern basic propositional forms or combinations of these put together by using combinatorial elements that make the truth of the complex statements dependent, in regular and predictable ways, upon the truth or falsity of the component simple statements making up the combinations.

There are two basic points to get clear on here, one about the way this study of reasoning interprets ordinary talk and the arguments made from it, and the other about how one can use this interpretation to get at the validity or invalidity of the argument so interpreted. Consider the linguistic interpretation point first.

This approach to arguments says that every statement is either a basic statement or a combination of basic statements. A basic statement is one that says of one thing—a person, a group, a material object, a day of the week, and so on, that it is this way or that. It is raining. The ground is getting wet. The moon is made of green cheese. The moon smells. This is the body shop. The service shop is through that door. That football team is large. (How would you correct the ambiguity in that statement?) These are all basic statements in the sense intended. *They all say something*—one thing, *about something*—one thing. And they can all be combined to say other things by being put together with various connectives.

For example, one can say *it is false* that it is raining—and this is different from saying it is raining.

One can say that it is raining *and* the moon is made from a paint can lid. Or one can say that it is raining *and* the ground is getting wet.

In context, one would think the first "and" statement weird—what has the weather to do with moon material? The second is not at all weird—well it is raining, and the ground *is* getting wet—so what did you expect? When it rains the ground gets wet, or it is false that it is raining and the ground is not getting wet. So what's the surprise? Well having noticed it, the discussion can postpone talking about that weirdness for a short while.

Again, one can say, *Either* it is raining *or* the ground is not getting wet.

Or one can say, *If* it is raining *then* the ground is getting wet.

Notice that these examples change or combine some basic statements into others by using "it is false," "and," "either-or," and "if-then." And notice that one could even go beyond combining basic statements and could combine compound or previously combined statements to get even more complicated non-basic or compound statements. One might say, Either, if it rains then the ground gets wet, or elephants can fly. Here the first **disjunct** (the statements on either side of the "or" in an "either-or" statement) is an if-then compound out of two basic statements. And these (the component statements of the if-then statement) are combined by either-or with another basic statement to make a further compound statement.

Now what happens to the truth or falsity of the original component statements when basic statements are combined in these ways? Suppose one starts with truth and adds "it is false," then the resulting statement is false. Or suppose it is true that it is false that elephants can fly, and one adds "it is false" one more time. Then the result is the cumbersome double negative all English teachers warn against: "it is false that it is false that elephants can fly." What is really being said is that "the statement that *it is false that elephants can fly*" is itself false, and that is the same as saying that it is true that elephants can fly, or simply that elephants can fly.

> So "it is false that" just changes the truth of the original statement from
> true to false or false to true, depending upon which a thinker starts off with.

Thus changing and combining basic statements (or compound statements) in this way, will not only yield a new statement, but it will also yield a statement that will be true when the original was false and vice versa.

What then about the other devices for combining statements to make new statements? How do these combining devices of "and," "either-or," and "if-then" affect the truth of the original component statements? Well, they do not change the truth or falsity of the original statements but they do result in *another* statement whose truth one can tell definitively from the truth or falsity of the component statements *and* the way the combining device works. This is a lot easier than it sounds!

Think of the word "and." When one says something is true *and* something else is true that person means to say that *both* of them are true. Anything less—with only one of the combined statements true, or neither of them true, that person would not be saying what the word means.

Thus "and" works to join two or more statements in such a way that the resulting statement is true when all the combined statements are true, and otherwise the whole statement is false.

This information is usually displayed in what is called a **truth table** or *a matrix showing all the possible assignments of the values true or false to the statements put together* with "and"—the conjuncts. The truth table shows how the value of truth or falsity of the combined components—that is of the entire statement, is related to the truth or falsity values of the component statements.

P	Q	P and Q (also expressed "P & Q")
T	T	T
T	F	F
F	T	F
F	F	F

This display just records what we already have said in English. We want the "and" combination device to yield a combined statement that is true when and only when *both* the combined statements are true. That is just what we mean when we say that: It is raining and the ground is getting wet—namely that *both* of these are true. So that illustrates the conventional understanding of the operations of the "and" combination device.

That said the truth table for the "~" which is called a ***tilde*** and is read as "it is false that" is as follows:

P	~P
T	F
F	T

This table is read as saying that when P stands for a statement given a truth value of true or "T", then ~P is to be given the value of "F." And if P is given the value of F, then ~P is to be given the value of T.

For the "**either-or**" combination device one wants to make sure that the combined statement is true when and only when **one or the other of the alternatives one is combining is true.** If one says today is Monday, or elephants can fly, one means to say that one of these statements is true, *at least.* This does not rule out both being true. After all one could say either the forest fire will get worse or we will have to spend more money fighting it. And the intention might be to allow that both of these alternatives can be true. Regardless, a thinker is saying that at least one will be true in saying that either this is so or that is so. And this means that:

The convention should make the "either-or" device work so that the resulting statement is true when at least one combined statement is true, and false otherwise.

The truth table thus looks like this

P	Q	P or Q (also expressed "P v Q")
T	T	T
T	F	T
F	T	T
F	F	F

Finally, the device for "if-then" combinations says that if the first statement of the combination (the antecedent of the hypothetical or if-then statement) is true then the second (the consequent of the hypothetical) is also. If it rains then the ground gets wet. That is just the natural progression of things. So this immediately reveals two features of the "if-then" combination device—first:

If the first statement is true and it is also the case that the second is true at the same time, then the whole is true. And if the first statement is true and the second is false, then the whole is false.

That is just what one means to say when he or she says that if something occurs, then something else will occur.

But what if the first statement is false, in fact, perhaps always false? So suppose someone says that if humans run at fifty miles per hour, then humans get tired running. In this crazy example, the antecedent statement (the "if" statement) is false and the consequent statement (the "then" statement) is true. Humans do not run fifty miles per hour and they do get tired running.

Or what if one says that if it gets to 300 degrees in the fields of corn, then the corn will pop on the ear. In normal conditions, neither of the basic statements making up this compound statement is true. Both are false. What about the if-then statement made up of both of these? What should the combining device do in that case?

Well there is much that can be said here. One way to look at these two conditions when the antecedent—the "if" part—is false and the consequent—the "then" part—is true, or when both the antecedent and the consequent are false, is to ask *whether the truth or falsity of these component statements makes the hypothetical false*. Does the fact that humans do not run at fifty miles per hour make false the whole statement which says that if they do then they will get tired? No. But then what should the truth assignment be? If it is not going to be false then the only option left is to make it true. Similarly, the fact that cornfields do not get to be 300 degrees Fahrenheit and corn does not pop on the ear (when attached to the plant and growing in the field), does not make it false that if the temperature did get that high, then the corn would pop that way. Again, by default, it seems that the best thing to do is to assign a truth value of "true" to hypothetical statements that have a false antecedent and a false consequent. And that is just what the convention calls for.

> **Accordingly, when the antecedent of an "if-then" or hypothetical statement is false, then the whole compound statement is true. And when both antecedent and consequent are false the whole is true.**

That is unsatisfying because it is somewhat conventional, yes. But the discussion would need to turn into a course on philosophical logic to straighten out the problem, let alone begin to solve it!

So with that said, the truth table for the combined "if-then" statements looks like this:

P	Q	if P then Q (also expressed "P→Q")
T	T	T
T	F	F
F	T	T
F	F	T

INTER-DEFINABILITY OF THE MAIN LOGICAL CONNECTIVES. Having set out the truth tables for each of the commonly used logical connectives, it might help fix ideas to note that these connectives are inter-definable. For example, the if-then connective can be "defined by" or shown *to be equivalent* in truth to an expression using only "~" and "&", or else "~" and "v." This can be seen by using truth tables for the connective to be defined and showing that the truth table for the defining expression yields a combined statement form that is true and false *under exactly the same truth assignments to the component statements.*

p	q	p→q	=	~(p&~q)
T	T	T t T		**t**(T **f** F)
T	F	T f F		**f**(T **t** T)
F	T	F t T		**t**(F **f** F)
F	F	F t F		**t**(F **f** T)

Thus if the lowercase "t" and "f" are understood to give the truth or falsehood values of the combinations of basic statements, and the uppercase "T" and "F" to give the truth values assigned to the component basic statements, then it is clear that the two statement forms will have the same truth values in all rows of their truth tables. *They can be exchanged, one for the other, and nothing in terms of truth values of the combined statement forms will have changed.* Notice here that in assigning the values for ~q in the second combined expression, ~(p&~q) the conversion of the truth values assigned to q was performed in assigning the ~q truth value. And notice that ~(p&q), or for that matter ~(x v y) and ~(s→t), includes within its scope the combined statement contained within the parentheses, so whatever that combined statement's truth value is, the truth value *of the whole* is changed from T to F or from F to T by the addition of the "~" sign.

With all that in mind then, consider the following equivalent forms and their truth tables:

p	~p	~~p
T	F	T
F	T	F

p	q	p→q	=	(~p v q)
T	T	T t T		F t T
T	F	T f F		F f F
F	T	F t T		T t T
F	F	F t F		T t F

p	q	p&q	=	~(~p v ~q)
T	T	T t T		t(F f F)
T	F	T f F		f(F t T)
F	T	F f T		f(T t F)
F	F	F f F		f(T t T)

p	q	p v q	=	~(~p & ~q)
T	T	T t T		t(F f F)
T	F	T t F		t(F f T)
F	T	F t T		t(T f F)
F	F	F f F		f(T t T)

Now notice that what statement variable letter is used does not matter as long as the form of the statement is the same and the use of the variables is consistent. Thus (s v t) can be expressed as ~(~s&~t), and (q→r) can be expressed as ~(q&~r) or as (~q v r), and so on. "p," "q," "r," "s," "t," "u," "w," are just variables that take the place of statements when the discussion is focused on the form not the content of a statement.

TO FIX IDEAS. Work through the following equivalencies.

1. express p→q using just "~" and "&".

2. express p&q using just "~" and "→".

3. express p→(q v r) using just "~" and "&".

4. express [(p&t) v w] → s using just "~" and "v".

5. express {[p→(q & s)] → (w v s)} using just "~" and "→".

Notice in number (4) that the expression (p&t) is a component statement form within another component statement form [(p&t) v w]. Thus "( )" are less inclusive than "[ ]", and "[ ]" are less inclusive than "{ }" found in (5). There will be virtually no occasion in this book to use any signs of partitioning of component statements more inclusive than the braces "{ }", and usually no need to use anything stronger than the brackets "[ ]".

Expressing Arguments as Truth Functional Compounds and Assessing Them by Reference to Truth Tables and the Short-Truth Table Method

This much gives you the equipment to express statements in terms revealing that they are truth functionally basic or are truth functionally compound. As well there is a standard way to understand just how compounding statements out of basic statements and the forms of connection examined above results in a new statement with a truth value dependent upon the truth values of the component statements. These various truth value determinations can be set out in a truth table for complex statements such as the following:

If Herman wins the race, then either Herman gets the spoils or Herman refuses the spoils. This statement is one made up of three basic statements connected by "if-then" and "either-or". The first basic statement is Herman wins the race. The second is Herman gets the spoils. And third is Herman refuses the spoils.

Herman wins the race can be symbolized as "w".

Herman gets the spoils as "s". And,

Herman refuses the spoils as "~s".

Then the whole statement can be put into the following form:

w→(s v ~s)

And a truth table can be set up to show all of the possible forms of combinations of truth value assignments and whether the combined statement would be assigned a "T" or "F" under these various assignments to the component statements. Again the lowercase "t" or "f" will signify the truth value of the component statement.

w	s	w → (s v ~s)
T	T	T t (T t F)
T	F	T t (F t T)
F	T	F t (T t F)
F	F	F t (F t T)

This truth table is interesting in itself as well as an illustration of the idea of giving a truth table for a truth functional statement. Notice that there was no way to make the component statement (s v ~s) false. And with that feature the hypothetical statement, with w as its antecedent and the always true (s v ~s) as consequent, is itself true—any statement always implies or is in a true if-then relationship with a true statement. This was clear from looking at the truth table for "→" but it is interesting to see it at work in larger statement form.

Perhaps that will give the idea of a truth table for a statement with two different statement variables, but what about statement forms with three statement variables? The idea is exactly the same. All that is increased is complication and the number of rows of the truth table needed to show all possible truth value assignment combinations—a number that is 2 to the nth where n equals the number of separate statement variables. Thus for a statement with three statement variables, there would have to be eight rows to show all of the possible combinations of truth value assignments to the component basic statements. Thus consider the statement that:

If Beatrice bought The Bobbsey Twins books, and Brenda bought *An Introduction to Welding,* then Belinda's Books of Brooklyn had a big day.

Let "r" signify Beatrice bought *The Bobbsey Twins*.

Let "w" signify Brenda bought *An Introduction to Welding*.

And "s" signify Belinda's Books of Brooklyn had a big day.

Then the statement in question would be symbolized:

[(r & w) → s]

The truth table would look like this:

r	w	s	(r & w)	→	s
T	T	T	T t T	t	T
T	**T**	**F**	**T t T**	**f**	**F**
T	F	T	T f F	t	T
T	F	F	T f F	t	F
F	T	T	F f T	t	T
F	T	F	F f T	t	F
F	F	T	F f F	t	T
F	F	F	F f F	t	F

There are two things to take special note of here.

First , after the truth values are assigned according to the assignments made to the individual statement variables to the left, then the truth value of the component complex statement form is worked out according to the truth table for "and."

Thus where the statement variables "r" and "w" both have the assignment of "T", then the compound (r & w) requires the assignment of "T". But in every other case where there is an assignment of "F" to either "r" or "w" or both, then the whole compound requires an assignment of "f". This is just like the basic truth table for "&".

Then, working out from the component statement form "(r & w)" to the whole "(r & w) → s", the truth values are assigned to the combination of the premises "(r & w)" and "s" according to the truth table of "→" so that only when the compound "(r & w)" receives a "t" and the "s" receives an "f", will the whole require an "f". Otherwise it will require a "t"—just as if "(r & w)" is "p" and "s" is "q" in the truth table displayed for "p & q".

The second thing to notice is that the text has put in bold the one row of the truth table for this statement form in which there is an "f" assigned to the whole form. This is just to highlight that the truth table method will show the case in which a statement form will receive a truth value assignment of "f", if there is one. This point and the row or rows where such an assignment would be made will figure prominently in the first test of validity.

And these are all the essentials. Things do not change in nature or differ in kind for doing the truth tables for any other statement forms, no matter how complex. They only become less or more complicated. If the above is understood as an illustration of how to proceed then the technique should be clear in all of its details. Notice one more time: the truth table sets out the truth values basic or compound statement forms would have depending upon the truth values of the component statement forms making them up. They are not trying to say or represent what are the facts of the world concerning some event or state of affairs.

To fix ideas, write the truth tables for and reflect on the following:

1. $(p \ \& \sim p) \rightarrow s$
2. $\{[(p \rightarrow q) \ \& \ (q \rightarrow r)] \rightarrow (p \rightarrow r)\}$
3. $\{[(p \ v \ q) \ \& \sim q] \rightarrow p\}$
4. $[(p \ v \ r \ v \ s) \ \& \ (p \ \& \ t)] \rightarrow (q \ \& \ s)$
5. $\{[p \ v \ (t \ \& \ s)] \ v \ [t \ v \ (p \ \& \ s)]\}$
6. Highlight and study the relationships in the above that produce truth tables with **no rows** showing the statement form to receive an "f" as a whole.
7. Highlight and study the above statement forms with rows showing the form to have the value of "f" as a whole.
8. What are the differences between the two situations referred to in (6) and (7)?

Techniques for Representing Arguments as Statement Forms _____

So far the discussion has provided the techniques of representing forms of statements and of examining their truth values as determined by the values assigned to component statements and the working of various logical connectives. Now things really start to get exciting! The above has given a way to interpret statements in English as either basic or combinations of basic statements and to figure out their truth when the truth-value of the basic statements is given. *Since statements can be combined into strings the truth of which is a function of the truth-value of the component parts, and since arguments are made up of statements,* **arguments themselves can be understood as other long statements combined out of the premises and the claim or conclusion.**

Notice that what one is trying to say in deductive reasoning is that if one has a good or valid argument then, if the premises are true, the conclusion has to be true also. That sounds analogous to what was said about hypothetical statements. They are true unless the "if part," the antecedent, is true, and the consequent part is false.

So imagine stringing the premises (as antecedent) together with the conclusion (as consequent) into an "if-then" statement. Then, if the truth table of the resulting "if-then" showed a row in which the premises (the antecedent) were true and the conclusion (the consequent) were false, one would know the argument is *not* valid. That is, the falsity of the hypothetical statement where the premises are the antecedent and true, and the consequent is the claim and false, this falsity of the whole statement turns out to indicate the invalidity of the argument in question.

If, on the other hand, there is no way to assign truth values to the component statement forms so that the statement form for the antecedent of the hypothetical (the premises) was true, while that of the conclusion (the consequent) was false, then any argument of that form could not have true premises and a false conclusion. Thus any such argument would be valid.

Thus, the technique of looking at the truth value for compound statements gives a short way to check the validity of arguments made up of basic statements or combinations of them.

How about an example or two: If Stalin reads Marx, then he is a Communist. Stalin was a Communist. So he read Marx. Now consider the display of this argument in terms of single letters for each basic statement and then in terms of their combinations into one big hypothetical statement.

So first—If *Stalin reads Marx,* then *he is a Communist.* The same conventions already introduced will hold here: The first basic statement then is "s". The next call "c". SO you have

If s then c

Now the second premise is c, Stalin was a Communist.

And the conclusion is Stalin read Marx or s.

So now the argument is

$$s \rightarrow c$$

$$\underline{c}$$

Therefore s

And now try putting the entire argument into an if-then form with the premises in the "if" position and the conclusion in the "then" position.

(s→c), and c, Thf. s Or **[(s→c) & c]→s**

Now what? Well, now the argument is valid if, when the premises are true, the conclusion has to be true also. And it is invalid when the premises are true and the conclusion is not true. So a good *rule of thumb* is: ***A check of the validity of the argument can be formed by trying to find assignments of truth-values for the letters of the combined***

statements such that the premises are true and the conclusion is false or the whole hypothetical formed of premises ("if") and conclusion ("then") is a statement form assigned an "f".

In order to apply this test of trying to make the hypothetical combining premises and conclusion false, one starts with truth-value assignments that will make the conclusion false. So the argument form written as a statement is: **[(s→c) & c]→s.** And what would be an indication of invalidity would be an assignment of truth values of the following pattern:

[(s→c) & c] → s

T   F yielding a truth value for the whole of

F

Is there a combination of truth values assigned consistently that will make the premises true and the conclusion false? Notice that an "f" has already been assigned to "s," the conclusion symbol. That means, as the truth table for if→then shows, that "s→c" will have to get a "T" for its truth value, no matter what is assigned to its component part "c". So if the premises are going to be made true c will have to be assigned "T" so that when s→c is combined with c using the "and" connective as in its truth table, the result will be a true conjunction or a true "and" statement of the premises. But then that is it. If one puts in the truth-values needed there is a progression showing that there is an assignment of truth-values such that the premises can be true and the conclusion is false.

[(s→c) & c] →s

F T T F

T and T

T   F

F

The "F" indicates that the whole hypothetical is false and so that the premises have been given legitimate truth value assignments that make them true while the conclusion has an assignment making it false or an assignment of "F"—true premises, false conclusion, and thus an invalid argument form. This is an indication that the argument form yields only invalid arguments.

How about another example? Either he picks up trash on Tuesday or he picks up on Wednesday. He does not do it on Tuesday. Therefore he does it on Wednesday.

Either Tuesday or Wednesday. Either t or w. ~t Thf. w

Using the conventions set out above the argument shapes up this way:

$$[(t \lor w) \& \sim t] \to w$$

Now is there a way to make this hypothetical false? You know that "w" will have to be false, or F. And "(t v w)" as well as "~t" will have to be "T," or true. Can you do that? Suppose we assign T's and F's as follows:

$$[(t \lor w) \& \sim t] \to w$$
$$\textbf{F} \quad \textbf{F} \qquad \textbf{T} \qquad \textbf{F}$$

Then the "either-or" statement is false and so this does not make the premises true and the conclusion false.

But consider the alternative truth-value assignment running this way:

$$[(t \lor w) \quad \& \quad \sim t] \to w$$
$$\textbf{T} \quad \textbf{F} \qquad \textbf{F} \qquad \textbf{F}$$

Well, again, there is a problem because one cannot make the premises true while the conclusion is false. In this case the first component premise is assigned the value of true but the second "~t" is not. But these two patterns are the only possible assignments of truth values to these statement forms. The problem comes in because we have a "t" (Tuesday) in the either-or premise and a "~t "as the other premise. These will always have opposite truth values and so if the "w" has to have a truth value of F to show the argument is invalid, then there is no way to assign truth values to the premises and conclusion of an argument with this pattern and show it is invalid.

But if it is not possible to make it invalid, then it has been shown to be valid. So this argument pattern is valid!

Consider one more invalid argument. If Colonel Mustard committed the murder in the dining room, then Miss Scarlet was innocent. But Colonel Mustard did not commit the murder in the dining room. Therefore, Miss Scarlet is not innocent.

If Colonel Mustard then Scarlet innocent. Not Colonel Mustard. Therefore not Scarlet innocent.

Or: p→s innocent, Not-p. Therefore Not-s innocent. Strung together into a hypothetical statement with the premises in the antecedent and the conclusion in the consequent, the resulting symbolization is this:

$$\{[(p \to s) \& \sim p] \to \sim s\}$$

Now using the procedure already sketched to check for validity by making the conclusion false and the premises true, this is what comes along:

$$[(p{\rightarrow}s)\ \&\ {\sim}p]\ \rightarrow\ {\sim}s$$

T   F

Then:
$$[(p{\rightarrow}s)\ \&\ {\sim}p]\ \rightarrow\ {\sim}s$$

F   T   T   F

Then:
$$[(p{\rightarrow}s)\ \&\ {\sim}p]\ \rightarrow\ {\sim}s$$

F   T   T   F

T   T

Then:
$$[(p{\rightarrow}s)\ \&\ {\sim}p]\ \rightarrow\ {\sim}s$$

F   T   T   F

T   T

T   **F**

F

In other words, the premises can be given consistent assignments of truth values making them true as the conclusion is made false—given the conventions to interpret and make true or false combination statements out of true or false basic statements using the connectives whose truth tables are described above. *Since one can give the premises a truth value of T while giving the conclusions one of F, and the whole hypothetical with premises in the antecedent and conclusion in the consequent is false, then the argument is shown to be invalid.*

Now one might well be asking how he or she can just assign T's and F's to these letters for basic statements. Of course, the technique shown here is not just assigning these values any old way. Basically it is reproducing the row of the truth table for the whole statement form that shows the premises true and the conclusion false—or it is showing that there is no such row. If the argument is valid, then if the premises are true the conclusion has to be true.

§ So if one can start with the conclusion and make it false and then using consistent assignments make the premises true, the argument is shown to have a counterexample or to be not valid.

§ It does not matter what basic statement letter is given a "T" or an "F" as long as this is done consistently so that every occurrence of the same statement variable receives the same assignment and as long as you make the assignment so that the conclusion is false.

§ The object is to find whether any such assignment can consistently be made using the ways the connectives of "either-or," "and" and the rest operate (as illustrated above with the truth tables).

This approach to checking validity is a version of the so-called "short truth table method." It has the benefit of being purely mechanical, for the most part.

Follow these steps to carry out a short-truth table check of validity:

1. Put the argument in proper symbolic form symbolizing each premise and then the conclusion.
2. Link the premises by "&."
3. Link the premises and the conclusion by connecting with an "→."
4. Assign an "F" to the conclusion directly, to a basic statement, or appropriately to the component basic statements if the conclusion is a compound statement form.
5. Assign the same value(s) to the occurrence of the statement variable(s) of the conclusion that are found in the premises.
6. If possible, assign a "T" to the basic statements standing alone in the conjoined premises. If it is not possible to do this, then you are done since it will be impossible to make the premises true and the conclusion false.
7. Carry the assignments made in step 6 to individual statement variables through the remainder of the premises where the same statement variables occur.
8. Fill out the remaining portions of the premises by assigning "T" or "F" to the remaining portions of the premises. If this can be done in a way that makes the premises true while the conclusion is false, the argument form gives a structure of invalid arguments. If it cannot be done, then the argument form is one for valid arguments.

Mastery Exercises VIII.1

SELF TEST   *Comprehension Questions*

1. Why can you assign "T" or "F" however you want as long as you respect the rules in the three bullets on pages 302 and 304?

2. What is the meaning of the term "valid?"

3. Why can you consider an argument as an extended statement of an if-then form, if you want to check its validity?

4. If you cannot make the "if" portion true and the "then" portion false in an argument's symbolization, is that argument form one for valid arguments?

⸮ *Mastery Exercises VIII.2*

SELF TEST

Short-Truth Table Method Practice

Show the validity or invalidity of the following argument forms by using the short truth-table method. In the case of a valid argument, there will be no possible way to assign an "F" or the truth value of "false" to the conclusion while properly assigning the truth value of "true" to the premises. In the case of an invalid argument, you can write the truth-values under the letters and the connectives to show that one can assign truth to the premises and falsity to the conclusion. For example:

$$[(P \rightarrow Q) \& \sim P] \rightarrow \sim Q$$

	F	T	T		F
		T	T		F
			T		F

1. $[(a \rightarrow b) \& (c \rightarrow d) \& (b v d)] \rightarrow (a v c)$

2. $[(p v q) \& (q v r)] \rightarrow (p v r)$

3. $[(p \rightarrow q) \& (q v s) \& (s \rightarrow r)] \rightarrow r$

4. $[(q \rightarrow q) \& \sim q \& q] \rightarrow \sim p$

5. $\{(p \rightarrow q) \& (\sim q v r) \& [\sim (r \& \sim s)] \& \sim p\} \rightarrow \sim s$

6. $\{(p v q) \& [(\sim p \& \sim q) v r] \& \sim r\} \rightarrow \sim q$

7. $[(p \rightarrow q) \& (p v s)] \rightarrow s$

8. $[(r \rightarrow q) \& (q \rightarrow p)] \rightarrow (r \rightarrow p)$

9. $[(p v s v r v q) \& \sim r \& \sim q \& \sim p] \rightarrow s$

10. $[(s \& p) v (q \& r)] \rightarrow \sim s$

SECTION 4

Natural Deduction and Checking Validity by Proofs

As the discussion proceeded, you might have noticed that valid argument forms can be thought of as rules of inference allowing the appropriate conclusion to be drawn from premises of the right form. Thus in the examples just given, number 8 gives such a rule that is so familiar in thought that it has a name of its own—hypothetical syllogism. That argument form, $[(p{\rightarrow}q)$ & $(q{\rightarrow}r)] \rightarrow (p{\rightarrow}r)$ allows thinkers to consolidate two hypothetical premises into one, dropping out, so to speak, the middle or shared statement variable. Why does this work? The truth table for this argument form is one you worked out in number 2 of the truth table exercises above. That much of it should be clear. But there is more of an explanation available as to why this argument form should hold up. Notice that in an if-then form of statement, *the truth of the if-portion, or antecedent, gives what is sufficient for the truth of what is in the consequent.* That is captured nicely in the truth table since there *if the antecedent is true and the consequent is false then the whole statement is shown to be false; if the truth of what is stated in the antecedent of a hypothetical is not accompanied by the truth of what is stated in the consequent, then the statement of the whole claim is false.* So hypotheticals give what are sufficient conditions for the truth of the consequent.

Now this means that whenever the antecedent is true the consequent is also, or from another angle, if the consequent is not true then the antecedent cannot be true. *The truth of the consequent of a hypothetical is necessary for the truth of the antecedent.* For example:

If it rains, then the ground gets wet.

So suppose it rains, what would one expect that is sufficient for—the ground getting wet. But suppose the ground stays dry. Then one would have to say that it has not rained, or not recently anyway.

Noticing sufficient and necessary conditions being expressed in the antecedent and consequent of a true hypothetical statement gives an understanding of why hypothetical syllogisms work and why such reasoning patterns should have their own name. Note that the consolidation of two hypotheticals into one trades on the fact that the consequent stating the necessary condition in the first is the same as the antecedent stating the sufficient condition in the second. Thus the if part of the first will not be true except when the consequent of the second is also true. *Or, the consequent of the second hypothetical is necessary to the truth of the antecedent of the first. So it is possible to consolidate the two into one.* Now there are so many relationships like this in the world, and it is such an economy to understand and compress, or telescope, these by thinking them through hypothetical syllogisms, that it is familiar to every thinker to proceed this way. No wonder there is a name for doing so.

> ***For example:*** "If I take out my garbage early, then surely cats will get into it and spread it everywhere. If cats get into it and spread it everywhere, then I'll have to clean it up. So if I take out the garbage early, I'll just have to clean it up."

A simple, even homely example, perhaps, until you go out to get into the car to head for work and there is the garbage to pick up before you leave. Now, ten minutes late, you take off with yesterday's ham sandwich unnoticed on your shoe—well you get the idea.

Hypothetical syllogism is not the only such highly useful and frequently used argument form that is explained in terms of necessary and sufficient conditions. Look back up at the last example worked through before summing up the section on the short truth table method.

$[(p{\rightarrow}q) \mathbin{\&} {\sim}q] \rightarrow {\sim}p$ called "modus tollens"

Here the first premise sets out a relationship between two statements so that the one, q, is necessary to the truth of the other—p. The second premise denies the truth of the consequent, of that necessary condition—~q. And the conclusion has to be that what requires the truth of that statement is itself false—~p. Think of trying to apply the pattern of reasoning of Mill's Method of Residues to trying to figure out why the car will not start. "Well, if it runs it has spark. Yes, it is getting spark—it shocked my little brother pretty good when he held the spark plug wire. If it runs it is getting air. Yes, it has air, I just replaced the air cleaner with a new one and I know that it is in the right place not blocking anything. If it runs, it is getting gas. Let's see—son of a gun, there's no gas! No wonder it's not running." This pattern of reasoning—if the necessary condition in a hypothetical is false then you may conclude the falsity of the antecedent also, is so familiar and so useful it is no wonder that it has its own name—modus tollens.

As it turns out, there are many such patterns of reasoning. These are so much a part of our ordinary reasoning day in and day out that they have names and are known as valid argument forms. They are patterns which thinkers would naturally or commonly take advantage of as so many rules in thinking about things. These rules, though perhaps not for that reason, are often referred to as patterns of natural deduction, or ordinary reasoning. And by knowing what these are, not only are thinkers better equipped to formulate good arguments themselves, but also they are in a better position for understanding and checking each other's reasoning. If an argument is meant as deductive and follows *only* along the lines of these rules of natural deduction, then as depending upon only valid forms of inference, the argument is itself valid. Thus it is useful for checking validity to know these patterns of reasoning and a couple of invalid rules that often trip up thinkers. These rules will be introduced and shown to be valid (invalid) by the short-truth table method.

1. *Modus Ponens* $[(p{\rightarrow}q)$ and $p] \rightarrow q$

Try to make this false—the first thing to do is assign F to the conclusion, that is to q. And then try to adjust the others to make the whole hypothetical false.

$$[(p{\rightarrow}q) \text{ and } p] \rightarrow q$$
$$\quad\quad\quad\quad F \quad\quad\quad\quad F$$

Since, in order to make the whole argument hypothetical false one has to make the premises true, then one has to make the first hypothetical statement "(p→q)" true. And since "q" is already made F or false to make the conclusion false, then "p" has to be F or false also. Now the result is:

$$[(p{\rightarrow}q) \text{ and } p] \rightarrow q$$
$$\quad F \;\; F \quad\quad F \quad\quad F$$

But then,
$$[(p{\rightarrow}q) \;\&\; p] \rightarrow q$$
$$\quad\;\; F \;\; F \quad F \quad\quad F$$
$$\quad\quad\;\; T \quad\quad F$$
$$\quad\quad\quad\;\; F \quad\quad\quad\quad F$$
$$\quad\quad\quad\quad\quad \mathbf{T}$$

What this shows is that the only possible assignments of truth-values to make the hypothetical false (the argument invalid), really will show it to be valid. That is, one cannot make the premises true and the conclusion false in this pattern. So Modus Ponens is a valid pattern of inference. Any argument that might be symbolically expressed by the Modus Ponens pattern is valid.

2. *Modus Tollens*   [(p→q) and ~q] → ~p

Now let us try to make that false   [(p→q) & ~q] → ~p

                                                                           F

So then   [(p→q) & ~q] → ~p

                                          T   F

And then   [(p→q) & ~q] → ~p

                                      T T   F   F

So: [(p→q) & ~q] → ~p

                                      T T   F   F

                                          T   F

                                              F   F

                                                T

So because of having to make the "p" statement T in the first embedded hypothetical, it is necessary to make the "q" in that hypothetical T and then "~q" turns out to be false, so the conjunction of the two premises turns out to be false and that in combination with the false consequent, according to the truth table for "if-then," makes the whole statement (premises and conclusion) true. So there is no way to show any argument with this pattern is invalid and thus any argument in this pattern will be valid.

For the rest of the basic rules in the text—the first nine rules all together, only the last line of this sort of reasoning is given, that is the argument pattern is stated with all of the possible truth values assigned. They all will start with the conclusion or the consequent of the argument hypothetical being marked F, and then as you think about them, work backwards from there.

3. *Hypothetical Syllogism*

                                [(p→q) & (q→r)] → (p→r)

                              T T   T F   T F

                                  T   F   F

                                      F   F

                                        T

And
$$[(p{\rightarrow}q)\ \&\ (q{\rightarrow}r)]\ \rightarrow\ (p{\rightarrow}r)$$

T	F	F	F		T	F
	F		T			F
			F			F
			T			

Notice that no matter how one assigns values to "q", the whole argument hypothetical will come out true.

4. *Disjunctive Syllogism*

This example is also illustrated above in the discussion of the short-truth table method. Check back to see how this works.

$$[(p\ v\ q)\ \&\ {\sim}p]\ \rightarrow\ q \qquad\qquad [(p\ v\ q)\ \&\ {\sim}q]\ \rightarrow\ p$$

T	F	F		F		F	T	F	F
	T			F			T	F	F
		F		F				F	
			T					**T**	

Notice the same result comes about no matter how complex "p" and "q" are. It would be the same if the argument form was

$$\{[(p{\rightarrow}r)\ v\ (q{\rightarrow}s)]\ \&\ {\sim}(p{\rightarrow}r)\}{\rightarrow}(q{\rightarrow}s)$$

5. *Simplification*

(p&q)→p clearly since both of the statements "p" and "q" are supposed to be true, then neither one of them may be false, while the conjunction is true

$$(p\ \&\ q)\ \rightarrow\ p$$

F	T/F	F
	F	F
	T	

6. *Conjunction*

If p, q then (p & q) clearly no matter which of the conjuncts in the conclusion portion of the argument hypothetical we make false the antecedent conjunction in the argument hypothetical will be made false also and thus the whole will be true—there would be no possibility of making the conclusion false and the premises true at the same time.

7. *Addition*

(p) → (p v q) Notice this says that if one knows one statement is true, the premise, then one knows the disjunction of that statement and any other is also true. Remember that the expression "p v q" says at least one statement is true, "p" or "q". So one only needs one of these to be true for the whole "(p v q)" to be true. Can you do the short truth table for this, showing its validity?

8. *Constructive Dilemma*

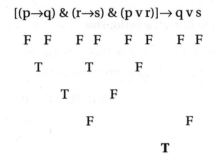

$$[(p{\rightarrow}q) \,\&\, (r{\rightarrow}s) \,\&\, (p \vee r)] \rightarrow q \vee s$$

F	F		F	F		F	F	F	F

(see diagram)

9. *Destructive Dilemma*

$$[(p{\rightarrow}q) \,\&\, (r{\rightarrow}s) \,\&\, ({\sim}q \vee {\sim}s)] \rightarrow ({\sim}p \vee {\sim}r)$$

(see diagram)

Well, ok, all of these argument patterns are valid. And, in addition, there are two common patterns in need of recognition, even though they are invalid—Affirming the Consequent and Denying the Antecedent.

Affirming the Consequent	*Denying the Antecedent*
p→q	**p→s**
q	**~p**
Thf. p	**Thf. ~s**

Try to use the short truth table method to show that these are invalid patterns.

With this much you have a very potent set of tools for checking the validity of many deductive arguments. You can either cast them into symbols showing the way basic statements are combined into compound statements and then use the short truth table method to check the validity, or you can cast the arguments into symbols showing the ways the basic statements involved are combined into compound statements and then check to see if the argument shows any of the valid or invalid patterns just presented. And if it does, then one can see by reference to the validity or the invalidity of the patterns just reviewed whether the argument is valid or not. (Any argument that has only valid argument patterns within it is valid. And any complex argument with even one invalid argument pattern within it is invalid.) To fix ideas, consider the following examples. The first is a familiar one in the study of logic.

> **(A) Only the good die young. Someone is good. So someone will die young.**

First let us get this into symbols. Only if p, q, really is If q then p. "Only if" is language introducing a necessary condition. "Only if there is enough oxygen will we be able to breathe at that depth. No, really we'll need nitrogen at that depth." So the second person is saying, "if we are able to breathe at that depth, then it will be through the use of nitrogen." "Only if the Colonel is free of appointments, will he be available." "If the Colonel is free of appointments, then he will be available (for an appointment)." So the first thing to do to symbolize the argument in A) is to symbolize "Only the good die young" in the following step:

"Only the good die young" goes to "If someone dies young then someone is good."

This can be symbolized as If p (for dies young) then q (for good).

The second premise is that Someone is good—q.

The conclusion is Someone will die young—p

So the argument comes out as If Y then G, and G, Therefore Y or

$$p \rightarrow q$$

$$\underline{q}$$

Thf. q   Does that look familiar? It should since it is a case of affirming the consequent, a pattern known to be invalid.

> **(B) If it rains the ground gets wet or the air is too dry. It is raining. Therefore the ground is getting wet or the air is too dry.**

The first premise is r (for it is raining) $\rightarrow$ (w v q) (w for ground gets wet, q for the air is too dry for the ground to get wet.)

The second premise is It is raining, or r. The conclusion is (w v q)

So the argument pattern is r→ (w v q)

<u>   r   </u>

Thf. (w v q)   Look familiar? It should. It is a case of Modus Ponens and so we
know the argument is valid

> **(C) Either the settlement is incorporated or it is part of Toledo. It is not part of
> Toledo. So: It is incorporated. But then, now I understand why the taxes are so
> high, since, If the settlement is incorporated then the local government needs
> lots of money and if it needs lots of money then taxes will be very high. So: If
> it is incorporated then taxes will be high. And it is incorporated—so, well there
> you are, taxes are high.**

Wow, that is a complicated argument! What one has to do is break it down into
bite sized chunks and then assess the part and the whole from there. The first part of
the argument is clearly a **Disjunctive Syllogism:**

Either the settlement is incorporated or it is part of Toledo	p v t
<u> It is not part of Toledo </u>	<u>~t </u>
Thf. It is incorporated	Thf. p

And this is a valid argument pattern—so far so good.

Now the second argument is buried along the way. It has to do with what chains
of connection there are between the incorporation of a settlement and how high
taxes are.

If the settlement is incorporated then the local government needs lots of money	p → q
<u> If the local government needs lots of money, then taxes will be high. </u>	<u>q → r</u>
Thf. If the settlement is incorporated then taxes will be high	Thf. p → r

That pattern of reasoning, a **Hypothetical Syllogism,** is valid, so that part of the
longer argument is ok. Now let us bring it home looking at the last part of the argument. This has to do with why taxes are so high. This sub-argument uses a conclusion
of one of the earlier sub-arguments to establish its conclusion.

If the settlement is incorporated then taxes will be high.	p → r
<u> The settlement is incorporated. </u>	<u>p </u>
Thf. Taxes will be high.	Thf. r

So we now see that we have a chain of reasoning the last part of which involves Modus Ponens, itself a valid form of inference. Notice that the form of the general argument is that the conclusion of the first part combines with the conclusion of the second to serve as premises from which one generates the main conclusion. Now one would not accept the results of the first and second arguments as giving premises from which to get a third conclusion (the main conclusion) if these arguments were not valid. But these first two arguments do give us those conclusions validly. Thus one can accept these as premises from which to derive the third or main conclusion. Thus the whole argument is acceptable. There are two independent and valid arguments converging into one to generate the main conclusion. That was not so bad, was it?

The general rule is this: ***Any time you find a number of arguments strung together to eventually add up to a main conclusion, the overall argument will be acceptable only if all the arguments along the way are valid.***

How about another example?

> **(D)** Sesame Street is a successful, long-running TV show. If Sesame Street had not been a successful, long running TV show, then the creators would not have made lots of money. But then if the creators made a lot of money, they lived in big homes. So the creators of Sesame Street lived in big homes. So it looks like here again is a complex argument involving a couple of sub-arguments.

First sub-argument: If *Sesame Street* is not a successful long running show then the creators would not have made lots of money. *Sesame Street* is a successful long running TV show. So the creators did make lots of money.

Notice that in the non-symbolic version in the narrative, this conclusion was not stated either here, where it is a conclusion, or in the next sub-argument where it is a premise!

$\sim$s $\rightarrow$ $\sim$t

$\underline{\text{s}\qquad}$

Thf. t   Does that look familiar? This is a case of Denying the Antecedent and one knows that that is an *invalid* argument pattern. But the argument does not stop there.

The next step has to do with the connection of making lots of money and living in big houses.

Second sub-argument: If the creators made lots of money, then they lived in big homes. They made lots of money. So they lived in big homes.

t $\rightarrow$ q

$\underline{\text{t}\qquad}$

Thf. q   This is a case of Modus Ponens, which is a valid pattern of argumentation. And, as far as that goes, the argument is good.

But the argument relies in its first part on Denying the Antecedent which is invalid. And that first sub-argument is supposed to generate a conclusion that can be used as a premise in the next sub-argument. But if one did not validly derive the conclusion in the first sub-argument, it is not available to use as a premise in the second sub-argument. That second sub-argument would be valid. But one cannot assume that the argument will go, as one does not have the premises needed. So then the total combination of the two sub-arguments does not work, the total argument is no good over all.

The whole argument is an unacceptable chain of argumentation. Once again the rule is: Any time you find a number of arguments strung together to eventually add up to a main conclusion, the overall argument will be acceptable only if all the arguments along the way are valid.

In order for it to be a combination of valid arguments, each part has to be valid. But since it is not, then we know the overall argument is not going to work. It is not a combination of valid arguments. One can show this by stringing together the two arguments making up the whole and seeing by the short truth table method whether they will be acceptable together. They will not, as the short truth table method for the Denying the Antecedent argument will show that the Denying the Antecedent pattern invalid. But maybe it will be interesting to see the two side by side and see that their conjunction is false.

$$\{[(\sim s \rightarrow \sim t)\ \&\ s] \rightarrow t\} \quad \& \quad \{[(t \rightarrow q)\ \&\ t] \rightarrow q\}$$

F	T	T	F		F	F	F	F
	T	T	F			F		F
		T	F			F		F
			F					T
			F					T
		F						

The point of this section so far has been to familiarize you with several of the deductive patterns of reasoning familiar to everyone and in that way show the beginnings of another method for seeing that arguments are valid or invalid—even complicated arguments where several deductive argument patterns are used together. Now there is some more to talk about here. And of course there are many, many more valid deductive patterns. But this is enough for the moment. With this much said there is already a pay off. The patterns of reasoning just explained can be used to understand some of the reasoning in planning.

PLANNING AND DEDUCTIVE REASONING. There is much that goes into the process of thoughtful planning. But at the basis of several of the standard steps of reasoning in planning are some of the basic patterns of deductive reasoning just spoken about. Understanding these patterns can then help with understanding several features of planning and so help directly in life.

General Picture of the Steps of Planning

1. **Vividly Identify Your Options by Identifying Their Likely Consequences:** This step is known to us all. All planning begins with getting some idea of what one can do, of where one might go on vacation, of what one wants to accomplish—in a lifetime or over the weekend. But how, in terms of the above thought patterns, does this work? Certainly one aspect of identifying options is thinking about various things and understanding them in terms of their consequences. "Well, if I go to medical school, then I will have to study hard for five more years and go into debt a lot further. So let's assume that I am going to medical school. Wow, think of all those weekends studying and all those student loans!! That is what I will be stuck with!!" Here the thought pattern is obviously that of Modus Ponens:

> If I go to medical school, I will have to study hard for five more years and go much further into debt.
>
> I am going to Medical School.
>
> Thf. I am stuck with all that studying and all that debt!

2. **Narrow Down These Options by Their Unwanted Consequences:** Now clearly it is thinking like this that "gets one thinking"! One might realize that he or she really does not want that option. The work is not a worry. But one is coming from a poor family as it is and one cannot stand the thought of a lot of debt waiting after school. So one rejects that option. And what pattern of thinking does that? Modus Tollens is the ticket.

> If I go to medical school. I will have to study hard for five years and go into debt much further.
>
> I reject the debt so I reject the debt and study combination.
>
> Thf. I will not go to medical school OR I reject medical school also.

3. **Arrive at One Major Objective or Chosen Option:** If one learns enough about all of one's options, he or she might be able to narrow down to only a couple for further thought. And, after all, one can give these further thought and then one might be able to reject one of these, leaving oneself with only one best option. The pattern of reasoning we would be using is Disjunctive Syllogism.

> Either I will become a concert pianist or a landscape architect.
>
> I will not become a concert pianist (not enough money, many in my family have arthritis in their hands, I do not like to travel that much).
>
> Thf. I will become a landscape architect.

4. Link Together the Several Steps One Will Have to Take in Order to Achieve That Goal: Having settled on the life option one wants to pursue, one can now think about how to get there and what various steps must be linked together to get there. The pattern of reasoning involved is the Hypothetical Syllogism.

> Well, if I am going to be a landscape architect, then I need to go to an agricultural school with a strong arts and architecture program.
>
> If I go to a school with such programs then I will have to go to the University of Illinois.
>
> If I go to the University of Illinois, I will have to pull up my SAT's and get good grades as well as intern somewhere.
>
> If I pull up my SAT's and get good grades as well as intern somewhere, I am going to have to become much more efficient with my use of time.
>
> If I become more efficient with my use of time, then I need to get a good daily planner.
>
> So if I am going to be a landscape architect I had better get a good daily planner and learn how to use it, pronto!!

And so it goes. Again, there is much more to planning. But that much is there and it shows just how much one uses and takes for granted valid deductive patterns of reasoning. This might also suggest how much deductive reasoning is involved (along with inductive reasoning) in reasoning about what to do—in reasoning in morality and law. In chapter X, the discussion will hint at some of the complexities there. And that will be that. In the meantime, one needs lots of practice in using these techniques for checking the validity of deductive arguments.

ILLUSTRATIONS OF ARGUMENTS USING THE ABOVE FORMS OF REASONING, FOR STUDY AND COMPLETION

1. "If you do that one more time, I'm out of here. Whoa, there you go again. I'm history."

   p   q   p   Thf. q

  1. $p \rightarrow q$

  2. p /thf. q

Notice if one wanted to write down just what served as the source of the conclusion and what pattern of reasoning got the thinker from the source to the conclusion, one could add a third line like this:

  3. q 1,2 MP

Line (3) states the conclusion, and then gives the numbers of the premises that served as sources, and finally gives the pattern of reasoning that was used—modus ponens (MP)

2. Roses are red and violets are blue. So roses are red.

    r   t   r

1. r & t   /thf. r
2. r 1 Simp.

So this display indicates that roses are red—r follows from roses are red and violets r & t are blue, from premise 1—the only premise after all, and by the reasoning pattern of simplification.

3. "If you wish to try, you may. Yes, you have my permission to do that. I guess you want to try."

    w   p   p   w

1. w → p
2. p   /thf. w
3. w 1,2 AC

Here the argument proceeds again by one inferential step to the conclusion. That inferential step is affirming the consequent—which, by the way, is known to be invalid. So setting out the proof in this way to show that an invalid form of inference was involved showed that the argument was invalid, just as in the first two cases, showing the way the argument worked by only using valid forms of inference showed the argument to be valid.

4. "Either it was Jim or Ellen. If it was Jim, then it was done by a man. It was done by a man for sure—look at the size

    p   q   p   →   r   r

of that footprint! So I conclude that Jim is the culprit."

                              So, p

1. (p v q)
2. (p→r)
3. r   /thf. p
4. p 2,3 AC

Notice that not every premise in an argument needs to be used. Secondly, note that this argument is invalid. Why? Because it trades on an invalid form of inference, affirming the consequent. Also note that there is a sub-argument in this argument—that since the footprint is big and belonged to the criminal, the criminal is male. There are a lot of things taken for granted in that argument, but for the purposes of understanding the main argument, it was fine to ignore the sub-argument. So these complexities can be set to one side.

5. If it is crystal "p" then it is either lead crystal "q" or "~q". It is not crystal "~p". So it was not lead crystal ~q.

There is much that is left out of this argument but it is straightforward enough.

1. p → (q ∨ ~q)
2. ~p   /thf. ~q
3. ~(q ∨ ~q) 1,2 DA (or denying the antecedent)
4. ~(q ∨ ~q) = (~q & q) 3   by definition of (p ∨ q)

(See above in the definitions at the end of the introduction of truth tables)

5. (~q & q) 4   by definition
6. ~q 5   Simp. (Simplication)

As complex as this argument is, setting it out in this way clearly shows that it is invalid since it relies on an invalid form of inference, Denying the Antecedent.

6. "Thirty years is a long time at any job. Herb has been emptying out parking meters for thirty years. He has been at the job a long time."

1. t → r (if on the job for thirty years that is a long time)
2. t   /thf. r
3. r 1, 2 MP   valid

7. "It is just false that I made fun of your mother. I agree that if I did that, then I would not be very nice. So I must be very nice—do not you think?"

1. ~p
2. p → ~t   /thf. t
3. t 1,2 DA   invalid

8. If your computer has a hard drive then you risk losing all your data to a virus. This computer does not have a hard drive. So it is safe from data loss.

1. p → r
2. ~p   /thf. ~r
3. ~r 1,2 DA

9. Henrietta knew she would have to defend herself "p". And she knew that if she would have to do that, she would have to have a good alibi "p→s". So she went to Tony to get him to lie "s". "You're the only one who can help me. Just say I was at the dance all evening. That's all you have to do." But Tony was honest and said that he would not lie "~s". So I guess Henrietta is not going to be able to defend herself "~p".

First, notice that the conclusion here is introduced by a term for conclusions, or a conclusion indicator word "SO". Having found the conclusion then the argument shapes up as follows.

1. $(p \rightarrow s)$
2. $\sim s$ /thf. $\sim p$
3. $\sim p$ 1,2 MT   (modus tollens)

This way of setting things up shows the interpretation that might have to go into reading an argument correctly. Here, the fact that Henrietta knew she needed an alibi is not itself a part of the argument, but rather part of the explanation why she would go to Tony and ask him to lie. What she said to him is just that, and again not a part of the argument as to why she has no alibi—except that Tony was her only hope. Since Tony was *the* only hope and he refused, the argument write up need not include that information. And with that simplification the argument is seen to work in one step using modus tollens, a valid from of reasoning. Alternatively, the argument could have been set up to include Tony in the picture by saying if she gets an alibi, then it will come from Tony (1*), and if it comes from Tony, then he would have to lie (2*). At this point the argument could go one of two ways. Either the conclusion could be derived by two uses of modus tollens. Or it could be derived by a use of hypothetical syllogism and then one use of modus tollens. Fill in the numbers (4*) and (5*) with these two alternatives.

1*. $(p \rightarrow t)$
2*. $(t \rightarrow s)$
3*. $\sim s$ /thf. $\sim p$
4*.
5*.

10. "If Herb is a Mormon, then his name is recorded in the archives at Salt Lake City. Either Herb is a Mormon or he is not recorded there. He's not there, we checked. So he's not a Mormon."

1. $(p \rightarrow r)$
2. $(p \lor \sim r)$
3. $\sim r$ /thf. $\sim p$
4. $\sim p$ 1,3 MT

Notice that one might have tried to derive the argument's conclusion using the either-or statement in (2). But that would not have fit the pattern of Disjunctive Syllogism. So it would not have been a correct use of that pattern or a valid argument.

11. Herb and Henrietta knew each other many years ago. It was 1983, in fact, when Herb asked her to marry him. If someone asks another to marry him/her, then he/she loves that other person, at least when he/she asks. So Herb loved Henrietta—at least in 1983.

1. p   (Herb asked Henrietta to marry him.)
2. p→ q   /thf. q
3.

Complete this and indicate whether this is a valid argument.

12. But Henrietta wanted a career. She applied to the Treasury Department to become an agent. Her first duty was to trace down a counterfeiting ring. She knew that either Clarence or Sid ran the gang. She then carefully traced Sid's movements on the night of the drop and found it could not have been him in the car. So she started to get together a list of Clarence's associates besides Sid. And when she started questioning them she found that no one else in the mob was ready to protect Clarence. So with implicating testimony from eleven others, she confronted Clarence. You are the one— I have proof!

The first thing to do in approaching this thicket is to find the conclusion in it— Clarence ran the gang. Next look over the reasoning and note that this is really a combination of two arguments for that conclusion—it is either Sid or Clarence and it is not Sid so it is Clarence. And—if his associates implicate Clarence, then he is running the gang. His associates implicated him. So he is running the gang. By now these two patterns of argument are familiar as the valid forms of inference, Disjunctive Syllogism and Modus Ponens.

TO FIX IDEAS: Set up these two natural deduction proofs for the conclusion that Clarence is the leader of the gang. And, say why they validly show the derivation of that conclusion.

So, there is a second pattern of proof of a conclusion being valid, namely that one can show a natural deduction proof of that conclusion in which no matter how many steps there are, each involves a valid form of inference. If the proof is set up and shown to involve an invalid form of inference then the proof itself is invalid. And, of course, if there is no way to make the derivation of the conclusion in question from the premises given, except to use an invalid form of inference, then the proof is going to be invalid no matter how it is set up.

Mastery Exercises VIII.3

SELF TEST

Comprehension Questions

1. What is the definition of a valid argument?

2. Why can valid arguments be good and have false premises?

3. Why does one always start a short truth table check of validity by making the conclusion false?

4. Under what circumstances is a conjunction false?

5. The consequent states which—the sufficient or the necessary condition? Explain what this means and relate it to one of the natural deduction rules, and to one of the steps of planning.

6. What is the difference between validity and soundness?

7. Affirming the consequent operates a lot like the valid form of inference, modus ponens. Explain the difference in terms of necessary and sufficient conditions.

8. Denying the Antecedent operates a lot like the valid form of inference, modus tollens. Explain the difference in terms of necessary and sufficient conditions.

9. Why does one try to make every premise in a short truth table check of validity have the truth value assignment of "true"?

10. What is the one natural deduction rule that allows one to introduce a new statement variable into a proof?

11. What two other rules—used together—does constructive dilemma resemble?

12. How many rows must there be in a full truth table for each single statement expression?

13. Describe how the rule, hypothetical syllogism, operates.

14. If it is impossible to assign truth values so that the statement forms of the premises come out "true" and that of the conclusion "false," what should this lead one to conclude about the argument form in question? Explain.

Mastery Exercises VIII.4

Natural Deduction Proofs

In what follows, there are a number of relatively straightforward examples of arguments the validity of which you can check by the rules of natural deduction and by the fallacious forms of affirming the consequent and denying the antecedent. They are symbolized and you should review this to get a further sense of how that part of the process goes. After studying the symbolization, complete the proof in the pattern illustrated above. Notice that in order to make these problems more intuitive, the symbolization used suggests some key term in the basic statement signified, as opposed to sticking to the conventional set of statement variables the discussion has been working with. The abbreviations for the reasoning patterns are either clear or are ones introduced above.

A. "If I want to get to the conference on time, I must fly. I do want to get there on time this year. So I guess I will fly. I wonder how long it takes in security these days."

If Want then Fly. Want. /thf. Fly

1. $W \rightarrow F$
2. W   /thf. F

B. "If I am to see the Dead Kennedys, then I must have my tickets by now. I haven't gotten them yet. So I will not see them."

If See then Have tickets now. ~H /thf. ~S

1. If $S \rightarrow H$
2. ~H   /thf. ~S

C. "If she loves philosophy, then she will read philosophy books. She reads philosophy books. So she loves philosophy."

If Loves, then Reads. Reads /thf. Loves

1. If $L \rightarrow R$
2. R   /thf. L

D. This letter says that to keep my scholarship I must either maintain an overall 3.0 GPA, take 16 hours this semester and achieve a 3.8, or write an award winning poem. I'm not taking 16 hours; I can't raise my GPA to a 3.0 even with straight A's. So I had better start writing poetry, I guess.

Either a 3.0 GPA-O, or sixteen hours-X, or Award winning poetry. But not X and not O. /thf. W

1. Either O v X v A
2. ~O
3. ~X   /thf. A

E. To be successful, one must be motivated. To be motivated, one must be enthusiastic. So to be successful, one must be enthusiastic.

If Successful then Motivated. If Motivated, then Enthusiastic. So If Successful, then Enthusiastic.

1. If S → M
2. If M → E   /thf. S→ E

F. If the monsoons come early, the rice paddies will not be prepared. If the rice paddies are not prepared, the rice crop will not be abundant. If the rice crop is not abundant, the people will not have enough to rice to eat. So if the monsoons come early, the people will not have enough rice to eat.

If Monsoons, then ~Prepared. If ~P then ~ A. If ~A then ~Enough. So if M then ~E.

1. M → ~P
2. ~P → ~A
3. ~A → ~E   /thf. M → ~E

G. "She said that she would go to the party only if she had all her telephone calls made and had responded to the needs of her young child. At last report, she hadn't finished returning the calls because her child is sick. So, I guess that's why she's not here."

If Party, then (Telephone calls and Responded to her young child). ~ (T&R). So, ~Party.

1. P → (T & R)
2. ~(T & R)   /thf. ~P

H. "Kids need emotional support, if they are to grow up healthy and strong and secure. Since it's not possible to do everything in life because we are limited by time and other constraining factors, I guess I must either choose to be the kind of father who arranges time to provide the emotional support a child needs or depend upon someone else for that or I just must not have children. I can't see finding the time to be with a child myself. I can't see passing on that responsibility to someone else. So, I guess it's hopeless; having a child is just not in the cards for me."

Arranges time v Depend v ~H. ~A. ~D. So, ~H

1. A v D v ~H
2. ~A
3. ~D   /thf. ~H

I. "In order to obtain a doctorate, I have to pass a foreign language exam. To pass such an exam, I'd have to study night and day because learning languages is the most difficult thing I can do. It's even worse than writing literature exams. Well, I do want a doctorate, so I guess it's night and day studying for me."

Doctorate → Pass a foreign language exam. P → Study night and day. D. /thf. S

1. D → P
2. P → S
3. D   /thf. S

J. "My pastor said that God said: If you keep my commandments, then you love me. The other day, when Heather asked me whether I thought she is a good artist, I told her I think she is, even though actually I think her work is pretty much average. I just couldn't bring myself to tell her the truth; after all, it's only my opinion and what do I know about art anyway? But I broke God's commandment not to lie, I guess. So, I guess I do not love God."

Keep commandments → Love. ~Keep. /thf. ~L

1. K → L
2. ~K   /thf. ~L

K. There will be peace unless all lose control. And it is also the case that there will be peace unless some lose control—that is either there is peace or some or all have lost control. But there is not peace. So some or all did lose control.

Peace v All lost. P v Some lost. But ~ P. So, Some v All.

1. P v A
2. P v S
3. ~P   /thf. S v A

Mastery Exercises VIII.5

SELF TEST   *More Practice Exercises on Deductive Logic*

SHORT TRUTH TABLE EXERCISES: Set up the following symbolizations in the proper from and complete a short truth table method proof of validity or invalidity. Answers are in Appendix II.

1. ‖{[(p v q) & (r v s)] → [(p v s) & (q v r)]} & (~ p & ~s)‖ thf. r

2. [(p v q) & ~(~p & ~q) & (r v p)] thf. r

3. {p → [r & (q v s)]} thf. (p → r)

NATURAL DEDUCTION PROOFS: Complete the following natural deduction proofs showing validity or invalidity. Answers are in Appendix II.

A. 1. p & ~r & q
   2. ~r → ~s   /thf. ~s

B. 1. (p v q) & ~ (~p & ~q)
   2. p → s
   3. q → t   /thf. s v t

C. 1. [p & (s v t)] → (r v s)
   2. p
   3. t   /thf. (r v s)

TRANSLATIONS AND NATURAL DEDUCTION PROOFS: Translate the following underlined arguments into symbols and then show the validity or invalidity by the natural deduction technique.

D. Herb saw Henrietta with Sid. He wondered if she had gone over to the enemy since he knew that she had suspected Sid of running the gang. He thought he could find out as follows: <u>If Henrietta had gone over, then she would pay a pretty penny to have Herb keep quiet. Herb threatened her with telling his story. She immediately offered to pay him a pretty penny to keep quiet. So he concluded that she had gone over.</u> He said, "now I've got you!"

E. Henrietta, seeing that she was going to be in big trouble, pleaded with Herb to meet her at midnight. Herb agreed wondering if she was going to try to bribe him some more. When they met, Henrietta told Herb that he did not have her at all. Sid was a secret agent—really one of Henrietta's fellow agents and they were working the case together. She said then: <u>You have three choices Herb, keep on threatening me and get locked up until the sting operation is over; just shut up; and third try to get away without picking one of these first two. Herb was not going to land in jail for an unknown period of time. And he was not going to keep silent since this was the perfect opportunity to get back at Henrietta for leaving him. So he made a break for it.</u> She said to herself, "<u>If he gets away, I'm sunk. I'm not giving up my career for that twerp. So he's not going anywhere.</u>" And at that point, she pulled a gun and shot him in the back.

F. Henrietta checked in shortly after the shooting occurred, saying that she had been attacked by this crazy who saw her with Sid and when she would not give him money to keep quiet, he went ballistic. "Since he was an ex-agent himself, I thought he would understand. I told him: '<u>If you run to the agency, my cover will be blown. And, if you confront Sid (since you are known to the mob and you are being watched), my cover will be blown.</u>' <u>Now I knew that either he was going to run to the agency or he was going to confront Sid. Therefore my cover was sure to be blown.</u> When I pointed this out to him he went nuts—you know how he was about logic. And he pulled a gun on me. We struggled, and just as I was getting a grip on the handle while I had his arm up behind his ear, the gun went off and he was shot in the back of the head. It was self defense." The investigating team said it could have happened that way, so she got off.

CHECKLIST FOR USING THE RULES OF INFERENCE TO CHECK FOR VALIDITY. In order to check for validity using the rules of natural deduction (and the two fallacious patterns denying the antecedent and affirming the consequent) one is basically trying to construct a proof along the lines set out above. In doing this, and assuming that the argument is symbolized and arranged properly as in the model arguments discussed, there are several steps one might follow to work through these problems.

1. Find the conclusion or some form of it in the premises.

2. Find how, by using one of the rules, you can separate out the conclusion from its place in the premises and end up with the expression in the right positive or negative form—the same as the conclusion, in other words—and write that down.

3. Find what else—what other premises or parts of premises you need to get the conclusion free and in the right positive or negative form using any rule that you think will work (remember that much of this work is pattern matching).

4. If you have a premise that is nothing other than that part that you need, then use the rule on it to get the conclusion and you are done—write the premise number and the rule abbreviation as in the patterns in the examples and that is it.

5. If you have what you need as a premise part—not a separate premise—then you need to use one of the nine rules to get that needed part out of the rest of the complex premise where it is embedded. Find out how, by using the rules of natural deduction, you can separate out that premise part and what else you need to be able to use that rule. If what you need is itself a stand-alone premise, then do the job, write it up, go on to use the part you freed up and the rule you need to get out the conclusion, and then write it up and you are done. If what you need to separate out the premise part that you need in order to get the conclusion is not by itself but is part of another premise, then you have to repeat the steps just outlined.

6. By proceeding in this way, you will have a series of derivations that lead to the conclusion being separated from some part of the premises by using one or more of the rules, one or more steps in the series, and you will have written them down to keep track of what you are doing—like making a map of where you have been so you can find your way home by the same path you came on. So at this point all you need to do is write the steps in reverse order with the derivation of the conclusion itself as the last step and then you are done.

Mastery Exercises VIII.6

SELF TEST

More Practice Exercises on Deductive Logic

HERB AND HENRIETTA, THE EARLY YEARS. Symbolize these arguments into proper forms and then, using the natural deduction technique, show whether they are valid or invalid. Answers are in Appendix II.

A. (1) Either Herb loves Henrietta or he does not. Now I know that (2) if Herb really loves Henrietta he will not care about whether she is rich or not. But (3) he does care, and he cares a lot! So he does not love her.

  1. Herb v ~Herb
  2. Herb→~Care
  3. Care   /thf. ~Herb

B. Henrietta has a cousin, Sal, who has just met Herb. I think Herb loves Sal. Sal is a shiftless scoundrel who will lie to anyone just to get money. Thinking Herb is rich, Sal told Herb that she is rich and Henrietta is a pauper, when just the opposite is true! So Herb loves Sal. After all, we know that (1) Herb cares a lot about money and so it seems that (2) if he loves someone, then he will think that that person has lots of money. But (3) Herb thinks that Sal has a lot of money, so he must love her, right?

  1. Cares
  2. Herb loves→Thinks
  3. Thinks   /thf. Herb loves

C. Now Henrietta is no dummy. She thinks that something has gone wrong in her try for Herb. She reasons in this way. "(1) If Herb is attracted to me, then he will fall in love. (2) He is definitely attracted to me—in fact he said so and I have no reason to doubt his word. So he does love me or something is blocking the way. But (3) nothing could be blocking the way since the only thing that happened lately is that he met Sal and I know Sal would not try to mess me up. So he must really love me— maybe he is just worried about something. I'd better talk to him soon."

  1. Attracted→Loves
  2. Attracted   /thf. Loves or Block
  3. ~Block   /thf. Loves

D. Herb has been thinking about things lately. He knows that (1) if someone is smart, then that person will eventually make lots of money. And (2) if a person eventually makes lots of money they will someday be rich. So he is led to conclude that if someone is smart, they will someday be rich.

1. Smart→Make (lot of $)
2. Make→Rich / thf. Smart→Rich

E. Herb has great evidence that Henrietta is smart. After all (1) if someone avoids studying and never pays attention, then they will fail to be smart. But (2) Henrietta studies all the time and is forever paying close attention to what her instructors say. So she will not fail to be smart.

1. Avoids→~Smart
2. ~Avoids   / thf. Smart

F. But if Henrietta just were not so shallow! Henrietta thinks that (1) if someone is attracted to her that person will fall in love with her. She knows that (2) Herb is attracted. So she thinks that Herb loves her. Does she not know that there is so much more to it than that?

1. Attracted→Loves
2. Attracted   / thf. Loves

G. Henrietta has decided to marry Herb. Maybe he does not realize he loves her yet. But he will. All she has to do is strengthen the attraction and he will not be able to help knowing he loves her. Now she thinks that (1) if she buys a horse and that new leather jacket, then she will be irresistible to Herb. And everyone knows that (2) if someone is irresistible to someone—Henrietta to Herb, then he will fall in love with her and know this.

1. Horse→Irresistible
2. Irresistable→Love / thf. Horse→Love

H. Little did Henrietta know that Herb is violently allergic to horses. So when he sees her on the horse and in her new leather riding jacket he is devastated. He looks at it this way: "(1) If I could live with her, then I could have all that money when she gets a great job and invests smartly. But I cannot stand to be around horses and so (2) I can't live with her. I guess I won't get all that money after all. I wonder what hobbies Sal has."

1. Live→Have
2. ~Live   / thf. ~Have

Please note that these exercises try to zero in on the reasoning involved and do not try to capture all of the descriptions and other rhetoric used in the passages. You have to do that as you construct an interpretation of what the reasoning is in some case you are thinking about. So keep that in mind as you proceed on the test. Find the conclusion and then seek what is relevant to its support. The rest is window dressing—usually, even though it can help you understand the premises in the argument sometimes.

There is another way I will check your progress on the technique of natural deduction proofs. This has to do with questions posed as multiple choice questions. Some of these will be set out below. But as an aid to dealing with questions of this sort, there is a second set of tech tips to offer here.

Once again, assume that the argument is set up in proper form as shown above, and then follow the steps below:

1. First, make sure you understand what the conclusion is. And find it in the premises—even if it is a part of one or two of the premises (for example, p is part of (q → p) and (r → s) is "part of" the two premises (r → t) and (t → s)

2. Second, see how (by the valid or invalid rules you have studied) you might be able to get the conclusion out of the premises—this might take two or more steps which means you will have to generate one or more results which you then use again to generate the result you are after. If the conclusion is (s&t), and the premises are (p→s) and p, and (t&r), then one can get r from (t&r) by simplification, and can get s from (p→s) and p by modus ponens, and then once one has s and one has t, one can put them together by conjunction to get (s&t) and so prove the conclusion (s&t) in this way by these three steps. And remember to sequence these correctly. In this problem it does not matter whether you do the modus ponens or the simplification first, but you have to do the conjunction last. So as you work backwards and find the conclusion in two different premises, s in one, and t in another, and you see that if you had them freed-up you could conjoin them into the conclusion as your last step, then you should ask, "well, how do I free them up?" And these are your second and first steps of the proof. (Yes, I can count—but remember you are working backwards and the right order of the steps will be the reverse of the steps one figures out as one works backwards).

3. Third, make sure you check the patterns of letters to make sure that the inferences you think you found are really going to work properly.

4. Write down for yourself the steps you took to find the conclusion and then write them in the right order—the order in which you would proceed to construct the proof, just like in the model problems you have done.

5. Then, among the multiple choice possibilities, find the answer which says these steps in the right order. And if they are all valid the answer will say the argument is valid, whereas if it is not the answer will say it is invalid.

Now remember, you will use some of the statement forms you deduce to generate others you need to make the proof. That is ok. And remember that really as you take a test or do exercises with problems of the sort we are discussing, you are working out which one or more of the suggested answers will give you the conclusion. You might see another way to make the proof—one that is not mentioned in the suggested answers. In *all* of these proofs there are multiple ways to do them. You need only find among the suggested answers one legitimate way of constructing the proof.

Mastery Exercises VIII.7

SELF TEST   *More Practice on Deductive Logic*

SECTION I   **SHORT TRUTH TABLE EXERCISES.** Select the best answer to each question and place the letter for that answer in the appropriate spot in the answer template below. There is at least one correct answer, maybe more, in each of the sets of possible answers. You need only put down one correct answer. Some of the possible answers are false or just plain bogus so please read them carefully! Answers are in Appendix II.

1. $\{[q \rightarrow (p \& r)] \& {\sim}s \& (s \vee q)\} \rightarrow [p \& (t \vee {\sim}t)]$

    (i) valid because ~s has to be true and so s has to be false and then q has to be true, and since p in the conclusion has to be false, there will be no way to make the premises true and the conclusion (p) false; (ii) valid because q will be true and r can be true so all the premises can be true and the conclusion false; (iii) invalid because since q will be true and r can be true we can make all the premises true and the conclusion false.

2. $[(p \vee q) \& (s \rightarrow p) \& (t \rightarrow q)] \rightarrow (s \vee t)$

    (i) valid because s and t have to be false and p and q can be made true and then all the premises can be true and the conclusion false; (ii) invalid because s and t have to be false and if you make p true and q false, then all the premises are true and the conclusion is false; (iii) valid since s and t have to be false, even if you make p and q false.

3. $[(p \rightarrow q) \& (r \rightarrow q)] \rightarrow (p \rightarrow r)$

    (i) since p has to be true and r has to be true to make the conclusion (p→r) false, then you can make the premises true and the conclusion false; (ii) since p has to be false and r has to be false to make the conclusion false, then you cannot make the premises true and the conclusion false; (iii) since p has to be true and r false to make the conclusion false, and since q can be true making both of the premises true, there is a way to make the premises true and the conclusion false, so the argument form gives invalid arguments

4. $[(p \& q \& r \& s) \& ({\sim}s \rightarrow t)] \rightarrow t$

    (i) since t (the conclusion) has to be false, and since ~s has to be false if s in the first premise is to be true so the whole of the first premise can be true, then, the premises can be true and the conclusion false and so the argument is invalid; (ii) since t has to be false, then ~s has to be false, and then s will be true and we can assume p, q, r are true and end up with true premises and false conclusion or an invalid argument; (iii) since t has to be false, this means that ~s cannot be true so the second premise is going to be false and so you can not have true premises and false conclusions and so the argument is valid

5. [(p→q) & (q→s) & (s→t) & t] → p

(i) since p (the conclusion) has to be false, and t has to be true, and s can be true, and q can be true, then p would have to be true, but it can not be so the premises cannot be true and the conclusion false, so the argument form is valid; (ii) since p has to be false and t true, if s and q are made true then all the premises can be true [since the first compound premise (p→q) will still be true when p is false and q true] and the conclusion will be false, so the argument is invalid

SECTION II

CHECKING VALIDITY WITH THE RULES OF NATURAL DEDUCTION. Select the correct answer to each question and place the letter for that answer in the appropriate spot in the answer template on page 337. There is only one correct answer, no more, for each question.

A. 1. (p v q v r v s)
   2. (~p & ~q & ~r & ~s) / t

(i) valid by, first, addition of t to 1, and then simplifying 2 into component parts and then repeated uses of Disjunctive Syllogism employing the premise 1 with its addition and the components of 2; (ii) valid by addition of t to 1 and then repeated uses of Modus Tollens; (iii) invalid because there is no way to make the derivation except by affirming the consequent

B. 1. [q v (s & t)]
   2. ~q   /thf. t

(i) invalid because the only way to make the derivation is with the use of denying the antecedent; (ii) valid by using 1 and 2 to derive (s & t) by disjunctive syllogism and then simplifying t out of the resulting (s & t); (iii) invalid because the argument does not use only one of the first nine rules

C. 1. (~p v ~q)
   2. (s→p)
   3. (t→q)   /thf. (~s v ~t)

(i) valid by constructive dilemma; (ii) valid by destructive dilemma; (iii) invalid because it relies upon the gambler's fallacy

D. 1. (p→t)
   2. (t→s)
   3. (s→q)
   4. ~q   /thf. ~p

(i) valid by one use of modus tollens; (ii) valid by one use of hypothetical syllogism and one use of modus tollens; (iii) valid by three uses of modus tollens

E. 1. (p v q)
   2. (q→s)
   3. ~p   /thf. s

(i) invalid due to the need to make two uses of denying the antecedent; (ii) valid by using first modus ponens and then disjunctive syllogism; (iii) valid by using first disjunctive syllogism and then modus ponens

Answer Template

Name _____

Section I.

1. _____

2 _____

3. _____

4. _____

5. _____

Section II.

A. _____

B _____

C. _____

D. _____

E. _____

Mastery Exercises VIII.8

SELF TEST

Deductive Reasoning Unit Test

The test is made up of three parts. Answer all questions in each of the sections. The first section is on definitions and identifications. Your score here counts for 20% of the total. The next section is concerned with proving validity or invalidity by the short truth table method. Your score in this section counts as 40% of the total. The third section is concerned with proving validity or invalidity by the natural deduction technique using the first nine rules explained in our text, plus the rule against affirming the consequent and the rule against denying the antecedent. Your score here will count as 40% of the total. (Answers for this Trial Test are in Appendix II.)

SECTION I

IDENTIFICATIONS. Put a (one) letter with each numbered blank correctly identifying the meaning or idea of the terms written after that number. Record that number in the correct spot in the answer template below.

1. _____ Conjunction

2. _____ Disjunction

3. _____ Valid

4. _____ Soundness

5. _____ Inductive Strength

6. _____ Denying the Antecedent

7. _____ Truth Table

a. when the premises are true and the argument valid

b. when two people are separated or divorced from each other

c. when two or more planets are close to each other

d. the fallacy of arguing that since the consequent is true the antecedent is true

e. a consideration that challenges one of the premises or the reasoning to the conclusion

f. a display of all the possible truth values of a statement in relation to the truth values of the component statements

g. a statement made up of more than one basic statement, true only when all component statements are true

8. _____ Affirming the Consequent

9. _____ Modus Ponens

10. _____ Rebuttal

h. a statement made up of more than one basic statement, true except when all component statements are false

i. an argument such that if the premises are true the conclusion has to be true

j. disowning the first born in a family

k. an argument that has two premises, one affirming the antecedent of the other

l. the table they put the lie detector on during a test

m. recognizing as a legal heir the off-spring of a family

n. the way of the pony (betting term)

o. an invalid argument form of two premises in which one is the negation of the antecedent of the other

p. what argument patterns have if they are good and are not valid

---

SECTION II

SHORT TRUTH TABLE METHOD CHECKS FOR VALIDITY. *Carefully* look over the following symbolic representations of argument forms. Using the short-truth table method determine whether each is valid or invalid *and then* select the correct answer from the possible answers for each question. Record the number of the correct answer in the answer template below.

11. [(p→q) & ~q] →[~p & (q v ~q)]

(i) this is valid because if we make the conclusion false by making ~p false and then (q v ~q) can remain true, then p in the premises will be true, and then if we make q false the (p→q) will be false, but if we make q true, then the ~q will be false—so we cannot make the premises true and the conclusion false; (ii) this is invalid because if we make the conclusion false by making ~p false, then p in the premises will be true, and then if we make q false the (p→q) will be false, but if we make q true, then the ~q will be false—so we cannot make the premises true and the conclusion false; (iii) this is invalid because we have both q and ~q in the premises and these are contradictory; (iv) this is valid because the conclusion contains the expression (qv~q), which cannot be made false, so the conclusion can not be made false and so you cannot make the premises true while the conclusion is false.

12. [(p v q v r) & ~p & ~q] →~r

(i) this is valid because if we make ~r false then r has to be false, but p and q are also false so all the premises would be false if the conclusion is false; (ii) this is valid because if we make ~r false, then r has to be true and then we must make p and q false so that ~p and ~q can be true and then the premises can be true while the conclusion is false; (iii) this is invalid because if we make ~r false, then r is true and then ~p and ~q can be true and so all the premises can be true and the conclusion false.

13. {p & r & [(t v s)→q] & ~(~t & ~s)} →q

(i) this is invalid since the argument contains both t and s and ~t and ~s; (ii) this is invalid because if q is made false then we can make ~t and ~s true so (~t &~s) is true and then t is false and s is false so (tvs) is false but since q is false [(tvs) → q] is true and p and r can be made true also so we have true premises and false conclusion; (iii) this is valid because if q is made false then we can make ~t and ~s true so (~t &~s) is true and then t is false and s is false so (tvs) is false but since q is false [(tvs) → q] is true and p and r can be made false so some of the premises end up false and so we do not have true premises and false conclusion; (iv) this is valid since if q is made false then (tvs) has to be made false by making each of the two component statement forms false—that would be what we have to do if we are going to carry through the test to try to get true premises and false conclusion to show invalidity. But if we make both t and s false, then in the expression ~(~t&~s), t and s will both be false so, ~t and ~s will be true and so the whole expression will be false. So there is no way to make all the premises true and the conclusion false so it is valid.

14. (p & ~p) → q

(i) this is invalid since the premises (the material to the left of the main arrow) contain both p and ~p and this is contradictory—inconsistent premises then invalid argument, we saw that above; (ii) this is valid since when there is a contradiction in the premises any conclusion will follow; (iii) this is valid since if we make q false then we have to make p true or false and whatever we make p we have to make ~p the opposite, so the premises (the part to the left of the main arrow of the expression) will never be true so we cannot have true premises and a false conclusion; (iv) this is invalid since if you make p true then you make ~p false and the whole statement of the premises is false, but q is false by assumption, so the whole expression (p&~p)→q would be true and so the argument is invalid.

15. (p v r) & (q v s) → (p v q) & (s v r)

(i) this is invalid since if we make s false and leave p and q true then the conclusion would be false and also all the component premises (except s) and also then the combined premise would be true—true premises and false conclusion; (ii) this is valid since if we make s false and leave p and q true then the conclusion would be false and all the component premises and so the combined premise would be true; (iii) this is valid since if we make p and q false and s false and r false, then the premise expressions would be false, but (qvs) would be false and so the whole combination of the premises would be false and the conclusion false; (iv) this is invalid as is shown by making either (pvq) false (by making both p false and q false), or by making (svr) false by making s false and r false. Either way, as long as the truth value "t" is assigned to the elements of the conclusion not made false then the premises will be true and the conclusion false.

SECTION III

CHECKS FOR VALIDITY THROUGH THE USE OF THE RULES OF "NATURAL" DEDUCTION. Carefully look over the following symbolic representations of arguments. Using the valid forms of inference or rules of "natural" deduction from our textbook, and the two invalid forms of inference, affirming the consequent and denying the antecedent, check to see whether the conclusions of each of these argument forms can be deduced from the premises stated. If either of the two invalid forms have to be used, then the whole argument is invalid. If not, if the conclusion can be derived using only the valid forms of inference, then the argument is valid. Then select the correct answer from the possible answers for each question. Record the number of the correct answer in the answer template below.

Please note that these problems are in effect questions in *pattern recognition*. Match the patterns named with those discussed in the textbook and then determine if the answer makes sense and is correct. Do not be thrown if the letters in the questions are used in orders not matching those in the textbook illustrations (~s is the same as ~p or ~t for all practical purposes, and p→q, p /q is the same pattern as ~s→t, ~s /t). It is the basic pattern that counts; that and whether statement letters are used consistently within the pattern.

16. a. p v q
   b. ~p
   c. r & s /thf. q & s

(i) This is valid because (a) and (b) can be combined in disjunctive syllogism to yield q, and s can be taken out of (c) by simplification and then q and s added to get the conclusion; (ii) This is valid because (a) and (b) can be combined in disjunctive syllogism to yield q, and s can be taken out of (c) by simplification and then q and s can be put together by conjunction to get the conclusion; (iii) this is invalid because it involves affirming the consequent; (iv) this is valid because of disjunctive syllogism, and then conjunction, and that is enough to get the conclusion by valid steps.

17. **a.** q & r & s

   b. (~p & t) v ~s   /thf. ~p

(i) this is valid because s can be simplified out of (a) and then used in disjunctive syllogism to generate the conclusion ~p; (ii) this is valid because s can be simplified out of (a) and then used in affirming the consequent in (b) to get the conclusion; (iii) this is valid because s can be simplified out of (a) and then used with (b) in disjunctive syllogism to generate the conjunction of the conclusion and another statement expression, and that result can be simplified into the conclusion.

18. **a.** p → q

   b. q → r

   c. (r v s) → t

   d. p   /thf. t

(i) this is valid by constructive dilemma; (ii) this is not valid because r and s do not occur together in the premises; ((iii) this is valid because (a) and (b) can be combined by hypothetical syllogism to yield (p→r), and this can be used with (d) by modus ponens to get r, and r can be used with addition to yield (r v s), and then this result can be used to derive t by modus ponens—from (c); (iv) this is valid because d can be used with a to get q by modus ponens. And this result can be used with b to get r by modus ponens. And that second result can be used in conjunction to get r v s. And that result can be used with c to get the conclusion by modus ponens.

19. **a.** p & s

   b. q & r

   c. (p & r) → t   /thf. (t & q)

(i) this is valid because (a) and (b) can be simplified into component parts and then two of these can be combined by conjunction and used to affirm the antecedent of (c) and derive t by modus ponens, and then t can be combined by conjunction with q from (b) to get the conclusion; (ii) this is valid because (a) and (b) can be simplified into their component parts and then two of these can be combined to derive t from (c) by modus tollens; (iii) this is valid because (a) and (b) can be simplified into their component parts and then two of these can be combined by addition and the result used with disjunctive syllogism to generate t and then this can be combined by addition with q which was simplified out of (b) to get the conclusion.

20. a. p v q
   b. ~p & ~t
   c. q → (s→t) /thf. ~s

(i) this is valid because the conclusion can be deduced by destructive dilemma; (ii) this is valid because the conclusion can be deduced by first disjunctive syllogism, and then using the result of this first deduction in modus ponens with (c) to generate a second result, and then the conclusion follows by simplification of that second result; (iii) this is valid because the conclusion can be deduced by the use of simplification on (b) and then disjunctive syllogism to generate a result that is then used in modus ponens to get a result that is combined with another part of (b) by modus tollens to get the conclusion.

Answer Template

Name _____

1. _____	11. _____
2 _____	12. _____
3. _____	13. _____
4. _____	14. _____
5. _____	15. _____
6. _____	16. _____
7. _____	17. _____
8. _____	18. _____
9. _____	19. _____
10. _____	20. _____

CHAPTER IX

Making Sense and Meaning of It All, Personal Views and Public Insights

SECTION 1

The Culture of Assessing Reasoning

The discussion so far has covered lots of ground, moving from the forest to the trees, inspecting many trees close up, and now it is time to bring the forest back into focus before the next and final chapter, ten. It is time for a tentative picture of the overall form and character of judgments assessing critical thought—a picture of the view that has been emerging from the discussion. Some orienting remarks on the culture of assessing reasoning will get things started. Then a brief summary will bring the forest back in focus, and prepare the way for introductory remarks on the assessment of thought.

Rationality is sometimes named as the goal of critical thinking. And this is often understood as conforming one's thought to patterns of reasoning that are inductively strong, or deductively valid (as well, ideally, as having true premises). But the discussion here makes much more of rationality; indeed, it makes of it an expression of a certain sort of character and a certain set of attitudes and feelings. Rationality cannot be understood as merely using good or logical patterns of reasoning to marshal what (perhaps after careful reflection all would consider to be) true evidence in support of beliefs, decisions, and actions.

Rationality, rather, is a matter of living a certain way in the light of reason:

§   it is a form of life chosen and undertaken; even if its outward expressions are expected by others, it is not just imposed by the expectations of others, rather it is a personal project of the thinker;

§ it is a way of life in which a person strives to exercise some degree of authority in critical judgment and living

♦ expressing good reasoning in belief and action, and

♦ participating in the project of articulating and maintaining the *reasoning pespective* of one or more communities of discussion.

Critical thinking is not just something one does. It is a project of the way one is and becomes. Mere conformity to rules without interest, or without need, and without seeing the point—without caring and without making critical reasoning a part of one's own values and life—is just being a certain kind of automaton, not being the creative being in whom critical thinking comes to life. *It is reasoning as a calculator, not as a critical thinker.* Being rational is living in a reasonable way and with good reasons for one's beliefs and actions. Being irrational is being unreasonable or else believing or acting for bad reasons. And so merely conforming to rules for good arguments or merely avoiding fallacies mechanically is being arational or not a rational being.

Socrates thought that if one knows what is good, one will pursue it. Presumably this would hold of pursuing the benefits of critical thought as well as other good things. On this view, being irrational would be a failure to achieve that which one sought, or a reflection of ignorance of what is good. Being irrational would be a failure to live fully within one's mind or mental capacities; a way of being out of one's mind! This is not to say the critical thinker is lost to the world by being caught up in elaborate abstractions of logic and rhetoric. Rather it is to say that critical thinking is woven into the very fabric of everyday living and it is part and parcel of striving to derive the most from life that a commitment to reason can deliver. Critical thinkers are not out of their minds and so out of this world, they are in their minds and, precisely through that, are deeply and richly in this world. This will be no surprise to those who have read this book. But, as promised, *it is time to summarize some of the preceding discussion* to remind the reader of where in the world the critical thinker is.

Inquiry, The Doorway

Inquiry is sometimes understood in a narrow way to signify the sort of investigation of possible wrongdoing or malfeasance recently undertaken by the 9/11 Commission. That is not the understanding of inquiry that this discussion has taken up. The first lexical definition in the *Merriam-Webster's Collegiate Dictionary,* Tenth Edition marks inquiry as any investigation into what is the case or into the basis of claims (see p. 604) and, while this is closer to where the discussion has gone, it is not quite the same. What is left out of that dictionary definition is the purposiveness of critical thinking. What is included in the Grand Jury or Senate Committee Hearing sense of inquiry is that it has a special focus. Inquiry as understood here falls somewhere in the middle of these two.

> It *is* purposive investigation, but it is constant and ongoing, a piece of every action, every observation, every reflection. It is more a matter of paying close attention and seeking to fully understand and reason through, rather than just a special occasion of that; it is more an investigation caught up in life concerns, as opposed to possibly removed from these as the dictionary definition seems to suggest.

Now this might seem a little overly enthusiastic since surely it is strange to say that critical thinking is working in observation. But no, this is not strange at all. The work is, of course, behind the scenes. Yet clearly it is there. Everyone has had the experience of learning something without bringing it consciously to mind. This is clear in what is sometimes called one's powers of observation. Some are more observant than others. Police, thieves, artists, surgeons, and other professionals with special reasons for taking in a lot without consciously thinking through the details all show that powers of attentive observation and the critical, discerning thought that goes with it can be learned and sharpened by training and experience. In such observation, the powers of attention and distinction leading to interpretation and even assessment are all enabled and used without conscious reflection. Imagine, for example, looking for your keys in a toolbox where they have fallen. You do not scan and consciously take explicit note of each and every item in the toolbox until the keys are noticed. There is scanning without such conscious discernment until, out pop the keys; and the popping out of the keys is not something separate from and preceding the finding of the keys. It is the finding of the keys without the self-talk, or other conscious accompaniments there would be if "finding the keys" signified a conscious, deliberate act. One looks and finds the keys. Along the way, one might have noticed that particular screwdriver that he or she had been looking for—a bonus; now you know where that is as well. But here the recognition need not even have been conscious in the way it was in the keys "popping out." Here the screwdriver is noted and remembered for where it is, without this placement having been consciously noted at all—at least not in any form that involved articulate recognition. The same occurs, no doubt, when one watches someone else doing something and learns how to go about that task or go through those motions without a word being exchanged, or when one walks through a room, overhears a conversation without paying attention, and remembers the contents of the room in great detail or remembers the conversation in detail without articulating any of it at the time, only later, if at all. Think of hearing a song that is in the background and not an object of conscious attention, only later to find oneself humming the tune or remembering that riff in the chorus. So called "incidental learning" suggests that when one acts or is otherwise paying attention, for example viewing art, listening to a concert, watching a movie, and so on, much is taken in and processed. It is seen for what it is, placed within a coherent life narrative of what the agent is up to at the time (or what the characters are up to in the story line of the movie, play, or opera), even more it is interpreted as significant to the agent, or not—seen as portraying prejudice, revealing a prejudice of the agent, or just reinforcing one's opposition to that form of partiality and thus involving an emotional response, sometimes leading to a change of heart or a change of belief on the spot, all without conscious or deliberate reflective thought. Critical thinking can occur at times and in circumstances without the conscious, deliberate work of reflection. It can occur intuitively and prior to articulation. It can occur as one makes sense of things in observation, in preparation for articulation.

During that articulation where one puts into words what he or she has seen or felt, or thought, one selects and emphasizes particular aspects of what one has observed or what one knows and remembers, or what one feels about something, what one hopes for, fears, looks forward to, and so on. *This putting into words allows for creativity, indeed to some extent the same creativity that allows thinkers to put what is observed into some coherent whole.* Sometimes it is the occasion of wordsmithing— of forging new terms to describe what was seen or felt, or of capturing an occurrence or mood in a figurative use of language. This is the work of poetry or of good evocative description. Other times it is a matter of thoughtfully (not necessarily—though maybe—reflectively) putting something into words that are available and carry the weight of common concepts and common perspectives. Poetry only carries so much standardization and precision. Sometimes, it is important to **convey** rather than to **capture** in words. And in using common terms one is highly constrained to the words and phrases that are the common property of reasoning in a social perspective or a more particular community of discussion. The constraint is also sometimes a matter of fashion or of a social group's style—eh?, can you dig it?, know what I'm sayin?, comprende?, savvy?, I so totally hear that!, affirmative! These stylistic and community limitations on concepts and terms for them all limit not only what one can use as modes of expression, but also what one can see, feel, or otherwise observe and convey. Some cultural differences in what can be said are quite famous. But these also provide windows on the world that are not shared across cultures. For example, talk to a person who has never been skiing but who shovels snow and get around to how many kinds of snow there are. Talk will turn, perhaps from difference in snowfalls—blizzards to flurries, to that heavy wet stuff in the spring as opposed to that light dusting in late November, or that big flakey, fluffy stuff that falls late in December if children are lucky. Now compare this with the talk of snow that comes from a knowledgeable and avid skier. The differences will be clear, not only in what is said about snow in these two groups, but also in how members of the two groups see the world differently. The Detroit snow shoveller does not see the snow in the same ways as does the skier. This is not to say that the snow itself is different. Nor is it to say that the Detroiter could not be brought to see in the same ways the skier does. It is only to say that available and common language can limit what one bothers to try to articulate. And, if it becomes the customary medium for articulation, its limitations can lead to habits of articulation that block observers from being aware in some ways that they might otherwise be.

Articulation, then, is selective and expresses styles of speech and conceptualization that are sometimes common across many communities of discussion and sometimes are indigenous to only narrow and particular communities of discussion. *The critical thinker will seek to be as little limited by these possible constraints as he or she can. But resistance is no guarantee of success. One must choose a limited number of communities of discussion in which to live and move and have her being.* These choices can be harmless if they are not fenced off by bias, prejudice, lack of charity or respect and the other fallacies identified in earlier chapters. If these choices are limited by such fallacies, especially by the lack of respect and the tendency to make one's own views and concepts fighting points, then critical thinking, and so rational living, will be out of reach for that person.

Critical thinking is then:

§ creative, but it is conducted within the limits of coherence and reasonableness,

§ interpretative but articulated and expressed within the limits of conceptual and dominant styles of expression.

Critical thinkers cannot be expected to say it all or to find some "just right" way of saying it. Nothing counts as saying it all, or saying just the right thing, except in the sense of what best serves the purposes at hand such as expressing precisely, or sympathetically, or romantically, or suggestively what needs to be said.

Further, the critical thinker will be responsible to what he or she really believes and feels. He or she will seek not only to be honest and forthcoming and so express what is called for by the context, but to also select and articulate what needs to be said in a way that he or she can endorse and stand behind by giving reasons to support. Thus, what is said must square not only with what is expected by the canons of good reasoning or cutting edge research or proper debate technique, but also must square with what the thinker feels is the appropriate way to capture what was observed and put the observation in a light showing the emphatic significance it held for her or him, if that is relevant. *Observing and expressing oneself, seeing the world from within and speaking or writing that world as a responsible member of multiple communities of inquiry or discussion is no small task then.*

So in speaking or writing personal articulations, one shoulders the further responsibility to stick by these beliefs or decisions, and to defend them while also holding them open to unbiased and impartial examination. What one has concluded comes to be available for future use as a premise in one's arguments. But also it is a further addition to the beliefs and decisions for which one is accountable. One is accountable within (and to some extent) outside one's communities of discussion. Within one's communities one searches for truth or other forms of acceptability and credence. Outside of communities one searches for the most coherent and functional perspective to take toward problems of a certain kind. *And,* one searches for that perspective that will fit most harmoniously with the perspectives of other communities to the extent that charity or respect demands this. *Thus, in living as a critical thinker, one takes on the task of representing, participating in, and also standing for or challenging and revising the perspectives of one's communities of discussion.* Most thinkers have the task of defense, and challenge only rarely and locally in the practice of a perspective. Some are entrusted with the global articulation and maintenance of one or more of those perspectives. These latter individuals are those authorities to whom members of communities look for an understanding of the perspective and for an understanding of the best practices of reasoning within the work of the group. Such authorities themselves thus become sources of evidence as well as being experts on the definitions, background assumptions, knowledge base, and processes of thought and examination that make up the perspectives and the accumulated wisdom of the communities. *All of these sources are drawn upon and brought into play along with the creative applications of the individual thinker who comes to issue public expressions of the thinking of communities. These public expressions extend one's personal take on things and put it into the form of a full dress explanation or argument.* Such public expressions of knowledge within or about the community put into everyday work and play the public forms of the life of reason found within those communities. They make meaning of it all in public insights.

This summary should orient the further elementary discussion of how, in general, assessments of explanations and arguments work in the activities of critical thinkers. Before saying something about argument, the discussion turns to explanation.

SECTION 2

Finding the Best Explanations

The discussion of chapter VI introduced the topic of explanations by stipulating what will be meant in speaking of an explanation.

> **When one tries to explain what has happened (or what will happen), he/she is assuming that something has occurred (or will occur) and is trying to understand what brought it about, or is trying to understand why someone decided in a certain way—what made that person decide in that way. Explainers are looking for what in the world produced the thing of interest or for some way to understand or make intelligible what happened, and not for reasons for believing that in fact it did occur or reasons for deciding on a certain option as the best one open.**

Explanations serve the need to understand why, how, and exactly what has happened. But appeals to explanations also serve another purpose for critical thinking. One of the ways in which thinkers argue to the truth or the acceptability of a belief or an interpretation is by showing that the truth or acceptability of such a claim is the best explanation of what happened. *Since it did happen, and that explanation makes sense of it happening, and does so better than all the other possibilities, it must be true or correct or acceptable.* Thus, in the understanding of what might count as good—as opposed to bad—or even the best explanations, there is a fair amount at stake for critical thinkers. In what follows, the first thing to do is to contrast two different families of explanations and to say a bit about how they proceed.

There is no agreement on how to classify explanations:

1. Moore, B. N., and Parker, P. *Critical thinking* (6th ed.). (2001). Mountain View, CA: Mayfield Publishing Company: **Physical explanations** point to some physical thing

or pattern showing why something came about. The thing pointed to is what does the explaining—so a change in temperature caused the rain by condensation and precipitation.

Behavioral explanations point to a single action, reason, or intention, or else to a pattern of human or other agency which brought about what one is explaining— so it was just jealousy that led her/him to kill him, just jealousy plain and simple.

Functional explanations point to a goal or aim or function served by something, and this goal or aim or function is then the explanation of why that other thing occurred—so her/his desire to teach at the college level is what explains her/his going to graduate school (behavioral), but her/his realizing that long study was necessary to reach the goal is what explains the long hours in the library (functional). The difference is perhaps roughly the difference between what moved you forward in a certain direction—behavioral—and the thing that draws you forward and organizes your activity—functional.

2. Aristotle, a philosopher who lived in ancient Greece and was the teacher of Alexander the Great, talked of four causes of things—**the material, the efficient, the formal,** and **the final.** The material is the stuff things are made of. The efficient cause is the force or process that brings about changes ending in what is now. The formal is the design or the organization of things that makes them the kind of things they are. The final cause is the perfect end or the good toward which things tend.

3. Jason, G. (2001). *Critical thinking, developing an effective worldview.* Belmont, CA: Wadsworth/Thompson Learning: suggests that explanations are: **deterministically causal** in so far as they proceed by invoking generalizations about the causes of things to explain why in certain circumstances some event came to pass—the iron crystallizing made the gate collapse; **statistically causal explanations** invoke statistical generalizations suggesting a significant correlation—the SARS virus came from Cantonese, live bird markets because of the correlations narrowing it down to there; **intentional explanation** invoking a person's reasons for undertaking some course of action—Barbara wanted the money she thought the jury would award so she sued the tobacco company; **functional explanations** relying on the kind of physical work done in a system by what is being explained—humans have a heart to pump blood throughout the body; and **historical explanations** giving the unfolding of some state out of earlier conditions—recently the reason why the United States becomes involved in small wars that grow to large ones is that political or economic interests send advisers to the troubled area and then these folks get into trouble calling for a further response and through gradual escalation the nation finds itself in a large conflict.

4. Toulmin, S., Rieke, R., and Janik, A. (1979). *An introduction to reasoning.* New York: Macmillan Publishing Co., Inc.: suggest that there are: **explanations by type** in

which questions about why something has taken place are answered by reference to the type of thing that is behaving and the typical forms of behavior for that sort or kind of thing—that sort of bird lays her eggs in the nest of other birds and thereby increases her chances of having surviving offspring; **explanation by material composition**—the drink fizzed over because of the carbon dioxide in it and the release of the pressure on the liquid; **explanation by history** in which events are explained by their occurrence in a series of events or in cycles of events—the passing of the dictator was followed by chaos that ushered in another reactionary leader; and **explanation by goal** in which what something serves or what one is trying to accomplish is brought out as what makes sense of something occurring—she went to all that trouble cooking the dinner in order to impress her father with the goodness of organic products and that led to another line of Newman food products. For Toulmin these explanations all have generalizations of the appropriate sort serving as warrants in the arguments presenting them in public dress. (In all cases interpretations and examples are the author's.)

There is no need to dispute any of these arrangements. Each has its merits. Instead, the discussion to follow tries to recognize two large families of explanations that include all of the above. The division between the two has to do with whether the explanations seek to provide a personal story or public argument about the *genesis or coming to be of some event, or one about the character or the significance of what is going on. Is the thinker after an account of what brought something about, or an account of how to understand or make intelligible what has come about?* This division incorporates the above. Explanation by material composition and by cause are certainly genetic sorts of explanations or are intended to be. Explanation by history of the operation of physical processes is certainly something to include in the genetic category. Other explanations by history (at least those not relying on the operation of physical mechanisms like an explanation by evolution), explanations by intentions, by goals, and to some extent explanations by type (those indicating the typical sorts of things that items in a type do) are all explanations of intelligibility. Consider a small imagined case of each type to help fix ideas.

Genetic Explanations

Suppose, as someone walks along with a European tour group, he or she comes upon an outdoor restaurant filled with people in what seem to be local traditional costumes. Among these, two in particular stand out. Their dress is even fancier that that of the rest. They are accorded the privileged place at the table, and, as the group watches, the couple initiate a series of movements accompanied by music, describing patterns and spatial relations to music the likes of which the tour group members have never seen before. Curious, someone asks the guide to explain just what is going on. The local guide, himself into dance, eagerly launches into an elaborate description of the movements, telling the crowd how one pose or movement in the series leads into the next through a complex repeated pattern with three different variations on the basic step. He ends the commentary by noting that this is how people hereabouts have traditionally danced something like a polka.

Here then is an explanation of the events observed. They are orderly, flowing one out of the other in a finite number of ways that are limited by local custom or convention. There are local rules for dancing the polka-like step, rules that, in effect, identify the basic step and patterns of turns made throughout, limit or constrain the popular turns or partner configurations that may be used in making those steps, and dictate what sequences of variations are to be danced when. *By knowing the dance steps and applying them to the movements, the observers can see the order that earlier had eluded them. One can now see why the couple moves just so, because of the conventions and the fact that they had previously moved in that way. The genesis, or origins, of the movements are given and thus the observers can understand why those that they notice come when they do.* The explanation provides the materials needed *to see and understand the development of the dance.* Thus the steps and turns become orderly and connected, and even within limits allowing for individual style, predictable, just as do a series of natural events when one comes to understand the physical or chemical laws or generalizations recording or modeling the patterns of their occurrence. The explanation of the dance would be a form of genetic historical explanation, while the explanations by reference to physical or chemical generalizations would be physical ones.

One thing that explaining amounts to then is giving a genetic account of the occurrence of some event. The account points out the normal order of the event in relation to other events (recorded in the rules of the steps of the dance and the causal or other generalizations of nature), and points to earlier events in the sequence, the **antecedent events** from which the one to be explained flows naturally as recorded by the statement of the regularity of the normal order of things. The grasp of this sequence of things makes the flow understandable and easy to fit into a personal life narrative as what one would expect. (Unlike what Hume said, this does not have to be the work of habit.) This personal understanding can be noted and remembered so as to prepare the observer by providing something specific to expect, in the presence of the antecedent events of the right sort. The thing to expect is the event that these antecedent conditions explain by the narrative made possible by the regularities covering events of this kind. And seeing an event of the sort explained by that regularity allows the observer to retrodict to the occurrence of the antecedent events which the regularity links with the explained event. *Thus observers are taken into the sequence of things in the world as they go about their affairs and can construct their life narrative and then their understanding accordingly. But these explanations provide not only personal views, they also provide public insights.*

The statement of such an explanation can be expressed as an argument to a conclusion stating the occurrence of the event to be explained. The premises of the argument would cite the regularity in question *and* the statement of the existence of some prior event which the generalization says normally precedes the one to be explained. Thinking of those cases in which the regularity appealed to is a law of nature (that is, an unrestrictedly universal and nonaccidentally true statement of the connection between events of different sorts), some philosophers have called arguments of these sorts **deductive nomological**—ones in which the statement of the event to be explained is deduced from a statement of a law (*nomos*) of nature and a statement of antecedent conditions.[1]

The dance example's regularity is a *conventional* rule for the proper sequence of dance steps, not a law of nature. Still the reasoning involved at the explicit public level of forming an argument expressing the explanation is of the same pattern as when a thinker appeals to such a law. The underlying deductive pattern is that of modus ponens. The warrant is the statement of regularity—the dance steps and turns and sequences, for example. The grounds are given in the affirmation of the prior event's occurrence. And the claim is the statement of the occurrence of the event to be explained. Reflecting this variation by speaking more generally, one might talk in terms of **deductive regularity,** or **DR explanations.** Such statements of explanations would also include ones where the generalizations involved in stating the warrant are statistical or causal generalizations.

The DR explanation is just the sort Galileo would be expected to give of the experiences he had upon looking at the moon through his spy glass. Here the argument would proceed from grounds to the effect that the moon has shadows with tips of light within them and that the terminator, or the line between the dark and light portions in less than a full moon, is irregular or not smooth (the way it would be if the surface were smooth) through the warrant that mountains and craters on the moon would produce experiences just like these, to the claim that he was experiencing what seemed to be mountainous regions on the moon. This is the very genetic explanation that so many of Galileo's detractors rejected.

Interpretive Explanations or Explanations of Intelligibility

Genetic explanations are not the only ones, however. Returning to the European tour, suppose one says to the guide that, while happy to now understand the movements of the dance, he or she would really like to know the larger significance of the gathering. And suppose that the guide went on to explain that the festivities were a celebration of a wedding. Here is a different sort of explanation, one that proceeds by providing an interpretation of the party's social significance as opposed to an account of what brought about the goings on at the gathering. Here the reasoning of the explanation would be presented in order to help the members of the tour group understand what values, conventions, and related social practices give the party some special meaning for the people involved. That reasoning could be stated by conjoining a set of descriptions of the group's religious beliefs, values, and related practices, with a claim that the set of events that the tour is observing is a case of those practices coming into play. This would allow the individual members of the tour group to take it in and mix it with their own memories or imaginings of weddings they know of, and traditions they keep to; and otherwise to build it into their individual personal life narratives, bringing it to a personal understanding. This personal view could also be accompanied with a moment of public insight as the group discusses it over lunch and arrives at a common set of statements that form an argument to the effect that what they saw was a wedding celebration. That is, it could be expressed in terms of an argument to the conclusion that the gathering was a wedding party, where one infers this from a description of the beliefs, practices, and values in question (the grounds supplied by the guide), and the warrant statement that hereabouts such a gathering counts as a wedding, or, that is, a warrant statement that points out the particular social or personal significance of the party to those gathered there.

Here the warrant would be something of the form: If people believe in public commitments of love, devotion, and shared fortunes, and they value this and gather on the occasion of such a public commitment and celebrate this in certain traditional dress and dances, and the rest, then this counts as a wedding party. The grounds would be that those beliefs and values and practices were present. Therefore, this was to count as a wedding party.

Again the basic pattern of inference could be a case of modus ponens. But the argument would differ from that of a genetic explanation in appealing to premises of values and beliefs and facts of social practice all forming a constellation of a certain form of social significance.

Such might be called a **significance typology,** *or* **ST explanation,** *expressed as an argument. In the framework of values, beliefs, and customs, behaving in such a way, among some people, or in some societies counts as celebrating a wedding. And these people are behaving this way expressing those values and beliefs within the community of thought of one such society. Therefore they are celebrating a wedding.* The same form of argument would inscribe the public insight of what counts as a baseball game, an entry into the faithful of a certain religion, and so on.

Once again notice the personal place of such an explanation. Through inscribing in behavior and feelings, and beliefs, and customs, the significance of such a gathering and its goings-on, this explanation allows observers to interpret the events observed as having a certain unity as a whole with a special significance. What they are doing is celebrating a wedding which is a point of intersection of the relationships of the beliefs, values, family ties, possibly power and wealth, and certainly support systems, as well as customs of the group in question. They are not celebrating an engagement, the harvest, a bowling tournament, an election, or anything else with a still different significance. With this explanation, one can interpret the special significance of some of the elements of the affair, the costumes, the presence of the religious official, the gifts, and so on. *One is able to interpret the significance of the affair rather than seeing how it came to pass in relation to the events that brought it about.*

This is the sort of explanation that Yerma was driven to give of Juan's treatment of her. She did not accept it until, in the end, Juan himself insisted on it. But, the explanation puts into perspective, one might say, his avoiding her, his spending so much time in the fields, postponing her plans for a baby, asking her to wait, telling her to be happy with other things. This allowed her to understand, to make intelligible, and to bring into one coherent account his behavior, strange as that was for a young married man in the region where they lived. It allowed her to put it into an argument for all in the town square to hear moving from those facts as ground, through the warrant that people who act that way and want marriage to be an economic relationship are trying to keep others from having children. And it led her to the dreaded conclusion that Juan was trying to keep her barren, trying to avoid having children. It was this kind of explanation that Yerma would not let herself accept in trying to understand her barren life. Such an explanation allowed her to interpret Juan's actions and to make sense of them or render them intelligible. But she rejected that significance. *Thus this sort of explanation will be referred to as an interpretive explanation. Alternatively one might speak of explanations of intelligibility.*

Assessing Both Genetic and Interpretive Explanations

Such explanations have two roles, a personal one and a public one. They can be assessed by how well they serve those roles. To explore how to assess explanations with reference to the first purpose—that of making the world intelligible—would take the discussion in the direction of a study of understanding and judgment, rhetoric and power, conventions and communicative relationships, and then to the application of this study to individual cases. This part of the discussion must be left for another time, although what can be said about the assessment of the public mission of explanations is not irrelevant to, indeed is constrained by, needing to fit with the personal side of explanations. No matter how good the expression of a public insight of explanation it will be useless if it does not record what makes the events explained intelligible.

Still the discussion has plenty to do in looking at the assessment of the public expressions of explanation. Here the aim will be to understand what is the best explanation expressed as a public insight. Once the question is put this way, the challenge is to find warrants of arguments expressing explanations that are best by comparison with other candidates—best at the job of linking what is to be explained with what explains that event(s).

There are three different, but related, circumstances under which one would have to answer the question, "what is the best warrant to appeal to in order to explain this occurrence?"

§ Sometimes, one explanatory hypothesis providing origins or intelligibility is more appealing than another because it is part of an explanatory system with certain clear practical advantages—**best by pragmatic virtues.**

§ Sometimes one does not have multiple explanatory hypotheses to choose among, but needs to find a plausible candidate hypothesis. Here one might rely on what will be called particular tests or procedures to determine what is relevant to the genesis of what, or what counts as having what, significance—**best by tests of relevance or significance.**

§ Sometimes one does not have an hypothesis to explain what has been observed, but this emerges out of trying to fit the occurrence into a coherent picture or pattern of events—**best by test of coherence.**

BEST BY PRAGMATIC ADVANTAGES OF AN EXPLANATORY SYSTEM.   Sometimes one knows what alternative explanations he or she could provide, what sorts of genetic regularities, or interpretations one could bring into play. The problem is that there is an embarrassment of riches. What is not clear is which of the available accounts is the best one. This would be a problem, of course only when the alternatives are equally plausible on the available evidence. And this sort of problem arises in either of two different situations. On the one hand competing explanations might belong to different communities of discussion. They might have been reached against different background assumptions and by the use of different procedures for determining the origin or significance of events. But they seem to be in competition with no agreed upon inter-community set of procedures by which to settle on the better explanation. For example, as was the case in the early 17th century, from the standpoint of revelation within the Catholic tradition, the way to best explain planetary motion might be through Ptolemaic astronomy, and the best way to explain Galileo's observations of the moons of Jupiter or of the surface of Earth's moon is as the result of illusion or hoax. From the standpoint of contemporary empirical science of the day, however, the best hypothesis of planetary motion might turn on the Copernican revolution or the best explanation of Galileo's observations might be that the objects were really there. Asking for a choice between these two explanations calls for moving outside both of the competing traditions and looking for an objective perspective impartial to both the church and emerging empirical science. *Was there such a framework? Well, what did the competing frames hold in common? The answer seems to be that they both held common purposes of using reason to give, in this case, a genetic explanation.* There are several such purposes to consider. One list goes as follows:[2]

§ Explanations should force thinkers to give up as few previously held beliefs as possible. Explanations should be *as conservative as possible.* For example, to reject the mountains on the moon hypothesis in favor of a view according to which telescopes are unreliable would force the surrender of many claims about optics and perception—for example that these work the same in looking at the stars as they do in looking at mountains on Earth. The mountains of the moon hypothesis is, in this regard, much more conservative than its competition.

§ Explanations *should function as simply as possible in one's system of beliefs.* An hypothesis that explains the experience of mountainous appearances, for example, and does so **without some special mechanism,** one that in this way operates more simply, would serve the efficient pursuit of the ends of a community of scientific discussion.

Simplicity in function, though hard to define precisely, is extremely influential in deciding between hypotheses. The mountains of the moon hypothesis allows the same explanation that is accepted for earthly mountainous appearances to work for lunar appearances. The appeal can be seen clearly when that hypothesis is compared, for example, to the reply one Aristotelian made to Galileo, namely that Aristotle was right, the Moon is a perfect sphere, but it is just glass-like and reveals mountains beneath its surface!

§ Explanations should allow one to explain the most that can be explained. That is, one would want *the most powerful explanations available,* other things being the same. The mountains on the moon hypothesis extended terrestrial explanations to heavenly bodies and, perhaps forever, changed the accepted mode of inquiry into all celestial phenomena. This came about by making more general the current explanations of terrestrial phenomena such as seeing sunlight on the tip of a high place first in the morning, so as to include within their scope heavenly bodies—objects which before Galileo were generally said to be subject to different laws and explanations. This greater generality made Galileo's hypotheses more powerful and then more appealing. More explanatory work could be done with these generalized hypotheses and so the work of explanation could be done more efficiently. On the other end of the spectrum of power (perhaps even the limit of power in an explanation) fall **circular explanations** which just amount to saying that something is explained by its being what it is. For example: The dancer tripped on her/his costume because he/she stumbled. Or for example: The flu victim felt so crummy because he/she was sick. A circular explanation has no power since it is just the repetition of the statement that the event (to be explained) occurred, but a repetition in other words.

§ Explanations also should be *as modest as possible* working more closely than alternatives with currently held beliefs, departing least from currently held beliefs. To the Aristotelians of the church, whose ultimate and pervasive power would be threatened if the universe was not made and regulated for humans to marvel at, Galileo's work was anything but modest. For this very reason it was difficult to embrace. Had it not been for the greater simplicity of his explanations, the increased generality of his hypotheses, and his success in leading people to restrict explanatory hypotheses concerning physical phenomena to those testable by experience, the immodesty of his claims might well have proven their downfall! Note that this is different from the explanation being conservative for, as Galileo pointed out, one could hold both the church views about "how to go to heaven" and take up his views about "how heaven goes." But in doing so one is not working closely with what views the church and tradition have to offer, but rather working with a different set even, in the case of Galileo, while trying not to give up the older views—conservative, but not modest.

§ Finally then, explanations in science, for Galileo, had to be answerable to the court of sense experience and mathematics. Explanations of physical phenomena would be subject to rejection should they conflict with, or fail to account for, something thinkers experience. Thus Galileo made the physical sciences *testable or refutable* by experience, unlike what they were as subject to the church supported authority of a long dead philosopher.

Thus the competing explanatory hypothesis that fits in a system of beliefs most virtuous in these regards would give the best explanation other considerations weighing equally. This leaves the earlier question. Would this sort of test decide between explanatory hypotheses from different and competing communities of discussion? If power, simplicity, and the rest are present to the same degrees, for the same reasons in differing communities of discussion, then in these pragmatic virtues one would have a good candidate for deciding between competing explanatory hypotheses from different communities. That is, if the perspectives understood these virtues in the same ways then, yes, these virtues would give a good test. But it is not clear that things ever work out that way.

What is most simple in the Roman Catholic Church tradition need not be most simple in the tradition of empirical science, for example. What might be open to the test of revelation and authoritative interpretation need not be open to the test of scientific observation, and so on. *Thus while appeal to the pragmatic virtues just identified might help decide on the best hypothesis **within a single community of inquiry,** it looks unlikely to help across such communities.* Indeed what is an explanation at all let alone the one fitting in the system most powerful, simple, and so on will depend upon the community in question. The church challenged Galileo on the point that the Bible says that God stopped the movement of the heavens in order to allow the favored to win a battle more decisively. But then the Sun was standing still, as opposed to moving. And Galileo's Copernican view would have had the Earth moving and the Sun standing still in relation to each other. So in this case the basic assumptions of the perspectives were in conflict. But also the personal views of members of the community differed. Those of the church persuasion saw the world as divinely controlled, and those of science saw it as blindly moving by causal laws one can get at by observation and mathematical models. Thus, what will even count as an explanation in the one view of things would not make sense to the members of the other community, and conversely. So a *good rule of thumb* is: ***What is the best explanation—or even what is an explanation—is a judgment made, it appears, within a community of inquiry. And if this is so, then looking for the best explanation across communities is not promising.***

However, things need not be much better within a single community of discussion, at least when the appeal to find the best explanation is taken up by looking for one that best serves the purposes of: *being simple, modest, powerful, conservative, and testable*. There is no guarantee that there will be only one such hypothesis about the genesis or significance of what is to be explained. If there is not only one, then to the extent possible, the critical thinker should withhold judgment and continue to inquire. However, if delay is not possible, where should a thinker turn? Such is what makes for differences of research programs within a single community of inquiry. There is no clear answer to give, other than to proceed ahead on the basis of one's best judgment even if it has no good claim to being finally correct. Eventually perhaps, as with Stephen Hawking's bet over black holes, things will clarify in one direction or another.

BEST BY TESTS OF RELEVANCE OR SIGNIFICANCE. Not all situations are ones with such an embarrassment of riches. Sometimes one is just looking for any hypothesis that is a likely candidate for a good explanation. What then? How does one decide what to take up in such cases as that? Consider two cases.

One might know that Galileo's telescope had lenses that were relatively primitive and distorting; that the moon was farther away than any other object ever observed through the spy glass; the telescopic image was subject to distortion by factors such as heat; that Galileo was interested in recognition, position, and financial security; and that other times when the spy glass yielded experiences apparently of mountains, mountains were being observed. What one would not know, is which of these circumstances should be taken as indicating the true character of lunar mountain experiences. Was it aberrations due to the telescope's construction, the distance to the moon, environmental interference, Galileo's ambition, or really mountains on the moon that produced those experiences? Or again, one might know that the Oedipus story is one of people ironically trapped into self-destructive actions by their own inadvertent ignorance. What might not be known is what literary significance is assigned to such works—is there a special category of such stories, what other such stories are of this type, and how does that type or genre highlight and clarify the significance of individual episodes of the story of Oedipus or the way the play was constructed? And in the case of Oedipus particularly, what means are there for interpreting the behavior of Oedipus and the problems that befell him? What is needed to answer such questions are procedures for separating the explanatory sheep from the goats.

What are the procedures for identifying the true origins or significance of events? What sorts of tests are there by which to identify the real genetic and interpretive relationships among events? Of course *there is no single answer here*. Mill's Methods, for example, are aimed at helping thinkers find the real genetic account of events. And these are highly appropriate to occasions when thinkers can experiment with the events of interest. Thus they include the very methods (especially the combined methods of agreement and difference) that thinkers would use to narrow down the possibilities in the Galileo example, to the view that Galileo's experiences were caused by mountains on the moon. However, they will not be of use in communities of discussion where questions of the origins of things are not settled by empirical means.

Similarly, when a thinker asks what possible interpretation of an event is the one that really explains its significance, there are various procedures one might rely on for an answer. These differ depending upon whether, for example, one seeks to give a psychiatrist's analysis of a slip of the tongue, or seeks to explain some allusion of the chorus in an Euripedian tragedy, or is just to determine which of several structural formulae for various literary genres fits the example under study. These tests can be formulated as the warrant or the backing of a warrant in an argument to the best explanatory hypothesis by saying that the series of events and their circumstances fit a certain genetic regularity, or the structure or the character and plot development fit a certain genre or interpretive pattern giving the significance of a play or other representation or event. Thus, there are tests by which to identify the appropriate explanatory hypothesis to appeal to when stating a public insight into the proper explanation.

If these tests single out an hypothesis, then all is well and good within the community of discussion in question. If they identify multiple good hypotheses, then the situation shifts back to the one examined in the previous sub-section and pragmatic tests need to be used. In fact, whatever explanations the tests of genetic relevance and of interpretive significance single out as true, these explanations will have to fit well with other beliefs (or decisions) in a package that serves well the purposes of explanation. The hypotheses must pass those tests, but also must fit as modestly and conservatively as possible into a whole that is as simple and powerful as can be achieved. Otherwise the explanations would fail to pass pragmatic muster and would be subject to rejection. Thus a full specification of how good an explanation of some event is, even in circumstances where one does not have multiple equally relevant explanations to choose among, must bring to bear both tests of relevance or significance, *and* pragmatic tests for how well what the test certifies fits into a system of belief (or decisions).

BEST BY CONSIDERATIONS OF COHERENCE. What if the tests of relevance or significance do not help because you are trying to explain a strange or new phenomenon, an anomaly? Here what is needed is a way to create a possibly worthy or credible explanatory hypothesis and this is not something that will be provided thinkers by the tests of what circumstances account for the genesis or significance of the event in question. An example that includes both questions of genesis and significance is found in the work of Sir Arthur Conan Doyle, in particular in the story, *The Sign of Four*, Chapter 1, "The Science of Deduction." Here Watson is challenging Sherlock Holmes to a test of the latter's powers of observation and explanation. Holmes had said that any object someone uses regularly will come to have the impression of its owner on it and so be identifiable as such. Watson produces a watch that Holmes correctly identifies as having belonged to Watson's older brother (from the initial) and something that came down to the oldest male child from his father—hence the older brother. But Holmes goes on from there to say that the brother was:

"very untidy and careless. He was left with good prospects, but he threw away his chances, lived for some time in poverty with occasional short intervals of prosperity, and finally, taking to drink, he died. That is all I can gather."

I sprang for my chair and limped impatiently about the room with considerable bitterness in my heart.

"This is unworthy of you Holmes," I said. "I could not have believed that you would have descended to this. You have made inquiries into the history of my unhappy brother, and you now pretend to deduce this knowledge in some fanciful way, you cannot expect me to believe that you have read all this from his old watch! It is unkind and, to speak plainly, has a touch of charlatanism in it."

"My dear doctor," said he kindly, "pray accept my apologies. Viewing the matter as an abstract problem, I had forgotten how personal and painful a thing it might be to you. I assure you, however, that I never even knew that you had a brother until you handed me the watch."

"Then how in the name of all that is wonderful did you get these facts? They are absolutely correct in every particular."

"Ah, that is good luck. I could only say what was the balance of probability. I did not at all expect it to be so accurate."

"But it was not mere guesswork?"

"No, no: I never guess. It is a shocking habit—destructive to the logical faculty. What seems strange to you is only so because you do not follow my train of thought or observe the small facts upon which large inferences may depend. For example. I began by stating that your brother was careless. When you observe the lower part of that watch-case you notice that it is not only dinted in two places but it is cut and marked all over from the habit of keeping other hard objects, such as coins or keys, in the same pocket. Surely it is no great feat to assume that a man who treats a fifty-guinea watch so cavalierly must be a careless man. Neither is it a very far-fetched inference that a man who inherits one article of such value is pretty well provided for in other respects."

I nodded to show I followed his reasoning.

"It is very customary for pawnbrokers in England, when they take a watch, to scratch the numbers of the ticket with a pin-point upon the inside of the case. It is more handy than a label as there is no risk of the number being lost or transposed. There are no less than four such numbers visible on the inside of this case. Inference—that your brother was often at low water. Secondary inference—that he had occasional bursts of prosperity, or he could not have redeemed the pledge. Finally, I ask you to look at the inner-plate, which contains the keyhole. Look at the thousands of scratches all round the hole—marks where the key has slipped. What sober man's key could have scored those grooves? But you will never see a drunkard's watch without them. He winds it at night, and he leaves these traces of his unsteady hand. Where is the mystery in all this?"[3]

Well, Holmes perhaps went beyond the bounds of probability, but this passage very clearly illustrates the idea of looking to coherence to create a hypothesis that explains the occurrence in question—here a hypothesis that fits the watch into a very general biography of Watson's brother. Thus, on this view, a good—indeed since there is no other, the best—explanatory hypothesis serving as the warrant of a genetic or interpretive explanation of the phenomenon in question, will be the one that fits into the most coherent set of beliefs one might construct. Watson's older brother was careless, late in life a drunk, and so on. But exactly what is meant by "coherence" here? This is not something that is settled and well worked out. As noted in an earlier chapter, coherence goes beyond consistency and includes explanatory power. But what is needed here is a bit more than that since the question is when does coherence have explanatory power. One approach regards the question as showing under what conditions the explanatory hypothesis when added to a consistent base set of beliefs raises the probability or else the credibility of all the beliefs in the entire set. But the details of such a proposal are not worked out fully. Questions remain about what should serve as the base set of beliefs and how their probability should be assigned or their credibility determined and then how the addition of the explanatory hypothesis should be understood as raising the probability or believability of all the beliefs in the set. Further this approach might seem to side-step the question of how the explanatory hypothesis should be assessed as a satisfactory explanation. Thus, what Watson wanted to know was how Holmes thought that the various claims he made explained what was seen in and on the watch, and because of that had credibility.

Thus one more try might be worthwhile. The interesting thing about Sherlock Holmes is that his explanations do not come out of thin air but are based on the facts he observes and their commonly understood significance. And they are put together in a way that fits them with what is known and is taken for granted about people, about the world and about the way the one operates within the other. For example, "What sober man's key could have scored those grooves? But you will never see a drunkard's watch without them. He winds it at night, and he leaves these traces of his unsteady hand." Thus there are beliefs that serve as reference points against which thinkers need to orient their stories of what fits together coherently. If Watson had no brother, or if drunkards rose early and with full coordination went on to wind their watches in Victorian England, then no matter how consistently Holmes's beliefs fit together and put the marks on the watch into a coherent story of genetic and interpretive explanation, the hypothesis would not be accepted. If Watson had really wanted to challenge Holmes, the former should have found a watch with the right initials, residing in a museum, and turned Holmes loose on that. But no matter. The lesson is well taken. In so far as one's explanatory narrative fits the pieces together coherently and in a way that ties them consistently and neatly to assumed truths about relevant features of the world and life, then that hypothesis has a good claim to be accepted—at least provisionally. Credibility comes from this fitting in and fitting with; it comes from reflective equilibrium.

Thus, for example, if one is after an understanding of the physical origins of some perceptual experience, then the hypothesis, that, for example, "lunar mountains were being observed by Galileo," must fit with a set of beliefs about how the sense of sight works and about how in this case, it might have been appropriately stimulated by light reflected from the moon's surface. If one is after an explanation of the origins of some human action then the hypothesis must fit consistently with a set of beliefs about what leads people to act, for example, beliefs about their motives and beliefs (or the biochemical correlates of these in the brain). On the other hand, if one is after an hypothesis about the legal or moral significance of some event, then the explanatory hypothesis must fit with a set of beliefs about what is legally or morally wrong. If one wants to get at the significance of a bit of language entirely new to the reader or auditor, then any acceptable hypothesis must fit consistently with a set of beliefs about how that language in question might function in other related contexts of communication. Or if one wants to understand the meaning of some new or unusual passage of literature, then one will need an hypothesis that fits with the facts of what similes, metaphors, or other symbolic devices might be at work in the literature and how they might produce the piece of work. Some of these other beliefs would be about the series of events in question, about what else is in fact now valued, or what else is being said. But also some of the beliefs would be prior views about the value systems, legal traditions, or causal histories in the world and how these things work. The latter would be the beliefs one would adjust the hypothesis to in order to get a coherent view that not only hangs together, but also, on reflection, fits in equilibrium with what was known of the world before.

Now this is not to say that what fits into a coherent story with a claim to a high degree of reflective equilibrium will deserve to be treated as what is true. It might cause such disruption in the wider system of beliefs or values that its immodesty would be disqualifying. And in any event hypotheses that are best by coherence are subject to revision as inquiry moves ahead. Still, relying on coherence and reflective equilibrium to create hypotheses for strange circumstances is a third important source of best explanations.

At this point then, a summary is in order:

§ Explanations are good when they serve the personal purpose of clarifying or engendering understanding and are something one can state in a defensible argument as public insights. The understanding is either genetic or interpretive, the arguments might be either DR or ST arguments.

§ The purposes of giving genetic accounts or interpretive accounts that engender understanding, and of recording public insights, are tied in their details to the character of the problems in three different kinds of situations:

- ◆ Settling competitions between plausible hypotheses within or between communities of discussion.

- ◆ Identifying hypotheses by tests of relevance or significance.

- ◆ Formulating hypotheses by fitting them into coherent systems of belief (or decision) that enjoy a high degree of reflective equilibrium.

§ To meet the problems of the first sort, explanations need to most completely meet conditions of the pragmatic virtues of conservatism, simplicity, modesty, power, and testability or refutability. These, however, are not necessarily decisive.

§ To meet the problems of the second sort, explanations need to pass tests of relevance or significance that are appropriate to situations of the sort in question and to the community of discussion in which the explanation is being offered.

§ To meet the problems of the third sort, explanations need to fit coherently into a set or system of beliefs (or decisions) and this system needs to be grounded by being in reflective equilibrium with other beliefs (decisions) common in the community of discussion.

§ Clearly in meeting problems of the second and third sorts, the explanatory hypothesis needs also to fit with a system of beliefs (or decisions) that meet the pragmatic virtues, as much as possible. Though there is no guarantee that this will happen.

§ Finally, explanatory hypotheses supported in these ways will not achieve the status of final truths in a community of discussion where inquiry is ongoing.

Mastery Exercises IX.1

SELF TEST

Comprehension Questions

1. What is a genetic explanation? Can you give the details of one from your own experience?

2. What is an interpretive explanation or one of intelligibility or significance? Can you give the details of one from your own experience?

3. What is the procedure for showing that a candidate is the best explanatory hypothesis according to the advantages of an explanatory system of beliefs?

4. Identify from one of your other courses tests of relevance or significance that help one identify an appropriate explanatory hypothesis in some situation.

5. Discuss how one might show that an explanatory hypothesis is good or the best by considerations of coherence.

6. Looking at the patterns of reasoning in items 3–5 just above, can you explain the differences between occasions on which each of these procedures would be the most appropriate to use?

7. How are explanations stated as arguments—what are the patterns of those arguments?

8. What is the point of explanations?

Mastery Exercises IX.2

SELF TEST

Explanations, Arguments, or Neither (or both)

Separating Arguments from Explanations. For each of the following statements or set of statements, identify whether it gives an explanation or an argument. If it is an argument, place an "A" in the blank provided. If it is an explanation, place an "E" in that spot. If the statement set is unclear so that there is no way to tell which it is or whether it is both explanation and argument you can indicate that by the letter "C". If you feel you have to explain your answer to show your interpretation of the situation, do so in no more than one short sentence. (Answers in Appendix II.)

_____ i. "The police officer and judge both said I was speeding. That's why I'm guilty."

_____ ii. "The car-jacker jumped in the car and told me to drive as fast as I could until I was out of town. That's why I was speeding."

_____ iii. The reasons why Lance Armstrong is such a good bike rider are that he has an unusual genetic make-up and he trains really hard.

_____ iv. The reasons why Armstrong won his fifth Tour De France are that all the judges and officials agreed he had the fastest overall time.

_____ v. "Well, but the real problem last year was that the Marshall University football team has never lost a championship game on their home field. That's why the University of Toledo lost last year."

_____ vi. "My car stopped because it ran out of gas."

_____ vii. "My lawyer stopped because the judge sustained the objection against her line of questioning."

_____ viii. Dennis Rodman stopped dying his hair at this point in time because if you look at all the pictures of him after that date, his hair was its original color.

_____ ix. "The victim stopped here because I can see the tracks and the pool of blood, and I can see another set of tracks leading here from the woods and then leading off to the river with signs of a body being dragged."

_____ x. "Why did I stop? Well, I stopped because this is the last question in this section so it is time to stop, that's why."

SELF TEST

Explanation Assessment by Pragmatic Virtues

Assessments Appealing to the Pragmatic Virtues of Explanations. Assess the following explanations in terms of whether they have or lack the pragmatic virtues of conservatism, simplicity, power, modesty, and testability. Then select the best answer from among the possibilities listed. (Answers in Appendix II.)

1. "That circle of greener grass around the old maple tree out back—the circle where the mushrooms grow every spring is what is known as a fairy circle. This is a ring that is put in by fairies and it is one of their special gathering places. The mushrooms are both umbrellas when it rains and seats when they have dances there. I know this because this is the best explanation for this particular sort of growth of grass and mushrooms." (a) not conservative since it would lead to giving up a number of beliefs about the forms that life can take and the powers that various life forms have; (b) not simple since it requires the postulation of questionable things—fairies; (c) not powerful by comparison with other explanations which can account for the same result by rainfall patterns and mushroom spores and propagation which also account for a number of other kinds of events as well; (d) it is not modest since it does not work with current theories; (e) it is a good explanation; (f) it is a bad explanation for all the above reasons except (e).

2. "The cat attacked the mouse because mice are very telepathic and cats are sensitive to that. It is like blowing a dog whistle which irritates dogs. The cats go nuts when the mice beam on them with their telepathic powers." This explanation is: (a) bad because of being nontestable; (b) bad because of being not very powerful since it does not explain much more than the hatred between cats and mice; (c) good; (d) bad because it is immodest in not working with what else we know about cats, namely that they are hunters and the mice look like prey to them, even though they do not eat the mice; (e) bad because of (a), (b), and (d).

3. "Horse flies, if they can, hang around barns with horses because they are like the guy who robbed banks because that is where the money is. The horse barns are where the horses are!" This explanation is: (a) good; (b) weak because it is not very simple; (c) weak because it is not very powerful is circular; (d) weak because it is not very conservative; (e) weak because it is not refutable.

4. "The invention of moveable type and printing with that explains the affordability of books and the spread of literacy beyond the wealthy and those associated with libraries. This explanation is: (a) bad because not very powerful; (b) bad because not testable; (c) bad because not simple; (d) good; (e) bad because not very conservative.

5. "There must be aliens and they must travel in flying saucers. How else would you explain all the sightings? This is not to beg the question and just assume that these were really sightings of flying saucers staffed by aliens. But it is just to point out that there have been sightings all over the world. And they all pretty much agree on what they have seen even though they don't know each other. What else would explain that?" This explanation is: (a) good; (b) not good because not conservative; (c) not good because not powerful; (d) not refutable and so not good; (e) not good for more than one of the above—name which ones.

6. Humans have always had art as a way of relating to the world and giving them the feelings of controlling it since they can make images and thus bring the things imaged into a kind of existence any time that they want. This explanation is: (a) good; (b) is bad because it is not powerful; (c) is bad because it is not testable; (d) bad because it is not modest.

7. "The reason those people win the lottery? Well, that is simple. You might think it is fixed. But that would be too much of a conspiracy theory. So what is it then? Well I'll tell you—they are singled out by God to be favored in this life." This explanation is: (a) good; (b) not good because it is not testable; (c) is not good because it is not modest; (d) is not good because it is not powerful.

8. "Why did all those people get cancer if it wasn't the cigarettes? It must have been the cigarettes. That is what explained it. The cigarette paper had some nasty substance in it that caused the cancer." This explanation is: (a) close but no banana; (b) good; (c) not good because of not being conservative; (d) not good because it is not testable; (e) not good because it is not simple.

9. "The moon being full is what explains it. Every time the moon is full there are more killings and more accidents and more crime than other times in the month. What happens is that moon beams have a particularly disturbing influence on the minds of some people." This explanation is: (a) good; (b) so much moonshine; (c) bad because it lacks power—is circular; (d) bad because it is not simple in a way that is modest; (e) both (c) and (d).

10. "People get depressed or sad anyway in the winter because of lack of light. The lack of light makes the fluid in people's minds heavier and thicker. This causes them to be depressed or sad. In the summer the added light makes the mind fluids lighter and their spirits lighter." This explanation is: (a) not good because it is not testable; (b) is not good because it is not conservative; (c) is good; (d) is not good because it is not powerful; (e) not good because it is not modest; (f) not good for multiple reasons mentioned—state which.

SECTION 3

Finding the Best Arguments

Much of this book—at least since chapter VI—has been devoted to the subject of understanding and assessing arguments in some detail. Thus, it is time for a summary review putting the pieces of the discussion into some whole approximating a procedure. Of course, there is no strict procedure for assessing arguments any more than there is for assessing explanations, if that means an algorithm or check list or recipe which could be employed with assuredly reliable results. Assessing arguments is an art form. It is a matter of coming to understand them and their point, individually and in context, and thus involves interpretation. It also involves getting a fix on what the author was up to in issuing the argument in the first place. At times this can be furthered by understanding why the author expressed the argument as he or she did. Only after coming to understand in this way the author's arguing does it make sense to identify the conclusion and the premises and to check their truth or acceptability and their logical relations as thinkers are so often advised to do. This book has offered that advice too. At the end of chapter VI, the advice was to determine whether the argument was deductive or inductive, then check the premises for acceptability and then check the logic of the argument to see if the premises provide strong inductive support or a sound argument for the conclusion. But now it is time to take a little larger look at assessing arguments. The following summary will seek to do this by way of several reminders. After each summary reminder of an important orienting point, a question is asked that could be used in the assessment of arguments at the appropriate stage.

1. Arguments are living/almost organic expressions of someone's views of connections in the world. These are views from the standpoint or perspective of a particular community of discussion.

First question: Have you, in making your assessment, interpreted the argument in its context of being a personal understanding representing a community's perspective, aimed at stating a defensible gathering of evidence for some claim?

The difficulty here is seeing the argument form as a living communication. As such it is liable to problems like incompleteness of expression and the thinker's selection of some aspect of an event or state or trend to emphasize. Such selections will reflect the thinker's community—where he or she is "coming from." This will tell a good deal about what is relevant as assumptions and processes or reasoning, and what is not. But the selection can also slant ideas and arguments, and can result in arguments supporting partial, and so biased or distorting, views of things. Still thinkers cannot consider all that is relevant and no argument presents the whole of the reasons for a belief or a decision nor does it suggest all the implications of looking at things in a certain way or from a certain perspective. There are dangers in arguments because of the selections that they express and the perspectival context in which they occur. Still that is the life of arguments as thinkers know and practice them.

Much discussion about critical thinking, including that in the preceding chapters, might be seen as suggesting that the argument is a fixed thing, somehow existing in a one-to-one correspondence with the terms and logic of the statements used to express it—one argument for one form of expression. But this is not the case. The language comes alive and conveys an argument in the context of exchange between the one issuing the argument and either a particular individual or the discourse of inquiry at a time within the appropriate community of inquiry. This is one reason why it is so difficult to reconstruct a thinker's arguments in the history of thought. What is needed is an account that places the reader in the time and community in question so that the issues that were current and their particular significance are brought to bear in interpreting the argument and understanding what its implications and meaning were thought to have been.

2. Arguments are aimed at giving the public face of reasoning on an issue where the object is to address a question focused on some commonly understood problem, and the approach expresses an emphasis that is common to those in a community of discussion.

Second question: Does the argument address a question understood and approached in the way *usual for those exchanging views in the relevant community of discussion?* If not, what is the understanding of the problem and of the approach? What are the reference points defining a context of interpretation and assessment? If there are some, then what perspective do these fit into? If there is none then the argument would be marked as either something critical thinkers should remain silent about, until the perspective becomes clear, or it should be marked as not rational.

Arguments are matters of public reason-giving, often proceeding by giving an account of what one believes, has decided, or done, and seeking to defend it by marshalling support for it. They proceed within and between the members of communities of discussion, normally, a single such community, though not necessarily so. Also the approach of the argument—what it takes as important and needing support as opposed to what can be assumed or ignored, while a matter of some creativity on the part of the thinker, is also likely to reflect the emphasis of the community on certain aspects of the issue at hand as opposed to others. If an argument strays far from these common understandings of what is important and needed, for example to take issue with the views of the group or of another representing the group, then it is incumbent upon the thinker to let others know that. And it is incumbent upon the person assessing the argument to enter into the flow of that reasoning, lest he or she would be guilty of a studied misunderstanding or a straw figure fallacy (see chapters IV and III respectively).

3. Arguments are responsive to real problems and not just "cooked up."

    Third question: Does the argument address a problem that has real salience for those in the exchange—another particular individual or the membership of the community in question, at large? If so then the interpretation can be informed by the implications of the claim of the argument. If not, then the argument's assessment should be set aside as lacking a crucial reference point.

    It may be the case that a thinker becomes carried away and loses sight of the personal side and importance of arguments, as Holmes claimed to do in the selection quoted above. But arguments are not without purpose (as discussed much earlier in this book). They are undertaken in order to address some problem that is of real consequence to the thinker(s) involved. The arguments might fail to make this clear themselves. But within the community of discussion where they are offered, it will be clear. The inconsequential or silly argument needs no response, plays no role in offering support for a claim of public insight. One can joke, putting it in the form of an argument, but it need not be taken seriously, nor as such need it meet the other conditions on giving arguments in critical thinking.

4. Arguments, then, are purposive and serious. As such they give an appeal that is to be taken seriously and so should be put in a form that is commonly accessible within the community for which it is intended. In setting out an argument then, the thinker takes responsibility for integrity as a member of some community of inquiry, and respects others who, either within or outside the group, might take issue with what is claimed and the reasons for it.

    Fourth question: Is the argument formulated in such a way that it is approachable by the standards, expectations, and patterns of reasoning within the appropriate community? If so then the person offering the argument has shown proper integrity of thought as a member of that community. If not, then does the argument challenge the perspective of the community in question? And if so, from what standpoint, and does the arguer show integrity there? If the arguer is challenging the perspective of the community and is doing so from no recognizable perspective, then there is no way to approach that argument as an exchange. So it should be set aside. Furthermore, if the thinker is not seriously approaching an issue within the purview of a community, because of committing one or more of the fallacies discussed in chapter II, then the thought should be analyzed to make clear its fallacious character and then set aside.

5. Thinkers offering an argument seek to forward the project of dealing with some problem and are not engaged in an intellectual combat. Indeed they are in a mutual undertaking of building knowledge of or within a perspective of a community of inquiry. Offering an argument is not the only way in which to further the community's thought on some subject or to make it real to the thinker or others involved. Reason giving also takes place within the framework of narratives ranging from myth to personal commentary in essays, letters, or journals, and in shared explorations of what one thinks on some matter. Also it is found in developing patterns of concepts introducing conceptual order into a field of inquiry, for example, in the design of a taxonomy. But argument is an important way of giving reasons for beliefs, decisions, or actions, especially in public contexts of accountability.

    Fifth question: Does the argument actually provide reasons for believing, deciding, or acting in some way? Or does it seek to manipulate or overpower another's thinking (and so her or his beliefs, decisions, or actions)? (See the fallacies discussed in chapter III.) If it does, do these reasons move forward the project of dealing with some problem recognized within the community of inquiry in question? Does the argument constitute a contribution to the thought of the group, or a further employment of that thought, or a real challenge to the thinking of the group in question? If it does not then it need not be considered other than to analyze the fallacies or other mistakes in it.

6. Thus it is important that thinkers offering arguments are understood, and that they put forward their best thought on the matter at hand. It is incumbent upon thinkers offering arguments to be honest, forthright, forthcoming, clear, communicative, and to articulate the argument as part of the inquiry process.

    Sixth question: Does the argument express serious inquiry or does it fail in this regard by committing one or more of the fallacies discussed in chapter IV? If it fails in such a way, then it should be analyzed so as to show that and set aside. If it is an expression of serious or responsible inquiry, then it should be assessed on its merits.

7. Thinkers offering arguments will need to make proper uses of sources and maintain integrity relative to the appropriate community of discussion. Thus those making arguments will show the proper effort to gain only *merited* credibility for their views. And this is a social act, in the sense that it involves interacting with others in ways that bring them along. It is not just a matter of producing what is logically successful or successful all alone or standing on its own. Critical thinking is the creative and judicious use of sources of belief, decisions, and actions so as to explore the personal and perhaps bring it to the public in the form of argument. When critical thinking does come to expression in an argument, the use of sources should be made clear as grounds in the argument and the propriety of this use should be made clear in the backing of the argument.

Seventh question: Does the argument make appropriate and effective appeals to sources for the evidence marshalled in the premises of the argument? Does the argument rest on and record observations correct within the ways of proceeding in the community in question? Does the argument rely on authority only to the extent that there is expertise and this is properly drawn on? And so on. If it does then the argument can be reviewed for the use it makes of these sources. If it does not then it should be set aside after an analysis of the misuse it makes of sources.

8. Further, it is important that thinkers offering arguments not try to shift the burden of proof but instead take it on and shoulder it.

Eighth question: Does the thinker inappropriately seek to shift the burden of proof? Although this question will have been addressed at an earlier stage (see the sixth question above), it needs to be revisited now, in order to determine whether or not the thinker is relying overly on the thoughts of others or is fully undertaking the job at hand.

9. In taking on the burden of proof, thinkers offering arguments take responsibility for the truth or acceptability of the premises, and for the warrants having backing, for the argument not being overreaching in what it claims, and for the proper level of detail and sophistication of the evidence adduced. Also thinkers take responsibility for the patterns of associating premises counting in the communities involved as providing logical support for the argument's claim. That is, they take responsibility for adducing evidence and for properly inferring a claim.

Ninth question: Does the argument proceed from acceptable premises to a conclusion bearing a proper logical relationship to those premises? And are these at such a level of sophistication as to move the project of the community forward on the particular occasion at hand? Finally, has the one offering the argument personally taken on the task of identifying and checking premises and reasoning in support of the claim?

10. Further, thinkers take on the responsibility of adducing evidence and properly inferring a claim in a way that appeals to others in the community. The aim is to invite and guide consideration and to lead to one or both of two changes in the beliefs and decisions of those receiving the argument: either they come to recognize the authority of the one offering the argument as sufficient to determine the acceptability of a belief, decision, or action on the matter at hand, or else they, themselves, come to accept the belief, decision, or action that the arguer was supporting. Good arguments are aimed at securing uptake by those who become aware of them—uptake either in the form of endorsing the arguer's participation in moving forward the work of the community of inquiry, or uptake in the form of a change of belief, decision, or action themselves in response to the argument. Good arguments are accessible from and flow out of communicable emphases placed on aspects of life narratives (personal experiences). As a result uptake of them and their conclusions is transferable from arguer to those to whom the argument is given, *if* that other person comes to share in the personal narrative or life experience out of which the argument flows. *This sharing comes about whenever there is respect for or sympathy with the person who gives the argument.*

Question 10: Does the argument succeed in so far as, assuming proper respect for the one offering the argument, the person offered the argument would be moved by reflection:

- ♦ to credit and recognize the authority of the author of the argument to determine a well-supported belief, decision, or action, and to express it by that argument; or,

- ♦ to accept and take up the claim itself on the basis of that evidence?

The pay-off of a good argument is a movement toward feeling, thinking, and living well by reason. As pointed out, argument is not the only way to be carried along on such a journey. But it is one. And this is the point of argument, as opposed to some intellectual gaming or combat. But this aim is shared; as is the work of critical thinking itself. It is an end that those who offer arguments help move others toward by those arguments. If this is not so, then what is the point? Nothing. So it would seem that reason and the exchange of reasons is needed. But it is clear that no one will be brought to this end if he or she is not open to this influence and no one will be open to this influence if not through the respect for, if not sympathy with, the one giving the argument.

Sometimes this respect or sympathy for other thinkers, or even the openness to it, must be built up by one's own life experience—thus Aristotle thought that only those with significant life experience should be allowed to study ethics. Other times it can be enabled by the patience and goodwill of the one giving the argument. And at still other times it must be gained by purposive work—as in Pascal's suggestion about what one should do if he or she has heard the arguments for the existence of God, but has not been able to take them to heart[4]:

> Concentrate then not on convincing yourself by multiplying proofs of God's existence but by diminishing your passions. You want to find faith and you do not know the road. You want to be cured of unbelief and you ask for the remedy: learn from those who were once bound like you and who now wager all they have. These are people who know the road you wish to follow, who have been cured of the affliction of which you wish to be cured: follow the way by which they began. They behaved just as if they did believe, taking holy water, having masses said, and so on. That will make you believe quite naturally, and will make you more docile. . . .

> 419 Custom is our nature, anyone who grows accustomed to faith believes it, and can no longer help fearing hell, and believes nothing else.

This is not to say that Pascal is correct, or that what he said could be carried over directly to talk about preparing one to be open to argument as a critical thinker. Still, perhaps he is right about faith. And perhaps Pascal's suggestion could be adapted so that by habituation thinkers open themselves to each other and thus to the thought of others. Sometimes thinkers do not listen to or pay close attention to each other. This is not the way of critical thought, however. In fact, the critical thinker will not only listen but will take seriously the argument offered. In that atmosphere, if the previous questions are answered to the credit of the argument, it should prevail upon the listener in one of the two ways indicated. It should be accepted as the act of an authoritative person or it should move the listener to accept the belief or decision or action in question. Thus for the assessment of arguments one final, or really one first, question m   u   s   t be answered:

> *Question 11:* Are you open, and ready to hear, and ready to seriously consider the arguments that others offer—to really consider them with understanding and impartiality?

This, of course, takes the discussion back to the beginning and raises the need for all involved to be critical thinkers and for their interdependence in that project. There are no recipes here, just hard work and the need for both courage and perseverance.

Mastery Exercises IX.4

SELF TEST

The Assessments of Arguments

Consider the following arguments. Assess them following the above suggestions for assessing arguments. You might have to fill in the details of a context to do some of this work. Write out your assessment in no more than 500 words. In your write-up, indicate how the above points about assessing arguments come into play.

1. At the recent zoning meeting of the incorporated village of Traditionville, the zoning board recommended that the Council accept the request to turn a local historic site into a small shopping mall. The historic site was the location of a regionally important battle and contains a small burial ground which the developers propose moving to another site they would pay for. The developers urge that turning the site into a strip mall would increase the tax base and bring more business into the village since the mall will have a small sports bar/restaurant and a video store—both high traffic items. Currently, the site is used for a small interpretive center run by the local historical society and a playground which only costs the village money. The developers are asking for tax abatement (no taxes) for the first 10 years. But the village has its own sales tax so it will get taxation from the consumption at the strip mall. Residents close to the site do not want extra traffic and noise. Environmentalists do not want the destruction of the green space. Local historians do not want to lose the site of the battle to another parking lot for a strip mall. And the village government wants the tax money. Overall the zoning board recommends approval since it would move the site up to a "best use" as the land use planners call the more developed uses of property.

2. "The President said of his re-election opponent's position that he would be happy if Saddam Hussein were still in power. What the other candidate really said was that in light of the cost in lives and property and government spending, and the present mess the situation is in, the United States might have made a mistake in invading when we did without further support and better planning and more troops. The President was here clearly committing a studied misunderstanding of his opponent's words."

3. "Senator Kerry has several times said he needs to wait until he becomes President to say exactly how he would feel about some problem or to say exactly what he would do about it. The President's campaign interprets this as further evidence that Senator Kerry is dangerously indecisive. The President's campaign is right about this."

4. "Humans are selfish. Look, we all know that people do a lot of stuff in order to look out for themselves. But if you look at the cases where there seems to be caring for someone else besides the agent it is always the case that beneath the surface appearances, there is a selfish motive working. Would a parent help a child if he or she did not get pleasure from doing so? Would a soldier help a buddy if he or she did not want to avoid feeling bad after not helping? Would anyone stop to help a stranger if no one else was looking? All of this proves that people, even in those cases where they seem to demonstrate caring for others, are really selfish."

5. "Humans are not all selfish. It might look to some people as though every human action has some ulterior and selfish motive. But that is because those who look at the action want to see some ulterior motive. Well, let's assume that a soldier never helps a buddy, or a parent never helps a child except because it will make them feel better if they do than if they don't. This might be true for two reasons: (A) because the agents really care for the children or the buddies and so when they help them they feel good because they have benefited them—a nonselfish act; (B) because the agents don't really care for the others but they do care for looking like they do—they really are self-centered and helping others makes them feel good because they will look good to other people. In the case of (A) the examples really prove the point against selfishness. In the case of (B), why should you accept (B)? There are lots of cases in which parents are hurt or soldiers injured and even risk their lives to benefit the others and no matter how much they might want to feel good by others thinking highly of them for helping, it will do no good if they are dead or seriously hurt. So it seems implausible to say there aren't cases in which some people really do things for others out of caring for those others and so not selfishly. They risk losing everything to help others—isn't that real caring? You might reply that no, it is not real caring since there must be some selfish motive that is overpowering even the fear of death and injury. But to say that at this point is just question begging. So if you don't beg the question there must be some cases of real caring for others and that proves the point that not all people are selfish all the time."

6. "Oedipus needed to be a critical thinker. If he had been, then he would have avoided killing the king in the first place and none of the troubles would have come about. He would have been in control of what happened to him and fate would not have gotten him. Why did he kill the king? Because he was a hot-head. That's why. He needed to be a critical thinker and things would have been ok."

7. "Yerma needed to be a critical thinker. If she had been then she would have seen that there are worse things than adopting a child or going childless. Killing another person is one of these. She lost all perspective because she insisted on making her perspective and its assumed values fighting points. Juan was no better. But Yerma was clearly reflecting on all of her options in the course of the play. Juan was just stubborn. Yerma came close to avoiding trouble. But she did not go far

enough as a critical thinker in the end. She was consumed by the need to be right and to live out the perfect version of her community's vision of the good life for women. It cost her, her son."

8. "There should be no concealed weapons allowed on people who are not police officials or other law enforcement agents. While the right to bear arms is protected by the Constitution, this does not guarantee that there be hand guns or that you be allowed to carry them concealed on your person. Those who work for law enforcement agencies have special mandatory training and are under very strict rules with very strict penalties for drawing and misusing a concealed weapon. But there is not any way to require that everyone given a concealed weapons permit will get the training and do what it teaches other than punishing those people for having the weapon if it is used to commit a crime. Police training and continuing education would be too expensive to support. So if not allowing concealed weapons to be carried by non-law enforcement officials does not take away the right to have arms, and cannot be properly supported, then what is the point? It will only bring into being a new crime—the criminal activities of hot-head cowboys who race to use the weapons they carry in order to make themselves feel powerful and important."

9. "Equal funding for schools is not going to be worked out by requiring the state to redistribute funds from one school district to another. And yet it has to be worked out. Anything less is really biased or prejudicial and hurts those who can least afford to avoid being hurt. So my plan is to tax those from districts where students receive more than 10% more than the least well funded students do across the state. The taxes would be in addition to the taxes the better-off school district members already pay and would not erode the tax base of the better-off schools. But it would be an equity tax since it would go directly to a fund to be redistributed to bring all schools up to a higher level that is closer, for all the underfunded, to being equal. The basic idea says that if your children are going to be advantaged, then you need to pay for it so other children are not disadvantaged by that. Seems fair, right?"

10. "Cold fusion is a hoax. The reason is that it violates the laws of classical physics and the tests cannot be duplicated in other labs besides where they were first claimed to take place. Of course, it might be something that physicists want to come back to at some later date if they have independent evidence suggesting it is possible. But right now, there is no unchallenged evidence on behalf of cold fusion. In fact, there are only the claims of those scientists who claimed they did it."

Wrap-Up

Thus there are paths to follow to assess both explanations and arguments. They are not simple ones; for the first thing that the thinker must do is open up to the arguments and then think her or his way into the situation to see what thought is being offered. Once there, the explanation or argument must be articulated after interpretation. And then, with the context properly understood, the tech tips for explanations or the eleven questions just set out for assessing arguments can be worked through and a judgment reached. Having said all of this, it should not be surprising that both explanations and arguments can be assessed by well-meaning individuals proceeding according to the same guidelines, and the judgments on the worth of the explanations or arguments can differ without either party being wrong. The facts are complex. The method of assessment is complex and calls for interpretation at crucial places. Is it any wonder that well-meaning and informed persons can disagree in their assessments? Thus once again the discussion leads to a reminder of the importance of openness and respect, of cooperation and perseverance, and of a strong commitment to a life led by the guidance of reason.

This is the requirement in dealing with each other through argument and explanation when thinkers move from the personal of life narratives, or what is commonly called experience, into the public realm of explicit articulate reasoning. How much more is this requirement a part of thinking about reason applied to ethics and the determination of well supported ways to interact?[5]

Notes and References

[1] For a contemporary expression of this sort of view see, Copi, I. M., and Cohen, C. (2004). *Essentials of logic.* Upper Saddle River, NJ: Pearson Prentice Hall.

[2] For a classical discussion of the pragmatic virtues of explanations, see the discussion in Quine, W. V., and Ullian, J. S. (1978). *The web of belief* (2nd ed.). New York: Random House.

[3] Doyle, A. C. (2003). The sign of four in *The complete Sherlock Holmes,* volume I. New York: Barnes and Noble Classics, 103–104.

[4] Pascal, B. (1995). *Pensées* (rev. ed.) (trans. by A. J. Krailsheimer). London: Penguin Books. 418–419, pp.124–125.

[5] Some of the material on explanation in this chapter was developed for my Reasoning in Context: An Introduction to (the General Theory of) Critical Thinking, which comprised the first portion of *Teaching Critical Thinking In Secondary Humanities Courses, The Manual of Wyoming's Critical Thinking Project.* (Copyright, Charlie Blatz, 1985.) Wyoming's Critical Thinking Project was funded by the National Endowment for the Humanities, whose support is gratefully acknowledged.

CHAPTER X

Conclusion: Living Well and Thinking Well, Taking Care of Yourself and Others

SECTION 1

The Culture of Ethics and Its Relation to Critical Thinking

200 H 3. Man is only a reed, the weakest in nature, but he is a thinking reed. There is no need for the whole universe to take up arms to crush him: a vapour, a drop of water is enough to kill him. But even if the universe were to crush him, man would still be nobler than his slayer, because he knows that he is dying and the advantage the universe has over him. The universe knows none of this.

Thus all our dignity consists in thought, it is on thought that we must depend for our recovery, not on space and time, which we could never fill. Let us then strive to think well; that is the basic principle of morality.[1]

Could the activity of thinking as such, the habit of examining whatever happens to come to pass or to attract attention, regardless of results and specific content, could this activity be among the conditions that make men abstain from evil-doing or even actually conditions them against it?[2] [Commenting on the banality of evil—that is, its being due to thoughtlessness.]

If thinking—the two-in-one of the soundless dialogue [with oneself in reflection]— actualizes the difference within our identity as given in consciousness and thereby results in conscience as its by-product, then judging, the by-product of the liberating effect of thinking, realizes thinking, makes it manifest in the world of appearances, where I am never alone and always too busy to be able to think. The manifestation of the wind of thought is not knowledge; it is the ability to tell right from wrong, beautiful from ugly. And this, at the rare moments when the stakes are on the table, may indeed prevent catastrophes, at least for the self.[3]

Ethics as an expression of critical thinking has multiple dimensions that are inter-related and interdependent. The task of this chapter will be to look at some of these and to consider how one could be a critical thinker in living ethically. The short answer is that:

1. In living ethically one continuing task is the reintegration of beliefs, decisions, plans, and actions in the face of a changing world and in ways that take into account what matters.
2. A second task is to prepare oneself to create arguments that give a public presenta-tion of reasons in support of one's beliefs, decisions, and actions concerning what matters.

This chapter will look at ways to approach both of these tasks and will give some considerations in favor of one over the others of these approaches. Also, the chapter will discuss the context of ethical thinking and the source of the connections holding thinkers together even when dealing with something as volatile as what is right and wrong, good and bad. The first order of business is to gain some understanding of the two tasks facing critical agents in the arena of ethics and the relationships between these two tasks.

The Place and Task of Reintegration in Ethical Thinking

Thinkers live in a world charged with significance. Things matter, for the most part, and those that do not are not processed or remembered in any detail. Thinkers encounter the world not just intellectually but also and always, emotionally and in terms of whether what they find is good or bad, predicted or unusual, useful to or hampering their efforts, something they want to follow-up on or something that can be ignored, something beautiful or something ugly, and so on for a number of other evaluative contrasts. The world is changing and thus its significance to thinkers is dynamic, shifting, and evolving. People have to make sense of the moment, and keep track of how it all fits together, through a life narrative. And this life narrative is not just a story that proceeds as just one thing after another—"and then this happened, and then this other thing happened, and then something else happened." Rather the story pieces together occurrences in terms of the thinkers' own undertakings, their continuing projects, the unfolding of their history, the expectations upon them from themselves and others, their hopes, their fears, and so on; in short, the narrative records events in terms of the threads of all the various significances that things have for them. What looks good one moment can be a difficulty later as things change. What is a great misfortune can become a cloud with a silver lining as things continue to evolve. That person whom one wanted to be with but who went with another turns out to be a person anyone would be glad not to be with. That job that one lost to another applicant turns out to be a terrible place to work. One loses a child, or a spouse. One finds a new love. Or these things go some other way. People must try to adjust to these changes and go on. *The point, then, is that life is a dynamic and interwoven set of changing circumstances and tendencies that thinkers are constantly adjusting to in order to make the most sense of things and to fit them into the best life.*

One major task thinkers face through ethical thinking, then, is to continually adjust their understanding of how they are doing, where they are going, what is next, and how it all fits together so as to make the best of what is presented and what is undertaken.

What thinkers themselves do, and what others do, and the way the wind blows, and the fortunes of the stock market or other economic markets, and a million other things, all provide the environment in which the thinker is continually adjusting and reintegrating her or his life plans, life narrative, and current and ongoing undertakings and commitments. How does one carry out this personal reintegration of life circumstances and individual agency?

Arendt's suggestion quoted above is that this work involves **judgment,** not deliberate and calculating reflection. The task seems to be one of making sense of or finding how to make intelligible one's life, in light of the changes encountered; that, as opposed to the task of providing a fully developed argument giving the reasons for why this or that judgment is correct or proper. **The task seems to be more one of creative interpretation and revisioning the future, rather than one of argument.**

Think of all that people must consider and integrate:

§   expectations from others,

§   demands from her or his own present plans and current activities,

§   what is required by her or his own history and way of seeing things in addition to her or his own principles (integrity),

§   attitudes toward living and levels of wellness,

§   what is known as possible about the open options,

§   the regard thinkers hold others in that makes their well-being more or less important in itself—that is morally, or as a matter of law, or as a matter of prudence,

§   the degree of involvement with others on the part of the thinker (are these others ones the thinker identifies with, or sympathizes with, or empathizes with, respects or merely recognizes as one requiring deference or noninterference),

§   impartiality toward the others involved in the situation so as to meet them on their own terms balanced against the ethical integrity of the thinker. (See chapter III.)

Ethically speaking, being open to considering others and their welfare is something that must be approached impartially in critical thinking or else the thinker is going to beg the question concerning how important that welfare is, or the thinker is going to be inconsistent, or is going to rely on stereotypes, or other fallacious forms of regard discussed in the earlier chapters.)

Thus the physical realities of the world, expectations on the agent, personal history and agenda, regard of others and openness toward them, all factor into and color what options the thinker sees or can imagine and what the thinker feels about them. And then in a hidden or non-conscious way, all these complexities are woven into a unified vision of the future course of action that makes coherent sense of what the agent is about and trying to do and of what other concerns the agent faces. As Arendt suggests, *the thinker reaches a judgment of what is right and good and what should be undertaken in the face of the changes that precipitated the disintegration of the person's thinking and called for reintegration.* This sort of reintegrative modeling of a future coherently including all the various pressures upon the thinker thus isolates a best or preferred goal to undertake in the changed circumstances. And the judgment is made. In light of this judgment the thinker can see her or his way clear into a future that makes sense in light of all the various constraints that are operating. There is what has been called an intuition of the right and proper and good thing to try to do or to achieve.

This recognition in judgment is reached perhaps with a good deal of non-conscious jockeying back and forth between various models of what could coherently fit the various pieces together and meet all the demands or constraints at work. *Some ethicists speak of this sort of reintegrative reasoning as reaching a decision in reflective equilibrium.* This judgment of reintegration is not necessarily one that is reached by conscious reflection. Indeed, by what procedure or calculative device might all these various factors be fitted together in a way that links the commitment and motivation of the thinker with the course of action decided upon? The judgment is more like creating an interpretation of what will happen next in the face of all these demands. And if the demands are weighted properly the vision or interpretation of that future will be acceptable. But how does all that work so that the demands are weighted properly?

This question calls for the mention of one other constraint in ethical judgment. The outcome of the judgment must fit into a pattern of giving reasons to support a decision in some polished and public form that is a good argument. As thinkers work with other people or reflect themselves on how to articulate the various things that entered into the setting of their current direction of action, they select certain features of what they are up to, to put forward as what should recommend this undertaking to others as well. These favored features of actions often show up in grand principles of ethics.

Possible basic principles include for example:

§
The action promises to **do the most for social welfare or the good of all affected.**

§
The action **shows the greatest respect for all concerned** of all those options open to the thinker.

§
The action **expresses most fully the principles or stands that the thinker wants to represent** herself.

§
The undertaking seems to **most appropriately express care for all those affected.**

And there are many other possibilities, of course. Here, thinkers operate not unlike the situation in which they select from experience those factors that seem salient in finding the cause, or the correlation, or the correct observation, or the best appeal to authority in order to settle some question of belief about the world. But the aim here is not to find the warrant and grounds for an argument concluding in some claim of a matter of fact. The claim here concerns what is proper, correct, justified, or, that is, defensible behavior. But the process of selection and emphasis as a reason for asserting that claim is the same in its making the present situation part of a coherent movement into the future. Thus, however the judgment process works in its psychological depths, the outcome must be fit to serve as a claim of an argument where the leading features of what the person is up to, or of what the person is trying to accomplish in her or his undertaking, can serve as reasons for that claim.

THE PLACE AND TASK OF ARGUMENT IN ETHICAL THINKING.   This brings the discussion to the second task for critical thinking in ethics. *The first is one of interpretation of the tendencies of things so as to reach a judgment fitting together a coherent future from the possibilities and one's place in the present.*

> **The second major task is to prepare oneself to give arguments that provide a public presentation of reasons in support of the thinker's beliefs, decisions, and actions about what matters.**

Now, just as the first task had to be handled in a way that fits with the second task, this second must match the first. *The conclusions and statements of reasons that make up arguments justifying decisions and actions must themselves express points that are salient to the agent whose action is being assessed. In addition they must be found acceptable by other thinkers at least out of respect for the agent.* Otherwise, they will not express the real reasons of anyone and will not be taken up to make a difference to the beliefs, decisions, or actions of those thinkers. Without uptake on the part of the agent involved, that is without really meaning something to the agent, the argument would misrepresent her or his reasons for acting. And without acceptance (at least of the credibility of the reasons given) on the part of the others to whom the argument is made, the argument will be no more than an exercise in logic. This is not to say that the argument, if successful, must be logical, based in premises that are defensible, *and also* must move others to action. That, of course, is not the way things work. Not everyone has to do just the same things on similar occasions since the pressures facing them are not the same. *But the argument must at least be credible in so far as it is a legitimate exercise of the authority of the thinker. Those to whom the argument is made must be brought to see either that the thinker was exercising proper integrity in the argument, or was reasoning in a way that charity or respect would have to credit as legitimate.* Maybe the reasons the thinker appeals to are not the principles or the grounds of the others to whom the argument is offered. But these others must see the legitimacy of the thinker's making that argument in so far as the reasons:

§ *either are the same as these others would use as their own reasons,*

§ *or else they show*
- ◆ *proper impartiality,*
- ◆ *regard for the well-being of others affected,*
- ◆ *at least a respect for others affected,*
- ◆ *can be seen as coherently pulling together the various expectations and personal commitments of the thinker,*
- ◆ *and fit into an argument where the logic is acceptable.*

Falling into one or the other of these cases is just what makes the action proposed or undertaken acceptable, defensible, or creditable as based on adequate reasons. If the grounds and warrants of an ethical argument meet either of these conditions, then they will be reasons for both the argument maker and for those other persons for whom the argument is made, or they will be the reasons of the argument maker and will be respected by those for whom the argument is made as a legitimate use of the agent's authority as a critical thinker in ethics. *In either case the argument's premises and conclusion will: (1) emerge from the thinker's judgment and its inputs so the judgment will fit with the public reasoning of the argument, and (2) be such that public reasoning grows out of the personal commitments and undertakings of the thinker making the argument.* There will be a mutual constraining influence between the way the task of reintegration and the task of argument are each carried out. In reasoning in ethics, personal views and public insights will be attuned to each other.

Thus the culture of critical reasoning in ethics is not just about reasoning logically to a conclusion from ethical premises as some have said. And it is not just about responding to the world through emotions or sentiment as others have said. Both logic and sentiment are involved in critical reasoning in ethics. The discussion has just revealed how arguments need to fit with an agent's responding to the world through emotions and sentiment. Still this does not reveal what defensible standards are and how they fit into arguments in ethics. The story of Yerma certainly raises this question since it seems to pit against each other two different sets of principles, two different visions of life's meaning, and two very different sets of aims. What importance is to be accorded each individual's aims and how much weight are these to be given when they conflict with the aims of others? These are two of the questions underlying the frustration Juan imposes upon Yerma, and she upon him. And they are the underlying cause of the conflict between Antigone and Creon. The issue of standards, their origins and their operation in arguments to support evaluations, needs to be discussed further.

Galileo's situation raises a different sort of ethical question. What constitutes ethical community and what allegiance does a member of that community owe to the goals and ideals of the group? Did Galileo turn his back on the religious and social community where he lived? Did he turn his back on the scientific community of his day? Was this all in the name of forming another community of inquiry to which he owed, ethically owed, his allegiance? Did he go far enough or did he ethically fail as Bertolt Brecht alleges in his drama *Galileo,* playing it safe by capitulating to the church concerning the Copernican view of our planetary system? And how does membership in an ethical community fit in with the two tasks of ethical thinking just described?

Oedipus, on the other hand, tragically poses the question of when we are obligated to do something. He is portrayed as believing that he has an obligation as king to relieve Thebes of the suffering it is under. He has an obligation to his subjects to identify and punish the killer of his predecessor. Creon and Jocasta urge him to set aside this burden. But he cannot. Can one help but wonder about the nature of obligation, as his perceived obligation impelled Oedipus on to his destruction?

These three issues, principles, or standards by which to argue for the worth of individual aims, the nature of an ethical community, and the nature of obligation, are central to any ethic—to any set of considerations that guide the formation of beliefs and decisions about what one should do. The remainder of this chapter explores these and related issues with an eye to the role that critical thinking can play in deliberations on what people should do.

SECTION 2

Standards of Individual and Relative Personal Worth

The place to begin is with an investigation of just how thinkers might determine the relative worth of the aims of other individuals. The personal side of this has been approached just above in discussing the place and task of reintegration and argument in ethics. Still there is another dimension to this question of acceptable standards. This is the issue of what arguments might be brought to support evaluations and even the standards or judgments people use. Are there any general positive principles that can serve as warrants of ethical assessments stated as arguments? Just above, it became clear those standards or ethical judgments are: common to a certain ethical community, or are ones that a thinker endorses impartially, with a proper regard for the welfare of others, and a proper respect for those others, and are ones that pull together that thinker's experiences, aims, and expectations. The question remains, what substantive principles, if any, will order ethical arguments and meet the conditions just spelled out? And what do these arguments look like? Consider that second question first.

Far and away the greatest amount of philosophical attention has been paid to argument strategies—even to the point of understanding rationality in ethics as a matter of evaluations being the claims of logically good arguments for some assessment. And in fact most attention has been given to argument strategies proceeding toward particular evaluative conclusions through the use of modus ponens. Such arguments have even been given the name of **verifications** of (particular) evaluations.[4]

Verifications of evaluations raise a further important question. Look at the following example:

If a farm woman is barren, then she is lacking in personal worth.

    Yerma was barren.

Thf. Yerma was lacking in personal worth.

This example, like all uses of modus ponens, will establish its claim soundly, under the assumption that its premises are acceptable. The premise providing the grounds of this argument is beyond question, within the confines of the story of the play. And, generally, in establishing an ethical conclusion from particular grounds about what nonethical feature an act or person has, one faces relatively few problems in being able to certify those grounding premises.

Unfortunately, the same cannot be said about the warrant or bridge principle of the argument in which possession of a certain nonethical feature is linked with the truth of a certain ethical claim. If it is true that barrenness in farm women is sufficient for lacking personal worth, then the above strategy will establish Yerma's lack of worth. But is there this connection between barrenness and lack of worth? The warrant asserting that there is—at least in Yerma's community—is one the playwright puts before us. But is it supportable? That is one of the questions the play raises.

What is sometimes offered in support of warrants (those as dubious as this and others much more plausible) is another argument rather like verification, but called by a different name; a **validation** of the warranting standard or rule or principle appealed to. Thus, for example, one might seek to argue for the warrant of the previous argument in this way:

If a farm woman does not contribute to the farm's work force, then she is lacking in personal worth.

    If a farm woman is barren, then she is not contributing to the farm's work force.

Thf. If a farm woman is barren then she is lacking in personal worth.

In this validation the argument appeals to a norm linking failure to contribute to a farm's work force with being someone who lacks personal worth. The argument also appeals to another general claim linking being barren to failing to contribute to the work force. Here, in the context of the play, the link seems to rest on the meaning of the term "barren." It also might rest on the factual claim as in the secondary validation running as follows:

If a farm woman does not increase the productivity of the land, then she lacks personal worth.

    If a farm woman does not contribute to the work force then she does not increase the productivity of the land.

Thf. If a farm woman does not contribute to the farm's work force, then she is lacking in personal worth.

In this validation the conclusion links failing to increase the work force and lacking personal worth. One might support this claim by appealing to a link between increasing productivity and having personal worth as well as one between farm women increasing the land's productivity and their having children. If the premises of this argument are true or acceptable, then the conclusion has to be true or acceptable as well. Thus some such validation is what one would need to support the warrant of the validation previously considered and then, ultimately, to support the verification with which this string of arguments began.

What this much makes clear then is the process one might engage in to support the warrants of ethical verifications. The question raised is, how does the process ever stop or come to an end? Where does one find the ethical norms or standards with which to begin the process of arguing in support of those warrants needed to argue in support of an ethical assessment? The process of validation cannot go on indefinitely. If it were to do so, the justification of a particular evaluation would never be finished and available. The best that could be said is that something is right or good *if* something else is, and that other is *if* yet something else is again, and so on. But no one, critical thinkers included, lives by postponing the support of their rules or standards in this way. The search might be directed to definitions of key ethical terms in an ethical community. Perhaps Lorca had it right and in the tradition represented by Yerma in the play "barren" means "bad or worthless like a handful of thorns"? But then the question just shifts to why should a critical thinker that is impartial and respectful of others accept such a definition? So the problem remains: How might one establish those ultimate beginning points of justifying arguments in an ethic? That is the pressing problem raised by a review of verification and validation of ethical norms.

If it is no good to appeal to other norms or standards or to definitions as ultimate sources of norms, then what kind of a problem do thinkers face here? One possibility is that ethics just have no good beginning point—if one chooses some principle(s) and a set of definitions or associations specifying what is good or right, then that is all there is to it. But this is to say that critical thinking has no systematic role to play in ethics just because it cannot use arguments relying on ethical standards to support all ethical standards. Are there not other possibilities? Earlier parts of the text have shown that this approach to argument and rationality is not the only one—in particular one might try to give a pragmatic justification of a warrant of an ethical argument by showing that it meets the functional conditions demanded of such norms. (Compare this with looking for the best explanatory hypotheses by appealing to pragmatic virtues.) In this way the argument for ultimate norms lying at the basis of validations of general rules (and then of verifications of assessments of particular actions) would rest in showing that the norms efficiently and effectively meet the needs there are for such norms. What might some of these pragmatic considerations be?

Ethical arguments involve norms, standards, or principles, so as to marshal support for saying that some ethical standards or some ethical assessment of particular actions are defensible as opposed to others. These arguments record practical wisdom in choice situations. Thus if agents had no real choice between incompatible actions, if agents operated on instinct or for some other reason were locked into a single track, then they would need no guidance. *Ethics are for those exercising choice influenced by reason. And indeed their reliance upon reasoning introduces the element of creativity in which agents are exercising their authority as critical thinkers to find and support the most defensible undertaking in the circumstances in which they find themselves.* To the extent they are not just being arbitrary when they exercise free choice, they are law givers to themselves or are autonomous beings.

Furthermore, if the choices were not of consequence to thinkers, guidance would not be needed. It would not matter which choice was made. And critical thinking would be out of place.

Beyond this, thinkers need to remember that ethics expressed in arguments provide guidance for recurring problems. Ethical guidance offered in arguments is expressed in concepts that abstract from the particularities of individual lives. The public differs from the personal, as discussed earlier. Ethical wisdom recorded in arguments and offered as guidance identifies what *kinds* of acts or ways of being are right or wrong, obligatory or not, expressive of good or bad characters, and so on. If the problems people face did not lend themselves to general characterization by agents selecting salient features to mark the right from the wrong and so on, then there would be no place for abstract general guidance. Ethics would not have a public side offered in arguments supporting assertions of assessments or evaluations.

Further, ethical argument is for beings with limited and somewhat standardized means to achieve their ends. If agents could get what they were after with magic or in technologically unlimited ways, then there would be no hard choices to make, either individually or between people who come in conflict while pursuing aims.

Thus ethical warrants and arguments support and serve as guides for: free, autonomous agents, faced with incompatible options of sorts that make a difference to them and which have salient features that regularly recur. These agents must choose and are partly limited by the means with which to pursue their options. This much already has serious implications for what acceptable ethical warrants could be like.

Acceptable ethical warrants:

§ **should not be systematically relativistic,** varying what is right or wrong/good or bad in spite of the acts or persons assessed being similar in salient ways;

§ **should be teachable and enforceable** otherwise the general guidance would not be carried forward (since it is not teachable), and it would not be taken seriously (since without enforcement its guidance would not have the status in society of an expectation);

§ **should be what critical thinkers could endorse without fallacy or other loss of integrity as critical thinkers,** thus these warrants should be something they can endorse without begging the question, without inconsistency and without introducing inconsistency into their reasoning, without stereotyping, without committing to acting out of power as opposed to reason, and so on;

§ **should arise out of, or be open to being accepted as the personal vision of, critical agents.** Thus they must show proper regard for the welfare of others, respect for others, impartiality, all while making coherent sense of a future combining personal aims, history including prior commitments, and the expectations they act under—that is, the public must be acceptable as the personal.

This short list of requirements for warrants of ethical arguments to serve the purposes of critical thinkers has real implications for which ethical warrants might seem acceptable. Consider some of the leading contenders:

ETHICAL EGOISM. Ethical egoism, the view according to which each person is to maximize her or his own welfare, is unacceptable as an ethical warrant according to the above. On this view, either one person is chosen as the reference point by which to determine what is justifiable, or everyone serves as one such standard. Either way, however, the question is begged as to whether the aims of certain people are worthwhile by themselves or when in conflict with the aims of others. If one person is the reference point, then the aims of every other are considered worthless in themselves and of secondary importance in a conflict. But if everyone is allowed to serve as a reference point, it is as the reference point of her or his own personal ethic from the standpoint of which no one else's aims matter. Thus by making everyone the reference point the result is to substitute many question begging ethics in place of one. Ethical egoism, then, is unacceptable as question begging. One example of this approach to ethics can be seen perhaps in Lorca's play *Yerma*. Juan kept his true views on marriage and sex from Yerma, thereby allowing her own very different views of marriage and sex to serve his own ends as and when he saw fit. He did not have to manipulate and regulate her behavior so much as keep her at arm's length except when he wanted something. His behavior raises the question of just who was he to so thoroughly control and live for another? By what right did he assert his own concerns over those of the people closest to him? Egoism and its question begging restriction of just who is worthwhile to the agent seems perfectly fit to serve as the ethic used by the oppressor Juan. The question begging ignoring of Yerma's value seems exactly the explanation needed of the moral outrage Juan's behavior calls forth.

RIGHTS ETHICS. Perhaps a rights approach to individual worth is what Lorca was suggesting to the reader? Individuals have rights in that it is unjustifiable for others to interfere with the rights holder. In addition, in the case of some rights, possession entitles one not just to the noninterference of others but to the assistance of others. For example, Yerma had a right to a life of her own choosing if she wished. Subject to an arranged marriage and a husband with no room in his personal agenda for hers, Yerma lacked rights of any significance to her within the marriage. How much Lorca was faulting his culture for its treatment of women on the ground that their rights are subjugated to those of husbands or other family members is not clear. But it certainly seems reasonable to view his tragic plays in this light.

If that is the message, however, is it acceptable? Is it satisfactory to simply say that ethically everyone counts, everyone has a right to a life or her or his own? Unfortunately it seems the answer is no. In the first place, how is one to support the claim that people have rights or that it is wrong for others to interfere with their pursuits? Or rather, how does one do so without just begging the question? Perhaps one could take a pragmatic approach as outlined just above? Perhaps. Traditionally, however, advocates of rights ethics have not been pragmatists, choosing instead to appeal in one way or another to what is self-evidently true about when others may interfere.

A deeper problem awaits once one grants that people do have rights to certain things. The question is, how does one decide who has rights to what? Is it that each person has a right to whatever he or she chooses? If so, then there is no useful guidance to be found in talking about rights. What each of us should do is stay clear of everyone else, in every way that might bear upon their choices. This sounds like a counsel of inaction and as such is worthless ethical guidance—such a warrant would justify no action. An ethic needs to tell agents what is justifiable, not just that all acts or ways of being are unjustifiable. Should a rights ethic be more discriminatory, however, it will have to decide between conflicting individuals saying just which one has no right to what he or she aims at, and which one does.

Either way, one will need to supplement a rights ethic with some other ethical standard that assigns rights to people or decides the relative weight of rights in a discriminating way. Yes, Yerma had rights as well as Juan. It is unjustifiable to deny this as Lorca's plays make clear. But still, one needs a standard of individual worth that does not give everyone a right to all, and that resolves conflicts of rights setting aside the interests, aims, or pursuits of some, in favor of those of others.

UTILITARIANISM. Utilitarianism seems to fill at least the last portion of the bill. According to such an ethic, right action consists in doing what has the best results for utility or social welfare for all those affected by an act (or acts of a certain type—in so-called "rule utilitarianism"). Utility has been said to be a number of things such as monetary gain, happiness, pleasure, absence of pain, or more generally, satisfaction of individual aims or interests. With that much said it should be clear why utilitarianism is appealing in the light of the failings of the rights approaches. This view does provide a perspective on how to weigh individual conflicting claims. No individual is ever more important than another, and individuals are less important than the social goal of a maximum amount of utility. Thus one can resolve conflicts or individual differences by trying to get the most happiness, satisfaction, or, in general, utility, for all affected, out of each of our acts or policies.

This perspective surely does seem to provide a way to understand Lorca's dissatisfaction with the culture represented in Juan's suppression of Yerma. John Stuart Mill, one of classical utilitarianism's most sophisticated proponents, discussed at length the subjection of women in an essay named after its subject matter.[5] The final section is devoted to the benefits to social welfare that would come about as a result of the cessation of women's subjection. This subjugation would pass, apparently, upon affording women: the vote; equal opportunity and reward in education and in the job market; equal or fair shares of child rearing responsibilities, equal property rights, division of labor and other aspects of partnership with males in marriage or family situations; an end to female sexual subjugation and any physical abuse in or out of marriage; and (for both men and women) a right of free association with friends for any legitimate purpose. The justification he offers for these liberating policies rests, it seems, with the greater happiness that would be enjoyed by marriage partners capable of being real partners, the greater happiness afforded society by the influence of women in business and government where they are now not allowed to flourish as leaders, and the lessening of pain suffered by women subjected to abuse and frustration as well as by those in society whom women's leadership could have benefited.[6]

Perhaps Lorca would have found Mill's analysis acceptable. Perhaps it pinpoints ethically objectionable aspects of Juan's treatment of Yerma? Perhaps, but utilitarianism faces other challenges. First, if utility is said to be something specific like felt pleasure, then one must ask why not other values? Why should an individual's aims count only to the extent that such pleasure is at stake? There is no nonarbitrary or nonquestion begging way to select only aims with certain objects as worthwhile any more than there was a nonarbitrary way to select only certain people as having worthwhile aims in Ethical Egoism. Also if utility is said to be something specific like pleasure, how is it to be measured? Considering the differences in values and degrees of maturity between different persons, for example, how much relative pleasure does any act give to each and every person? No utilitarian has yet to solve such measurement problems.

Suppose that utility is something general like satisfaction of individual aims or interests. This seems an improvement. Still, this view is biased. Why after all should one favor only satisfaction or success? If Yerma sought to have a child of her own but, unknown to her was really unable to do so, is her aim any less worthwhile than that of a woman who could succeed? Surely the very process of aim or goal pursuits is as ethically important as is the product of aim satisfaction? Put another way, the aim of freely living a certain way, striving for a goal, even when this is unlikely to be achieved, is as good or ethically important, other things being equal, as the aim of reaching some end or satisfying some desire for a product separate from action. Indeed, there is no nonarbitrary way to favor a product over a process kind of ethic. And so it seems the only defensible thing to do is leave behind utilitarianism's production orientation.

Finally, utilitarianism has no need to be fair in its ethical decisions; no matter whether these are decisions of individual actions or large social policies. Perhaps the greatest amount of good was produced by Juan's conduct of running the farm and ignoring Yerma's desires and perspective. Then, utilitarianism would say, that is the way things should be. The individual freedom or autonomy of Yerma does not matter in itself. Rather the general welfare, that faceless social goal, is all that really matters. Thus in distributing good and in distributing pain, utilitarianism can be unfair.

SOCIAL JUSTICE STANDARDS. This might lead to the proposal that a defensible ethical warrant would be one that decides questions of individual worth (absolute and comparative worth) in ways that are fair or just. People should be given what is fair. Then all will be well. Maybe Lorca's play illustrates the need for social justice, not social welfare. Maybe, but then what does this amount to? Some have said that all should be treated equally. But people are not equal and could not benefit from or be recognized for whom they are by treating them the same—if that is what equal treatment means. Yes, people should be treated the same in so far as they are the same ethically. But who is the same in ethically important ways? When it comes to fairness and just deserts, what matters ethically about people? That is the question of individual worth all over again.

Aristotle said that merit is decisive: the more virtuous people should get more and the most virtuous should get the most. This, however, only pushes the problem back, because now one needs an ethical test of when someone is virtuous. Also, not everyone has the same opportunities to be virtuous. Why penalize those who do not have a good shot at being the best?

Some say that people should be given only what they need and should contribute all they can. This socialist ideal is also flawed. How does one decide what people need in any real detail? To do so another ethical warrant is needed; and what is that? Secondly, why should people contribute all they can? Is it not right that people be able to keep much of what they earn or produce? Well, this is so at least in individualistic cultures today—but why not? Third, why should people have to contribute to others, if the others are not working up to their capacity? What does it mean to say that everyone should contribute all he or she can? What if one cannot meet her or his full potential through no fault of one's own?

More in the spirit of Western industrial countries, an alternative suggestion has been that people deserve only what they earn in a free marketplace. But the marketplace has never been free and open in the economist's sense. Not everyone can get into good schools, borrow money to open a business, find a good location, and so on. And there seems to be no way to provide everyone with equality of opportunity either. Further, it is clear that not all are interested in business as a career. So recognizing that people should be allowed to keep some of what they make or produce, what is the standard of fairness?

John Rawls, late a professor of Harvard, suggested a two part test.[7] First each is to be allowed as much liberty of action as is consistent with everyone else having the same, and second, no one will use up the scarce opportunities in society without those who are shut out being compensated in a way they would agree to.[8] This view also has its troubles. First, what is to count as equal liberties when society has people going in different directions requiring different sorts of educations and financial access and so on. How are we to weigh one person's liberties against those of another? Secondly, what compensation is there for missing out on one's first choice? Yerma wants to be a mother above all else and this is central to her value perspective, her identity, and her sense of self-worth. Her husband does not want a family and instead wants her as a business partner. How should she be compensated? How should society be restructured to serve both of their interests? What would compensate those who lose out in that restructuring? Third, what if one is willing to settle for a situation that thwarts her or his development? Is this impossible? Is there any compensation for such a person— any compensation that does not amount to corrupting the integrity of that person?

Finally, this view faces the basic problem with all tests of justice. Since these standards will end up favoring some people over others, one must ask, how can one show that this (or any standard of justice) is nonarbitrary and defensible? Rawls claimed that his standards are ones that all self-interested parties would agree to, if they did not know what their social and economic position is.[9] (Supposedly not knowing that position will make their agreement unbiased, though that seems highly questionable. If they are selfish to begin with, that will carry through when they pick a test of fairness not knowing their social or economic position. They simply hedge their bets in favor of themselves, as Rawls himself suggested.) Why should one tie a standard of justice to selfishness, however? Ethically speaking, selfishness is not the only or even the most plausible basis for standards or the only regard in which ethical beings might hold the welfare of others.

The debate about justice does not seem to provide an acceptable standard upon which to decide between conflicting interests, aims, and claims. Yes one wants to be fair in assessing individual worth in and out of conflicts. The question remains, however, how one determines what is fair. And, it now looks as though one cannot decide that issue without determining individual worth in and out of conflicts.

HARMONIZED GOAL PURSUIT ETHIC. Another approach that emerges out of the above might be called the harmonized goal pursuit ethic. According to this view, right action consists in people pursuing those goals they have chosen autonomously, that is after a review of the options and in recognition of the risks, and without the choice being due to social or biological determination. Further the right action is one that meets the constraints of impartiality, respect, regard for the welfare of others, and coherently blends all of this with the agent's personal agenda, history, and the expectations upon her or him. The public stand should then incorporate the personal constraints on ethical judgment already explored. When people's aims conflict, what is called for is that line of action creating circumstances allowing for a maximum of harmonious goal pursuits. The proper resolution of the Juan and Yerma struggle would have been the course that facilitates each of their chosen lives to the maximum extent possible. What might be that social structure and policy with respect to marriage and business that would respect and include the pursuits of women and men both? Of course, that social structure might be one that neither Juan nor Yerma would have recognized and immediately endorsed. But, all the same, it would provide a vision of a harmonious direction for them to work toward and in the bargain at least induce respect and consideration in each—making for something less than the fighting points they each lived by. What they would have worked out is not subject to some formulaic statement. Like ethical life itself, it would have required critical thinking as the mode of interaction between members of their ethical communities and the respect to go with that, making for the social conditions of ethical thinking in that community.

This view, like the rights approach, takes each individual's aims or goals seriously, unlike the faceless aim of producing a maximum of social welfare or utility. Also this view does not arbitrarily favor just one population's aims, or aims with only a certain object, such as felt pleasure, or happiness. In this way, it avoids the bias found in the rights approach, the utilitarian ethic, and some suggested standards of justice. Further this view can be set up to reflect individual differences as it resolves conflicts. The fact is that actions and policies hurt or help people to different degrees and in different ways, sometimes changing their whole lives, sometimes only costing them some nominal fine of money. For example, Juan would have had to change less of his life aims to accommodate Yerma, than would Yerma for Juan. Utilitarianism can measure such relative costs, but how these are spread around legitimately is a question that theory does not answer. The harmonized goal pursuit ethic approach seeks to avoid that problem in its being process not product oriented. It seeks to assist all in their pursuits (at least those that are harmonious with the pursuits of others). Thus it favors the best opportunity possible for all to seek their goals as they would define these, and it will not thwart people in their pursuits by denying them the fruits of their labors. Thus it agrees with what many theories of justice have said. Finally, in restricting whose or what aims are worthwhile or might win in conflicts, it avoids question begging outside of and inside conflicts. And in doing this, the theory fits with the constraint of ethical standards being subject to uptake in the personal life of every agent. Since the standard endorses as much of each person's and each community's aims as is possible to pursue with respect and regard for others, it would naturally be one that the personal perspective of a critical thinker in ethics would accept.

However, all of that said, this discussion only scratches the surface of seeking to identify warrants for arguments supporting ethical assessments that will efficiently and effectively serve the purposes of such standards. Still, in an introduction to ethical arguments, a serious beginning is better than nothing. Much more needs to be said about each of the positions mentioned. Much more needs to considered about the defensibility of ethical standards. But for present purposes, perhaps this will suffice.

SECTION 3

Community and Critical Thinking in Ethics

In section 1 the discussion made clear that there are two basic tasks of critical thinking with respect to ethics. The first of these is to form a judgment of right/wrong or good/bad of some particular act or option of character or desire formation. This judgment should coherently fit the act or person's traits together with her or his own history, current actions, impartial and respectful consideration of others, and so on. In doing so, a coherent sense of the situation the thinker is in and a vision or model of the future of that thinker must be formed so that the thinker commits to that direction of living. Now, as mentioned, this first task of ethical thinking is often performed silently, with the quicksilver speed and elusiveness of mercury. It may be only when the thinker finds herself or himself acting or speaking to others explaining what he or she is doing or tending toward that the judgment is articulated. Or it might be that the judgment is articulated as the judgment that this or that is right or good. And subsequently, it is rationalized by the agent selecting some feature of the approved action or trait by which to praise it while saying that the act or trait described in that way or as having that feature is what he or she is committed to and striving toward. Only then do we have the thinker/agent's reason for what he or she is doing, a reason offered up also as the support of her or his doing or becoming that. And only if that reason is found to be acceptable or offered as though it is acceptable as support, only then does the agent move toward the public insight of what is right or good in the situation he or she is in.

For example: Someone, say Bennett, a physician, has promised to not tell the patient's family how sick she is. She will die quickly and then the family can catch up with their troubles. In the meantime, the patient's wish is not to be a burden. The doctor has a history of keeping her word and also of being concerned about her patients and her patients's families. She discovers that the patient will leave teenaged children who will be devastated by the death and will feel cheated if they cannot talk to and comfort their mother before she dies. Also, the physician knows that the patient is not paying attention to financial matters which need to be cleared up so the family will have money to live on without interruption. She has a difficult decision—keep the promise, or tell the family and the patient's lawyer. She is sure that her patient is dying. There is no doubt. And she is sure that it will be quick—a matter of a few months—and that deterioration will not be noticeable until the very last when the patient collapses. What should she do? Legally she cannot tell the lawyer; morally, by one consideration, she cannot tell the family. There is an older child who could intervene and talk to the lawyer and to the family and the teenaged children might be able to keep a secret and just spend more time with their mother and give her the comfort of closeness without revealing that they know. Still she gave her word. She is not at all clear what would have the best consequences for the happiness of all involved, or even what would serve to give all the parties involved the greatest harmonious goal pursuits possible in the situation. She cannot rely on a standard to figure out what to do. The situation is too complex. She reflects. Her respect and moral concern for the patient and family as well as her desire to continue with a deep degree of involvement with these people as well as expectations all play a role in her thinking. After a while, this cluster of influences comes together into the judgment that she has to tell someone and to urge that person to let the family know and the lawyer know so that all can work together to form a future that is one they all participate in the vision of. She tells the oldest child, a sensitive and conscientious person in his own right. And she says that she will stay involved to the extent needed and wanted.

The oldest child speaks at length with her trying to get at the physician's motives and vision of what should be done. The child concludes that the physician did not have more in mind than looking out for the interests of the family and cannot even articulate exactly what makes her action right. He works with her to help in that regard and finds that this overall seems to best fit together all the various pressures and concerns that are working and most assuredly sets up the circumstances in which the maximum of harmonious goal pursuits of the family could come out—no guarantees, but that seems to be a salient direction of the doctor's actions. That is the reason and the justification the doctor and oldest child settle on for her action of telling him. And with that sense of things, the child shoulders the responsibility of bringing that to pass in his own way and in the fashion of the family.

The example illustrates the performance of the first task of ethics and its relation to the second task. But it serves to make one other thing clear. Critical thinking in ethics (as made clear generally in chapter I) is very much a social activity. The way this plays out here is that others are needed to help thinkers articulate the selected features in terms of what they have made intelligible in their judgments, so as to give reasons for their acts and ways of becoming. This assistance on the social playing field of ethics might be no more than confirmation or reassurance. Or it might be a fully fledged assistance in exploring the thinker's ruminations. In either case, it occurs in the relationship of **accountability** in which the thinker is called upon to give reasons and to assert the credentials of her or his use of critical thinking in forming an ethical judgment. And this relationship is sometimes adversarial, sometimes perfunctory, sometimes supportive and mutually reassuring. Still it is pivotal to the linking of the personal and the public aspects of critical thinking about ethical issues. It is the place where others can remind the agent of accepted reasons for doing or being some way. It is the place where the thinker can participate in challenging and perhaps changing the accepted reasons for being or acting in some way. And it is the reason community is so important in ethical thinking. Possibly, it was the absence of such a community that led Juan and Yerma to sound-bites and frustrations in their dealing with each other.

Thus membership in an ethical community is vitally important to being a critical thinker in this area of human undertaking. Thinkers need to be in a relationship in which all the individuals are accountable to each other to follow or live under or else justify their actions and ways of being in spite of a shared set of rules. But being in such relationships will be costly—it will require that individuals stay out of the way of each other, that they extend various forms of aid to each other to enable them to live as they would, and that they hold each other to account in order to explore with them their reasons for acting. What justifies all of this inconvenience and interference? What justifies people being treated as though the rules, teaching, and burden of the maintenance of an ethic apply to them? Yes community membership is useful, perhaps necessary to thinkers using reason to guide their lives. But is that enough? Is there more that might be said to justify lumping people together in terms of ethical expectations of these sorts? The answer seems straightforward. Any ethic that did not, or any view by which certain people are exceptions to such groups, would favor those exceptions arbitrarily and so ethically would be indefensible. The only way to avoid an ethical bias is to group people together in ways governed by rules aiming at keeping them from interfering and requiring them to aid each other, to the extent that this maximizes all the harmonious goal pursuits affected (or some other, defensible standard). Seeking to avoid such bias is what justifies treating people as members of ethical communities, as members of groups whose organization facilitates such goal pursuits.

The Problem of Conflicting Communities

Still these things are never simple. What if someone is a member of conflicting ethical communities, facing expectations from both? Is he or she still beholden to both, assuming that neither is unjustifiable in its demands? This brings us back to Galileo.

Bertolt Brecht, in his play *Galileo,* shows the importance of ethical community and raises the question of just what makes for such communities. In the play, Brecht seems to accuse Galileo of having sold out his scientific community in favor of the church when he capitulated to the Inquisition's pressure to recant. The play even portrays Galileo as recanting only to save himself the agony of torture or a fiery death at the hands of the Inquisition. (Perhaps not a bad reason, Brecht notwithstanding.) His interest in the church's beliefs is not allowed to be a factor as Brecht portrays the situation. Is this assessment defensible? Was Galileo a member of the scientific community and not of the church community? Did he abandon the one while not embracing the other, all just to save his skin? And would that have been an indefensible line of action? Or was Brecht wrong? Did Galileo really choose the church over science when the two seemed on a collision course? Perhaps instead, he affirmed both science and religion—giving as much to each as he could? How might one understand Galileo's action of recanting Copernicanism, and once understood, how does that action reflect on Galileo, favorably or unfavorably? And what does it tell us about critical thinking in the face of membership in conflicting communities?

Certainly, Galileo was a member of the scientific community. In fact arguably he was one of those forming the community of modern science. And he seems to have been considered and to have considered himself a member of the Roman Catholic community. Throughout his publications and personal correspondence Galileo expressed his allegiance to the church community, and expressed his concern to stay a member of that community. Brecht in his cynicism seems to refuse to give this any credence, making the only concern Galileo faces the one of doing science and finding the truth versus a concern to avoid being tortured. The sincerity of the scientist's concern for the well-being of the church and for his continuing membership in it seems genuine, however. And so it must be taken as a concern for the impact on his religion which his not recanting supposedly would have. In the judgment of the church authorities, heterodoxy, especially in a widely known and respected figure, must be stopped because of its potentially destructive influence upon the community of the faithful. By recanting, as things were at the time, as seen from the standpoint of a faithful member of the religion, Galileo could have been said to have avoided interfering with, or perhaps even have been said to have positively aided the pursuit of the purposes of his religious community. Thus, from that standpoint (and even if he had not been a believer himself), Galileo could have been seen to be under the jurisdiction of the church community's ethical authority.

If this much seems right, then the next question is whether Galileo could be faulted for recanting. Whatever else is so, the man cannot be faulted for making a public stand of abandoning science just to save himself. This ignores the human condition, just as Brecht's treatment of the issues ignores the possibility of the sincerity of Galileo's expressed faith. Brecht might question the legitimacy of the church as a community of individuals with certain pursuits. He could not deny them all legitimacy, however, without begging the question against the value of their aims.

The relative importance of the demand of these two communities remains another question; one Galileo himself chose not to accept as a question he had to answer. Instead he attempted to affirm the legitimacy of both, relative to different and, as he saw it, nonconflicting sets of aims. (See chapter VI above.) But surely Brecht's own political views led him to color Galileo's options in a certain way that the scientist would not have accepted. Galileo was not just abandoning science to save his own skin. Indeed some of the things he said provide strong inductive evidence for accepting an explanation of intelligibility according to which Galileo, in deciding to recant, had considered the impact his decision would have on the church and was seeking to minimize the harm coming from his choice.

Viewing Galileo's choice as one between two ethical communities in each of which he was a member who could interfere with and in fact withhold positive aid to the memberships, could he be faulted for doing what he did? Such a question is difficult and uncertain, of course. Still in one light the decision comes off very well. The decision allowed him to complete important work in spite of failing health. It was not incompatible with that work's being published outside of the influence of the church. Refusing to recant might have allowed for neither of these things. All things considered, in his circumstances at any rate, his action seems to have been just the thing to maximize all the conflicting goal pursuits and as such would seem to be justified by one sort of ethical standard. Had the man acted merely out of cowardice, then perhaps he would deserve criticism. But evidence seems to speak against that in favor of seeing his act as an attempt to balance the conflicting calls upon him and do best by all concerned.

In the end, since Galileo's intentions and the lived circumstances involved are beyond reach, there is no way to say that he was above reproach. But in such matters one should be content to rest with inductive arguments for what seems to be the best explanations and then accept the implications of those. Even Brecht grudgingly admits, in one place, that Galileo was courageous, apart from the demands of the Church. Even according to Brecht, then, it seems Galileo did not utterly fail in his obligations.

Unfortunately, not every case is one in which the demands of conflicting community memberships are so easily dealt with as to choose a course serving both to the greatest extent possible. What then? Short of some way to bring them together on the same course, one must choose. And short of any clarity favoring one or the other in public reasons, one must fall back on the personal. One must exercise her or his authority and creativity as a critical thinker forming ethical judgments to the best of one's critical ability. Others need to recognize this and forgive one's shortcomings with respect to one community as long as they are shortcomings shown while striving to further critical thought in ethical living. Critical thinking can ask no more. The human condition is one in which multiple and sometimes conflicting community memberships are all but inevitable. What more could be asked beyond responsibility in creatively exercising one's judgment? That must be the basic obligation of critical thinkers always.

SECTION 4

Obligation and Critical Thinking in Ethics

This brings up the third and last item of attention for the present discussion. What is ethical obligation as far as critical thinking is concerned? The question is raised in a useful way in connection with Oedipus's tragic quest for the truth. The driving force of the play's tragic figure is in part Oedipus's earnest desire to relieve Thebes of its troubles. He seems really to have felt obligated to do this, as its king, as the husband of the former slain ruler's queen, and as a member of the political community of Thebes. Had he been concerned as a politician, then the impact of the play would not have been that of tragedy so much as a story of just deserts. Acting out of obligation, however, he is once again the tragic victim. His community called upon him. It was up to him to prevent further harm to its citizens, indeed, to aid them. This obligation he willingly undertook and, though it destroyed him, Oedipus seems never to have regretted answering the call. What is the nature of this bond of obligation that links the members of an ethical community into a unit and imposes as requirements living by the rules of that community? What is the social relationship of people who are obligated one to another? There are three views to consider.

MOTIVATIONAL VIEWS. Some have held that for an act to be obligatory is the same as those for whom it holds to be motivated toward performing the obligated act, or decision.[10] One typical line of such a view pictures this motivation as being external in the sense that it is in the control of people other than the obligated agent. Thus, for example, for someone to have an obligation is for there to be a set of penalties imposed upon those who wrongly omit an act of the sort in question, and for that to have motivated the agent to act in that way. This seems to fit the situation of Oedipus, though in his case the sanctions are, as John Stuart Mill would have called them, internal, that is, coming from Oedipus's own desire to prevent further harm to the citizens of Thebes.

No one was threatening him and providing external sanctions to motivate him. However, this view will not hold up. It would leave free of obligations those who just did not give a hang because they could avoid penalties or just did not care. Just being king and being able to avoid penalties if he put off the investigation does not relieve Oedipus of his obligation. The story makes clear his obligations independently of his behavior and of Jocasta's warnings, and all the rest that cranked up the drama of the play. The motivational view falls short of the mark.

JUSTIFIED PENALTY VIEWS. If motivation is not the thing, perhaps what makes for obligation is that if the agent did not do what was called for then penalties would be justified? Well, maybe the view to be considered is that penalties would be justified in the absence of any acceptable defense of not doing what was called for? After all someone might have an obligation and yet not deserve penalty since he or she has a legitimate excuse. But even with this qualification the view will not work. It overlooks the fact that one might have an obligation when he or she has no good excuse for not doing so and yet punishment or penalty is not justified because it all turned out for the best. At one point in the play Oedipus believed that Creon did the dirty deed and yet he did not act. Had he done so it would have made matters worse, and yet it makes sense to say he had an obligation to act against Creon. Here Oedipus was lucky, ethically speaking. And though perhaps he could be blamed for delaying, that is different from being justifiable in treating Creon as a traitor. Here, there would be an obligation where there would not be justifiable punishment if one did not meet the demand, even with no good excuse. But perhaps the problem is that this view goes too far— something short of justifiable punishment guarantees obligation?

ACCOUNTABILITY VIEWS. Those with obligations are accountable or answerable for not doing what they are obligated to do. That is, it is justifiable for some others (or perhaps even for the agent) to call upon the obligated person to explain the omission with an eye to showing, if possible, why blame or punishment is not justifiable. The interference of having to explain oneself and the motivation to avoid that are the sanctions of obligations. Their threat is what one feels, at the least, whenever one feels the presence of obligations.[11]

On this view, then, ethical communities are accountability or A-groups. The mutual practice of holding to account, of explaining failures to meet ethical guidelines, negotiating over what those guidelines are and what they call for, of exploring and articulating reasons for actions or striving for ways of being, all of this is what is special about the social relationships of people in ethical communities. Such a view fits with a participant view of members of ethical communities and with a view according to which the rules of those groups are not fixed and final, but grow out of the personal and the life narratives individuals make intelligible and negotiate and reformulate both within and across communities of ethical discussion. For what it is worth, it also fits with the harmonized goal pursuit standard to the extent that it sees ethical agents as goal-seeking individuals interacting in potentially harmful and helpful ways with those with whom they live. As well, it fits with the social wisdom of denying full membership in ethical communities to children except and until and to the extent that they can take part in the critical thinking within and across communities. Thus it fits with not holding them to account until they have the maturity and self-control to influence their behavior by the reasons for action that emerge and enter into shared accounts exchanged in the social context of communities.

Much more needs to be said on the subject of obligation as well as on ethical communities and standards and ethical argument. This has been only the beginning of what needs to be reflected in critical thinking on ethical matters. Still, perhaps, for an introduction to some of the elements of critical reasoning in ethics and as a larger case study of what this discussion has said about critical thinking, this will do.[12]

Mastery Exercises X.1

SELF TEST

Comprehension Questions

1. What are the two tasks facing individuals in reaching ethical assessments?

2. What are the main difficulties with the utilitarian view?

3. Why does egoism illustrate the fallacy of inconsistent premises or begging the question?

4. Can rights ethics be considered complete in themselves?

5. What difficulties does a social justice approach to ethics face?

6. What is the difference between a process and a product approach to ethics?

7. Why cannot obligation be understood in terms of the justifiability of punishment or blame if the obligated person does not perform up to expectations?

8. What is the role of accountability in community unity?

9. What is the role of accountability in the linkage of the two main tasks of ethics?

10. How does critical thinking in ethics show the social character of critical thinking?

Mastery Exercises X.2

SELF TEST

Creating and Understanding Ethical Assessments. Consider the following situations or questions. Construct what you believe are acceptable ethical views in response to them. And defend your views. You might have to fill in the details of a context to do some of this work. Write out your assessment in no more than 500 words. In your write-up, be sure to indicate how the relevant points of this chapter come into play.

1. Suppose that you really believe in the agenda of a particular political party and fear that all the good it could produce would be lost if the election went the wrong way. Would it be right or ethically defensible to use funds to put out false or smear advertising to try to discredit your candidate's opponent?

2. Could cheating in a class or in a sales transaction ever be defensible or justified? In your answer compare and contrast the utilitarian and the harmonious goal pursuit positions.

3. Can we think critically about whether it is justifiable to claim women have a right to abort their pregnancies?

4. Imagine a society has a choice between jobs training and education on the one hand and leaving people alone with their money and erecting more prisons to protect people from criminals on the other. Which of these choices should be made and why?

5. Should one's own family come first ethically? Why?

6. Is it possible to defend the death penalty in light of the facts of the state killing innocent persons, of the penalty falling more heavily on the most disadvantaged, and the penalty seeming to lack deterrent value? Why or why not?

7. Can one show by critical thinking that it is right or best to live by critical thinking in the area of ethics?

8. Can you think of circumstances in which, and a justification showing that, it is sometimes right to deceive?

9. If an act would compromise your integrity as a critical thinker by violating the ethical beliefs of your community, but would further ethical reasoning being generally present in society, should you go along?

10. A familiar case discussed in ethics courses, but with a twist: Two people need a scarce drug and there is no way to obtain or manufacture more in time. Only a full dose is going to be at all effective. Is there a way to make a decision here in terms of critical thinking? What would it be and how would that process of critical thinking turn out?

Notes and References

[1] Pascal, B. (1995). *Pensées* (Rev. ed.). (Trans. by A. J. Krailsheimer). London: Penguin Books, p. 66.

[2] Arendt, H. (1978). *The life of the mind, one thinking* (One-volume ed.). San Diego: A Harvest Book, Harcourt, Inc., p. 5.

[3] Arendt, H. *The life of the mind, one thinking.* (just cited) p. 193.

[4] See Taylor, P. (1961). *Normative discourse.* Englewood Cliffs, NJ: Prentice-Hall, who distinguishes verification, validation, and vindications of assessments.

[5] Mill, J. S. (1970). *The subjection of women.* In A. S. Rossi (Ed.), *Essays on sex equality: John Stuart Mill and Harriet Taylor Mill.* Chicago: The University of Chicago Press, pp. 123 and ff.

[6] J. S. Mill, just cited, pp. 235 and ff.

[7] See the now classic work: Rawls, J. (1971). *A theory of justice.* Cambridge, MA: The Belknap Press of Harvard University Press.

[8] See J. Rawls just cited, pp. 60 and ff. Of course it becomes more complex than this. But for present purposes this should suffice.

[9] See J. Rawls, just cited, Chapter III.

[10] See for example, Hobbes, T. (1962). *Leviathan.* R. S. Peters (Selector and Introduction), and M. Oakeshott (Ed.), New York: Collier Books, Chapter 14 and especially page 105.

[11] See, Blatz, C. V. (1972). Accountability and answerability. *Journal for the Theory of Social Behaviour,* (10), 101–ff.

[12] Much of the structure and text of this chapter is derived and reworked from the discussion of ethics in my *Reasoning in Context: An Introduction to (the General theory of) Critical Thinking* which comprised the first portion of *Teaching Critical Thinking In Secondary Humanities Courses, The Manual of Wyoming's Critical Thinking Project.* (Copyright, Charlie Blatz, 1985.) Wyoming's Critical Thinking Project was funded by the National Endowment for the Humanities, and its support of this work is gratefully acknowledged. Portions of the work on ethics in the *Manual* also were adapted for part of my general introduction of Charles V. Blatz (ed.), *Ethics and Agriculture, An Anthology on Current Issues in World Context.* Moscow, Idaho: University of Idaho Press, 1991.

APPENDIX I

Quick Reference and Summary

Central Concepts _____

Ambiguity is present when a term or assertion has more than one meaning. As opposed to

Vagueness which is a dysfunctional lack of precision. **(Chapter V)**

Appeals to the Authority of Others always amount to reasoning that since the authority is an expert and is probably using her or his expertise, what the authority offers as credible or acceptable, is so. **(Chapter V)**

Argument: Any set of assertions or statements some of which provide evidence for one or more of the others. **(Chapter V)**

Assessing Arguments: One focal point is this: Good arguments are aimed at securing uptake by those who become aware of them—uptake either in the form of endorsing the arguer's participation in moving forward the work of the community of inquiry, or uptake in the form of a change of belief, decision, or action themselves in response to the argument. **(Chapter IX)**

Charity/Respect is a matter of thinkers standing ready to extend to others accountability for their own views, to seriously consider the views of others, and to allow them parity of reasoning. **(Chapter IV)**

Coherence includes but goes beyond consistency to what saves appearances and what explains the best, and fits the set together intelligibly into one consistent body of belief. **(Chapter V)**

Community of discussion is any group of reasoners sharing a common area of inquiry, commonly understood and holding each other to account for their thinking within that area or domain. They operate according to common definitions, background assumptions, and procedures of reasoning which constitute the community's perspective. Communities of discussion are the centers of thinking in which one properly finds assertions of truth and correctness of claims. **(Chapter V)**

Critical Thinking: The careful attempt to arrive at well-supported beliefs, decisions, and plans of action, and to take these to heart so that we live accordingly and well. **(Chapter I) Critical thinking is then:** creative, but it is conducted within the limits of coherence and reasonableness, interpretative but articulated and expressed within the limits of conceptual and dominant styles of expression. **(Chapter IX)**

Critical Thinking is one Option opposed to living through power (intimidation or force), manipulation or guile, or simple unthinking conformity. **(Chapter II)**

Deductive Arguments seek to provide demonstrations of the truth of their conclusions; they seek to show that the conclusion must be true because the premises are true and the reasoning pattern is such that if the premises are true then the conclusion has to be true. Such an argument is **sound.** If the reasoning is good because if the premises are true the conclusion has to be true, then the argument is **valid. (Chapters VI, VIII)** This is so regardless of whether the premises are true. Validity is a **hypothetical** feature—that is, it is a property that the argument has *under assumed certain conditions,* namely that the premises are true. Validity is approached here in terms of the relationships holding within sets of basic statements and truth functional compounds of these statements. The regular ways in which these truth functional combining operators work to make the truth of the whole a function of the truth of the component statements, under all possible assignments of truth values to the component statements, is displayed in a **truth table.** Truth tables can also show when statements are equivalent in their truth functional characters, namely when they have the same overall truth value under all possible assignments of truth values to the component statements. Arguments can be expressed as hypothetical statements in which the antecedent is made up of the premises conjoined together, and the consequent is the conclusion. This allows for the use of a truth table of the statement of an argument, so constructed, to be used to test the validity of the argument. If there are no rows in the truth table showing a possible assignment of truth values to the component statements that yields a value of false for the whole statement, then there is no way to make the premises (the antecedent of the argument hypothetical) true and the conclusion false. The short truth table method shows such results in a rapid way by trying to construct an assignment of truth values to the component statements in which the conclusion (the consequent) is false and the antecedent (the premises) is true. Truth tables also can be used to show that certain patterns of inference are valid/invalid so that any argument made in those patterns is valid/invalid. Thus one can establish a set of approved inference patterns so that if an argument can be shown to use only those patterns to derive the conclusion from its premises then it is valid. And if the derivation cannot be made except with the use of an invalid form of inference then the argument will be invalid. This gives a third way to test for validity or invalidity of arguments—by constructing proofs using the premises to infer the conclusions in question. This method can also be used to check the validity of complex arguments that involve several sub-arguments. **(Chapter VIII)**

Elements of Critical Thinking (Chapter I) include problems interpreted and understood in a certain way, by reference to shared assumptions of background knowledge and patterns of reasoning apt to identify and address cases of the problem as they arise, as well as shared patterns of reasoning used to assess the reasoning and inquiry devoted to these problems.

Ethics and Critical Thinking: Ethics are for those exercising choice influenced by reason. And indeed their reliance upon reasoning introduces the element of creativity in which agents are exercising their authority as critical thinkers to find and support the most defensible undertaking in the circumstances in which they find themselves. (1) In living ethically one continuing task is the reintegration of beliefs, decisions, plans, and actions in the face of a changing world and in ways taking into account what matters.

(2) A second task is to prepare oneself to create arguments that give a public presentation of reasons in support of one's beliefs, decisions, and actions concerning what matters. Those to whom the argument is made must be brought to see either that the thinker was exercising proper integrity in the argument, or was reasoning in a way that charity or respect would have to credit as legitimate.

Ethical Standards: should not be systematically relativistic; should be teachable and enforceable; should be what critical thinkers could endorse without fallacy or other loss of integrity as critical thinkers; should arise out of, or be open to being accepted as, the personal vision of critical agents. These concerns can be used to test a variety of candidates for the leading ethical standard. Ethical communities can be understood as accountability groups and obligation can be understood in terms of accountability for failure to do what is ethically called for. **(Chapter X)**

Explanations: Explainers are looking for what in the world produced the thing of interest or for some way to understand or make intelligible what happened, and not for reasons for believing that in fact it did occur or reasons for deciding on a certain option as the best one open. Explanations can be divided into two large categories: **Genetic Explanations and Explanation of Intelligibility or Interpretation.** The division between the two has to do with whether the explanation seeks to provide a personal story or public argument about the genesis or coming to be of some event, or one about the character or the significance of what is going on. Is the thinker after an account of what brought something about, or an account of how to understand or make intelligible what has come about? Explanations can be assessed in terms of considerations of: pragmatic virtues; tests of relevance or significance; the test of coherence. **(Chapter IX)**

Inductive Arguments are those that are intended to give some **strong** evidence for the conclusion but not evidence that demonstrates the conclusion beyond a shadow of doubt. Inductive premises try to start with true premises all right. But unlike deductive arguments they proceed by a process of reasoning that does not guarantee the truth of the conclusion even if the premises are true. Good inductive arguments are **inductively strong or cogent. (Chapter VII)**

Arguments from Analogy are always about specific individuals and proceed by comparing two or more individuals in one or more regards and then thinkers infer that since the individuals compared are alike in some regard they have experienced in both of them, they are also alike in a feature they have experienced in only one of them. **(Chapter VII)**

Arguments to a Generalization from a Sample proceed from the properties of the members of a sample to the properties of all or some percentage of the members of an entire group of things. They are good to the extent that the sample really represents the general population covered by the generalization. See the rules of thumb below for possible mistakes in this regard. **(Chapter VII)**

Identifications of Causes proceed in a number of ways summarized in Mill's Methods (see below). **(Chapter VII)**

Inquiry is purposive investigation, but it is constant and ongoing, a piece of every action, every observation, every reflection; it is more a matter of paying close attention and seeking to fully understand and reason through, rather than just a special occasion of that; it is more an investigation caught up in life concerns as opposed to possibly removed from these. **(Chapter IX)**

Integrity: in speaking or writing personal articulations, one shoulders the further responsibility to stick by these beliefs or decisions, and to defend them while also holding them open to unbiased and impartial examination. What one has concluded comes to be available for future use as a premise in one's arguments. But also it is a further addition to the beliefs and decisions for which one is accountable. One is accountable within (and to some extent) outside one's communities of discussion. **(Chapter IX,** also see **Chapter IV)**

Mill's Methods are patterns of inference used to identify the cause or part of the cause of an event. These were gathered by John Stuart Mill in the 19th century. They are comprised in the methods of agreement, difference, agreement and difference, residues, and concomitant variation. These are listed as rules of thumb below. **(Chapter VII)**

Necessary Condition: What is stated in the consequent of a true hypothetical statement. **(Chapter VIII)**

Sufficient Condition: What is stated in the antecedent of a true hypothetical statement. **(Chapter VIII)**

Outlining Arguments (See **Chapter VI)**

Personal Conditions of Critical Thinking (Chapter I)

Thinkers must be honest

Thinkers must seek appropriate clarity

Critical thinkers must ask "why?"

Critical thinkers must think for themselves

Critical thinkers must be ready to recognize and challenge authority when appropriate

Critical thinkers must think creatively

Critical thinkers must respect themselves and others as thinkers

Qualifiers: Terms or phrases used to limit a speaker/writer's commitment to some claim or assertion that he or she has just made. **(Chapter VI)**

Rationality is a matter of living a certain way in the light of reason. **(Chapter IX)**

Reportive Definitions attempt to state or to report the rules or the conditions for the correct use of a term in a language group. These are too broad when they include cases that do not belong and too narrow when they exclude cases that do belong. **(Chapter V)**

Stipulative Definitions indicate which of many possible meanings a term will be used with, a definition that picks out as the class of things referred to one from among the many the term might cover, or which makes more precise the application of some vague term. If a *stipulative definition* does its job of clarifying by précising or coining a new word, then it is a good one, if not then it is not. **(Chapter V)**

Persuasive or Emotive Definitions seek to attach some emotional tone to a term and thereby persuade the users of the term to share some value or attitude. If it is effective it will shift emotional tone and attitudinal response and if not, then it has failed as an emotive definition. Also such definitions, like the others mentioned, might fail by being revisonary. **(Chapter V)**

The Sciences use the sources of support for beliefs and decisions in the service of learning what can be discovered by controlled experience or observation, and then interpreted and expressed mathematically as regularities of process and connections between events and things of various sorts in our world. This work is in the service of understanding, predicting, and controlling events in the world. This differs from study in the **Humanities** which is what humans need to get clear about what beliefs and values they hold, what modes of inquiry they use, what understandings of humans and other beings they assume, in the communities of discussion where they "live and move and have their being." Also, study in the humanities is just what is needed to critically assess, modify, and reintegrate, at least for the moment, various sets of beliefs, value commitments, and assumptions. Thus the humanities can provide a critical theory of living well and the means to apply this theory by integrating its various threads. The sciences, by contrast, provide the broad content of living well in that they strive to reveal the limits nature places upon physical and social existence and thus, in effect, show the physical and social possibilities open for realizing or making concrete the life well lived. **(Chapter VI)**

Social Conditions of Critical Thinking (Chapter I)

The thinker is free and thus: basic needs have been met, the thinker enjoys sufficient self-esteem, the thinker has adequate and reliable personal security, and the necessary leisure to conduct inquiry

Open access to all needed information

Problem at issue is open to reason

Communication on the issue is possible

Thinkers are accountable to each other

Thinkers are ready and able to reach common decisions and so to make the effort and compromises necessary for that

Thinkers are able to coordinate their actions and cooperate as needed to follow through to the conclusion

The Spirit of Critical Thinking is one of openness and taking candidates for well-supported belief, decision, and action as they come, understood with respect if not sympathy. **(Chapter II)**

Fallacies

 FALLACIES OF OPENNESS (CHAPTER II)

Bias exists when a thinker is unable to consider fully evidence or reasons for a belief, decision, or action because of an inclination to believe, decide, or act contrary to what that evidence supports

> **Two Wrongs Fallacy** occurs when bias leads a thinker to accept doing or believing what is wrong because of a perceived wrong against the thinker

Prejudice occurs when a thinker forms a belief or decides or acts based on a pre-formed view of the situation or persons involved, not even seeing the need to consider the situation in critical thought

Bigotry is that stamp of character that means that the thinker has lost the capacity to be open to a fair consideration of the evidence and as a result characteristically disfavors all of those in some group

Stereotyping is responding from a standard and unreflective set of beliefs, decisions, or actions shared with other unreflective individuals

> **Ridicule** is seeking to lead others to bias or prejudice against a third party

Ad Hominem Abusive is seeking to fault someone's beliefs, decisions, or actions by a personal insult of that other

Ad Hominem Circumstantial is seeking to fault someone's beliefs, decisions, or actions by reference to their group affiliation, profession, or economic or other circumstances

Poisoning the Well is speaking against someone to block future consideration or adoption of her or his beliefs, decisions, or actions

 FALLACIES OF FAILED EFFORT IN INQUIRY (CHAPTER II)

Impatience in Inquiry (the quick-fix fallacy) is the mistake of concluding the reflection after only a cursory or rapid or incomplete look at the issue

Wishful Thinking is the mistake of refusing to accept what there is good reason to because doing so would force the thinker to give up beliefs, decisions, or actions he or she wants to keep

Slippery Slope is the mistake of refusing to consider or accept a belief or decision because it would lead to a string of consequences ending in an absurdity or clear error

Misplaced Abstraction is the mistake of inquiring into a particular or singular case while only considering it in terms of features it shares with others

> **Perfectionist Fallacy** is the mistake of refusing to consider something because it is not or cannot be articulated in a fully precise or complete way

> **Line Drawing Fallacy** is the mistake of refusing to consider something because it is not or cannot be precisely or fully separated off from other things with which it might be confused

FALLACIES OF UNMERITED CREDIBILITY (CHAPTER II)

The Fallacy of Appeal to the *Status* of a source is the error of being ready to rely on sources, without checking, just because of their status

The Fallacy of Appeal to Unexamined Expertise is the error of being ready to rely on someone's claimed expertise on a subject, without checking

The Fallacy of Appeal to Unsubstantiated Evidence Claims is the error of relying on assertions without checking on the reliability of the sources and methods of gaining that evidence

The Fallacy of Appeal to Popular Opinion is the error of being ready to rely on claims or to accept decisions just because others in a group of people (with no particular claim to expertise) do so

> **Appeal to Popularity, Common Belief, Peer Pressure** are all forms of this sort of mistake and differ in ways suggested by their names. A **Bandwagon Appeal** is another appeal to popular opinion wherein the idea is basically to push someone to acceptance so as not to miss out on a good thing

FALLACIES OF MISPLACED VALUES (CHAPTER II)

The Fallacy of False Values in Inquiry involves conducting inquiry because of reasons or from motives other than the desire to reach a well-supported belief, decision, or action

The Fallacy of Improper Ambitions in Inquiry is the error of proceeding in inquiry toward a degree of certainty that is unachievable in the sort of inquiry in question

The Fallacy of Improper Processes of Reason is the error of seeking to proceed in critical thought using a form of reasoning or proof that is inappropriate to the problem or subject area in which the thinker is operating

FALLACIES OF EVASION (CHAPTER III)

The Fallacy of Red Herring is a matter of introducing into the discussion or even into the characterization of the focal point of discussion something that is irrelevant and takes the discussion off subject

The Fallacy of Casual Dismissal is the error of setting aside the potentially significant views or decisions of someone or the significance of an event or occurrence for no reason that challenges their significance, but rather in order to evade the responsibility of seriously considering them

The Fallacy of Cover-Up or Spin is the error of redescribing or representing someone or her/his beliefs, decisions, or actions as less faulty or less good than they are, by putting a better or worse face on them without good reason and to influence reasoning

> **Dysphemism** (worse face version of cover-up or spin)
>
> **Euphemism** (better face version)

The Fallacy of Deception is the error of evading full participation in critical thinking by withholding or miss-stating information thought to be pertinent to the subject or inquiry at hand

FALLACIES OF MIS-FIGURATION (CHAPTER III)

The Fallacy of Persuasive Definition is the error of defining a term in such as way as to seek to manipulate others to approve or disapprove of what is being defined

The Fallacy of Persuasive Comparison is the error of offering a comparison so as to manipulate others to approve or disapprove of the target belief, decision, action, or person in the comparison

The Fallacy of Oversimplification of the Alternatives is the error of presenting the plausible or reasonable options of belief, decision, or action as fewer in number, or less complete than they really are

> **False Dilemma:** To present only some of the alternatives that need to be considered
>
> **Straw Figure Fallacy:** To present only a weakened or incomplete form of one of the alternatives, and in particular a weakened version of one of the alternative sets of reasons or views in question

⸙ FALLACIES OF SEDUCTION (CHAPTER III)

The Fallacy of Innuendo/False Suggestion is the error of leading another to reject or not take seriously a belief, decision, action or person by tapping into a pre-existing emotionally charged view that runs counter to that belief, decision, action, or positive assessment of the person in question

The Fallacy of Appealing to Flattery or Vanity is the error of leading another to accept or to take seriously a belief, decision, action, or person by tapping into a pre-existing positively emotionally charged view of her- or himself that the other feels so that he or she feels indebted or for other reasons eager to reciprocate by accepting the belief, decision, action, or positive assessment in question.

The Fallacy of Appealing to Pity or Sympathy is the error of leading another to accept or to take seriously a belief, decision, action or person by tapping into a pre-existing sympathy with or pity for it, pointing out how the pity or sympathy is deserved, but not giving any reasons for the belief, decision, action, or assessment itself.

⸙ FALLACIES OF SHOCK AND AWE (CHAPTER III)

The Fallacy of Scare Tactics is the error of leading another to accept or to take seriously a belief, decision, action, or person by causing fear in that other for the consequences of non-acceptance.

The Fallacy of Appealing to Anger or Indignation is the error of leading another to accept or to take seriously a belief, decision, action, or person by displaying anger or indignation over the possible or real rejection of that belief, decision, action, or person. Alternatively, the fallacy could work to lead another to reject a belief or decision.

The Fallacy of Hyperbole is the error of leading another to accept or to take seriously a belief, decision, action, or person by tapping into a pre-existing readiness to follow someone who displays certitude by inappropriately exaggerated emphasis.

⸙ FALLACIES OF CHARITY/FAIRNESS (CHAPTER IV)

The Fallacy of Studied Misunderstanding is the error of intentionally misinterpreting or of failing to expend the effort needed to correctly understand another thinker's belief, decision, or action before critically considering and replying to it.

The Fallacy of Shifting the Burden of Proof is the error of trying to avoid having to give reasons for a belief, decision, or action, by misassigning to someone else the requirement of giving that proof or evidence.

The Fallacy of Denying Reconsideration (or the "flip-flop" fallacy) is the error of faulting someone for inconsistency in her or his thought or actions when that person changes views or decisions after reasoned reconsideration.

The Fallacy of Denying Parity of Reasons is the error of some thinkers refusing to allow those with differing aims and ends of reasoning to use the same general sorts of procedures to support principles or conclusions as those critics do themselves.

The Fallacy of Rejecting External Accountability is the error of thinkers refusing to hold themselves and their ideas accountable to the reasoning of others in fields of study using methods different in detail from their own.

 ## FALLACIES OF INTEGRITY (CHAPTER IV)

The Fallacy of Rejecting Internal Accountability is the error of thinkers refusing to hold themselves and their ideas accountable to the principles, standards, and general expectations of reasoning facing all in their field of study or all who deal with problems of the sort they are dealing with.

The Fallacy of Mythic Images is the error on the part of thinkers interpreting and thinking through the questions/problems they address in terms of the images of myths that seem relevant, rather than trying to meet the problems/questions in a clear and reflective way on their own terms.

The Fallacy of Evading Integrity by the Use of Qualifications is the attempt to escape responsibility to stand for what one claims.

The Fallacy of Fighting Points is the error committed when thinkers protect their views or their principles or even their patterns of reasoning from critical review, insisting instead on their correctness and then holding them as slogans or dogmas.

The Fallacy of Relativism is the error of thinkers—individuals or groups, adopting or holding views that are idiosyncratic to them, or else, capricious—that is without having reasons for them, holding these views to be true or correct or worth holding just because they hold them. **Subjectivism** is holding that some belief, decision, or action is fine for the thinker even though others in the individual's reasoning group reject or question it.

FALLACIES OF EVIDENCE COLLECTION (CHAPTER IV)

The Fallacy of Arguing from Ignorance is the error of thinkers—individuals or groups—arguing that since no one has shown the belief, decision, or action in question to be faulty, then it must be considered critically acceptable, or, since no one has shown that it is not faulty, then it must be considered critically flawed.

The Fallacy of Appealing to a Sound-Bite is the error of thinkers— individuals or groups—providing information in such a form that (a) it lacks context and sufficient richness to guide interpretation and to understand the main point of the story, and (b) lacks sufficient richness to warrant or support inferences to conclusions it suggests.

The Fallacy of the Insider Appeal is the error of thinkers who substitute for evidence an appeal to the other reasoners who share acceptance or knowledge of the belief or decision in question.

The Fallacy of Begging the Question amounts to a thinker having as reasons for believing or deciding in some way, something he or she would have no reason to accept if he or she did not already accept the claim or decision he or she is trying to support.

To Argue in a Circle is to explicitly use the conclusion as part of the evidence.

The Fallacy of Inconsistent Premises amounts to a thinker proceeding in a way that allows in inconsistent statements of evidence or support for a conclusion.

FALLACIES OF MEANING (CHAPTER V)

Equivocation is the error of a thinker using a term in one of its meanings in one part of an argument, and in another of its meanings in a separate part of the argument so that the flow from evidence to conclusion is interrupted.

The Fallacy of Composition (a problem of vagueness) is the error of attributing to the whole any arbitrarily selected one (or all) of the properties of the parts making up the whole, just because they are properties of what make up the whole.

The Fallacy of Division (a problem of vagueness) is the error of attributing to the component parts of a whole, any arbitrarily selected one (or all) of the properties of that whole itself, just because they are properties of the whole itself.

FALLACIES OF INFERRING TO A GENERALIZATION FROM A SAMPLE (CHAPTER VII)

If a sample is not of an acceptable size then the generalization from it is said to commit the fallacy of being a **Hasty Generalization.**

If the sample does not reflect the influences present on the appearance of the correlation in the general population covered by the generalization, then it is **Biased.**

If the inference does not rely on a sample but only on an anecdote, that is a story relating the personal experiences of one or more individuals (usually the speaker or acquaintances) which suggests some correlation, and is taken as evidence for the truth of the generalization claiming that correlation—then it has committed the mistake of **Appealing to an Anecdote.**

⸮ FALLACIOUS CAUSAL IDENTIFICATION (CHAPTER VII)

The **Fallacy of Post Hoc Ergo Propter Hoc** is the mistake of inferring that because one event follows another the second is the cause of the first.

Rules of Thumb

CHAPTER III
A generally recognized rule of normal conversation is that people will offer up what they know on a subject and believe to be of interest and relevance to the subject.

CHAPTER IV
The riskier the outcome of the belief, decision, or action he or she wants to accept, the greater part of the burden of proof a thinker has. If the risk is low or relatively low, then the burden of proof can rest upon the person who accepts or is ready to accept the most implausible claim.

If claims and counter-claims are mutually implausible across the interacting viewpoints or fields of study, then both sides have a serious burden of proof.

Without fixed institutions or conventions assigning the burden of proof, the way of respect or fairness is to shoulder the burden of proof for the view that one is putting forward.

CHAPTER IV
What is an acceptable critical thinking procedure for one thinker also should be for others in similar circumstances.

CHAPTER IV
Each thinker must remain open to the possibility that her or his own methods of inquiry and thought need to be revised in light of those used by others.

CHAPTER IV
Critical thinkers should seek evidence whose credentials are independent of the acceptance of the conclusion. If this restriction on evidence is not respected, then begging the question is allowed and, in effect, that permits thinkers to assume the very thing that they are trying to prove in marshalling the proof.

CHAPTER V
Observation should be made in circumstances as close to ideal as possible for the mode of sense and for the sorts of properties to be experienced.

If one *is* seeking a sensuous experience of a certain kind, just as such, for example an experience of some sound or tonal quality, try to limit the impact of the other senses.

Recognize that emotional associations and conceptual distinctions are part of virtually all experiences even if they are not articulated.

If one *is* seeking to observe in order to form a judgment about the character of some event or the features of some object or process, identify an expert in the field where the judgment is called for and learn what that individual would suggest.

Remember that articulating one's experiences will only bring out part of what one has observed, which amounts to paying special attention to a feature of the observed.

CHAPTER V   **If another belief is inconsistent** with central or powerful beliefs, then that other belief should be rejected as false.

CHAPTER V   **In checking unsupported claims,** if a belief fits coherently and consistently with our background beliefs as well as our observations, while explaining best what we seem to have to take as fact, all of that together is some reason for accepting it.

CHAPTER V   Thinkers need a **personal narrative** focused on intentions and informed by both memory and awareness to take them through the world of their actions and experiences. But just as much, they need a **public narrative** so they can take part in recording and exchanging experiences, views, and claims so as to fully engage in the social process of critical thinking.

CHAPTER V   **Definitions** can convey information that can settle disputes and move forward inquiry itself as a source of information. Indeed, the very anchor pins of informational and value-laden outlooks are found in definitions.

CHAPTER V   **Rules for Appealing to Authority**
              There must be expertise on the issue in question
              The person appealed to must have this expertise
              The experts must not disagree
              The expertise must have been used in reaching the claim in question
              The expertise that was used must not have been compromised

CHAPTER V   **The Source Determining Proper Reasoning**—What counts as a common sense assumption, and who is an authority, and what is an acceptable procedure to follow to identify and solve or manage problems of interest, all are spelled out for thinkers by the operations and the operating rules of the communities of discussion they belong to. So what counts as good critical thinking about some problem or questions of interest, even what counts concerning whether someone formulates a question correctly or productively, depends on what community of discussion that individual belongs to.

CHAPTER V   **In the Case of Cross-community or Cross-cultural Conflicts**—Thinkers can seek a higher authority or a more inclusive community and perspective that brings the conflicting ones together and resolves their conflicts—for example the community of those sharing the spirit of critical thinking.
              Thinkers can try to separate out the conflicting authorities, definitions, or community perspectives and avoid the conflict.
              Thinkers can agree to disagree and go about their separate ways.
              Thinkers can continue the conversation between the conflicting parties trying to find common ground or a way to be apart.

CHAPTER VI   A thinker should proceed so as to supply as little as possible while making the argument as strong as possible. If something seems left out of the statement of an argument, follow "the principle of charity" that suggests that the best thing to do is to interpret and supply missing elements to the reasoning of others so as to make their reasoning as strong as seems warranted in the context.

CHAPTER VII **Rules for Assessing Arguments from Analogy**

The greater the number of cases where the comparison of interest holds up the stronger the argument.

The greater the number of similarities there are between the objects being compared the stronger the argument.

The greater number of cases where the comparison of interest holds up and what is compared is otherwise different, the stronger the argument.

The greater number of unexplained differences there are between the things compared the weaker the argument.

CHAPTER VII **Assessing Generalizations from a Sample**—Inductive generalizations are strong in so far as they rest on a sample that considers a sufficiently large number of cases of what is under examination and properly reflects all the possible influences on the correlation of interest that are to be found in the general population—the argument is not hasty and the sample is not biased.

The larger the sample the stronger the level of confidence that is justified.

If the population is homogeneous, then a thinker need only randomly select cases to sample using some method of picking them out which gives as much of a chance of being selected to any one case in the population as to any other case.

If the population is heterogeneous, then the researcher needs to make the sample reflect the sorts of differences in the population as a whole that might make a difference to the connections of properties that are being studied.

CHAPTER VII **Mill's Methods**

The **method of agreement** draws on multiple cases to identify the common features in the circumstances as the cause or part of the cause.

The **method of difference** compares a case where the occurrence of interest is found with one where it is not and looks for differences in the circumstances of the two cases. These are the cause or part of the cause.

The **combined method** uses agreements to find possible causes and narrows these down by the method of difference and then checks differences that are possible causes by the method of agreement, alternating until what is identified as the cause or part of the cause is always present when the effect is present and is such that its absence is always found with the absence of the effect.

The **method of concomitant variation** identifies the cause or part of the cause by spotting positive or negative co-variations in properties of co-occurrences.

The **method of residues** eliminates possible causes by using prior knowledge of relevant causes and effects, and narrows down to the cause or part of the cause.

CHAPTER VII   **When Is There a Causal Connection Between Two or More Events?**

A connection between cause and effect is one that has been confirmed in experience (see, for example, Mill's Methods), challenged with disconfirmation but so far is still holding up, and a connection that it is still of use to the thinkers accepting it: reliable, not disconfirmed, useful connections thinkers draw as they string together features of the world into their accounts or stories of what brings about what.

If this is a plausible account of cause and effect connections, then researchers should begin to think of causal connections as the connections thinkers settle on when their explanatory and predictive stories of how things are related are defensibly accepted and used within a group of thinkers as part of the group's perspective on the world.

CHAPTER VIII   **Using the Short Truth Table Method for Checking Validity**—In checking for the validity of an argument using the short truth table method, a check of the validity of the argument can be formed by trying to find assignments of truth-values for the letters of the combined statements such that the premises are true and the conclusion is false or the whole hypothetical formed of premises ("if") and conclusion ("then") is a statement form assigned an "f".

CHAPTER IX   What is the best explanation or even what is an explanation is a judgment made, it appears, within a community of inquiry. And if this is so, then looking for the best explanation across communities is not promising.

APPENDIX II

Answers To Exercises and Self-Tests

Chapter I

MASTERY EXERCISES I.1

SELF TEST

Answers to Mastery Exercise

1. lack of accountability
2. lack of necessary information
3. lack of support of freedom to think in terms of self-esteem
4. problems of people being able to reach common decisions and especially problems of people being able to coordinate their actions
5. lack of communication
6. topic or issue not really open to reasoning
7. lack of needed information and curtailing of necessary freedom
8. curtailing of freedom
9. lack of the chance to communicate
10. lack of willingness to work together on an issue (Condition VII).

MASTERY EXERCISES I.3

SELF TEST

Answers to Mastery Exercise

1. Not ready to think for her or himself, not thinking creatively, not showing self-respect, not asking why
2. Failure of honesty
3. Failure to ask why and find out whether the tire was defective or not. Maybe the company owes you a free tire!
4. Well, this is not really asking the tough questions is it? Failure of need to think for oneself as a critical thinker.
5. Looks like there was a failure to properly check out or challenge authority
6. Looks like a case of failure to respect others since there might well be the same sorts of reasons to take the Bible as literal truth as there are to take it as revealed but metaphorical or allegorical.
7. Should have asked to see the search warrant—failure to challenge authority, and perhaps a failure to think for yourself
8. Caveat Emptor—Buyer Beware. It is very important to practice the second personal condition of critical thinking—seek appropriate clarity. As my Grandmother used to say, "A fool and his money are soon parted."
9. Looks like a case of failure to be honest shaping up here.
10. Looks like a failure to get proper clarity, to think for yourself, to be skeptical, and a failure of self-respect as a critical thinker.

Chapter II

MASTERY EXERCISES II.1

SELF TEST

Answers to Mastery Exercise

1. stereotyping
2. bias
3. ad hominem abusive
4. ad hominem circumstantial
5. prejudice
6. poisoning the well
7. prejudice
8. stereotyping
9. bias
10. ridicule
11. ad hominem abusive
12. ad hominem circumstantial

MASTERY EXERCISES II.2

SELF TEST

Answers to Mastery Exercise

1. perfectionist fallacy
2. line-drawing fallacy
3. misplaced abstraction
4. impatience/quick fix fallacy
5. slippery slope
6. wishful thinking
7. wishful thinking
8. slippery slope
9. quick-fix fallacy—though it did not hurt the Model-T
10. misplaced abstraction

MASTERY EXERCISES II.3

SELF TEST

Answers to Mastery Exercise

1. appeal to the status of a source
2. unexamined expertise
3. appeal to popularity—generic
4. peer pressure
5. appeal to popularity
6. common belief

7. common practice
8. unsubstantiated evidence
9. bandwagon
10. appeal to the status of a source

MASTERY EXERCISES II.4

Answers to Mastery Exercise

1. false values in inquiry
2. improper processes of reason in inquiry
3. improper ambitions in inquiry
4. this is tough—if there is a fallacy it is one of false values in inquiry. But in research devoted to military purposes which are defensive, the motive indicated might suggest acceptable values of inquiry. The problem is that every defensive weapon is also an offensive weapon or has offensive capabilities.
5. Well, maybe Dr. Smith was being a little over-reaching in that estimation. False ambitions in inquiry
6. It might work for the Dogon, but not for us. Within our way of thinking this is a case of the use of improper processes of reasoning in inquiry.
7. This is clearly a case of improper processes of reason. The logic might be ok, if you could uncover it. But the pattern of explanation relies on superstition in a way that is not acceptable.

Chapter III

MASTERY EXERCISES III.1

Answers to Mastery Exercise

1. red herring
2. red herring
3. some would say that this is a deception since it involved a series of failures of oversight by a succession of high level officials
4. euphemism
5. dysphemism
6. euphemism and minimizing the importance of significant views
7. that, as the tapes revealed, was an out and out deception
8. the fallacy of spin
9. as we found out this was both spin and deception
10. dysphemism

11. another case of belittling or minimizing the importance of persons or their views. All of that could be true but the person might still have the key insight to the problem at hand.

MASTERY EXERCISES III.2

Answers to Mastery Exercise

1. looks like a persuasive comparison, and not too complimentary at that
2. oversimplification
3. oversimplification
4. false dilemma
5. false dilemma; unfortunately things are never this simple between persons. But it makes for interesting daydreams and speculations with daisies.
6. persuasive comparison
7. persuasive definition
8. persuasive definition
9. straw figure fallacy
10. straw figure fallacy

MASTERY EXERCISES III.3

Answers to Mastery Exercise

1. innuendo
2. vanity
3. sympathy or pity
4. innuendo
5. vanity
6. pity
7. flattery and pity

MASTERY EXERCISES III.4

Answers to Mastery Exercise

1. anger
2. scare tactics
3. anger
4. hyperbole
5. scare tactics
6. hyperbole
7. indignation

Chapter IV

MASTERY EXERCISES IV.1

SELF TEST

Answers to Mastery Exercise

1. denying parity of reasons
2. denying parity of reasons
3. rejecting external accountability
4. denying reconsideration
5. studied misunderstanding
6. fallacious shifting of the burden of proof
7. denying reconsideration
8. fallacious shifting of the burden of proof
9. a couple of things might be going on here but one is surely a studied misunderstanding
10. rejecting external accountability

MASTERY EXERCISES IV.2

SELF TEST

Answers to Mastery Exercise

1. fallacy of evading integrity by qualifications
2. fallacy of turning to fighting points
3. fallacy of mythic images
4. rejecting internal accountability
5. relativism
6. rejecting internal accountability
7. relativism
8. fallacy of mythic images
9. fighting points
10. fallacy of evading integrity by qualifications

MASTERY EXERCISES IV.3

SELF TEST

Answers to Mastery Exercise

1. arguing from ignorance
2. insider appeal
3. circular argument
4. one problem is that of an insider appeal
5. Really? How will the managers know what to do? This looks like a train wreck about to happen because of inconsistency in the boss's guiding principles.

6. Question begging. How are we so sure that these signs are signs of alien contact unless we believe that there are aliens contacting us?

7. Well, in our legal system there is a procedural principle that operates that way. But if that is not what the person was appealing to then it is arguing from ignorance. And if it was what that person was appealing to, why all the talk about circumstantial evidence?

8. looks like an insider appeal

9. circular

10. question begging

11. inconsistent premises or claims in the evidence

FALLACY IDENTIFICATION PRACTICE

SELF TEST IV-ST2 *Answers to Self Test*

1. studied misunderstanding
2. fallacy of mythic images
3. arguing from ignorance
4. begging the question
5. circular argument
6. shifting the burden of proof
7. rejecting internal accountability
8. denying reconsideration
9. rejecting external accountability
10. evading integrity by qualifications
11. relativism
12. denying parity of reasons
13. insider appeal in what the Governor said to Susan.
14. inconsistent premises
15. relying on the sound-bite
16. fighting points

Chapter V

MASTERY EXERCISES V.1

SELF TEST *Answers to Mastery Exercise*

1. The mother can't expect the child to tell her everything. Either this is just a way of showing interest and then it is not a serious request. Or it is a mistaken request for reporting observations. Why? Explain.

2. False. What's left out?

3. (a) inconsistent, (b) inconsistent by present definitions, (c) inconsistent, (d) it would seem to be inconsistent since time flows ever forward, (e) no contradiction—emotions are complex

4. No, since it is not coherent with common background beliefs about the existence of aliens, and all that is known about physics and space travel. Besides what is all of this about aliens and drilling teeth anyway?

5. No, at least as a critical thinker you should go back and rethink your observations, your interpretation, and the implications of these. The assumption is that the world is coherent or else one needs to rethink her or his conclusions from the source of observation.

6. Yes. Can you think of an example from your own life for that?

7. Bias is often a problem tainting observation. Explain how this happens and how it can be corrected for.

8. No. Some bias is cultural and this is just a reflection of how people in a group see the world—it is not necessarily a fault. Is it something that can be corrected for? That is one that requires a critical thinker to withhold judgment at this point. There is not enough clarity or evidence on the matter.

9. No, not really. If you want to listen to music, turn off the TV, for example.

10. Emotional background tone and specific emotional responses are parts of most forms of consciousness. The idea is to understand them and what they are telling you and use that in the interpretations that generate observations, and not be overwhelmed by them in a way that corrupts observation. You can't escape it, but that does not mean that observation cannot be objective and impartial.

MASTERY EXERCISES V.2

Answers to Mastery Exercise

1. Very briefly: The first of these narratives provides what makes possible interpretation in the generation of observation while the second makes possible the coordinated shared views and communication of critical thinkers. Please expand on this further.

2. They can be the place where basic shared beliefs of a culture or other groups of thinkers are stated.

3. Because computers are so commonplace today, this is a reportive definition.

4. Yes, it seems to be neither too broad nor too narrow. Explain

5. True. Well, not really since you could spraypaint your trees green or bluish green with long lasting paint and that would not make them evergreen trees.

6. Vagueness allows us to agree on subjects where there is great difficulty getting agreement on the details, but also, it can be a deficit since it can lead us to not give enough information when precision is needed. How do we get rid of it and when do we want to get rid of it?

7. It is vague. Explain the difference between ambiguity and vagueness.

8. This is a case of the fallacy of composition. Explain this fallacy.

9. That would be the fallacy of equivocation. After defining that fallacy in your own words, please answer the remainder of the question.

10. Definitions which change the meaning of a commonly used term from the way a language group or a special interest group uses it are revisionary. (Check the chapter text.) No; these are not always bad. Explain.

MASTERY EXERCISES V.3

SELF TEST

Answers to Mastery Exercise

1. No, Dr. Phil never claimed to know much about cars, and if you saw the movie *Drowning Mona*, you know he got it all wrong. Rule 2.

2. Best by what standard? To be sure Britney should know her own life and her expertise could come out in the book. But what does she know about non-fiction in general, and autobiography (presumably ghost-written) more particularly? And indeed, is there anything to know? Until a type or focus of non-fiction is picked out, no standards can come into play and so there cannot be any expertise that could come into play. Rule 2 or rule 5 if it is autobiography, that is in question. Rule 1 if there is no more specificity to the claim about the sort of non-fiction in question.

3. There is no expertise on good sleep for you personally is there? So this would fail on rule 1 on that count. But if there were why should we trust someone who is being paid to endorse a product? Rule 5.

4. Sounds too much like ambulance chasing. Probably the lawyer's motives are disqualifying. Rule 5.

5. Isn't music preference a matter of taste and isn't that what is in question here? Rule 1.

6. The experts are in disagreement. Better hold off making a judgment if possible. Rule 3.

7. Since the person is not a doctor or a pharmacist or anyone else in the know as far as the question of headache medications goes, the person lacks expertise and so could not have been using it. Rules 2 and 4.

8. Well, if they got it wrong once, what is to guarantee that they have gotten it right this time? But, setting that aside, can we trust the company when we can certainly believe that they have taken the cheapest way out to save money? They are in a state of conflict of interest so no, don't trust them. Rule 5. But what choice do you have? If the danger is serious enough, I'd call whatever government agency might know about these matters or try to talk to an engineer.

9. Well, it looks like this might be ok. There is expertise, the speaker has it, is resolving a conflict among experts at the highest level, presumably was using it in making

the reconsideration, and is acting in a way that is against his own interests to concede error. Looks good.

10. First off, I'd want to know a good deal about Dr. Knows. Does she know more than she demonstrated on the sister and brother in question? What is the good doctor's track record? Second, I would want to know what star I was going to look like and by whose standards I would be fabulously attractive. Third, can we trust a doctor that would do this for a fat fee from a television show—in effect as a "reality-show" stunt? Doesn't look good even if the doctor checks out. Rule 5.

MASTERY EXERCISES V.4

Answers to Mastery Exercise

1. No—explain. Most likely: fighting points, begging the question. But also possibly fallacious use of persuasive definitions, straw figure and fallacies of lack of respect.

2. Beliefs about the common problems of interest, about background assumptions of what exists, how it operates, and why it matters; procedures for diagnosing what problems of interest are currently occurring; procedures for managing or solving those problems

3. Within. Explain.

4. Authorities are persons authorized to interpret, explain, and maintain the perspective of the community as well as use it in addressing the problems of the group at the most sophisticated level. Everyone in a community has such authority to some degree. But people are not equal in this regard. Usually authorities are understood to be experts and have passed various tests to earn that recognition.

5. Integrity requires internal accountability to the perspective of a community. Explain.

6. Charity or respect requires external accountability to the thoughts of others from other communities, in so far as these thoughts bear on the defensibility and proper use of the thinker's own perspective. Explain.

7. Yes. What are some potentially competing communities you belong to?

8. Integrity demands that thinkers seek to defend the perspective of the community of which they are members. But just because the requirement is for the defense of that perspective it is incompatible with taking any of that perspective as fighting points. For critical thinkers, a defense proceeds by appealing in good arguments and without fallacies to reasons for believing, deciding, or acting.

9. Yes. Explain and give an example or two.

10. Yes! The common requirements of good critical thinking that run across all communities of discussion—these common requirements are the main points of discussion in this text.

Chapter VI

MASTERY EXERCISES VI.2

Answers to Mastery Exercise

1. E
2. E
3. E
4. E
5. E
6. O
7. E
8. E
9. A
10. O Note that this gives a reason to be careful, not a justification of the truth of any claim or strictly speaking an explanation of anything either, but an indication of why one would want to be careful and try to take care. It gives reasons for acting but not justifying reasons or explaining reasons.
11. E
12. E
13. E Though if one focuses on the fact that the member nations could justify the call to discuss this matter and bring it to a vote, this could be seen as an argument.
14. A
15. A

MASTERY EXERCISES VI.4

Answers to Mastery Exercise

1. (A) Suppose that the President has decided that he will send more troops to the Philippines only if he wants to invade the area held by the rebels. (B) We know he is sending more troops to the Philippines. So on that supposition, (C) he wants to invade the rebels' stronghold. (A) warrant; (B) grounds; (C) claim

2. (A) If you want to do well in critical thinking (CT) and get as much out of it as possible, then you should do the exercises in the textbook. (B) If you do the exercises in the textbook, then you will need to read the book and ask questions about what you don't understand. So, (C) if you want to do well in critical thinking and get as much out of the course as possible, then you will need to read the book and ask questions about what you don't understand. (Missing a warrant.) (A) and (B) grounds; (C) claim; *possible backing—If the "then part" of an if-then statement (the consequent, as it is called) is the same as the if part (the antecedent) of a different*

if-then statement, then you can combine the two statements, eliminating the common element. Possible warrant, if you want to do well in CT and get as much out of it as possible then you should do the exercises, and if you do the exercises then you will read the book and ask questions, and so, if you want to do well in CT etc., then you will read the textbook etc.

3. (A) The Pistons are off to a slow start for a former championship team. (B) Either they need to start winning a lot more of their games or they don't have a chance to be champions again. (C) They don't have a prayer of winning a lot more games with their present attitude and personnel, and these don't look like they will change. So (D) they are not going to be champions again. (A) and (C) grounds; (B) warrant; (D) claim

4. (A) In some places in Russia the pollution from fossil fuels and agricultural chemicals and the health care as well as food quality are so bad that the infant mortality rate is 100+ per thousand live births. (B) In Guatemala, the infant mortality rate is only 30–40 per thousand and in the U.S. it is much less. So (C) in the US and in Guatemala, pollution from fossil fuels and agricultural chemicals, health care, and food quality are not as bad as they are in Russia. (Missing a warrant.) Missing warrant: If the infant mortality caused by pollution and agro-chemicals in a country is less than 100+ per thousand live births then the pollution and agro-chemicals are not as damaging in that country as in Russia. (A) and (B) grounds; (C) claim

5. (A) (You ought to try an American car.) Why don't you try an American car? (B) All successful school principals have tried American cars and (C) I happen to know that you aspire to be a successful high school principal. (Missing an explicit conclusion or claim.) (A) claim; (B) warrant; (C) grounds

6. (A) Only if you use your mind and push it like athletes push their physical limits will you grow and become your best mentally. (B) Oedipus didn't grow and become his best mentally, nor did Juan and Yerma, so (C) these people did not use their minds and push them like athletes push their physical limits. (A) warrant; (B) grounds; (C) claim

7. (A) The word "philosophy" begins with "p". (B) If a name of a discipline begins with a "p" then it is intriguing and rewarding—think of political science and physics. Is it any wonder then that (C) philosophy is intriguing and rewarding? (A) grounds; (B) warrant; (C) claim

8. (A) If Jeep closes in Toledo, we should change the base of this city's economy. But (B) we all know that we should change the base of this city's economy regardless. So (C) Jeep is going to close. (A) warrant; (B) grounds; (C) claim

9. (A) If you go north five miles, then you will get to Michigan. (B) If you get to Michigan, then you will be in the land of Wolverines and other strange beasts. So (C) if you go north five miles, you will be in the land of Wolverines and other strange beasts. (Missing a warrant.) (A) and (B) grounds; possible warrant: If (A) and (B) then (C); (C) claim

10. (A) (There is no point in voting.) Why bother voting? (B) If your candidate is elected, he or she will only spend her or his time trying to get reelected. And (C) if someone is a good politician she won't spend time trying to get re-elected but will tend to the business of the people. So (D) either your candidate is good and won't be re-elected or your candidate is bad and is going to get re-elected. What's the point? Missing grounds and a warrant.) Possible warrant: There is no point in voting unless you can get a good candidate into office and keep her there. But (D) (which implies you can't elect and keep in office a good candidate) grounds; so (A) claim. (B) and (C) function to support (D).

Chapter VII

MASTERY EXERCISES VII.1

SELF TEST

Answers to Mastery Exercise

1. Stronger, rule 1
2. Stronger, rule 2 because of all the similarities going with the same brand and model
3. Stronger, rule 2
4. Stronger , rule 2
5. Stronger, rule 2
6. Stronger, rule 1
7. Weaker, rule 4
8. Weaker, rule 4
9. Stronger rule 3
10. Stronger rule 3

MASTERY EXERCISES VII.2

SELF TEST

Answers to Mastery Exercise

1. (c) because only restaurants in the best neighborhoods were sampled and these are where the newest equipment and best training and most information on inspections coming up would be likely to be found.
2. (d) because only five lanes in one location is not enough to give much certainty—so it is hasty; and biased because there was only one location sampled. Maybe temperature and humidity make a big difference. And only one third of the leading bowling balls were tested—let alone specialty makes of bowling balls.
3. (a) the samples were random, the conditions were common for all those factors that affect the readiness of the grapes so a random sample was fine and there was no reason to sample more vines since the vines and the conditions were uniform.

4. It is not anecdotal since George is a professional taster and he was asked to test only three wrappers for a single company and judge between them. The wrappers were presumably all the same or uniform to type, on the different cigars where they were placed. Presumably since they are all uniform, they were randomly selected and he presumably did not have to sample many to give a responsible judgment. But the judgment is biased (b) since he should have done a stratified sample, testing the taste in a number of settings that were truly representative of the proportion of beverage accompaniments the customers smoked with—60% with coffee, 30% with brandy, and 10% with nothing.

5. (e) is the answer—this might work for Henderson but not for someone with a different personality.

6. The answer is (d) Why?

7. This looks like a good one. 10,000 are way more than enough samples. And lightning is lightning no matter where, one would think, and as well air is air no matter where except for pollution. And if there was a lot of ozone in the air before the strikes then still there were very high concentrations of ozone after the strikes. So bias does not seem to be a factor here. The generalization is not the result of an anecdotal reflection. So it's a good one. Do you agree?

8. Well, at least (a) is true. Maybe the tests will be random, maybe not. We do not know from what is said. Further, this might include cows that arrive at the slaughterhouse in symptomatic condition. And if that is true and the total number of those cows is large enough then the sample size will be unacceptable to give any degree of reasonable assurance with respect to that population represented by the negative tests. Finally, since the disease is terrible and quite possibly fatal for victims, most would demand higher testing numbers for higher testing—if they could.

9. (e), this is only anecdotal, a story told by one person from this person's not so systematic sampling and experience.

10. Both biased and hasty—(d). First it is apples and oranges if the testers throw in trucks, so that biases the sample; and second, only thirty percent of brands of diesel personal car engines were tested against some undisclosed number of brands of gasoline car engines. Now whatever that number of brands of gasoline car engines was, more of the diesel car engines should have been tested unless we have some other assurance that the ones tested were truly representative of diesel engine equipped cars in general. After all, some new diesel car engines are quite clean running even when compared with average gasoline engines—either the sample should be stratified to include the proper percentage of those clean diesel car engines, or it should have been larger so as to ensure that those were represented since they are by no means the majority of car diesel engines yet in production.

MASTERY EXERCISES VII.3

SELF TEST

Answers to Mastery Exercise

1. G, 1
2. G, 3
3. G, 3
4. G, 2
5. B, 4
6. D
7. E—b, c
8. E—a, c, d
9. C
10. B

MASTERY EXERCISES VII.4

SELF TEST

Answers to Mastery Exercise

1. C
2. A
3. B
4. Concomitant variation
5. C
6. While you might be tempted to see this example as a case of the method of difference, there is really no reason to go that far. The reasoning seems to be that the speaker saw something follow something else and immediately thought that what preceded was the cause of what followed. That is the fallacy of Post Hoc, Ergo Propter Hoc. On the other hand we really cannot tell. Maybe the reasoning is that at first there was no light and all else remained the same except the bulb was changed. Then the light went on—by method of difference the cause was a bad bulb. Lesson: Sometimes we don't know what the reasoning is until we ask or investigate further.
7. It is no better as a case of causal knowledge about washing your car making it rain. It seems like a case of the use of the method of agreement, but what is agreeing—that the car was washed and it rained? No, the claim should be that his car was washed and it rained on *his* car. So we had better limit his claim to just that—which he does not do. This is not a use of the method of agreement to support all car washings causing rain showers. And the more we get serious about it, the more we would see that really the only agreement is that when he washed his car when it was about to rain, then it did rain later. So what might look like a remarkable correlation is really nothing more than a case of Post Hoc, Ergo Propter Hoc.
8. This is a case of the use of the method of difference—and a correct case.

9. This could be analyzed using the method of concomitant variation. The variation was between the degree of anger and the target of the anger saying anything.

10. —discuss

11. —discuss

12. —discuss

13. —discuss

14. concomitant variation

MASTERY EXERCISES VII.5

Answers to Mastery Exercise

1. O
2. J
3. A
4. M
5. D
6. S
7. R
8. Q
9. G
10. K
11. G, 3
12. G, 1
13. G 1, maybe 2
14. B, 4
15. G, 3
16. A
17. D
18. A
19. C
20. C, maybe d
21. F (b), ii
22. T (a), i
23. F (b), ii
24. T (a), iii
25. T (a), v

Chapter VIII

MASTERY EXERCISES VIII.2

SELF TEST

Short Truth Table Answers

1. [(a→b) & (c→d) & (b v d)] → (a v c)

```
     F          F              F  F
     F  F     F  T     F  T
       T         T         T
            T         T
            T                   F
```
                                        F-Invalid

2. [(pvq) & (q v r)] → (p v r)

```
     F          F     F  F
     F  T     T  F
       T         T
            T         F
```
                        F-Invalid

3. [(p→q) & (q v s) & (s→r)] → r

```
                        F       F
     T  T     T  F     F  F
       T         T         T
            T         T
            T              F
```
                                F-Invalid

4. [(p→q) & ~q & q] → ~p

```
     T                  F
     T  T/F  F/T  T/F
       T/F      F   T/F
            F            F
```
                        T-Valid

NOTICE THAT IT MAKES NO DIFFERENCE WHETHER ONE MAKES q TRUE OR FALSE, THE CONTRADICTION IN THE PREMISES (q AND ~q) WILL MAKE THE ARGUMENT VALID.

5. {(p→q) & (~q v r) & [~(r & ~s)] & ~p} → ~s

```
   T T     F T      T   F     F       F
    T          T      T          F
                 T                F    F
                             F        F
```
                                   T-Valid

NOTICE THAT IT MAKES A BIG DIFFERENCE WHETHER ONE ASSIGNS A T OR F TO p. IF ONE ASSIGNS AN F TO p, THEN ~p BECOMES T, AND THE PREMISES ARE TRUE WHILE THE CONCLUSION IS FALSE, OR THE ARGUMENT IS SHOWN TO BE INVALID! Thus:

{(p→q) & (~q v r) & [~(r & ~s)] & ~p} → ~s

```
   F T     F T      T   F     T       F
    T          T      T          T
                 T         T        T
                     T              F
```
                                   F-Invalid

AND SINCE ONLY ONE SET OF ASSIGNMENTS OF TRUTH VALUES MAKING THE PREMISES TRUE AND THE CONCLUSION FALSE IS NECESSARY TO SHOW AN ARGUMENT INVALID, THIS ARGUMENT FORM IS FOR INVALID ARGUMENTS.

6. (p v q) & [(~p & ~q) v r] & ~r → ~q

```
    T              F              F
  F T       T    F  T/F F/T
   T           F     T/F F/T
        F         T/F   F/T
                 F        F
```
                                   T-Valid

NOTICE THAT IT MAKES NO DIFFERENCE WHETHER ONE MAKES r T OR F. THE ARGUMENT IS GOING TO COME OUT VALID AS IT IS IMPOSSIBLE TO MAKE THE PREMISES TRUE AND THE CONCLUSION FALSE.

7. [(p→ q) & (p v s)] → s

```
              F    F
   T    T   T F
    T        T
        T        F
```
                                   F-Invalid

8. [(r→q) & (q→p)] → (r→p)

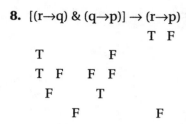

```
                              T  F
     T                   F
     T  F      F  F
       F         T
         F              F
```

T-Valid

NOTICE THAT ONE COULD MAKE q TRUE, BUT THEN THE SECOND IF-THEN WITH q IN IT WOULD BE FALSE AND SO THE PREMISES TOGETHER WOULD BE FALSE. SO IT IS IMPOSSIBLE TO MAKE THE PREMISES TRUE AND THE CONCLUSION FALSE.

9. [(p v s v r v q) & ~r & ~q & ~p] → s

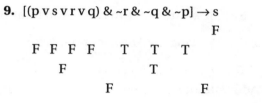

```
                                    F
     F F F F    T    T    T
       F              T
         F              F
```

T-Valid

NOTICE THAT IN ORDER TO MAKE TRUE THE ~r, ~q AND SO ON STANDING ALONE, ONE WOULD HAVE TO MAKE r AND q AND SO ON F. AND IF ONE REVERSED THAT ONE WOULD STILL END UP WITH FALSE PREMISES AND SO IT IS IMPOSSIBLE TO MAKE THE PREMISES TRUE AND THE CONCLUSION FALSE.

10. [(s & p) v (q & r)] → ~s

```
     T T    T T    F
       T        F
```

F-invalid

NOTICE THAT IF ONE HAD MADE p, q, AND r F, THEN THE PREMISES WOULD HAVE BEEN F AND ONE WOULD NOT HAVE SEEN THE INVALIDITY OF THE ARGUMENT.

MASTERY EXERCISES VIII.4

SELF TEST

Natural Deduction Proofs

A. 3. F   1,2 Modus Ponens or MP

B. 3. ~S   1, 2, MT or Modus Tollens

C. 3. L   1, 2, AC (Affirming the Consequent) invalid

D. 4. X v A   1, 2 DS (Disjunctive Syllogism)
     5. A   3, 4 DS

E. 3. S → E   1, 2 HS

F. 4. M → ~A   1,2 HS
     5. M → ~E   4, 5 HS

G. 3. ~P   1, 2 MT

H. 4. D v ~H   1, 2 DS
     5. ~H   3, 4 DS

I. 4. D → S   1, 2 HS
     5. S   3, 4 MP

There is at least one other way to prove this. Can you think of what it is?

J. 3. ~L   1,2 DA (Denying the Antecedent) invalid

K. 4. A   3, 1 DS
     5. S v A   4 Add (Addition)

Can you think of another way to prove this conclusion?

MASTERY EXERCISES VIII.5

SELF TEST

Answers to Further Exercises on Short-Truth Table Method, Natural Deduction, and Symbolization

1. ‖{[(p v q) & (r v s)] → [(p v s) & (q v r)]} & (~p & ~s)‖ → r
        F T   F T T F T   T F   T   F   F

Since s has to be true if (p v s) is to be true (and that is because p has to be false if ~p is to be true), then ~s is going to be F and, if the truth values of s and ~s are switched, then (p v s) would be false, so then it is impossible to find assignments of truth values making the premises true and the conclusion false—so the argument is valid.

2. [(p v q) & ~(~p & ~q) & (r v p)] → r
        T F   F   T   F T   F

This one is invalid. Can you complete the short truth table demonstration of this?

3. {p → [r & (q v s)]} → (p → r)
        T   F   T   F

Notice that in this problem, it does not matter what truth values are assigned to q and to s, since r has to be false and that means the whole conjunction (which is the consequent of the premise) is going to be false and so it is impossible to make the premises true and the conclusion false.

A. 1. p & ~r & q
   2. ~r → ~s   /thf. ~s
   3. ~r 1   Simp.
   4. ~s   2, 3 MP

B. 1. (p v q) & ~ (~p & ~q)
   2. p → s
   3. q → t   /thf. (s v t)
   4. p v q   1 Simp.
   5. s v t   2, 3, 4 Constructive Dilemma

C. 1. [p & (s v t)] → (r v s)
   2. p
   3. t   /thf. (r v s)
   4. (s v t)   3 Add
   5. p & (s v t)   2, 4 Conj.
   6. (r v s)   5, 1 MP

D. If Henrietta had gone over, then she would pay a pretty penny to have Herb keep quiet. Herb threatened her with telling his story. She immediately offered to pay him a pretty penny to keep quiet. So he concluded that she had gone over.

Henrietta gone over = p,
Pay a pretty penny = q

   1. (p → q)
   2. q   /thf. p
   3. p   1,2 Affirming the Consequent invalid

E. You have three choices Herb, keep threatening me and get locked up until the sting operation is over, just shut up, and third try to get away without picking one of these first two. Herb was not going to land in jail for an unknown period of time. And he was not going to keep silent since this was the perfect opportunity to get back at Henrietta for leaving him. So he made a break for it.

p = get locked up
s = shut up
t = try to get away

   1. (p v s v t)
   2. ~p
   3. ~s   /thf. t
   4. (s v t)   1, 2 DS
   5. t   3, 4 DS

And

"If he gets away, I'm sunk. I'm not giving up my career for that twerp—I'm not going to be sunk over this, in other words. So he's not going anywhere."

p = he gets away

q = I'm sunk

1. (p → q)
2. ~q   /thf. ~p
3. ~p   1,2 MT

F. If you run to the agency, my cover will be blown. And, if you confront Sid (since you are known to the mob and you are being watched) my cover will be blown. Now I knew that either you (he) was going to run to the agency or you (he) was going to confront Sid. Therefore my cover was sure to be blown.

r = run to the agency

s = cover will be blown

t = confront Sid

1. (r → s)
2. (t → s)
3. (r v t)   /thf. (s v s) (which is equivalent to s)
4. (s v s)   1, 2, 3 Constructive Dilemma

MASTERY EXERCISES VIII.6

More Practice Exercises on Deductive Logic

A. 1. Herb v ~Herb   (p v ~p)
      2. Herb→~Care   (p → ~q)
      3. Care   /thf. ~Herb   q   /thf.~p
      4. ~Herb   2, 3 Modus Tollens—Valid   ~p   2, 3 MT

B. 1. Cares   s
      2. Herb loves→Thinks   (p → t)
      3. Thinks   /thf. Herb loves   t   /thf. p
      4. Herb loves   2, 3 Affirming the   p   2, 3 AC
Consequent—Invalid

C. 1. Attracted→Loves   (r → t)
      2. Attracted   /thf. Loves or Block   r   /thf. (t v q)
      3. ~Block   /thf. Loves   ~q   /thf. t
      4. Loves 1,2 Modus Ponens (MP) notice you could have ended up thinking Loves or Blocks by virtue of deriving Loves and then adding the other alternative. In that case you would need to also use 3 and the previous in disjunctive argument to get Loves. Valid   t   1, 2 MP

D. 1. Smart→Make (lot of $)   (s → w)

    2. Make→Rich   /thf. Smart→Rich   (w → r)

    3. Smart→Rich   1,2 Hypothetical Syllogism   (s → r)
           —Valid

E. 1. Avoids→~Smart   (p → ~s)

    2. ~Avoids   /thf. Smart   ~p   /thf. s

    3. Smart   1, 2 Denying the Antecedent—Invalid   s   1, 2 DA

F. 1. Attracted→Loves   (t → s)

    2. Attracted   /thf. Loves   t   /thf. s

    3. Loves   1, 2 Modus Ponens—Valid   s   1, 2 MP

G. 1. Horse→Irresitible   (w → t)

    2. Irresible→Love   /thf. Horse→Loves   (t → s)   /thf. w → s

    3. Horse→Loves   1, 2 Hypothetical Syllogism   (w → s)   1, 2 HS
           —Valid

H. 1. Live→Have   (s→ r)

    2. ~Live   /thf. ~Have   ~s   /thf.   ~r

    3. ~Have   1, 2 Denying the Antecedent—Invalid   ~r   1, 2 DA

MASTERY EXERCISES VIII.7

SELF TEST

Answer Key

1. i		**A.** i	
2. ii		**B.** ii	
3. iii		**C.** ii	
4. i or ii		**D.** iii	
5. ii		**E.** iii	

MASTERY EXERCISES VIII.8

SELF TEST

Answer Key

1. G	**11.** i	
2. H	**12.** iii	
3. I	**13.** iv	
4. A	**14.** ii or iii	
5. P	**15.** iv	
6. O	**16.** ii	
7. F	**17.** iii	
8. D	**18.** iii	
9. K	**19.** i	
10. E	**20.** iii	

Chapter IX

MASTERY EXERCISES IX .2

SELF TEST

Explanations, Arguments, or Neither (or both)

    i. A
   ii. E
  iii. E
   iv. A
    v. C or it is an historical explanation of intelligibility
   vi. E
 vii. could be either E or A
viii. A
   ix. A
    x. A that is perhaps an E

MASTERY EXERCISES IX .3

SELF TEST

Explanation Assessment by Pragmatic Virtues

  1. (f)
  2. (e)
  3. (c) (it is circular)
  4. (d)
  5. (e)—(b) and (c)
  6. (d)
  7. (b)
  8. (c)
  9. (e)
10. (f)—(b) and (d)

Answer Templates

Chapter I

Name _____

Assignment _____

1. _____

2. _____

3. _____

4. _____

5. _____

6. _____

7. _____

8. _____

9. _____

10. _____

11. _____

12. _____

13. _____

14. _____

15. _____

16. _____

17. _____

18. _____

19. _____

20. _____

Chapter I

Name _____

Assignment _____

1. _____
2. _____
3. _____
4. _____
5. _____
6. _____
7. _____
8. _____
9. _____
10. _____
11. _____
12. _____
13. _____
14. _____
15. _____
16. _____
17. _____
18. _____
19. _____
20. _____

Chapter I

Name _____

Assignment _____

1. _____
2. _____
3. _____
4. _____
5. _____
6. _____
7. _____
8. _____
9. _____
10. _____
11. _____
12. _____
13. _____
14. _____
15. _____
16. _____
17. _____
18. _____
19. _____
20. _____

Chapter II

1. _____
2. _____
3. _____
4. _____
5. _____
6. _____
7. _____
8. _____
9. _____
10. _____
11. _____
12. _____
13. _____
14. _____
15. _____
16. _____
17. _____
18. _____
19. _____
20. _____

Chapter II

Name _____

Assignment _____

1. _____
2. _____
3. _____
4. _____
5. _____
6. _____
7. _____
8. _____
9. _____
10. _____
11. _____
12. _____
13. _____
14. _____
15. _____
16. _____
17. _____
18. _____
19. _____
20. _____

Chapter II

Name _____

Assignment _____

1. _____
2. _____
3. _____
4. _____
5. _____
6. _____
7. _____
8. _____
9. _____
10. _____
11. _____
12. _____
13. _____
14. _____
15. _____
16. _____
17. _____
18. _____
19. _____
20. _____

Chapter III

Name _____

Assignment _____

1. _____

2. _____

3. _____

4. _____

5. _____

6. _____

7. _____

8. _____

9. _____

10. _____

11. _____

12. _____

13. _____

14. _____

15. _____

16. _____

17. _____

18. _____

19. _____

20. _____

Chapter III

Name _____

Assignment _____

1. _____
2. _____
3. _____
4. _____
5. _____
6. _____
7. _____
8. _____
9. _____
10. _____
11. _____
12. _____
13. _____
14. _____
15. _____
16. _____
17. _____
18. _____
19. _____
20. _____

Chapter III

Name _____

Assignment _____

1. _____
2. _____
3. _____
4. _____
5. _____
6. _____
7. _____
8. _____
9. _____
10. _____
11. _____
12. _____
13. _____
14. _____
15. _____
16. _____
17. _____
18. _____
19. _____
20. _____

Chapter IV

Name _____

Assignment _____

1. _____

2. _____

3. _____

4. _____

5. _____

6. _____

7. _____

8. _____

9. _____

10. _____

11. _____

12. _____

13. _____

14. _____

15. _____

16. _____

17. _____

18. _____

19. _____

20. _____

Chapter IV

Name _____

Assignment _____

1. _____

2. _____

3. _____

4. _____

5. _____

6. _____

7. _____

8. _____

9. _____

10. _____

11. _____

12. _____

13. _____

14. _____

15. _____

16. _____

17. _____

18. _____

19. _____

20. _____

Chapter IV

Name _____

Assignment _____

1. _____

2. _____

3. _____

4. _____

5. _____

6. _____

7. _____

8. _____

9. _____

10. _____

11. _____

12. _____

13. _____

14. _____

15. _____

16. _____

17. _____

18. _____

19. _____

20. _____

Chapter V

Name _____

Assignment _____

1. _____

2. _____

3. _____

4. _____

5. _____

6. _____

7. _____

8. _____

9. _____

10. _____

11. _____

12. _____

13. _____

14. _____

15. _____

16. _____

17. _____

18. _____

19. _____

20. _____

Chapter V

1. _____
2. _____
3. _____
4. _____
5. _____
6. _____
7. _____
8. _____
9. _____
10. _____
11. _____
12. _____
13. _____
14. _____
15. _____
16. _____
17. _____
18. _____
19. _____
20. _____

Chapter V

Name _____

Assignment _____

1. _____
2. _____
3. _____
4. _____
5. _____
6. _____
7. _____
8. _____
9. _____
10. _____
11. _____
12. _____
13. _____
14. _____
15. _____
16. _____
17. _____
18. _____
19. _____
20. _____

Chapter VI

1. _____
2. _____
3. _____
4. _____
5. _____
6. _____
7. _____
8. _____
9. _____
10. _____
11. _____
12. _____
13. _____
14. _____
15. _____
16. _____
17. _____
18. _____
19. _____
20. _____

Chapter VI

Name _____

Assignment _____

1. _____
2. _____
3. _____
4. _____
5. _____
6. _____
7. _____
8. _____
9. _____
10. _____
11. _____
12. _____
13. _____
14. _____
15. _____
16. _____
17. _____
18. _____
19. _____
20. _____

Chapter VI

Name _____

Assignment _____

1. _____

2. _____

3. _____

4. _____

5. _____

6. _____

7. _____

8. _____

9. _____

10. _____

11. _____

12. _____

13. _____

14. _____

15. _____

16. _____

17. _____

18. _____

19. _____

20. _____

Chapter VII

Name _____

Assignment _____

1. _____
2. _____
3. _____
4. _____
5. _____
6. _____
7. _____
8. _____
9. _____
10. _____
11. _____
12. _____
13. _____
14. _____
15. _____
16. _____
17. _____
18. _____
19. _____
20. _____

Chapter VII

Name _____

Assignment _____

1. _____

2. _____

3. _____

4. _____

5. _____

6. _____

7. _____

8. _____

9. _____

10. _____

11. _____

12. _____

13. _____

14. _____

15. _____

16. _____

17. _____

18. _____

19. _____

20. _____

Chapter VII

Name _____

Assignment _____

1. _____
2. _____
3. _____
4. _____
5. _____
6. _____
7. _____
8. _____
9. _____
10. _____
11. _____
12. _____
13. _____
14. _____
15. _____
16. _____
17. _____
18. _____
19. _____
20. _____

Chapter VIII

Name _____

Assignment _____

1. _____
2. _____
3. _____
4. _____
5. _____
6. _____
7. _____
8. _____
9. _____
10. _____
11. _____
12. _____
13. _____
14. _____
15. _____
16. _____
17. _____
18. _____
19. _____
20. _____

Chapter VIII

Name _____

Assignment _____

1. _____
2. _____
3. _____
4. _____
5. _____
6. _____
7. _____
8. _____
9. _____
10. _____
11. _____
12. _____
13. _____
14. _____
15. _____
16. _____
17. _____
18. _____
19. _____
20. _____

Chapter VIII

Name _____

Assignment _____

1. _____
2. _____
3. _____
4. _____
5. _____
6. _____
7. _____
8. _____
9. _____
10. _____
11. _____
12. _____
13. _____
14. _____
15. _____
16. _____
17. _____
18. _____
19. _____
20. _____

Chapter IX

Name _____

Assignment _____

1. _____
2. _____
3. _____
4. _____
5. _____
6. _____
7. _____
8. _____
9. _____
10. _____
11. _____
12. _____
13. _____
14. _____
15. _____
16. _____
17. _____
18. _____
19. _____
20. _____

Chapter IX

Name _____

Assignment _____

1. _____
2. _____
3. _____
4. _____
5. _____
6. _____
7. _____
8. _____
9. _____
10. _____
11. _____
12. _____
13. _____
14. _____
15. _____
16. _____
17. _____
18. _____
19. _____
20. _____

Chapter IX

Name _____

Assignment _____

1. _____
2. _____
3. _____
4. _____
5. _____
6. _____
7. _____
8. _____
9. _____
10. _____
11. _____
12. _____
13. _____
14. _____
15. _____
16. _____
17. _____
18. _____
19. _____
20. _____

Chapter X

Name _____

Assignment _____

1. _____

2. _____

3. _____

4. _____

5. _____

6. _____

7. _____

8. _____

9. _____

10. _____

11. _____

12. _____

13. _____

14. _____

15. _____

16. _____

17. _____

18. _____

19. _____

20. _____

Chapter X

Name _____

Assignment _____

1. _____
2. _____
3. _____
4. _____
5. _____
6. _____
7. _____
8. _____
9. _____
10. _____
11. _____
12. _____
13. _____
14. _____
15. _____
16. _____
17. _____
18. _____
19. _____
20. _____

Chapter X

Name _____

Assignment _____

1. _____
2. _____
3. _____
4. _____
5. _____
6. _____
7. _____
8. _____
9. _____
10. _____
11. _____
12. _____
13. _____
14. _____
15. _____
16. _____
17. _____
18. _____
19. _____
20. _____